LEARN JAPANESE
NEW COLLEGE TEXT

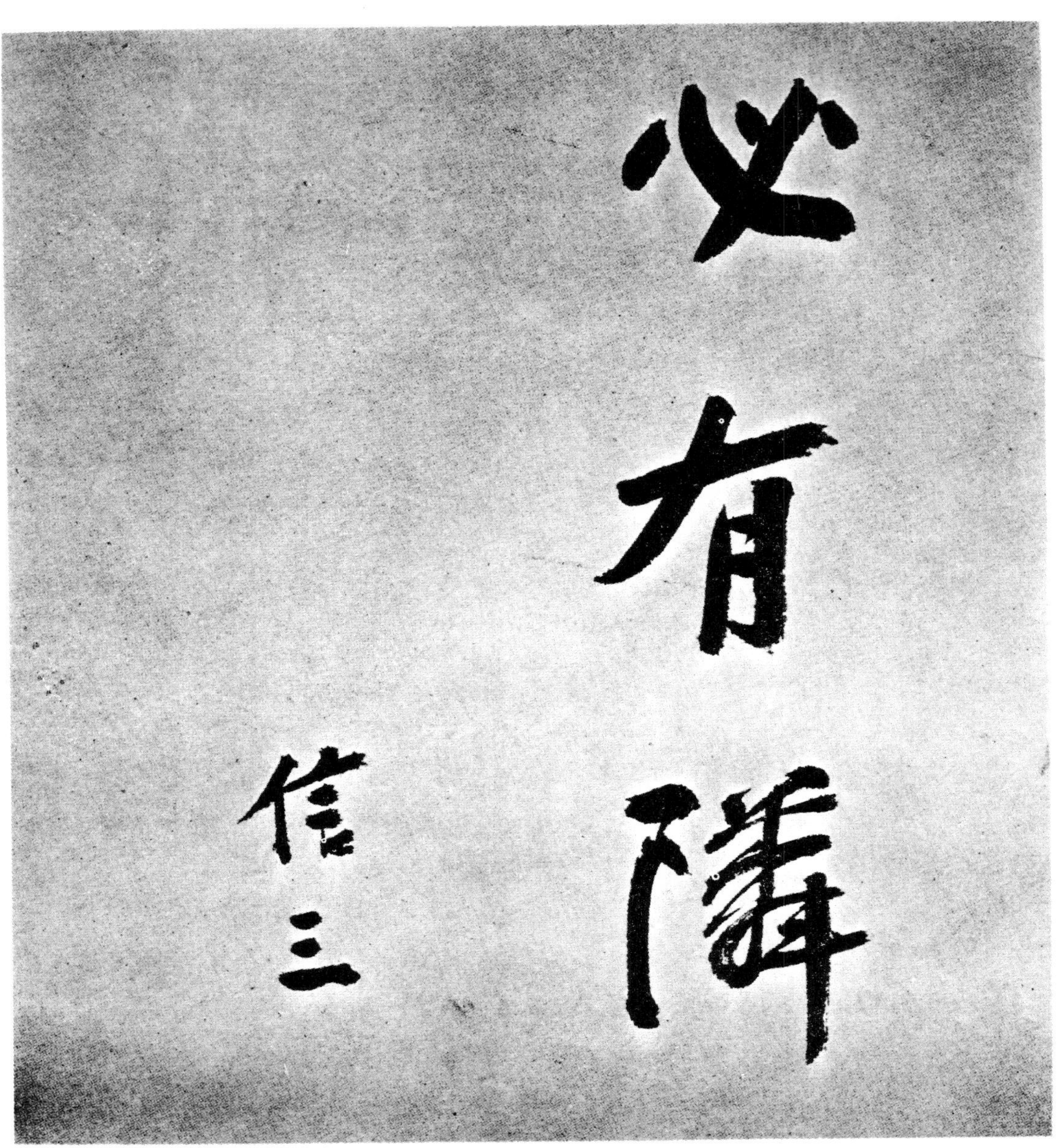

「必 有 隣」 信三

written by Dr. Shinzo Koizumi, who was formerly president of Keio University and tutor of the Crown Prince. Dr. Koizumi was awarded an honorary doctorate degree from the University of Maryland. He received in 1959 the "Bunka Kunshō," an imperial award to distinguished men of letters.

LEARN JAPANESE

NEW COLLEGE TEXT VOLUME III

John Young and Kimiko Nakajima-Okano

Published for
University of Maryland University College

University of Hawaii Press
Honolulu

This volume is another in a series of Japanese language textbooks prepared by the Asian Division of the University of Maryland University College and published by the University of Hawaii Press.

Manufactured in the United States of America

90 89 88 5 4 3

Library of Congress Cataloging in Publication Data
(Revised for volume III)

Young, John, 1920–
Learn Japanese.

1. Japanese language—Text-books for foreign speakers —English. I. Nakajima-Okano, Kimiko. II. Title.
PL539.3.Y64 1984 495.68'3421 83-18060
ISBN 0-8248-0859-2 (v. 1)
ISBN 0-8248-0881-9 (v. 2)
ISBN 0-8248-0896-7 (v. 3)

CONTENTS

ACKNOWLEDGMENTS

The authors are deeply indebted to the Japanese language faculty and administrative staff of the University of Maryland and of more than one hundred universities and schools who have used the original *Learn Japanese: College Text* and offered many invaluable comments in the preparation of this revised text. We are also very grateful to the staff members of the Institute of Far Eastern Studies and of the Asian Bilingual Curriculum Development Center at Seton Hall University for their assistance.

We also wish to mention the following people whose assistance was very valuable in the preparation of the original, *Learn Japanese: College Text:* Ms. Yoshiko Andō, Dr. Edgar A. Austin, Dr. Ivan Benson, Dr. Keiichirō Okutsu, and Mr. Shōzō Kurokawa.

Miagureba
Oou kage nashi
Mochi no tsuki
— *Seien* —

Looking up
I see all life revealed;
Unshadowed full moon of autumn.

INTRODUCTION

This is the third volume of *Learn Japanese: New College Text.* It begins where Volume II ends. The use of *roomaji*—roman letters—is limited to a minimum, with *kana* and *kan'ji* used instead.

In this volume, a total of one hundred new *kan'ji* characters, one *kan'ji* mark, and thirty-one new readings of *kan'ji* which previously appeared are introduced. Any *kan'ji* that has appeared in a preceding lesson with a different reading, or any compound *kan'ji* whose reading is especially derived as a result of a combination, is introduced with the number with which it was originally introduced. Such *kan'ji* with different readings are assigned numbers (such as 行 2.6.a) which are different from those numbers (such as 旅 2.6.1) assigned to newly introduced *kan'ji.* Most of the *kan'ji* first appear in presentations and dialogs, but there are some that first occur in notes or drills. They are identified with an asterisk in the *kan'ji* section.

As stated in Volume II, we are introducing some additional *kan'ji* for "passive" learning, and to these *kan'ji, furigana*—readings of the *kan'ji* in small *hiragana* characters—are attached. The student is required to identify and possibly reproduce the "active" *kan'ji,* but the "passive" *kan'ji* need not be memorized until they are introduced for active learning.

In many traditional *kan'ji* dictionaries, *kan'ji* are classified according to 214 *bushu,* or radicals. This kind of arrangement has generally been discarded by modern dictionary compilers because many simplified or modified *kan'ji,* as a result of the language reform measures taken since 1945, do not fit the various radicals. For example, the Agency for Cultural Affairs' *Dictionary of Chinese Characters for Foreigners* classifies *kan'ji* into 5 categories, namely, 丶, 丨, 一, 丿, and ㇇ and 247 subcategories called elements. In this text the term "classifier" refers both to radicals of traditional dictionaries and categories/elements of reformed dictionaries. The traditional classifiers appear in parentheses after the reformed classifiers. For example: Vol. 2, 1.6.6 六(3) classifier 亠 (八). The following popular dictionary is used in determining classifiers: Kikuya Nagasawa, *Meikai Kan'wa Jiten,* 1959, San'seidoo, Tokyo. Other reformed dictionaries might have different ways of grouping *kan'ji,* however.

It should be remembered that the introduction of *kan'ji* is not meant to interfere with the student's efforts in building up his oral-aural capability, which is still the focal target of this volume. Therefore, reproduction of *kan'ji* should not be overemphasized at this stage.

An introduction to styles has been incorporated in Lesson 1, and linguistic and cultural factors in helping the student to develop receptive comprehension, in Lesson 14. However, it is not the author's intention there to ask the student to practice the various styles, or receptive comprehension skills, which have been listed for cognitive or "passive" learning purposes. If necessary, these two lessons may be omitted.

Lessons 2 through 4, 6 through 9, and 11 through 13 constitute the main texts, while Lessons 5, 10, and 15 are review lessons.

As an attempt to add more notional/functional elements to this text, we have introduced a new section called Mike Harrison Series for Review Lessons 5, 10, and 15. The main goal of this section is to help the student develop comprehension skills through application conversations in a variety of situations. The student should study this section for "passive" learning purposes. Many types of drills and exercises have been included in this text for the sole purpose of offering learners as many options as possible. Please feel free to skip any item which is easy and concentrate on those which are difficult.

LESSON 1

1.1 GENERAL INTRODUCTION TO STYLES

In Japanese, there are many styles and levels of speaking and writing, depending upon the occasion. Age, sex, social status, sociopsychological differentiation, profession, education, class, seeking or giving favor, in-groupness, and even personality determine the style and level that the speaker uses. Usually Japanese call these *keigo*.

Generally speaking, a level is determined by the speaker's evaluation of the relative status relationship of the subject-person with other people or the object-person involved in his talk, and a style is determined by the speaker's relative status relationship with the listener.

The following symbols and abbreviations have been used here:

- ⓪ no person involved
- ① the speaker, the first person
- ② the listener, the second person
- ③ the third person or persons
- ⓧ the person referred to as the subject
- ⓧⓧ the person referred to as the object

- ↑ P promotion of ⓧ } level
- ↓ D demotion of ⓧ } level
- → F more formal or polite } style
- ← I more informal, familiar, plain or less polite } style

Thus, styles and levels can be described in the form of two axes with the speaker placed at the center.

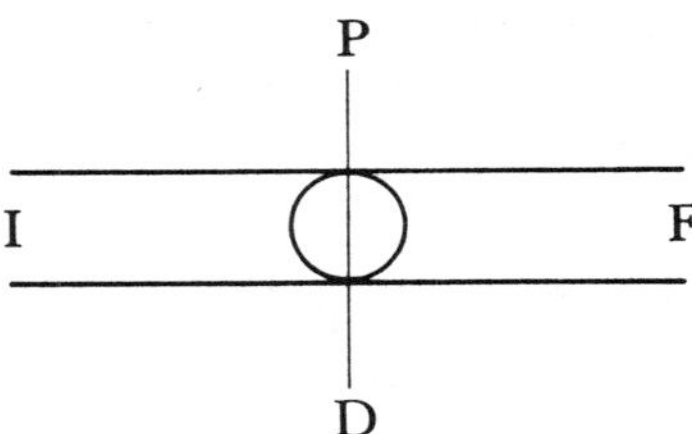

1.2 CLASSIFICATION OF STYLES

Styles are determined by the speaker's evaluation of the relative status of the speaker ① and the listener ②. They are distinguished mainly by the ending of sentences, although lexical items, contractions, deletions, Sentence Particles, nonfinal clause endings and even intonations are also considered.

Generally speaking, two styles may be described: (1) polite or formal style, and (2) plain or informal style.

The sentence endings of the polite or formal style are in formal forms of the Copula, a Verb, and an Adjective. Three types of the polite or formal style will be treated here: (1A) *desu* type, (1B) *de arimasu* type, and (1C) *de gozaimasu* type.

(1B) is used for public address or audience purposes and the *desu* family is replaced by the *de arimasu* family.

(1C) is used for honorific purposes and the *desu* family is replaced by the *de gozaimasu* family.

The sentence endings of the plain and informal style are in plain forms of the Copula, a Verb, and an Adjective. Two types of this style will be treated here: (2A) *da* type and (2B) *de aru* type. The latter type is used mainly for public writing or audience-written purposes and the *da* family is replaced by the *de aru* family.

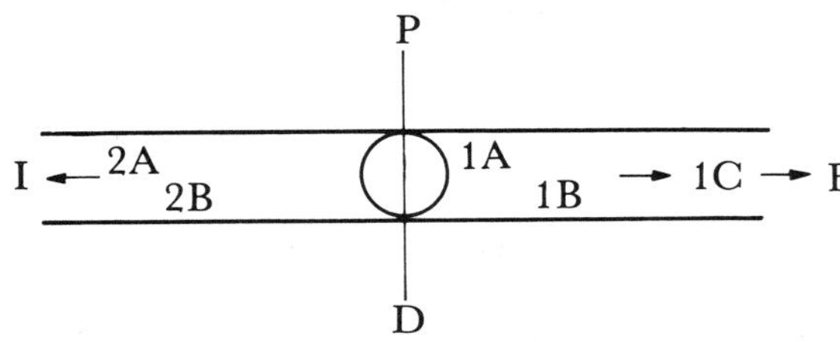

1.3 STYLES

1.3.1A Polite style – *desu* or normal type

1. Forms:

Desu, n(o) desu and *-masu* endings are used at the end of sentences or before some clause Relationals such as *ga, kara, keredomo,* or Sentence Particles. In all other positions, the plain form of Verbs, Adjectives, and the Copula are used.

Example: 私が　します。
すしが　食べたいんです。

②→

2. Usages:

This type of style is popularly used except when another style is suggested. This is the safest style, in the sense that it will not be regarded as excessively polite or rude. For a foreigner, this style has the widest application and is adaptable to most occasions.

3. Other features:

a) There are sentence-ending lexical items such as *wa, wa yo, wa ne, no, ne, no yo,* and so on that distinguish women's way of talking from that of men:

Example: 行きますわ。 …… 行きます。
そうですわね。 …… そうですね。

b) Other lexical items, such as *irasshaimasu, itashimasu, itadakimasu,* which are used in a more polite level of speech may be used as a part of this style of utterance.

Example: いらっしゃいますか。 …… いますか。
私が　いたします。 …… 私が　します。
おっしゃってください。 …… いってください。

c) Normally (1) the Stem form of a Verb plus *nasai,* (2) the TE form of a Verb plus *kudasai,* and (3) *nasai, osshai, irasshai,* or *kudasai* alone formulate the imperative form of this type of polite style.

Example: 食べなさい。　　はやく　おっしゃい。
食べてください。　　こっちへ　いらっしゃい。
べんきょうを　なさい。　　それを　ください。

1.3.1B Polite style – *de arimasu* or polite audience type

1. Forms:

The *desu* family such as *desu, deshita* are replaced by the *de arimasu* family.

Example:		
先生です。	⟶	先生であります。
先生なのです。	⟶	先生なのであります。
先生でした。	⟶	先生でありました。

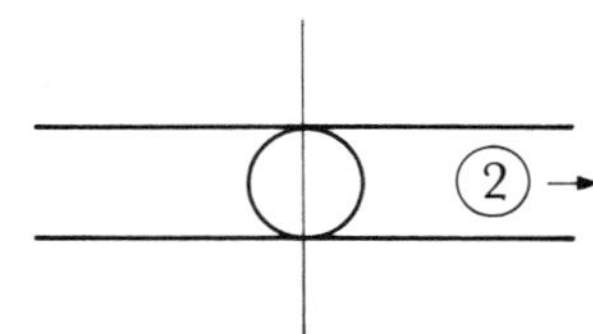

2. Usages:

In more formal lectures, radio and television announcements, and public speeches, this audience type is widely used.

3. Other features:

a) Sentence Particles like *yo* and *ne* are avoided.

b) Contractions like *ja* or *jaa* and the Pre-Copula *n* are avoided, and *de wa* and *no* are used instead.

Example:		
先生じゃありません。	⟶	先生ではありません。
行くんです。	⟶	行くのであります。

c) Instead of the TE form at the end of a nonfinal clause, the Stem form for Verbs and the KU form for Adjectives are often used.

Example:

山田さんは　先生で、　大川さんは　学生です。	⟶	山田さんは　先生であり、大川さんは　学生であります。
学校へ　行って、べんきょうしたのです。	⟶	学校へ　行き、　べんきょうしたのであります。
きょうは　あめが　多くて、さむかったです。	⟶	きょうは　あめが　多く、　さむかったのであります。

d) Humble words such as *itasu* (for *suru*), *mairu* (for *iku* or *kuru*) are often used to formulate this type.

Example:		
私が　行くんです。	⟶	私が　まいるのであります。
私が　するつもりです。	⟶	私が　いたすつもりであります。

e) *Zu ni* "without doing such and such" is used in place of *-naide* before a pause to formulate this type.

Example:		
学校へ　行かないで、べんきょうしました。	⟶	学校へ　行かずに、べんきょうしたのであります。

1.3.1C Polite style – *de gozaimasu* or honorific type

1. Forms:

The *de gozaimasu* family is used at the end of a sentence, replacing the *desu* family. Polite lexical items such as *itashimasu, meshiagarimasu* are more frequently used.

Example: さようでございます。

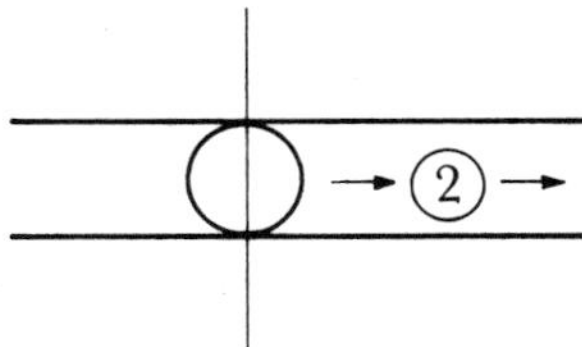

2. Usages:

This type is regularly used in such cases as an inferior talking to his superior, a merchant to his customer, or a servant to his employer. This style is also often used by women or by people who are very polite.

3. Other features:

a) The honorific type is characterized by the use of many lexical items which are normally used for more polite speech levels.

Example:

はい	⟶	はあ	します	⟶	いたします、なさいます
そうです	⟶	さようでございます	いいます	⟶	もうします、おっしゃいます
行きます	⟶	まいります、いらっしゃいます	います	⟶	おります、いらっしゃいます
			あります	⟶	ございます
来ます	⟶	まいります、いらっしゃいます			

4. The imperative form of this type of style ends in *-mase*.

Example: いらっしゃいませ。　　くださいませ。

1.3.2A Plain style – *da* type

1. Forms:

The plain forms of a Verb, an Adjective, and the Copula are used in all positions.

Example: 食べる。 or 食べるのだ。
しろい。 or しろいのだ。
先生だ。 or 先生なのだ。

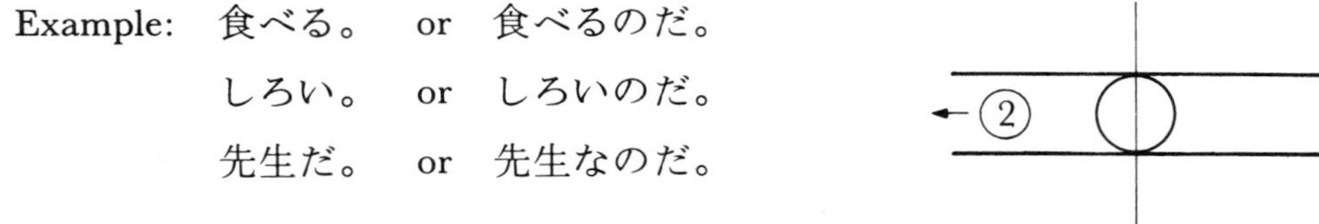

2. Usages:

This type of speech style is used within the family, with intimate friends, or with close associates. It is not necessary for a foreigner to use this style, but it will be useful for him to understand it, because he will hear it often.

3. Other features:

a) Omission of the Copula before *ka?* is obligatory in plain questions (*ka* is dropped when the female uses the plain form):

Example:

normal form		plain form			
先生ですか。	⟶	先生か。	そうですか。	⟶	そうか。
先生なのですか。	⟶	先生なのか。	そうなのですか。	⟶	そうなのか。

b) Omission of the Copula *da* is mandatory in women's talk after the Pre-Copula *no* or *n*. However, in the latter case *n* will become *no:*

Example: 行くのだよ。 ⟶ 行くのよ。
先生なんだよ。 ⟶ 先生なのよ。
東京から　来たのだ。 ⟶ 東京から　来たの。

c) Omission of Relationals *wa, ga,* and *o* is common:

Example: 先生が　いるか。 ⟶ 先生　いるか。
ごはんを　食べた？ ⟶ ごはん　食べた？
天気は　どうか。 ⟶ 天気　どう？

d) Omission of the Sentence Particle *ka* is common, especially when there is an interrogative Noun:

Example: いつ　行く？
学校(こう)から　とおい？

e) Sentence-ending lexical items such as *zo, ze, yo, ne,* or *sa* are frequently used by men, and *wa, wa yo, wa ne, no, no ne,* and *no yo* are used by women:

Compare:

行くよ。	……	行くわよ。	ぼくなんだね。	……	あたしなのね。
おいしいぞ。	……	おいしいわよ。	いいねえ。	……	いいわねえ。

f) Contractions are common in this style:

Example:
wa (Relational):

Den'sha wa kon'de ita yo. ⟶ Den'shaa kon'de ita yo.
Kore wa taihen da. ⟶ Korya taihen da.
Itte wa ikenai. ⟶ Itchaa ikenai.
Ikanakereba naranai. ⟶ Ikanakerya naranai.
Ikanakute wa dame da. ⟶ Ikanakucha dame da.
Ashita de wa dame? ⟶ Ashita ja dame?

-te (TE form) plus Extender:

Mite iru.	⟶	Miteru.
Non'de ita.	⟶	Non'deta.
Shite oku.	⟶	Shitoku.
Itte shimatta.	⟶	Itchatta.

g) *-tte,* and *-ttara* are used as *wa* substitutes:

Example:

ぼくは　だめだね。	⟶	ぼくって　だめだね。
あなたは　おかしい　人だ。	⟶	あなたったら　おかしい　人だ。

h) Instead of *to, -tte* is sometimes used as an informal quotation:

Example:

山田も　行くと　いっていた。　⟶　山田も　行くって　いってた。

i) Replacement of many lexical items which are used in a more polite situation with plain equivalents:

ぼく(＝私)、きみ(＝あなた)、山田くん(＝山田さん) is common among men, and まあ、あら、あたし、and so on, among women.

j) The Sentence Particle *na* is used by men to prohibit others from doing something:

Example: もう　食べるなよ。　　行くな。

k) Omission of *kure* after the TE form of a Verb is particularly common in women's talk:

Example: ちょっと　待ってくれ。 ⟶ ちょっと　待って(ね)。

ここへ　来てくれ(よ)。 ⟶ ここへ　来て(よ)。

1.3.2B Plain style – *de aru* or plain audience type

1. Forms:

The *da* family is replaced by the *de aru* family, including *no de aru.*

Example:	先生だ。	⟶	先生である。
	先生なのだ。	⟶	先生なのである。
	先生だった。	⟶	先生であった。

2. Usages:

In books, articles, and public writings, the Japanese often use this type. Normally the plain audience type is used only for writing purposes.

3. Other features:

a) Sentence Particles like *yo* or *ne* are avoided.

b) Contractions like *ja* or *jaa* and the Pre-Copula *n* are avoided, and *de wa* and *no* are used instead:

Example:

じゃあ、… ⟶ では、…　　行くんです。 ⟶ 行くのである。

先生じゃない。 ⟶ 先生ではない。

c) Phrase Relationals placed between two Nouns are often omitted:

Example:

東京や　大阪(さか)は　人口が　多い。 ⟶ 東京、大阪(さか)は　人口が　多い（のである）。

d) Instead of the TE form at the end of a nonfinal clause, the Stem form for Verbs and the KU form for Adjectives are often used.

Example:

山田(だ)さんは　先生で、　大川さんは　学生だ。 ⟶ 山田(だ)さんは　先生であり、大川さんは　学生である。

学校(こう)へ　行って、べんきょうしたのだ。 ⟶ 学校(こう)へ　行き、　べんきょうしたのである。

きょ年は　あめが　多くて、　さむかった。 ⟶ きょ年は　あめが　多く、　さむかったのである。

e) Formal words such as *itasu* (for *suru*), *mairu* (for *iku* or *kuru*) are often used to formulate this type:

Example: 私が　行くんだ。 ⟶ 私が　まいるのである。

私が　するつもりだ。 ⟶ 私が　いたすつもりである。

f) Women may use the *de aru* style for book and article writing, but they do not use it for speaking.

g) *Zu ni,* or "without doing such and such," is used following a Verb in the place of *-naide* before a pause to formulate this type:

Example: 学校(こう)へ　行かないで、　べんきょうした。 ⟶ 学校(こう)へ　行かずに、　べんきょうしたのである。

1.4 SPEECH LEVELS

Speech levels will be further analyzed in Lesson 1 of Volume IV. Since the characteristics of style and level of speech have been mentioned throughout our texts, we would like to restate briefly here three general traits which characterize the Japanese view of human relationships in society, with their implications for language behavior.

Groupism. As has been described previously, groupism involves in-groupness and out-groupness, as well as group solidarity. Japanese language behavior within the group is quite different from language behavior among groups. Also, styles and speech levels usually follow more polite and formal patterns outside the in-group. Within the group, speech is much more informal and plain. These considerations are, however, always subject to the second characteristic described below, namely, hierarchy.

It is interesting to note, however, that when dealing with total strangers, Japanese language behavior tends to differ again. Therefore, groups can be divided into (1) intimate groups such as the family; (2) formal groups such as colleagues, clubs, and associations; and (3) out-groups of strangers. The role of an individual would necessarily become less significant as compared with that of a group. The following chart might be helpful in understanding this relationship:

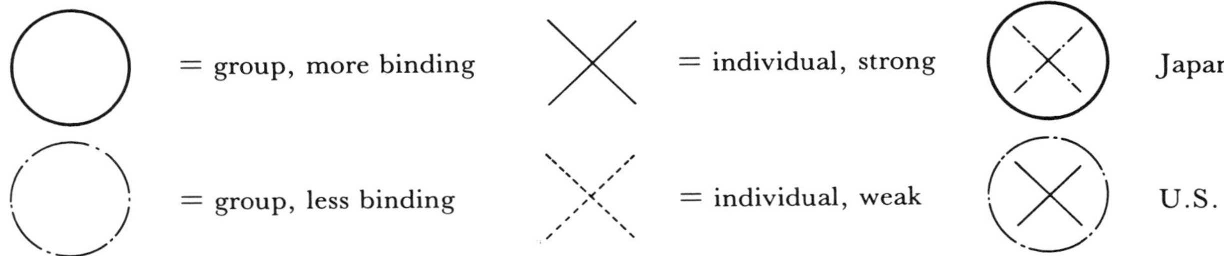

Hierarchy. A hierarchical system predominates both among various groups as well as within the group itself. In general, a more polite form is used toward one's superior, and a less polite form toward one's inferior. Considerations of hierarchy and groupism are very interconnected in language usage; therefore, the two terms are often combined to describe this phenomenon as hierarchical groupism, or vertical groupism.

Heteronomy. Heteronomy is the speaker's tendency to inflate or promote the second person while demoting himself as a first person. It is characterized by self-demotion, self-denial, and modesty in referring to oneself, while very polite reference is made to the second person. At the very least, the second person will be made the decision-maker, or the second person's status will be raised by the first person. At least the speaker must consider the second person's position in making an utterance.

The above three characteristics combined will determine the appropriate style and level of speech. For example, the plain audience style (*de aru*) is used to an undetermined, general audience, and not to any specific person. Therefore, such a style cannot be used when a specific second person is involved.

Japanese level and style of speech has had two lines of historical development: (1) absolute speech level and style; and (2) relative speech level and style. In using absolute speech level and style, the speaker makes no subjective evaluation which determines appropriate level and style; rather, an absolute status and rank is set. The speaker does not consider the relative status of himself and the second and third persons involved in the speaking. An example of this is the emperor's use of polite and formal forms before the Japanese defeat in 1945 when referring to himself. This practice resembles the Western "royal we" to a certain degree. Absolute style and level of speech appeared as early as the Nara and Heian periods in the *Man'yooshuu* and *Gen'ji Monogatari*, but they do not exist today.

Relative speech level and style also appeared as early as the *Gen'ji Monogatari* period, indicating social relationship, age, sex, professions, and even temporary power relationships, including favor giving and favor receiving. One of the relative usages governing male and female had appeared already in the *Man'yooshuu*; for instance, the word *kimi* was then used to refer to high-ranking women, but through change in use the present-day usage of *kimi* is in reference to low-ranking men, women, and intimate peers. Women's speech style also appeared early in Japan, persisting for centuries until the present day. This style is so distinctive that it is often possible, without a subject reference, to pinpoint whether the speaker is male or female.

1.5 VOCABULARY (for passive learning)

であります	de arimasu	......	C+E	copular expression used for polite audience purposes
でございます	de gozaimasu	......	C+E	copular expression used for honorific purposes

である	de aru	......	C+E	copular expression used for plain audience purposes
いらっしゃる	irassharu	......	V	more polite (deferential) equivalent of *iru*
いたす	itasu	......	V	more polite (humble) equivalent of *suru*
おっしゃる	ossharu	......	V	more polite (deferential) equivalent of *iu*
なさい	nasai	......	E	forms an imperative expression when used after the Stem form of a Verb
なさる	nasaru	......	V	more polite (deferential) equivalent of *suru*
まいる	mairu	......	V	more polite (humble) equivalent of *iku* and *kuru*
ずに	-zu ni	......	Dv+R	without (doing); instead of (doing)
さよう	sayoo	......	N	more polite or formal equivalent of *soo* ''so''
はあ	haa	......	SI	formal equivalent of *hai* ''yes''
ござる	gozaru	......	V	more polite equivalent of *aru*
もうす	moosu	......	V	more polite (humble) equivalent of *iu*
おる	oru	......	V	more formal or polite (humble) equivalent of *iru*
ませ	-mase	......	Dv	imperative form of *-masu*
ぞ	zo	......	SP	used among men
ぜ	ze	......	SP	used among men
さ	sa	......	SP	used mainly among men
な	na	......	SP	means ''prohibition'' when used after the Dictionary form of a Verb
くれ	kure	......	E	used among men as a plain imperative expression with the TE form of a Verb

LESSON 2

関西旅行

2.1 PRESENTATION

京都や 奈良[1]には 日本の 古い 文化が のこっている[2]。 京都・奈良を おとずれる 人々[3]は 歴史を 自分の 目で 見ることが できる。 しかし[4]、 前もって 歴史を 知って いれば、 京都などを おとずれる かちが もっと[5] ふえると[6] 思う[7]。

2.2 DIALOG

ロバーツ 「来週の 週末に 京都へ 行きたいと 思っています[8]。」

池田 「それは いいですね。 京都という[9] 所には 見る 物が おどろくほど[10] たくさん ありますよ。 寺[11]や 神社[12]が 千五百も[13] あるそう[14]です。」

ロバーツ 「そんなに[15] 多いんですか。 おどろきましたねえ。」

池田 「そうでしょう。 ホテル[16]は もう よやくしましたか。」

ロバーツ 「いや、 むこうで 小さい 旅館[16]を さがすつもりです。」

池田 「なぜですか。」

ロバーツ 「本当の 日本を 知りたいから、 日本風[16]の 小さい 旅館に とまりたいんです。」

池田 「それは いい 考えだ[17]と 思いますね。 洋風[16]の ホテルでは 日本の でんとうを あじわうことが できませんからね。」

ロバーツ 「ええ。 ところで、 奈良は 京都から 近いそうですね。」

池田 「ええ、 特急なら、 三十分ぐらいだそうですよ。」

ロバーツ 「そんなに 近ければ、 足[18]を のばしたいですね。 ぼくの 友だちの[19] ジョーンズさんは、 奈良の 大仏[20]が とても いんしょう的だった[17]と 言っていました。」[21]

旅行	人々	思う	来週	池田	寺	旅館	近い
足	友だち	大仏	言っていました				

2.3 PATTERN SENTENCES

2.3.1

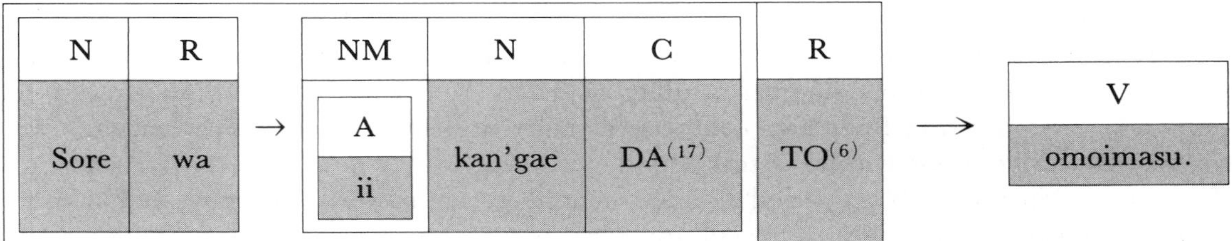

2.3.2

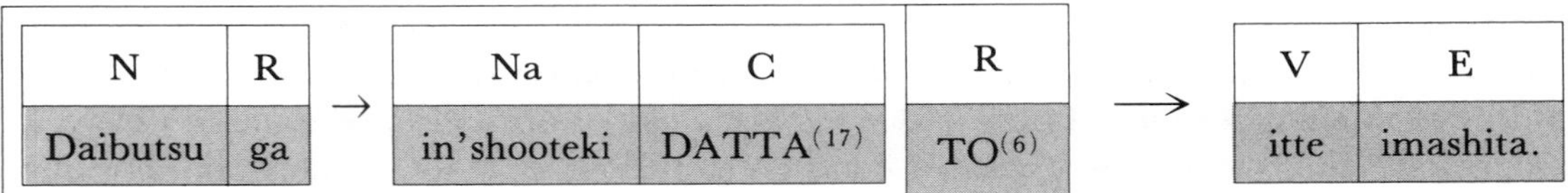

2.3.3

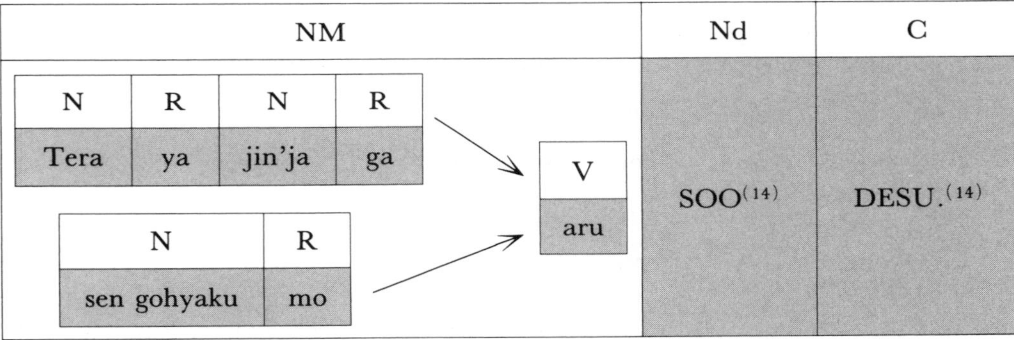

2.4 NOTES

2.4.1 Nara

Until 710, with the reign of Emperor Genmei (707–15), the capital traditionally had been transferred to a new location with each new emperor due to the Japanese belief that remaining at an old site would subject the new reign to impurities. With the increased power of the emperor and his court, a larger capital was necessary, which made it difficult to change sites each time a new emperor was enthroned. Emperor Genmei established his capital in Nara, where it remained for seventy years, thus becoming the first permanent site for a capital.

The city of present-day Nara covers only the eastern part of the old capital. The capital was modeled after the ancient Chinese capital of Ch'ang-an. All the streets were at right angles, with eight avenues crossing the main street (called Suzaku Ōji). The location of the palace was at the northern end of this street with the government offices surrounding it.

This era was culturally enriched by the civilizations of China and, indirectly, India and the West. The T'ang Empire of China was prosperous and powerful at the time, and with the establishment of diplomatic relations, Japan was greatly influenced by T'ang culture. Students and scholarly monks accompanied the ambassadors and brought back ideas and scriptures. The national consciousness of Japan was heightened by this widening of horizons, and national history began to be recorded.

This era has also been termed the golden age of Buddhism, as it exerted a great influence upon the lives of the people. The temples accumulated great wealth through vast estates, and the priests were held in reverence by the people. Nara itself had six different sects of Buddhism, whose priests participated in a number of different fields, from government administration to social work. What's more, Buddhism contributed many works of excellent craftsmanship and great aesthetic value to the culture of this period.

Thus, Japan during the Nara period attained great heights of power, prosperity, and culture. Another significant characteristic of the culture of this period, aside from the strong Buddhist influence, was the exclusive dominance of the role of the nobility within the capital.

2.4.2 When a plain form of a Predicate is used before a period of a sentence, the sentence is in the plain style. Plain-style sentences are common in writing for newspaper articles, reports, diaries, and the nonconversational portions of novels. See the explanations on styles presented in Lesson 1. This is because all of the above-mentioned items are aimed either at an unknown or an impersonal reader or at the writer himself for reading (as in a diary). When a more personal reader is involved—as in individual letter writing—a more polite style is usually employed.

2.4.3 人々 is read *hitobito* and means "people." Some Nouns consisting of few syllables often formulate their plural forms by repeating the Noun. Note that some of them make sound changes.

hito	......	hitobito	人々	"people"
kuni	......	kuniguni	国々	"countries"
ki	......	kigi	木々 (きぎ)	"trees"
yama	......	yamayama	山々	"mountains"

The mark 々 is used to show that the preceding *kan'ji* is repeated. Note that these plural forms appear more frequently in writing than in spoken language.

2.4.4 *Shikashi* is more formal and therefore used more often in the written style than its more colloquial counterparts such as *keredomo*, *keredo*, *kedo*, and *demo*.

2.4.5 *Motto* is an Adverb meaning "some more," "more," "longer," "farther," and so on. As already explained in Note 13.4.3, Volume I, another word for "more" is *moo. Moo* occurs with number words such as *ippai*, *gonin*, or numerals such as *hitotsu*, *yattsu*, while *motto* does not occur with them. *Motto*, however, may occur with other quantity words, Adjectives, Nouns, such as *takusan*, *yukkuri*, *omoshiroi*, *soba*. *Moo sukoshi* "a little more" is an exception.

Motto kudasai.	"Please give me some more."
Motto yukkuri itte kudasai.	"Please say it more slowly."
Motto takusan hoshii n desu.	"I want quite a bit more."
Koohii o motto atsuku shimashoo ka?	"Shall I make the coffee hotter?"

2.4.6 *Fueru to omou* means "I think that it will increase." *To* in this sentence is the quotation Relational, and is used to quote or report what one thinks, says, hears, writes, and so forth. The quotation Relational *to* is preceded by the Predicate of plain form normally to formulate indirect quotation or reporting. The Verbs that will follow the Relational *to* may be *omou* "think," *iu*, which should be pronounced as *yuu*, "say," *kiku* "hear; ask," *shiraseru* "inform," *kotaeru* "answer," *kaku* "write," and so on. The tense of the quoted sentence does not need to be the same as the tense of the Verb which follows the Relational *to*. The original tense is maintained. As explained before, the imperfect tense form shows that an action has not been completed while the perfect tense form means that the action has been completed.

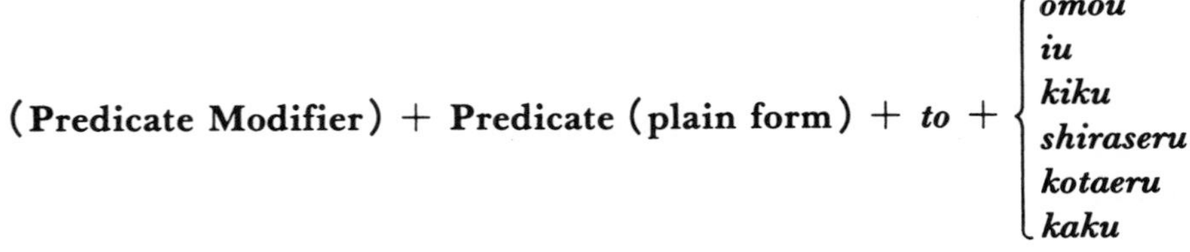

hoteru ni tomaru
hoteru ni tomaranai
hoteru ni tomatta
hoteru ni tomaranakatta

yasui
yasuku nai
yasukatta
yasuku nakatta

isha da*
isha ja nai *or* ~ de wa nai
isha datta
isha ja nakatta *or* ~ de wa nakatta

to

omoimasu
iimasu
kikimasu
shirasemasu
kotaemasu
kakimasu

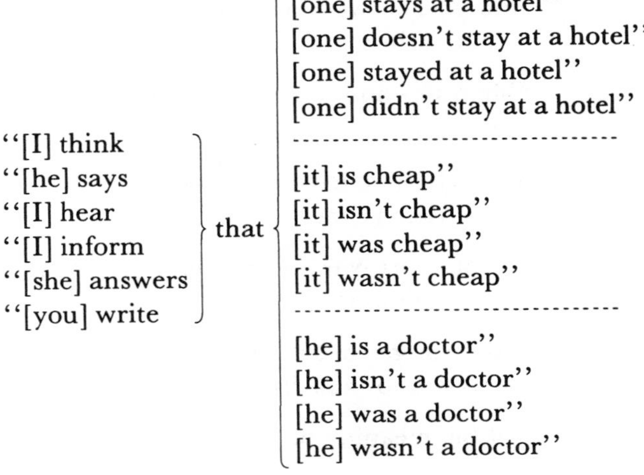

*The plain forms have been studied so far, except those of the Copula, *da, datta,* and so on. These will be explained in Note 2.4.17.

When some Predicate Modifiers, such as *sen'sei ga* as the subject of *iimasu* "say," *tomodachi ni* to show the person to whom one says or answers, *tomodachi kara* as in *tomodachi kara kikimashita*, occur, those Predicate Modifiers may occur after the quotation Relational *to* (Case 1), or they may precede the quotation phrase (Case 2). The order of the quotation phrase and other phrases is not definite: consequently, when some phrases modifying the final Predicate *omou*, *kaku*, and the like precede the quotation (Case 2), there may be some ambiguity to determine whether those phrases modify the Predicate in the quotation or the final Predicate.

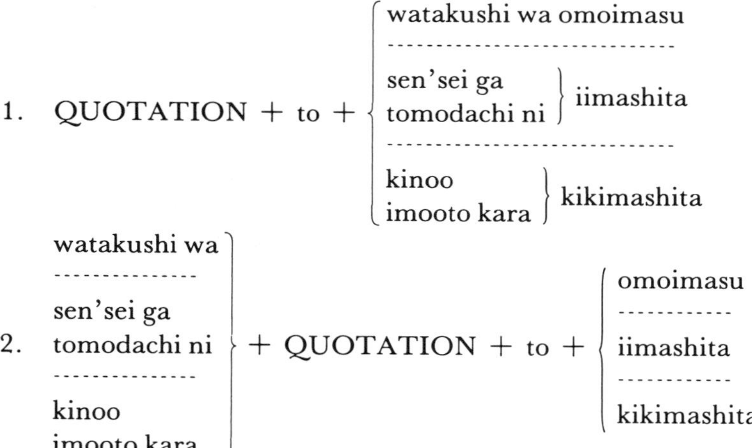

When the quotation phrase is rather long, the first pattern will be more common.

The tense of the quotation is never affected by that of the final Predicate. The so-called "sequence of tense" in English does not occur in Japanese. Therefore *iku to omoimashita* "[I] thought he would go" is different from *itta to omoimashita* "[I] thought he went." The former sentence uses imperfect tense form *iku* and the latter uses perfect tense form *itta*. In connection with the Verb *omoimasu*, both *~nai to omoimasu* and *~to wa omoimasen* are used. But normally the former is used, although the latter may be used when one has very strong evidence that indicates there is reason for strong doubt.

Pooru san wa sushi o taberu to omoimasu yo. — "I think Paul will eat *sushi*."

Ano yoyaku wa moo torikeshita to kikimashita ga. — "I heard that he already canceled that reservation."

Nihon'fuu no ryokan ni tomaritai to Buraun san ga itte imasu*. — "Mr. Brown says that he would like to stay at a Japanese-style inn."

Tomodachi ni hatsuka ni wa ikanai to shirasemashita. — "I informed my friend that I was not going there on the twentieth."

Kyooto yori Nara no hoo ga mushiatsui to omoimasu. — "I think it is hotter and more humid in Nara than it is in Kyōto."

Mori san ga shiken wa muzukashiku nakatta to iimashita. — "Mr. Mori said that the exam was not difficult."

*In the meaning of "say," *itte imasu* is used more often than *iimasu* with a quotation.

In addition to the indirect quotation, it is also possible to use the Relational *to* to quote one's utterance directly, to reproduce it as it is said, written, and so on. Sometimes it is not easy to distinguish the direct quotation from the indirect quotation.

Yamada san ga "watashi wa Nara ni tomarimashita" to iimashita.	"Mr. Yamada said, 'I stayed in Nara.' "
Haha ga "ban'gohan wa ton'katsu ni shimashoo" to itte imashita.	"My mother said, 'Let's cook pork cutlet for dinner.' "
Kokuban ni "shiken" to kakimashita.	"I wrote the word 'examination' on the blackboard."

2.4.7 Non-definite Expressions

As has been previously mentioned, the traditional Japanese tend to avoid definitive statements. The use of *to omoimasu*—"I think"—adds a softening effect to an otherwise definite or abrupt statement. Therefore, in discussing tomorrow's weather, one would not say *ashita wa ten'ki desu*—literally, "tomorrow is good weather"—but would use the less definite expression, *ashita wa ten'ki da to omoimasu*, which means "I think tomorrow will be good weather." Likewise, instead of saying *Nyuu Yooku e ikitai desu*—"I want to go to New York"—the Japanese would also say, *Nyuu Yooku e ikitai to omoimasu*—"I think I want to go to New York." Such an explanation of one's intentions sometimes might sound awkward in American English. The Japanese, however, prefer such non-definitive expressions, especially when revealing a first person's wish or desire. *~to omoimasu* may function similarly when the speaker expresses his own opinion.

The Japanese speaker will avoid asserting his own position on a matter. Therefore, *ikanai to omoimasu*—"I think he wouldn't go"—is preferred to *iku to omoimasen*—"I don't think he would go." In the former expression, *to omoimasu* serves as a softening adjunct to the statement, whereas in the second expression, it is not a softener, and in fact stresses the speaker's position. Consequently, the first statement is the more commonly used expression.

2.4.8 *To omotte imasu* is a common expression in Japan, and serves also to leave room for the listener to feel that the speaker does not show his wish or desire in an obvious way. While *to omou* in the preceding note indicates the speaker's answer to the question, *ikitai to omotte imasu* in this note is the speaker's own statement of wish, desire, or intention.

2.4.9 *Kyooto to iu tokoro* means "the place called Kyōto." The combination of Noun 1 *to iu* Noun 2 conveys the meaning of "Noun 2 called Noun 1" or "Noun 2 named Noun 1," and so forth. *Iu* is pronounced *yuu*. Generally speaking *to iu* is used because the preceding Noun is unfamiliar to the listener or it is being referred to in an unusual sense.

Mori san to iu hito	"a person named Mr. Mori"
nihon'fuu to iu kotoba	"the word 'Japanese style' "
San Furan'shisuko to iu machi	"a city called San Francisco"
Kiku to Katana to iu hon	"the book titled *The Chrysanthemum and the Sword*"

In order to ask the name of a person or of an inn, the meaning of a word, and so on, *nan to iu* plus a Noun is used.

Ano kata wa nan to iu namae desu ka?	"What is his name?"
"Yoyaku" wa nan to iu imi desu ka?	"What does the word *yoyaku* mean?"

"Reservation" to iu imi desu. — "It means 'reservation.' "

Yuumei na ishi no niwa ga aru no wa nan to iu otera desu ka? — "What is the name of the temple where the famous stone garden is?"

Ryooan'ji desu. — "It is the Ryōanji Temple."

Note that *iu* in the meaning of "called" or "named" is not normally written using the *kan'ji* 言, but in *hiragana*.

In this dialog, Ikeda refers to the city of Kyōto by using the phrase *Kyooto to iu tokoro*. Actually such a phrase, meaning literally "a place called Kyōto," is superfluous, and one can easily say *Kyooto e*, as Roberts does. Such a usage is, however, another example of the Japanese circumventional approach. By placing the expression *to iu tokoro ni wa* after a proper noun, one makes an otherwise definitive statement much less definite. It is understood that Kyōto is well known, therefore, *to iu tokoro ni wa* will not be necessary. However, Ikeda was talking to a foreigner, therefore Kyōto may not be as well known. With this feeling in mind, Ikeda used *Kyooto to iu tokoro ni wa*.

2.4.10 *Odoroku hodo* means "to such an extent that one may be surprised." The Relational *hodo*, preceded by a Predicate, may also be used in an affirmative sentence meaning "to such an extent that . . . " (See Notes 11.4.13 and 12.4.10, Vol. II, for *hodo* in a negative sentence.)

Kono gakusei wa oshieru koto ga dekiru hodo nihon'go ga joozu ni narimashita. — "This student became so proficient in Japanese that he could teach it."

Byooki ni naru hodo hatarakanaide kudasai. — "Please don't work so hard that you may become ill."

Kawa no mizu ga odoroku hodo fuemashita. — "The water of the river has increased surprisingly."

2.4.11 *Tera*, or Buddhist Temples

The construction of temples began as early as 592 in the reign of Empress Suiko. The Hōryūji, located near Nara, is one of the most famous. It is probably the oldest wooden building in existence today, and remains relatively intact. Most of the temples of this period consisted of a few buildings erected within enclosures and comprising a pagoda. The buildings usually house the sacred treasures and consist of a hall for preaching, a scripture house, the priests' quarters, a bell tower, and a hall where the image of the Buddha was kept. A corridor that surrounded the grounds in a square shape usually was connected with these structures. The foundations were of stone, the roofs were tiled, and the woodwork was always put together by means of wooden pegs, without the use of any nails or screws.

The Buddhist architecture introduced roughly in the period between 552 and 794, was basically a Chinese architectural style modified in ornamentation. Thus, the spread of Buddhist architecture throughout Japan resulted in a widespread influence of Chinese architecture in the building of palaces and shrines.

Following the Heian period, however, with the cessation of official communication with China after the tenth century, the architecture began to move away from the dominant Chinese influence and toward a traditional Japanese style.

2.4.12 *Jin'ja*, or Shinto Shrines

Architecturally shrines were extremely simple. They were intended for the worship of the gods rather than for preaching. They never faced the west or the north due to the unluckiness of these directions, and usually were built at a spot of scenic or historic beauty.

The styles of the palaces of the ancient days were used in the building of shrines, with the forests supplying all the materials used in the construction. The *Nihon'shoki*, or "Record of Ancient Matters," published in 720 says that the only type of wood that may be used is the Japanese cypress, or *hinoki*.

The shrine building consisted of the main shrine where the deity is enshrined, the front shrine, the *haiden*, or hall for public worship, the *hon'den*, or the inner sanctuary used by the priests and important people, and the symbol of the shrine, the *torii* gate. The front shrine was used during religious festivals for the seating of the people.

2.4.13 *Sen gohyaku mo* is "as many as a thousand and five hundred," "no fewer than a thousand and five hundred." The Relational *mo*, when used right after a number, means "as many as ~," "as long as ~," "as much as ~," "no less than ~," and so on.

Buraun san wa kan'ji o moo hyaku mo naratta soo desu.	"I understand that Mr. Brown has already learned as many as a hundred Chinese characters."
Kesa wa koohii o gohai mo nomimashita.	"I drank as many as five cups of coffee this morning."
Mukashi wa Tookyoo kara Sapporo made kisha to fune de nijuu yojikan mo kakarimashita.	"It took us no fewer than twenty-four hours by train and boat from Tōkyō to Sapporo in old times."

2.4.14 *Tera ya jin'ja ga sen gohyaku mo aru soo desu* means "I understand that there are no fewer than a thousand and five hundred temples and shrines there." When *soo* occurs after a Predicate or a sentence, it is the dependent Noun that conveys the meaning of "hearsay." The whole sentence followed by *soo desu* is equivalent to "I heard that . . . ," "They say that . . . ," "It is said that . . . ," or "I understand that . . . ." The forms of Predicate that precede *soo desu* are plain forms of a Verb, an Adjective, or a Noun plus a plain form of the Copula. *Soo* is always followed by the imperfect tense form of the Copula *desu* or *da*.

(Predicate Modifier) + Predicate (plain form) + ***soo desu***

hoteru ni tomaru	soo desu
hoteru ni tomaranai	
hoteru ni tomatta	
hoteru ni tomaranakatta	
chikai	
chikaku nai	
chikakatta	
chikaku nakatta	

hon'too da* hon'too ja nai *or* ~ de wa nai hon'too datta hon'too ja nakatta *or* ~ de wa nakatta *See Note 2.4.17 for *da*.	soo desu

"I heard "it is said "they say "I understand	that	[he] will stay at a hotel" [they] are not staying at a hotel" [she] stayed at a hotel" [they] didn't stay at a hotel" --- [it] is near" [it] is not near" [it] was near" [it] wasn't near" --- [it] is true" [it] isn't true" [it] was true" [it] wasn't true"

Kisha wa gogo goji ni tsuku soo desu.	"I heard that the train would arrive at 5 P.M."
Ichiroo wa kibun ga warui kara, hirugohan o tabenai soo desu.	"I heard that since Ichirō doesn't feel well he won't eat lunch."
Ikeda san wa Yokohama no ii ryokan ni tomatta soo desu.	"I understand that Mr. Ikeda stayed at a good inn in Yokohama."
Imooto wa Nara made ashi o nobasanakatta soo desu.	"I understand that my sister didn't extend the trip to Nara."
Yamada san wa isha ni naritai soo desu yo.	"They say that Mr. Yamada wants to be a physician."
Niigata wa fuyu yuki ga ooi soo desu.	"It is said that they have a lot of snow in Nīgata in the winter."
Byooin wa koko kara amari chikaku nai soo desu.	"I understand that the hospital is not very near here."
Ryokoo wa taihen tanoshikatta soo desu.	"I heard that he enjoyed the trip very much."
Getsuyoobi wa zen'zen isogashiku nakatta soo desu.	"I heard that he was not busy at all on Monday."

2.4.15 *Son'na ni ooi n desu ka?* means "Are there that many?" *Son'na ni* is used as an Adverb and means "so (many)," "that (much)," and so on. Likewise, *kon'na ni*, *an'na ni*, and *don'na ni* are also possible.

Michi ga kon'de imashita kara, Kyooto kara Nara made nijikan mo kakarimashita.	"Since the roads had heavy traffic, it took me a good two hours from Kyōto to Nara."

Son'na ni kakarimashita ka?	"Did it take that long?"
Anata no uchi wa eki kara kon'na ni tooi n desu ka?	"Is your house this far from the station?"

2.4.16 *Hoteru* is usually the Western-style hotel and *ryokan* is the Japanese-style inn. *Nihon'fuu* means Japanese style and *yoofuu* means Western style. The coexistence of both Japanese inns and Western hotels is a good example of "cultural pluralism and eclecticism" of Japan.

Cultural Pluralism

Cultural pluralism is one of the most dominant and important features of Japanese civilization. Before developing a definitive and prosperous culture of their own, the Japanese were exposed to the overwhelmingly more powerful and highly developed culture of the Asian mainland via China, Korea, and other channels. The Chinese culture to which they were thus exposed took the form mainly of Confucianism and Buddhism, as well as general life-styles. All of these foreign elements were added to the indigenous Japanese culture of ancient, pantheistic Shinto. Rather than totally replacing the older or native elements with the new or foreign ones, the Japanese kept all, digesting new forms according to the needs of the Japanese environment and society. Thus, a workable synthesis of new and old, native and foreign was created. Two features that have made Japan one of the most obvious cases of cultural pluralism in the world are: the Japanese eclectic tendency in absorbing foreign cultures, and the relative absence of any thorough revolutionary overthrow of rulers in Japanese history. (The existing society was never totally overthrown by new forces in Japan; rather, adjustment allowed for a gradual shifting into new stages.)

Shūichi Katō has described Japanese culture as a hybrid culture; the coexistence of various types of cultures in Japanese society, serving to complement each other. The term "hybrid" implies that the end result of such coexistence is not necessarily a new synthesis—a viewpoint which may be disputed.

Konan Naitō, on the other hand, has compared the manner in which Japanese culture developed with the relationship between bean curd material and bittern (*nigari*). He states that prior to the Chinese cultural invasion, the Japanese had no definitive cultural patterns. Rather, the Japanese had the materials for the bean curd (culture). It was only with the help of the bittern of Chinese culture that these bean curd materials became, in fact, bean curd.

Whatever theory we adopt, the relationship between the indigenous culture and the foreign cultures as well as its subsequent developments have had an important effect upon Japanese thought and the Japanese way of life, resulting in cultural achievements in the pluralistic manner. The transformed, imported foreign cultures became incorporated into a pattern of Japanese culture. Such cultural pluralism is the result of the Japanese eclectic approach in the selection of foreign elements, and marks one of the most important characteristics of Japanese culture.

Japanese clothing, food, housing, hotels, and inns—all evidence this cultural pluralism. Such manifestations can be found in every area of Japanese daily life. The criterion of practicality, however, seems to be guiding the assimilation of these foreign elements. For men, for example, one finds Western dress in use outside the home, where it is better suited to the demands of modern life; in the home, however, traditional dress is often preferred. The home itself also exhibits Western and traditional elements side by side: the more durable Western-style architecture may be used in the construction of buildings, enclosing a more traditional interior design. The Japanese diet has also felt the impact of new influences, injected with new types of foods and new methods of preparation.

Similarly, industry exhibits the coexistence of gigantic modern industry alongside the premodern small and medium size manufacturing concerns, and the modern concept of democratic government, including a parliament and cabinet, coexists with premodern political party operations.

Contemporary manners and customs in Japan are the products of a long period of development, cultural contacts, assimilation of non-Japanese elements and subsequent Japanization of such elements. At present, extensive cultural change is taking place in Japan due to westernization, with the result that traditional and Western elements exist side by side in contemporary Japanese life. As can be seen, the absorption and transformation of foreign cultural elements are not new to the Japanese, but only time will tell what type of synthesis will evolve from this new stage of cultural change.

Cultural pluralism covers not only "area concepts," such as Japanese, Chinese, Indian, and Western, but also covers "time concepts," such as primitive, medieval, modern, and current. All elements coexist with relative degrees of importance, and in many cases complement each other. Labor unions, for example, structured along the industrywide unions' lines are not necessarily as powerful as those unions built along the companywide arrangements which are more compatible with the traditional Japanese context.

From the point of view of the written language, Chinese characters coexist with *hiragana* which represents the conjugated portions of Verbs, Adjectives, Copulas, some prefixes, and Relationals and Sentence Particles. Both of these forms coexist with *katakana*, which in many cases represents Western loan words. The tremendous number of Western loan words currently in use in Japan is still another example of this cultural pluralism.

And finally, so basic is cultural pluralism that, when they marry, the Japanese could go to a Shinto shrine for the wedding ceremony, whereas, when they die, they might well be buried in a Buddhist temple cemetery ground according to Buddhist rites.

2.4.17 *Da* is the plain equivalent of *desu,* and *datta* is the plain equivalent of *deshita.* The plain negative equivalents of *ja arimasen* or *de wa arimasen* and *ja arimasen deshita* or *de wa arimasen deshita* are as follows:

Noun + *desu*	⟶	**~ + *da***
Noun + *ja arimasen*	⟶	**~ + *ja nai***
or ~ + *de wa arimasen*		**or ~ + *de wa nai***
Noun + *deshita*	⟶	**~ + *datta***
Noun + *ja arimasen deshita*	⟶	**~ + *ja nakatta***
or ~ + *de wa arimasen deshita*		**or ~ + *de wa nakatta***

Adjectives are never followed by the plain-form Copula *da.* Adjectives are plain forms as they are, and the normal-form Copula *desu* is needed only when Adjectives occur at the end of a sentence in polite-style speech.

These plain forms of the Copula are used in various patterns in polite style, as well as in plain-style Japanese, and the patterns introduced in Notes 2.4.6 and 2.4.14 both require the use of the plain forms *da, datta,* and so on.

~ da ~ ja nai *or* ~ de wa nai ~ datta ~ ja nakatta *or* ~ de wa nakatta	to omou to kiku to iu - - - - - - - - soo da

Sore wa hon'too da to omoimasu.	"I think that is true."
Yoyaku shita ryokan wa nihon'fuu de wa nai to omoimasu yo.	"I don't think that the hotel we have reserved is Japanese style."
Kyooto no furui tera ya niwa ga in'shooteki datta soo desu.	"They say that the old temples and gardens in Kyōto were impressive."
Inoue san wa byooki ja nakatta soo desu.	"I understand that Mr. Inoue wasn't sick."
Kore wa Michiko san no da soo desu.	"I heard that this is Michiko's."
Sore wa dame datta to Watanabe san ga itte imashita.	"Mr. Watanabe said that was no good."

2.4.18 *Ashi o nobasu* means here "extend the trip as far as such-and-such a place." Depending upon context, this can mean literally "extend one's leg" or "stretch one's leg." Likewise, *te o nobasu* can be literally "extend one's hand" or can mean "expand (one's business, etc.)." These expressions form part of the Japanese tendency to use vocabulary connected with concrete objects, such as the human body, to indicate generalized and abstract concepts. Examples of words used in this way are: *ashi o arau*—"wash one's hands off"; *te o kiru*—"cut off ties"; *te ga hayai*—"thievish"; *kubi* "neck," *kubi o kiru*—"fire," *kubi o tsukkomu* "be involved"; *kao* "face," *kao o tsubusu*—"lose face," *kao o kasu*—"spare a moment," *kao o tateru*—"save a person's face"; *mimi* "ear," *mimi ga itai*—"be ashamed to hear," *mimi o kasu*—"lend one's ear to"; *me o tsukeru*—"have one's eye on," *me o nusumu* "secretly."

2.4.19 *Boku no tomodachi no Joon'zu san* means "Mr. Jones, who is a friend of mine" or "my friend, Mr. Jones." The second *no* of this phrase is different, both in meaning and function, from the first *no* already studied. When a Noun plus the imperfect tense form of the Copula modifies the following Noun, there are two ways of formulating a Noun Modifier. If the Noun before *desu* is an adjectival Noun such as *kirei*, *gen'ki*, *desu* changes into *na*. (See Note 5.4.2, Vol. II.) However, when the Noun before the Copula is other than an adjectival Noun, the Relational *no* is used instead of any form of the Copula *desu*. This is called the appositional use of the Relational *no*.

Noun 1 + *wa* + Noun 2 + *desu*	⟶	**Noun 2 + *no* + Noun 1**
Sumisu san wa gakusei desu	⟶	gakusei no Sumisu san "Mr. Smith who is a student"
Joon'zu san wa igirisujin desu	⟶	igirisujin no Joon'zu san "Mr. Jones, an Englishman"
musuko wa hatachi desu	⟶	hatachi no musuko "twenty-year-old son"

There are times when it is difficult to distinguish this use of *no* from the possessive use of *no*. For example, *isha no musuko* can be "the doctor's son" or "a son who is a doctor." However, usually the context will make it clear which meaning is called for.

Da, the plain equivalent of *desu*, never modifies a Noun directly. Either *na* or *no* must be used. Note that this is applicable only to the imperfect tense form of the Copula, and *datta, ja nai, de* (*wa*) *nakatta* occur for other tense forms.

Noun + ***no***
(non-adjectival)
  〃 + ***ja nai*** **or** ~ ***de*** **(*wa*)** ***nai***
  〃 + ***datta***
  〃 + ***ja nakatta*** **or** ~ ***de*** **(*wa*)** ***nakatta***
} + **Noun**

byooki no byooki ja nai byooki datta byooki de wa nakatta	hito	"a person who	is sick" is not sick" was sick" was not sick"

Isha no musuko wa ima Oosaka ni imasu ga, hoka no wa min'na Tookyoo ni imasu.	"One of my sons, who is a doctor, is now in Ōsaka, but the other sons are all in Tōkyō."
Kono naka de gakusei ja nai hito wa Yamada san dake desu.	"Mr. Yamada is the only one that is not a student among these people."
Ishii san wa amerikajin no okusan to nihon'go de hanasu soo desu.	"I heard that Mr. Ishii communicates with his American wife in Japanese."

When the first Noun is an adjectival Noun and the second Noun is replaced by a Noun *no* "one(s)," the *na* should be used instead of the Relational *no*.

Noun + ***na*** + ***no***
(adjectival)

Kirei na no o kudasai.	"Give me the one that is pretty."

2.4.20 *Nara no Daibutsu*, or the Great Buddha of Nara

The largest Buddhist image in Japan is in Nara. Construction on it began in 745. The bronze image of the Buddha is over fifty-three feet tall and sits upon a lotus which is ten feet high and sixty-eight feet in diameter. The lotus has fifty-six petals, which represent the Buddhist universe. Frequent fires in the past have caused extensive damage to the Hall of the Great Buddha, and the only original portions of the bronze image that remain are the body and a few lotus petals.

2.4.21 From the "level and style" of speech in this dialog, it is possible to determine that Roberts and Ikeda are probably friends. From what Ikeda says in particular, he probably feels that Roberts does not know much concerning what to see, what is good and what is bad, as well as what to expect in Japan.

2.5 VOCABULARY

Presentation

奈良 (なら)	Nara	......	N	a historical spot in the Kansai area
文化 (か)	bun'ka	......	N	culture

のこって	nokotte	V	TE form of *nokoru* - remain; is left (intransitive Verb)
おとずれる	otozureru	V	visit (transitive Verb) (normally used in formal speech or in writing)
人々	hitobito	N	people (more commonly used in formal speech or in writing than *hitotachi*) (see 2.4.3)
しかし	shikashi	SI	however; but (formal equivalent of *demo*) (see 2.4.4)
前もって	mae motte	Adv.	in advance
かち	kachi	N	value
もっと	motto	Adv.	some more; more; longer; farther (see 2.4.5)
ふえる	fueru	V	increase (intransitive Verb)
と	to	R	quotation Relational (see 2.4.6)

Dialog

ロバーツ	Robaatsu	N	Roberts
池(いけ)田	Ikeda	N	family name
いう	iu (yuu)	V	is called; is named (see 2.4.9)
おどろく	odoroku	V	is surprised (intransitive Verb)
神社(じんじゃ)	jin'ja	N	Shinto shrine
も	mo	R	as many as; no less than; no fewer than (see 2.4.13)
そう	soo	Nd	I heard; I understand (see 2.4.14)
そんなに	son'na ni	Adv.	so (many); that (much) (see 2.4.15)
ホテル	hoteru	N	(Western-style) hotel
よやく	yoyaku	N	reservation
よやくしました	yoyaku shimashita	V	reserved (TA form of *yoyaku shimasu* ← *yoyaku suru*)
いや	iya	SI	no (used normally by men)
むこう	mukoo	N	over there; the other side
旅館	ryokan	N	Japanese-style hotel or inn
なぜ	naze	Ni	why?
日本風(ふう)	nihon'fuu	N	Japanese style
とまり	tomari	V	Stem form of *tomaru* - stop (at); stay (at) (～ *ni tomaru*)
考(かんが)え	kan'gae	N	idea; thought

だ	da	......	C	plain equivalent of the Copula *desu* (see 2.4.17)
洋風(ようふう)	yoofuu	......	N	Western style
でんとう	den'too	......	N	tradition
あじわう	ajiwau	......	V	taste; appreciate
特急(とっきゅう)	tokkyuu	......	N	limited express
のばし	nobashi	......	V	Stem form of *nobasu* - extend; stretch
の	no	......	R	(see 2.4.19)
ジョーンズ	Joon'zu	......	N	Jones
大仏(ぶつ)	daibutsu	......	N	a great image of the Buddha
いんしょう的(てき)	in'shooteki	......	Na	impressive
だった	datta	......	C	TA form of *da* (plain equivalent of the Copula *deshita*) (see 2.4.17)

Notes

知らせる	shiraseru	......	V	inform; let someone know
じゃない	ja nai	......	C+R+E	negative of *da* (see 2.4.17)
ではない	de wa nai	......	C+R+E	negative of *da* (see 2.4.17)
とりけす	torikesu	......	V	cancel
きく	kiku	......	N	chrysanthemum
かたな	katana	......	N	sword
いみ	imi	......	N	meaning
川	kawa	......	N	river; stream
汽(き)車	kisha	......	N	steam train; railroad train
こんなに	kon'na ni	......	Adv.	this (many; much)
あんなに	an'na ni	......	Adv.	that (many; much)
どんなに	don'na ni	......	Adv.	how (many; much)?

2.6 KAN'JI

2.6.1 旅 (1) RYO (2) travel; journey (3) classifier 方

(4) 丶 亠 方 方 方 方 方 旅 旅 旅 (5) 旅館(かん)、旅行

(6) many people ( ) under a flag (⟶) ⟶ moving around like military personnel

2.6.a 行 (1) KOO (5) 急(きゅう)行、旅行、銀(ぎん)行員
4.6.3, Vol. II

2.6.2 々 (2) This mark may be used for repeating the sound of the preceding character.
(4) ノ ク 々 (5) 人々、年々 [year after year]、国々(ぐに) [countries]

2.6.3 思 (1) *omo(u)* (2) think; esteem (3) classifier 田 (心(こころ))
(4) 田 田 思 思 思 (5) そう思います

2.6.b 来 (1) RAI (2) coming (5) 来年、来月、来週(しゅう) [cf. 先月、先週(しゅう)]
8.6.4, Vol. II

2.6.c 田 (1) *-da* (5) 山田さん、上田さん
13.6.5, Vol. II

2.6.4 寺 (1) *tera* (2) Buddhist temple (3) classifier 土 (寸)
(4) 一 十 土 寺 寺 寺 (5) 京都には寺が多い
(6) ankle (止) ⟶ leg plus hand (ㄓ ⟶ 寸); place to work ⟶ office ⟶ temple

2.6.5 館 (1) KAN (2) building (3) classifier 食 [eat; meal]
(4) 食 食 食 館 館 館 館 館 館
(5) 旅館、大使(たいし)館、図(と)書館、びじゅつ館、えいが館 [movie theater]
(6) 官 KAN is the phonetic component; homonym 官、菅、棺、管

2.6.6 近 (1) *chika(i)* (2) near; close (3) classifier 辶
(4) 丿 厂 斤 斤 䜣 䜣 近 (5) 近い
(6) one side of a crossroad (彳) and leg (止) ⟶ walking (彳止 ⟶ 辵 ⟶ 辶); homonym KIN 欣、斤

2.6.7 足 (1) *ashi* (2) leg; foot (3) classifier 口 (足)
(4) 丨 口 口 早 早 足 足 (5) 左足
(6) knee (○) and ankle (止); homonym SOKU 促

2.6.8 友 (1) *tomo* (2) friend (3) classifier ナ (又) (4) 一 ナ 方 友
(5) 友だち

2.6.9 言 (1) *i(u)* (2) say; express; remark (3) classifier 言
(4) 丶 亠 亠 言 言 言 言 (5) 日本語で言ってください

2.6.10 円* (1) EN (2) yen (Japanese monetary unit) (3) classifier 冂
(4) 丨 冂 円 円 (5) 八千九百六十二円

2.7　DRILLS

2.7.1　Transformation Drill

1. おとうとは　いしゃに　なります。思います。	→	おとうとは　いしゃに　なると　思います。
2. あしたは　学校を　休みます。友だちに　知らせました。	→	あしたは　学校を　休むと　友だちに　知らせました。
3. 1975年ごろ　ちちは　銀行に　つとめていました。聞きました。	→	1975年ごろ　ちちは　銀行に　つとめていたと　聞きました。
4. 日光まで　足を　のばしたいんです。思っています。	→	日光まで　足を　のばしたいと　思っています。
5. よやくは　とりけしました。林さんが　言っています。	→	よやくは　とりけしたと　林さんが　言っています。
6. 洋風の　ホテルには　とまりたくありません。ポールさんが　言いました。	→	洋風の　ホテルには　とまりたくないと　ポールさんが　言いました。
7. 京都まで　車で　三時間　かかりません。思っていました。	→	京都まで　車で　三時間　かからないと　思っていました。
8. ヨーロッパには　古い　文化が　のこっています。思います。	→	ヨーロッパには　古い　文化が　のこっていると　思います。

2.7.2　Transformation Drill

1. この　週末は　天気が　わるいです。ラジオで　言いました。	→	この　週末は　天気が　わるいと　ラジオで　言いました。
2. あの　ホテルは　あまり　ひろくありません。聞きました。	→	あの　ホテルは　あまり　ひろくないと　聞きました。
3. 「きくと　かたな」という　本は　すこし　古いです。ポールさんが　言っています。	→	「きくと　かたな」という　本は　すこし　古いと　ポールさんが　言っています。

4. 奈良(なら)の　大仏(ぶつ)は　おどろくほど　大きいです。聞きました。 → 奈良(なら)の　大仏(ぶつ)は　おどろくほど　大きいと　聞きました。

5. 日光(にっこう)なら、東京から　とおく　ありません。思います。 → 日光(にっこう)なら、東京から　とおくないと　思います。

6. いしゃに　なるのは　むずかしかったです。井上(いのうえ)さんが　言いました。 → いしゃに　なるのは　むずかしかったと　井上(いのうえ)さんが　言いました。

7. カリフォルニアの　ふゆは　さむく　ありません。聞きました。 → カリフォルニアの　ふゆは　さむくないと　聞きました。

8. 先週(しゅう)は　あまり　いそがしく　ありませんでした。思いました。 → 先週(しゅう)は　あまり　いそがしくなかったと　思いました。

2.7.3 Transformation Drill

1. つぎの　しけんは　五月三日です。聞きました。 → つぎの　しけんは　五月三日だと　聞きました。

2. 歴史(れきし)が　好きでした。大川さんは　言いました。 → 歴史(れきし)が　好きだったと　大川さんは　言いました。

3. ブラウンさんは　あまり　日本語が　じょうずじゃありません。思いました。 → ブラウンさんは　あまり　日本語が　じょうずじゃないと　思います。

4. それは　たぶん　池(いけ)田さんの　考(かんが)えです。思いました。 → それは　たぶん　池(いけ)田さんの　考(かんが)えだと　思いました。

5. 京都が　一番　いんしょう的(てき)でした。山田さんが　言っていました。 → 京都が　一番　いんしょう的(てき)だったと　山田さんが　言っていました。

6. あの　うちは　洋風(ようふう)じゃありませんでした。思います。 → あの　うちは　洋風(ようふう)じゃなかったと　思います。

7. なつ休みに　旅行するつもりでした。ぼくは　こたえました。 → なつ休みに　旅行するつもりだったと　ぼくは　こたえました。

8. ロバーツさんが　見たのは　鎌倉の　大仏です。思います。 → ロバーツさんが　見たのは　鎌倉の　大仏だと　思います。

2.7.4 Transformation Drill

1. 池田さんは　週末に　鎌倉へ　およぎに　行きます。 → 池田さんは　週末に　鎌倉へ　およぎに　行くそうです。
2. 外国人が　おおぜい　京都や　奈良を　おとずれました。 → 外国人が　おおぜい　京都や　奈良を　おとずれたそうです。
3. みち子さんは　ピアノを　ひくことが　できます。 → みち子さんは　ピアノを　ひくことが　できるそうです。
4. 新しい　電話番号は　みんなに　知らせません。 → 新しい　電話番号は　みんなに　知らせないそうです。
5. ポールさんは　日本文化を　勉強しませんでした。 → ポールさんは　日本文化を　勉強しなかったそうです。
6. 日本語の　学生が　ずっと　ふえました。 → 日本語の　学生が　ずっと　ふえたそうです。
7. 京都には　まだ　古い　でんとうが　のこっています。 → 京都には　まだ　古い　でんとうが　のこっているそうです。
8. ジョーンズさんは　日本風の　旅館に　とまりたくありません。 → ジョーンズさんは　日本風の　旅館に　とまりたくないそうです。

2.7.5 Transformation Drill

1. スミスさんは　もっと　やさしい　本が　ほしいんです。 → スミスさんは　もっと　やさしい　本が　ほしいそうです。
2. 歴史の　クラスは　とても　むずかしかったです。 → 歴史の　クラスは　とても　むずかしかったそうです。
3. この　カメラは　あまり　たかくありません。 → この　カメラは　あまり　たかくないそうです。

4. きのう　石井(いしい)さんが　見た　えいがは　おもしろくありませんでした。 ──→ きのう　石井(いしい)さんが　見た　えいがは　おもしろくなかったそうです。
5. 汽(き)車より　自動車の　ほうが　はやかったです。 ──→ 汽(き)車より　自動車の　ほうが　はやかったそうです。
6. その　旅館は　あまり　ひろく　ありません。 ──→ その　旅館は　あまり　ひろくないそうです。
7. 京都という　町は　古いです。 ──→ 京都という　町は　古いそうです。
8. 先週(しゅう)の　日曜(よう)日なら、つごうが　わるくありませんでした。 ──→ 先週(しゅう)の　日曜(よう)日なら、つごうが　わるくなかったそうです。

2.7.6 Transformation Drill

1. 一郎(ろう)くんは　今　びょう気です。 ──→ 一郎(ろう)くんは　今　びょう気だそうです。
2. きょ年の　ふゆ休みは　一月十日まででした。 ──→ きょ年の　ふゆ休みは　一月十日までだったそうです。
3. あの　旅館は　しずかじゃありません。 ──→ あの　旅館は　しずかじゃないそうです。
4. あの　かたの　うちは　日本風(ふう)です。 ──→ あの　かたの　うちは　日本風(ふう)だそうです。
5. その　名前は　本当(とう)ではありませんでした。 ──→ その　名前は　本当(とう)ではなかったそうです。
6. 神社(じんじゃ)や　お寺は　ひじょうに　りっぱでした。 ──→ 神社(じんじゃ)や　お寺は　ひじょうに　りっぱだったそうです。
7. 池(いけ)田さんは　洋風(ようふう)の　食べ物が　好きではありません。 ──→ 池(いけ)田さんは　洋風(ようふう)の　食べ物が　好きではないそうです。
8. 時間は　前もって　知らせるつもりです。 ──→ 時間は　前もって　知らせるつもりだそうです。

2.7.7 Expansion Drill

1. 食べ物屋が　多いです。 …… 食べ物屋が　多いです。
   おどろくほど …… おどろくほど　食べ物屋が　多いです。
   東京には …… 東京には　おどろくほど　食べ物屋が　多いです。
2. しないでください。 …… しないでください。
   しごとを …… しごとを　しないでください。
   びょう気に　なるほど …… びょう気に　なるほど　しごとを　しないでください。

3. 気分が　わるいんですか。 …… 気分が　わるいんですか。

いしゃを　よぶほど …… いしゃを　よぶほど　気分が　わるいんですか。

鈴木さんは …… 鈴木さんは　いしゃを　よぶほど　気分が　わるいんですか。

4. 買いました。 …… 買いました。

いろいろな　おみやげを …… いろいろな　おみやげを　買いました。

へやが　せまくなるほど …… へやが　せまくなるほど　いろいろな　おみやげを買いました。

5. 食べました。 …… 食べました。

すしを …… すしを　食べました。

みんなが　おどろくほど …… みんなが　おどろくほど　すしを　食べました。

ロバーツさんは …… ロバーツさんは　みんなが　おどろくほど　すしを食べました。

6. ありますか。 …… ありますか。

おかしが …… おかしが　ありますか。

たくさん …… たくさん　おかしが　ありますか。

みんなに　あげるほど …… みんなに　あげるほど　たくさん　おかしがありますか。

7. じょうずに　なりました。 …… じょうずに　なりました。

テニスが …… テニスが　じょうずに　なりました。

教えることが　できるほど …… 教えることが　できるほど　テニスが　じょうずになりました。

ジョーンズさんは …… ジョーンズさんは　教えることが　できるほどテニスが　じょうずに　なりました。

2.7.8 Expansion Drill

1. ふえるはずです。 …… ふえるはずです。

もっと …… もっと　ふえるはずです。

人口が …… 人口が　もっと　ふえるはずです。

来年は …… 来年は　人口が　もっと　ふえるはずです。

2. しらべなければなりません。 …… しらべなければなりません。

もっと …… もっと　しらべなければなりません。

ことばの　いみを　……　ことばの　いみを　もっと　しらべなければ　なりません。

つぎの　しけんまでに　……　つぎの　しけんまでに　ことばの　いみを　もっと　しらべなければなりません。

3. じょうずに　なりますよ　……　じょうずに　なりますよ。

もっと　……　もっと　じょうずに　なりますよ。

勉強(べんきょう)すれば、　……　勉強(べんきょう)すれば、もっと　じょうずに　なりますよ。

毎(まい)日　……　毎(まい)日　勉強(べんきょう)すれば、もっと　じょうずに　なりますよ。

4. 思っています。　……　思っています。

けんぶつしたいと　……　けんぶつしたいと　思っています。

もっと　……　もっと　けんぶつしたいと　思っています。

いろいろな　所を　……　いろいろな　所を　もっと　けんぶつしたいと　思っています。

5. ながいと　思います。　……　ながいと　思います。

もっと　……　もっと　ながいと　思います。

アメリカの　川は　……　アメリカの　川は　もっと　ながいと　思います。

6. あけてください。　……　あけてください。

まどを　……　まどを　あけてください。

もっと　……　もっと　まどを　あけてください。

いい　天気ですから　……　いい　天気ですから、もっと　まどを　あけてください。

2.7.9 Response Drill

1. あの　イギリス人は　何という　名前ですか。

   スミス　……　スミスという　名前です。

2. 何という　教科(か)書を　使(つか)っていますか。

   Learn Japanese　……　*Learn Japanese* という　教科(か)書を　使(つか)っています。

3. 何という　きっさ店(てん)へ　行きましたか。

   でんえん　……　でんえんという　きっさ店(てん)へ　行きました。

4. おとうとさんは　何という　大学へ　はいりましたか。

   メリーランド大学　……　メリーランド大学という　大学へ　はいりました。

5. 文化は　英語で　何という　いみですか。
   culture …… culture という　いみです。
6. あそこは　何という　所ですか。
   上野公園 …… 上野公園という　所です。

2.7.10 Transformation Drill

1. かん字を　百五十　習いました。 ⟶ かん字を　百五十も　習いました。
2. 池田さんは　さけを　十ぱい　のみました。 ⟶ 池田さんは　さけを　十ぱいも　のみました。
3. 駅まで　一キロ　あるきました。 ⟶ 駅まで　一キロも　あるきました。
4. 大阪から　ここまで　六時間　かかりました。 ⟶ 大阪から　ここまで　六時間も　かかりました。
5. ドイツ語を　もう　五年　勉強して　います。 ⟶ ドイツ語を　もう　五年も　勉強して　います。
6. 青木さんの　うちには　七人　子どもが　いるそうです。 ⟶ 青木さんの　うちには　七人も　子どもが　いるそうです。
7. 英語の　しゅくだいが　八ページ　あります。 ⟶ 英語の　しゅくだいが　八ページも　あります。
8. くだ物を　五千円　買いました。 ⟶ くだ物を　五千円も　買いました。

2.7.11 E-J Transformation Drill

1. 京都には　古い　でんとうが　のこっています。
   I think that …… 京都には　古い　でんとうが　のこっていると　思います。
   I heard that …… 京都には　古い　でんとうが　のこっていると　聞きました。
   I understand that …… 京都には　古い　でんとうが　のこっている　そうです。
2. 東京は　人口が　ふえました。
   it is said that …… 東京は　人口が　ふえたそうです。
   Mr. Ikeda said that …… 東京は　人口が　ふえたと　池田さんが　言いました。
   I think that …… 東京は　人口が　ふえたと　思います。

3. あの　ホテルは　やすくありません。

I heard that …… あの　ホテルは　やすくないと　聞きました。

do you think that …… あの　ホテルは　やすくないと　思いますか。

who said that …… あの　ホテルは　やすくないと　だれが　言いましたか。

4. あそこは　日本風の　旅館です。

I think that …… あそこは　日本風の　旅館だと　思います。

it is said that …… あそこは　日本風の　旅館だそうです。

Mr. Brown said that …… あそこは　日本風の　旅館だと　ブラウンさんが言いました。

5. よやくを　とりけしませんでした。

I heard that …… よやくを　とりけさなかったと　聞きました。

who is saying that …… よやくを　とりけさなかったと　だれが　言っていますか。

I think that …… よやくを　とりけさなかったと　思います。

6. 東京は　人や　車が　たいへん　多いです。

I thought that …… 東京は　人や　車が　たいへん　多いと　思いました。

I understand that …… 東京は　人や　車が　たいへん　多いそうです。

I heard that …… 東京は　人や　車が　たいへん　多いと　聞きました。

7. デパートの　店員の　ことばは　ていねいでした。

do you think that …… デパートの　店員の　ことばは　ていねいだったと思いますか。

my friend said that …… デパートの　店員の　ことばは　ていねいだったと友だちが　言いました。

I understand that …… デパートの　店員の　ことばは　ていねいだったそうです。

2.7.12 Response Drill

1. 山本さんは　あした　事務所へ　来ると　思いますか。

いいえ …… いいえ、(山本さんは　あした　事務所へ) 来ないと思います。

2. 加藤さんが　そんな　ことを　言ったと　思いますか。

いいえ …… いいえ、(加藤さんは　そんな　ことを) 言わなかったと　思います。

3. この　さんこう書の　せつめいは　よくないと　思いますか。
   はい　…… はい、（この　さんこう書の　せつめいは）よくないと　思います。
4. ロバーツさんの　考(かんが)えは　てき当(とう)だったと　思いますか。
   いいえ　…… いいえ、（ロバーツさんの　考(かんが)えは）てき当(とう)では なかったと　思います。
5. ぼくが　あげた　本は　やさしくなかったと　思いますか。
   はい　…… はい、（あなたが　くれた　本は）やさしく なかったと　思います。
6. 鈴木(すずき)さんは　ギターが　へただと　思いますか。
   いいえ　…… いいえ、（鈴木(すずき)さんは　ギターが）へたじゃないと 思います。

2.7.13 Transformation Drill

A. ジョーンズさんが　そう　言いました。

1. ジョーンズさんは　ぼくの　友だちです。　…… ぼくの　友だちの　ジョーンズさんが　そう 言いました。
2. ジョーンズさんは　アメリカ人です。　…… アメリカ人の　ジョーンズさんが　そう 言いました。
3. ジョーンズさんは　大学生です。　…… 大学生の　ジョーンズさんが　そう　言いました。
4. ジョーンズさんは　いしゃです。　…… いしゃの　ジョーンズさんが　そう　言いました。
5. ジョーンズさんは　パン屋の　店(てん)員です。　…… パン屋の　店(てん)員の　ジョーンズさんが　そう 言いました。

B. むすこは　今　ハワイに　すんでいます。

1. むすこは　おんがくの　先生でした。　…… おんがくの　先生だった　むすこは　今 ハワイに　すんでいます。
2. むすこは　東京大学の　学生でした。　…… 東京大学の　学生だった　むすこは　今 ハワイに　すんでいます。
3. むすこは　この　町で　ゆうめいでした。　…… この　町で　ゆうめいだった　むすこは　今 ハワイに　すんでいます。
4. むすこは　日本語が　じょうずでした。　…… 日本語が　じょうずだった　むすこは　今 ハワイに　すんでいます。
5. むすこは　軍(ぐん)人でした。　…… 軍(ぐん)人だった　むすこは　今　ハワイに すんでいます。

2.8 EXERCISES

2.8.1 Transform the following sentences into ～ *to omoimasu* and ～ *soo desu* endings:

1. あの　レストランの　ビフテキは　おいしくありませんでした。
2. 小山さんの　むすこさんは　せいが　とても　たかいです。
3. あの　たて物は　前　きっさ店でした。
4. ロバーツさんは　日本風の　へやを　よやくしました。
5. きょ年は　あまり　ゆきが　ふりませんでした。
6. 上野公園の　さくらは　たいへん　ゆうめいです。
7. むこうには　十時ごろ　つきます。
8. ロバーツさんは　今度の　旅行に　来ません。

2.8.2 Answer the following questions as guided in English:

1. なぜ　うみに　行きませんでしたか。

   Because I thought the weather will turn bad.
2. 奈良という　所は　どんな　所ですか。

   It is said that Nara is the place in which the ancient culture of Japan remains.
3. こんでいる　電車に　のるのは　そんなに　たいへんでしたか。

   Yes, it was so hard that I became sick.
4. 京都には　いくつぐらい　寺や　神社が　ありますか。

   I heard that there are no fewer than one thousand and five hundred.
5. ロバーツさんは　何と　言っていましたか。

   He was saying that he intends to make a reservation at a Japanese-style inn because he wants to know the real Japan.
6. どんな　本を　読みたいと　思いますか。

   I want to read the book titled *Yukiguni*.

2.8.3 Insert appropriate Relationals in the blanks:

1. これは　中国風（　　）あじですね。
2. 鎌倉（　　）も　古い　お寺（　　）たくさん　のこっています。
3. 駅（　　）そば（　　）ホテル（　　）とまりたいんですけど。
4. 沖縄（　　）足（　　）のばしました。
5. 「どの　中村先生ですか。」「いしゃ（　　）中村先生ですよ。」
6. 東京の　新宿（　　）いう　所を　知っていますか。
7. 「何日　関西（　　）旅行しましたか。」「十日です。」「十日（　　）？　いいですねえ。」
8. 手紙（　　）友だちに　行くことが　できない（　　）知らせました。

2.8.4 Answer the following questions depending upon the Dialog:

1. ロバーツさんは 「おどろきましたねえ」と 言いましたが、なぜ おどろきましたか。
2. 池田さんは 何が いい 考えだと 言いましたか。
3. ロバーツさんは どこへ 足を のばしたいと 言っていますか。
4. ロバーツさんは 奈良で 何を 見たいんでしょうか。
5. あなたなら、洋風の ホテルに とまるのと 日本風の 旅館に とまるのと、どっちが いいと 思いますか。どうしてですか。

2.8.5 Make sentences using each of the following:

1. そんなに（こんなに） 2. おどろくほど 3. 何という

2.8.6 Write the following underlined *hiragana* in *kan'ji*:

1. ふるい おてらを おとずれる ひとびとが とても ふえたと おもいます。
2. 池ださんが もっと ちかい りょかんを さがしてくださいと いいました。
3. ごひゃくえんだと おもいます。
4. らいげつ フランスへ りょこうしますが、できれば、ドイツへも あしを のば すつもりです。
5. ともだちの よしこさんは めが きれいです。

2.8.7 Distinguish the following *kan'ji*:

1. 寺、時、持
2. 食、館
3. 近、新
4. 言、語、読

2.8.8 Rewrite the following paragraph into the written style using plain forms.

Sen'shuu shigoto de Kyooto e ikimashita ga, eki kara chikai hoteru ni tomarimashita. Kon'do wa, nihon'fuu no ryokan ni tomaritai to omoimasu.

2.8.9 Rewrite the Presentation of Lesson 2 as if spoken by someone.

2.8.10 The following words all mean "but." Are they always interchangeable or is there any preference in the use of them according to the type of sentence?

1. けれども 2. でも 3. けれど 4. しかし 5. けど

2.8.11 Change the following written sentences into spoken utterances:

Raigetsu Kan'sai e ryokoo shitai to omou. Toku ni Kyooto e wa mada itta koto ga nai kara, mikka gurai machi ya otera o ken'butsu suru tsumori da. Kyooto no ryokan wa totemo takai soo da kara, ima kara yasui ryokan o sagashita hoo ga ii to omou.

2.8.12 Try to figure out some of the historical reasons behind Japanese cultural pluralism, especially in language.

2.8.13 When do you use the plain style in written Japanese?

2.8.14 Describe Japanese cultural pluralism in terms of clothing, housing, and eating.

2.9 SITUATIONAL AND APPLICATION CONVERSATION

2.9.1 Using patterns of "report" or "quotation," carry on the following conversation.

An American asks his Japanese friend if the Japanese has ever been to the United States.
The Japanese says he hasn't, but his older brother was in California from the spring of 1981 to the autumn of 1983.
The American asks the Japanese if his brother made a trip to the Grand Canyon, New York, etc., and asks his impressions about the places he visited.
The Japanese talks about what he has learned from his brother.

2.9.2 Go to a travel agency to make a hotel reservation. Tell them your preference in the type of a hotel, etc.

2.9.3 Talk with your friend about the places you have visited.

2.9.4 A: Chotto ocha o nomimasen ka?

B: Ee, ii desu ne.

A: Ii kissaten o shitte imasu ka?

B: Kissaten to iu tokoro wa itsumo amari hairimasen kara . . .

2.9.5 Yamada: Katoo san, anata no jimusho ni Hayashi to iu hito ga imasu ne?

Katō: Ee, imasu yo.

Yamada: Sono Hayashi to iu hito wa don'na hito desu ka?

Katō: Totemo ii hito desu kedo.

Yamada: Soo desu ka? Jitsu wa sono hito to uchi no musume ga tomodachi de . . .

2.9.6 Ishii: Nichiyoobi ni Hibiya Toshokan e itte mimasen ka?

Satō: Toshokan to iu tokoro wa doomo . . .

Ishii: Watashi mo amari suki ja arimasen ga, tokidoki wa ii to omoimasu yo.

2.9.7 Itō: Boku wa gaikokugo no ben'kyoo wa kirai desu.

Hayashi: Demo, Itoo kun, gaikokugo to iu mono wa, yoku ben'kyoo shita hoo ga ii to omoimasu yo.

2.9.8 Mrs. Higashi: Minasan, nani o tabemasu ka?

Mr. Suzuki: Sono mae ni tsumetai biiru o nomitai to omou kedo.

Mrs. Higashi: Jaa, soo shimashoo.

Mr. Suzuki: Demo, Ishii kun dake wa biiru o nomanai hoo ga ii to omoimasu yo, kuruma da kara . . .

2.9.9 Fujikawa: Moo ippai kudasai.

Nishimura: Fujikawa san, moo nomanai hoo ga ii to omoimasu kedo.

LESSON 3

漢字[1]

3.1 PRESENTATION

現代（げんだい）の　日本語で　よく　使う　漢字は　千九百四十五字　あります。これを「常用（じょうよう）漢字[1]」といいます。　小学校と　中学校では、　この　うち　九百九十六の　漢字を　教えますが、これは　「教育（いく）漢字[1]」と　いいます。

3.2 DIALOG

高橋（たかはし）　「クラークさん、　森（もり）さんが　話していましたけど、　日本語を　勉強しはじめた[2]そうですね？」

クラーク　「ええ。　でも、　まだ[3]　四か月[4]しか[5]　習っていません[3]。」

高橋（たかはし）　「一週間[6]に[7]　何時間ですか。」

クラーク　「六時間です。」

高橋（たかはし）　「今までに　漢字は　いくつぐらい　習いましたか。」

クラーク　「そうですねえ。　百ぐらいでしょう。　だから、　まだ　新聞や　本を　読む　ことが　できません。」

高橋（たかはし）　「そう、　まだ　少なすぎ[8]ますね。　漢字は　おぼえにくい[9]ですか。」

クラーク　「おぼえやすい[9]のも　おぼえにくいのも　あります。」

高橋（たかはし）　「ひらがなは　もう　ぜんぶ　おぼえましたか。」

クラーク　「ええ。　二週間で　おぼえました。　ひらがなを　おぼえるのは　わりあい　かんたんでした。　でも、　はじめは、〝あ〟と〝お〟や[1]〝ぬ〟と〝め〟などが　まちがえやすかった[9]です。」

高橋（たかはし）　「けっきょく、　漢字も　ひらがなも　毎日　れんしゅうすることが　たいせつですね。　日本には　〝石の　上にも　三年[10]〟　という　ことわざ[10]が　ありますよ。　がんばってください[11]。」

漢字（かんじ）　使（つか）う　小学校（しょうがっこう）　中学校（ちゅうがっこう）　話（はな）していました
勉強（べんきょう）　四（よん）か月（げつ）　一週間（いっしゅうかん）　新聞（しんぶん）　毎日（まいにち）　石（いし）

3.3 PATTERN SENTENCES

3.3.1

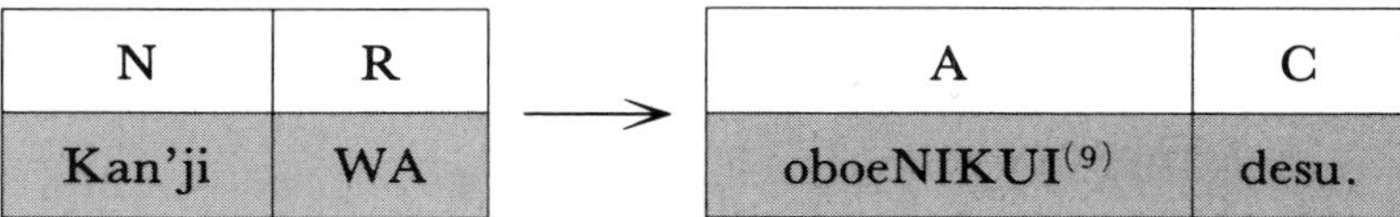

3.3.2

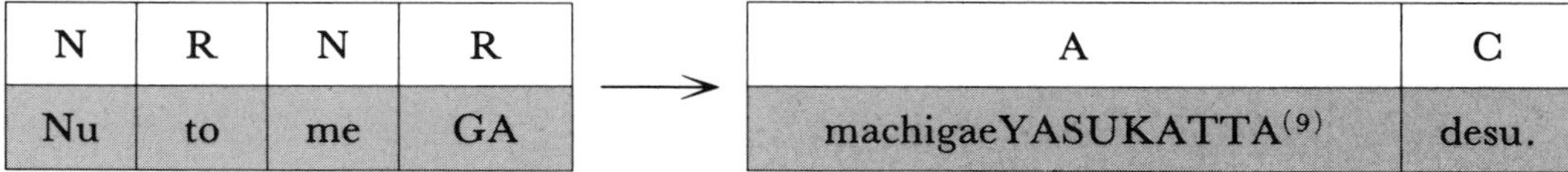

3.3.3

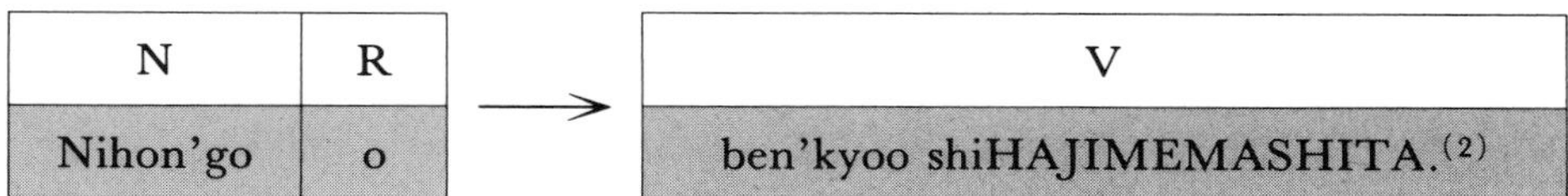

3.3.4

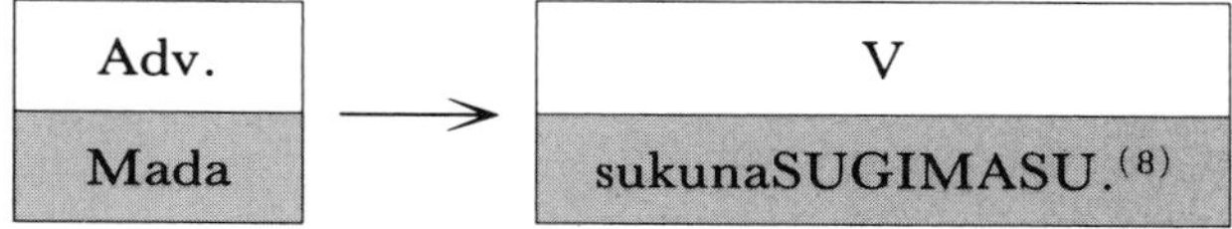

3.4 NOTES

3.4.1 *Kan'ji*

For many years a controversy has revolved around the elimination of *kan'ji*. The pros and cons of this controversy are too numerous to develop fully here. The main argument for such elimination, however, concludes that such a move would greatly reduce the effort now required in learning to read, since at present knowledge of some two thousand *kan'ji* is necessary to read, for instance, a newspaper. On the other hand, the fact that thousands of homonyms are contained in the Japanese language has led opponents to argue that elimination of the *kan'ji* would leave the language too ambiguous, and therefore difficult, to understand. Without the concrete symbolization of the *kan'ji*, meaning would have to be deduced from the context of the sentence. Opponents of elimination claim that the context is not, however, sufficient for complete understanding. Their argument may be supported by the fact that the Japanese seem to think occasionally in terms of *kan'ji*. For instance, a speaker may even trace a *kan'ji* on his hand to clarify what word or words he means.

A written language provides a frame of reference for the spoken sounds to which it corresponds. For instance, the speaker of a language which is represented by phonetic symbols will associate the sound of a particular word and its meaning with a particular collection of those phonetic symbols.

It would be interesting to investigate whether or not the Japanese think in terms of the Chinese characters which represent much of the Japanese vocabulary, or if they think only in terms of vocabulary without corresponding visual images. In other words, when the Japanese think about a particular noun—since Chinese characters have so many homonyms—do they conceive of this noun in terms of its pronunciation only; to what extent do they associate this particular pronunciation with the corresponding meaning, and with this meaning plus the Chinese character which visually supports this meaning? See Appendix V of Volume II.

3.4.2 *Nihon'go o ben'kyoo shihajimeta soo desu* means "I heard that you started studying Japanese." *Hajimeru* itself is a Verb meaning "begin," and, as a compound component, it may formulate a compound Verb preceded by the Stem form of a Verb. The compound Verb ~*hajimeru* will be equivalent to "start (do)ing" or "begin (do)ing." The compound Verb meaning "finish (do)ing" is formulated by the Stem (Pre-Masu) form of a Verb plus *owaru* "finish; end." Some more compound Verbs will be explained in this lesson and in later lessons.

(Predicate Modifier) + Stem form of Verb + { ***hajimeru*** / ***owaru*** }

tabehajimemasu	"begin eating"
tabeowarimasu	"finish eating"
hon o yomihajimemashita	"started reading a book"
hon o yomiowarimashita	"finished reading a book"
Suzuki san ga piano o hikihajimemashita.	"Miss Suzuki started playing the piano."
Gakusei wa moo kuni e kaerihajimeta soo desu.	"I heard that the students have already started leaving for home."
Rokuji made ni ryoori shiowaru to omoimasu.	"I think I'll finish cooking by six o'clock."
Ame wa ohiru goro furihajimemashita.	"It began raining about noon."
Yamada san no akachan wa moo arukihajimeta soo desu.	"I understand that the Yamadas' baby has already started walking."

3.4.3 The Adverb *mada* means "yet" in the negative sentence, as already introduced in Note 7.4.15, Volume I. The Adverb *mada* "yet" is used with a negative Predicate. Since *mada* "yet" is used to express that an action has not been completed or a state hasn't been started, the negative imperfect tense, instead of the negative perfect tense, should be used with *mada*. In order to stress that an action has not been completed, the TE form of a Verb plus negative imperfect *imasen* often occurs with *mada*. As already explained, the Adverb *moo* "already" contrasts *mada*. To answer a question with *moo*, a short answer *iie, mada desu* is also possible.

***mada* + negative Predicate (imperfect tense)**

moo oboemashita	"I have already memorized"
mada oboete imasen mada oboemasen	"I haven't yet memorized"
mada desu	"not yet"

moo yasumi ga hajimarimashita	"the vacation has already begun"
mada yasumi ga hajimatte imasen mada yasumi ga hajimarimasen	"the vacation hasn't begun yet"
mada desu	"not yet"

Hoteru o moo yoyaku shimashita ka?	"Did you already reserve a room at the hotel?"
Iie, mada shite imasen.	"No, I haven't yet."
Oosaka yuki no kyuukoo wa moo demashita ka?	"Has the express to Ōsaka already left?"
Iie, mada demasen.	"No, it hasn't left yet."
Kono zasshi o moo yomiowarimashita ka?	"Have you already finished reading this magazine?"
Iie, mada desu.	"No, not yet."

3.4.4 *Yon'kagetsu* means "four months." The *-kagetsu* is a counter for number of months. *Nan'kagetsu* is "how many months?"

1	ikkagetsu	5	gokagetsu	9	kyuukagetsu
2	nikagetsu	6	rokkagetsu	10	jikkagetsu; jukkagetsu
3	san'kagetsu	7	nanakagetsu		
4	yon'kagetsu	8	hakkagetsu; hachikagetsu		

Dono gurai Yooroppa ni imashita ka?	"How long were you in Europe?"
Rokkagetsu imashita.	"I was there for six months."
Akachan wa ima ikutsu desu ka?	"How old is your baby?"
Jikkagetsu desu ga, moo arukihajimemashita.	"He is ten months old now, and he has already started walking."

3.4.5 *Yon'kagetsu shika naratte imasen* means "I have been studying only four months." *Shika* is a Relational always followed by a negative Predicate, and the combination conveys the meaning of "only" or "nothing but." Note that it is the combination *shika* plus negative that carries the meaning of "only," but not the Relational *shika* alone. The Relational *dake* also means "only," but it may be used either in an affirmative or negative sentence, depending upon the context. Normally when *shika* is placed together with *ga*, *o*, or *wa* as a double Relational, *ga*, *o*, or *wa* should be omitted. The omission of *ni*, *de*, *kara*, *e*, and the like, may become optional in some limited cases. *Dake* merely limits the reference without any subjective evaluation while *shika* is used to stress that the number referred to is very small in the mind of the speaker.

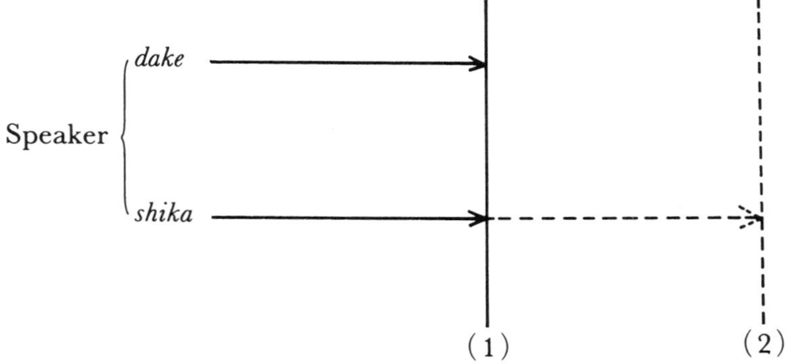

(1) point actually reached
(2) point expected to reach but failed

On the basis of the above diagram, it can be seen that *shika* involved the subjective evaluation of the achievement, whereas *dake* is merely an objective statement of the fact of a ceiling or limitation on the quantity under discussion.

yon'kagetsu dake naraimashita	"studied just four months"
yon'kagetsu shika naraimasen deshita	"studied only four months" (it seems to the speaker the study period was too short)
Takahashi san dake kimashita	"only Mr. Takahashi came"
Takahashi san shika kimasen deshita	"only Mr. Takahashi came" (the speaker expected more people to come)

Shika replaces the Relational *ga*, *o*, and *wa*, but it follows such Relationals as *ni*, *de*, *kara*.

Yonen'sei no naka de wa Katoo san shika shirimasen.	"I don't know anyone but Mr. Katō among the senior students."
Karate wa san'kagetsu shika ren'shuu shimasen deshita.	"I practiced *karate* for only three months."
Kyooto ni mo daibutsu ga arimasu ka?	"Is there a big image of the Buddha in Kyōto also?"
Iie, daibutsu wa Nara to Kamakura ni shika arimasen.	"No, big images of the Buddha are only in Nara and Kamakura."
Boku wa toshokan de shika ben'kyoo shimasen.	"I study nowhere but at the library."

Compare *yon'kagetsu shika naraimasen deshita* with *yon'kagetsu mo naraimashita*. The former indicates "how short" and the latter "how long." See Note 2.4.13.

3.4.6 *Isshuukan* means "one week." The *-shuukan* is a composite counter consisting of *shuu* "week" and *-kan* "period." "How many weeks?" is *nan'shuukan*.

1	isshuukan	5	goshuukan	9	kyuushuukan
2	nishuukan	6	rokushuukan	10	jisshuukan; jusshuukan
3	san'shuukan	7	nanashuukan		
4	yon'shuukan	8	hasshuukan; hachishuukan		

The dependent Noun *-kan* is indispensable to refer to "a period of weeks or hours," but it may occur or may be omitted in references to "a period of years, months, days, or minutes."

isshuukan	ikkagetsu *or* ikkagetsukan
ichijikan	futsuka *or* futsukakan
ichinen *or* ichinen'kan	ippun *or* ippun'kan

Hawai kara Nihon made fune de isshuukan gurai kakarimasu. — "It will take about a week by boat from Hawaii to Japan."

Nihon no shoogakkoo no fuyuyasumi wa nan'shuukan desu ka? — "How many weeks' winter vacation do you have in Japanese elementary schools?"

3.4.7 *Isshuukan ni nan'jikan desu ka?* means "How many (class) hours do you have per week?" The Relational *ni* following a number that shows time duration, such as *isshuukan* "one week," *ikkagetsu* "a month," *ichijikan* "one hour" means "per."

Isshuukan ni rokujikan nihon'go no kurasu ga arimasu. — "We have Japanese class six hours a week."

Kuraaku san wa ichinen ni nido gurai Nihon e kuru soo desu. — "I understand that Mr. Clark comes to Japan about twice a year."

Arubaito de ichijikan ni roppyakuen moraimashita. — "I earned six hundred yen an hour for my part-time work."

3.4.8 *Sukunasugimasu* means "they are too few." *Sugiru* is a Verb meaning "excess," and, as a compound component, it may formulate a compound Verb preceded by the Base form of an Adjective, the Stem form of a Verb, or an adjectival Noun. The compound Verb ~*sugiru* will be equivalent to "do too much," "be in excess," and so forth.

(Predicate Modifier) + { Base form of Adjective / Stem form of Verb / adjectival Noun } + *sugiru*

hayasugimasu	"is too early; is too fast"
oosugimasu	"is too much; are too many"
takasugimasu	"is too expensive"
hatarakisugimasu	"work too hard"
nomisugimasu	"drink too much"
shitsumon shisugimasu	"ask too many questions"
kan'tan sugimasu	"is too simple; is too easy"
hetasugimasu	"is too poor (at)"
himasugimasu	"have too much free time"

Kono heya wa atsusugimasu ne? — "This room is too hot, isn't it?"

Ano kata no kotoba wa teineisugiru to omoimasu. — "I think that person's language is overly polite."

Amari tabesuginaide kudasai.	"Please don't overeat."
Shuumatsu sukoshi asobisugimashita. Kon'shuu wa motto ben'kyoo shimasu.	"I did practically nothing but play during the weekend. I will work harder this week."

3.4.9 *Kan'ji wa oboenikui desu ka?* means "Are Chinese characters difficult to memorize?" When the Stem form of a Verb is followed by *nikui*, it formulates a compound Adjective carrying the meaning of "hard (to do)" or "difficult (to do)." The opposite expression "easy (to do)" is formulated by the Stem form of a Verb followed by *yasui* "easy." Both *nikui* and *yasui* may be used in the sense of physical and psychological difficulty. In this instance, *yasui* does not have the meaning of "inexpensive." Compound Adjectives *nikui* and *yasui* conjugate in the same way as an Adjective does.

(oboe)nikui	"is difficult (hard)	to memorize"
(oboe)nikuku nai	"is not difficult (hard)	
(oboe)nikukatta	"was difficult (hard)	
(oboe)nikuku nakatta	"was not difficult (hard)	

(kaki)yasui	"is easy	to write"
(kaki)yasuku nai	"is not easy	
(kaki)yasukatta	"was easy	
(kaki)yasuku nakatta	"was not easy	

In the pattern with *nikui* and *yasui*, the object of the Verb, if expressed, is never followed by the Relational *o*, but by *wa* (or sometimes *ga*). This replacement occurs since the Predicate of a Verb plus *nikui* or *yasui* is not verbal but adjectival. Other Relationals such as *to, ni, de* are also often followed by *wa*.

Noun + *o* + Verb ⟶

Noun + { *wa* / (*ga*) } + Stem form of Verb + { *nikui* / *yasui* }

Kono boorupen wa tsukainikui desu.	"This ball-point pen is difficult to use."
Taishikan e iku michi wa wakariyasui soo desu.	"It is said that the way to the embassy is easy to find."
Tookyoo wa mono ga takai kara, suminikui deshoo.	"I suppose it's difficult to live in Tōkyō, since things are expensive there."
Kuraaku san to wa issho ni shigoto ga shinikukatta desu.	"I had difficulty working together with Mr. Clark."
Katoo sen'sei no setsumei wa totemo wakariyasui desu.	"Professor Katō's explanations are very easy to understand."
Kotoshi no natsu wa suzushikatta kara, ben'kyoo shiyasukatta desu.	"Since it was cool this summer, I found it easy to study (during the summer)."

3.4.10 *Ishi no ue ni mo san'nen* means "Sit on a stone for three years, then even the stone will become warm" and implies patience and endurance. Japanese proverbs, or *kotowaza,* are indicative of the

Japanese attitude toward nature. In comparing Japanese and Chinese proverbs we find that the Chinese use many more abstract referents than do the Japanese, and that the Chinese approach is much more pedagogical. The Japanese use concrete objects or actions to imply abstract and generalized concepts, tending to accept all concrete objects as they are, each with its residing spirit, such as soul, mind, or god. Some scholars have termed this "phenomenalism." Such phenomenalism originates partially in animism and the so-called man-in-nature mentality of the Japanese. The traditional Japanese preference is to be subservient to nature, to be part of nature, rather than to control or modify it. Therefore, they personify nature while regarding human beings as an intrinsic part of nature.

From ancient times, the Japanese have been close to nature, and in the relative sense, are more involved with nature than with human matters per se. Especially in the context of art, nature is its theme and its material, and they sing of, describe, and state topics connected with nature.

Such attitudes have obviously been affected by Buddhism, which regards all human phenomena as part of the natural phenomena. Human life is seen as similar to the blooming and inevitable withering of flowers, of leaves that fall in the autumn, and of the stars that shine and falter. Human lives are given birth together with universal phenomena and die with them. Nature in Japanese is called *shizen*. *Shizen no mama* means natural and is regarded to be good, while *fushizen*, meaning unnatural, is regarded as a negative force.

To the Japanese, the process of nature is equated with the human process—for example, growth. Spring, summer, autumn, and winter, for instance, are used to represent a year, while combined with the stars and frost, they also represent years. Although Chinese also has this tendency and some vocabulary and expressions have been created in China, the Japanese particularly love them. The past several *seisoo*, or star-frosts, for example, refer to many decades past; the *fuusetsu*, or wind and snow of the human life, refers to the hardship of that life; and hearsay information is indicated by the phrase *kaze no tayori*, meaning "the winds talk." Even the titles of dictionaries always include references to nature: *Jikai* "Sea of words," for example; or *Kōjirin* "Woods of expressions" or *Jien* "Gardens of vocabularies." This Japanese association with nature is so pervasive that even names of special trains are affected, and names such as Matsukaze "Pine wind," Sakura "Cherry blossom," and Asakaze "Morning breeze" are popular. It is also interesting that the names of plants are utilized most often in such situations. This Japanese cultural trait can be called "naturalism."

The Japanese phenomenalism can also be seen in the tendency, as described previously, of the Japanese to often use body names for abstract concepts. Note the following examples:

Expression	*Literal Meaning and Connotative Meaning*
me ni kado o tateru	"establish a cornea in your eye"—is angry
me no naka ni irete mo itaku nai	"you don't feel pain even if you put someone in your eye"—implying affection and love for your own child
mimizawari	"disturbed the ear"—jarring noise
mimi ni hairu	"enter [your] ear"—[you] learn something
kubi ga mawaranai	"you cannot turn your neck" —[you] are unable to manage debts
hara ga futoi	"someone has a fat stomach" —[he] is generally broad-minded
hara ga tatsu	"stomach is standing"—[you] are angry

The proverb referred to in this dialog—*Ishi no ue ni mo san'nen*—reveals this characteristic Japanese phenomenalism by using the stone as a concrete object. *Nakittsura ni hachi*—"a bee stinging your crying face" ([you] are getting double trouble); *I no naka no kawazu*—"a frog in the water well" (you don't know the world); *Yabu kara boo*—"a stick from a bush" (sudden), are similar expressions used by the Japanese.

Two other proverbs worth noting at this time are *Chiri mo tsumoreba yama to naru*—"even dust when it accumulates will eventually become a mountain" (therefore, continuous efforts are necessary), and *Nodomoto sugireba atsusa wasureru*—"once the hot thing passes through your throat, you do not recall its heat" (therefore, you can easily forget hardship).

The Japanese language tends toward a concreteness which conveys abstract ideas by implication rather than directly through abstract terms. Some parallels exist in English; however, such English parallels are not forms of expressions which pervade the language as a whole in its day-to-day use. They occur more frequently in poetry and certain subcultures. Americans in general, however, are more accustomed to homilies than they are to such proverbs.

3.4.11 *Gan'batte kudasai* means "please hold out." The Japanese use this expression extensively to encourage the second person or persons. The word *gan'barizumu*, which means "hold-out doctrine," has even been coined in Japan.

Gan'batte kudasai.	"Please hold out!"
Hai, gan'barimasu.	"Yes, I shall do my best."

3.5 VOCABULARY

Presentation

現代(げんだい)	gen'dai	......	N	the present age; today
常用(じょうよう)漢字	jooyoo kan'ji	......	N	*Kan'ji* for Common Use
小学校	shoogakkoo	......	N	elementary school
中学校	chuugakkoo	......	N	junior high school
うち	-uchi	......	Nd	among; out of
教育(いく)漢字	kyooiku kan'ji	......	N	*Kan'ji* for Education

Dialog

高橋(たかはし)	Takahashi	......	N	family name
クラーク	Kuraaku	......	N	Clark
はじめた	hajimeta	......	V	started (doing) (TA form of *hajimeru* – start; begin) (compound component) (see 3.4.2)
四か月	yon'kagetsu	......	N	four months (see 3.4.4)
しか	shika	......	R	only; nothing but (see 3.4.5)
一週間	isshuukan	......	N	one week (see 3.4.6)
に	ni	......	R	per (see 3.4.7)
少な	sukuna	......	A	Base form of *sukunai* – is few; is little

すぎます	sugimasu	......	V	excess; over (do)ing; too (few); excessively (compound component) (see 3.4.8)
おぼえ	oboe	......	V	Stem form of *oboeru* - memorize; master
にくい	nikui	......	A	is hard (to do); is difficult (to do) (compound component) (see 3.4.9)
やすい	yasui	......	A	is easy (to do) (compound component) (see 3.4.9)
わりあい	wariai	......	Adv.	comparatively
かんたん	kan'tan	......	Na	easy; simple; short
まちがえ	machigae	......	V	Stem form of *machigaeru* - make a mistake; error; mistake (transitive Verb)
やすかった	yasukatta	......	A	TA form of *yasui* - is easy (to do) (see 3.4.9)
けっきょく	kekkyoku	......	Adv.	after all; in conclusion
れんしゅうする	ren'shuu suru	......	V	practice; drill
れんしゅう	ren'shuu	......	N	practice; drill
たいせつ	taisetsu	......	Na	important
ことわざ	kotowaza	......	N	proverb
がんばって	gan'batte	......	V	TE form of *gan'baru* - do one's best; buck up; persist (see 3.4.11)

Notes

おわる	owaru	......	V	finish (doing) (see 3.4.2)
あかちゃん	akachan	......	N	baby
か月	-kagetsu	......	Nd	counter for months (see 3.4.4)
週間	-shuukan	......	Nd	counter for weeks (see 3.4.6)
間	-kan	......	Nd	period (see 3.4.6)
ボールペン	boorupen	......	N	ball-point pen

Extra Vocabulary

(お)べん当(とう)	(o)ben'too	......	N	packed lunch; a lunch
オーストラリア	Oosutoraria	......	N	Australia

3.6 KAN'JI

3.6.1 漢 (1) KAN (2) China (3) classifier 氵

(4) 漢 (5) 漢字

3.6.2 使 (1) *tsuka(u)* (2) use (3) classifier 亻 (4) 亻 仁 佢 使 使
(5) 鉄（てつ）やアルミを使う

5.6.9, Vol. II
3.6.a 小 (1) SHOO (5) 小学校（こう）、小学生 [elementary school pupil]
(6) homonym 少、抄

3.6.3 校 (1) KOO (2) school (3) classifier 木 (4) 木 木' 村 杧 校 校
(5) 学校、中学校、小学校 (6) homonym 交、狡、絞

3.6.4 話 (1) *hana(su)* (2) speak; speech (3) classifier 言 [speech]
(4) 丶 亠 亠 言 言 言 言 言' 訁 訂 訐 話 話
(5) 日本語を話します、話しがじょうずだ

3.6.5 勉 (1) BEN (2) make efforts (3) classifier ク（力）
(4) ノ ク ク 々 各 色 缶 免 免 勉 (5) 勉強（きょう）
(6) 免 represents a woman giving birth to a child

3.6.6 強 (1) KYOO (2) strong (3) classifier 弓 [bow]
(4) フ コ 弓 弘 弘 弦 弹 強 強 (5) 勉強、強力（りょく） [strong; powerful]

3.6.7 週 (1) SHUU (2) week (3) classifier 辶
(4) 丿 冂 月 丹 用 周 周 凋 週 (5) 一週間、来週、今週（こん）、先週、週末（まつ）
(6) homonym 周

11.6.8, Vol. II
3.6.b 新 (1) SHIN (5) 新年 [new year]、新聞（ぶん） (6) homonym 辛、親

7.6.7, Vol. II
3.6.c 聞 (1) BUN (5) 新聞

3.6.8 毎 (1) MAI (2) every (3) classifier 𠂉（毎） (4) ノ 𠂉 勹 勾 毎 毎
(5) 毎日、毎週、毎月、毎年、毎時30マイル [30 MPH]

3.6.9 石 (1) *ishi* (2) stone (3) classifier 一（石） (4) 一 ア 石
(5) 大きい石、石屋 [mason]

3.6.d 今 (5.6.8, Vol. II) （1） KON （5） 今週、今月、今度(ど)

3.7 DRILLS

3.7.1 Transformation Drill

A. 1. ひらがなを　おぼえます。 ⟶ ひらがなは　おぼえやすいです。
   2. この　セーターを　きます。 ⟶ この　セーターは　きやすいです。
   3. ひらがなの　“ぬ”と　“め”を　まちがえます。 ⟶ ひらがなの　“ぬ”と　“め”は　まちがえやすいです。
   4. ここの　ピアノを　ひきます。 ⟶ ここの　ピアノは　ひきやすいです。
   5. この　新聞を　読みます。 ⟶ この　新聞は　読みやすいです。
   6. その　もんだいが　わかります。 ⟶ その　もんだいは　わかりやすいです。
   7. あかちゃんが　おどろきます。 ⟶ あかちゃんは　おどろきやすいです。

B. 1. 山本(もと)先生に　しつもんします。 ⟶ 山本(もと)先生には　しつもんしやすいです。
   2. あの　小学校へ　行きます。 ⟶ あの　小学校へは　行きやすいです。
   3. 図(と)書館で　勉強します。 ⟶ 図(と)書館では　勉強しやすいです。
   4. よし子さんと　話します。 ⟶ よし子さんとは　話しやすいです。
   5. あの　友だちから　かります。 ⟶ あの　友だちからは　かりやすいです。

3.7.2 Transformation Drill

A. 1. この　辞(じ)書を　使います。 ⟶ この　辞(じ)書は　使いにくいです。
   2. あなたの　電話(わ)番号(ごう)を　おぼえます。 ⟶ あなたの　電話(わ)番号(ごう)は　おぼえにくいです。
   3. よやくを　とりけします。 ⟶ よやくは　とりけしにくいです。
   4. おとうとの　字を　読みます。 ⟶ おとうとの　字は　読みにくいです。
   5. 漢字を　教えます。 ⟶ 漢字は　教えにくいです。
   6. この　ことわざの　いみが　わかります。 ⟶ この　ことわざの　いみは　わかりにくいです。
   7. 本屋の　前の　みちを　あるきます。 ⟶ 本屋の　前の　みちは　あるきにくいです。

B. 1. 週末(まつ)に　かえります。 ⟶ 週末(まつ)には　かえりにくいです。
   2. はしで　食べます。 ⟶ はしでは　食べにくいです。

3. うちで　れんしゅうします。 ⟶ うちでは　れんしゅうしにくいです。
4. 高橋(たかはし)さんに　知らせます。 ⟶ 高橋(たかはし)さんには　知らせにくいです。
5. ごご　三時までに　来ます。 ⟶ ごご　三時までには　来にくいです。

3.7.3 Transformation Drill

1. この　電話(わ)は　聞きにくいです。 ⟶ この　電話(わ)は　聞きにくかったです。
2. これと　それは　まちがえやすいです。 ⟶ これと　それは　まちがえやすかったです。
3. その　教科(か)書は　使いにくいです。 ⟶ その　教科(か)書は　使いにくかったです。
4. みち子さんには　話しにくいです。 ⟶ みち子さんには　話しにくかったです。
5. 高橋(たかはし)さんの　うちは　わかりやすいです。 ⟶ 高橋(たかはし)さんの　うちは　わかりやすかったです。
6. 教育(いく)漢字は　おぼえやすいです。 ⟶ 教育(いく)漢字は　おぼえやすかったです。
7. あの　へやの　まどは　あけにくいです。 ⟶ あの　へやの　まどは　あけにくかったです。
8. 漢字は　おぼえにくいです。 ⟶ 漢字は　おぼえにくかったです。

3.7.4 Transformation Drill

A.
1. 日本語を　勉強しました。 ⟶ 日本語を　勉強しはじめました。
2. あかちゃんが　いろいろな　ことばを　おぼえました。 ⟶ あかちゃんが　いろいろな　ことばを　おぼえはじめました。
3. むすこが　今月　銀(ぎん)行に　つとめました。 ⟶ むすこが　今月　銀(ぎん)行に　つとめはじめました。
4. さくらが　もう　さきました。 ⟶ さくらが　もう　さきはじめました。
5. 教科(か)書の　二十五ページを　読んでください。 ⟶ 教科(か)書の　二十五ページを　読みはじめてください。
6. ごはんを　食べてください。 ⟶ ごはんを　食べはじめてください。

B.
1. しゅくだいを　しました。 ⟶ しゅくだいを　しおわりました。
2. この　新聞を　読みましたか。 ⟶ この　新聞を　読みおわりましたか。
3. こたえを　書きました。 ⟶ こたえを　書きおわりました。
4. おべん当(とう)は　食べました。 ⟶ おべん当(とう)は　食べおわりました。
5. へやは　もう　よやくしました。 ⟶ へやは　もう　よやくしおわりました。
6. ばんごはんを　作りました。 ⟶ ばんごはんを　作りおわりました。

3.7.5 Transformation Drill

A.

1. あさごはんを　食べました。 ⟶ あさごはんを　食べすぎました。
2. ロバーツさんは　おさけを　のみました。 ⟶ ロバーツさんは　おさけを　のみすぎました。
3. いろいろな　本を　読んだ　そうです。 ⟶ いろいろな　本を　読みすぎたそうです。
4. きのうの　よる　テレビを　見ました。 ⟶ きのうの　よる　テレビを　見すぎました。
5. 子どもに　おかしを　やらないでください。 ⟶ 子どもに　おかしを　やりすぎないで　ください。
6. なつ休みに　はたらきました。 ⟶ なつ休みに　はたらきすぎました。
7. ごちそうを　作りました。 ⟶ ごちそうを　作りすぎました。
8. 先週　勉強しました。 ⟶ 先週　勉強しすぎました。

3.7.6 Transformation Drill

1. この　へやは　せまいです。 ⟶ この　へやは　せますぎます。
2. あなたの　辞書は　古いです。 ⟶ あなたの　辞書は　古すぎます。
3. 新聞の　漢字は　むずかしいです。 ⟶ 新聞の　漢字は　むずかしすぎます。
4. きみの　カメラは　たかいです。 ⟶ きみの　カメラは　たかすぎます。
5. この　しけんの　しつもんは　ながいです。 ⟶ この　しけんの　しつもんは　ながすぎます。
6. ここの　食事は　つめたいです。 ⟶ ここの　食事は　つめたすぎます。
7. この　カレーは　からいです。 ⟶ この　カレーは　からすぎます。
8. あの　いしゃは　ちょっと　わかいです。 ⟶ あの　いしゃは　ちょっと　わかすぎます。

3.7.7 Transformation Drill

1. この　しごとは　ひまです。 ⟶ この　しごとは　ひますぎると　思います。
2. あの　人は　ドイツ語が　へたです。 ⟶ あの　人は　ドイツ語が　へたすぎると　思います。
3. その　しつもんは　かんたんです。 ⟶ その　しつもんは　かんたんすぎると　思います。
4. あの　男の子は　しずかです。 ⟶ あの　男の子は　しずかすぎると　思います。

5. よし子さんの　ことばは　ていねいです。 ——→ よし子さんの　ことばは　ていねいすぎると思います。
6. その　石は　りっぱです。 ——→ その　石は　りっぱすぎると　思います。

3.7.8 Response Drill

1. おさけを　もう　いっぱい　<u>のんでもいいですか</u>。 …… ええ。でも、<u>のみすぎないでください</u>。
2. もっと　から手(て)を　れんしゅうしても　いいですか。 …… ええ。でも、れんしゅうしすぎないでください。
3. 八時まで　あそんでいても　いいですか。 …… ええ。でも、あそびすぎないでください。
4. たばこを　すっても　いいですか。 …… ええ。でも、すいすぎないでください。
5. もっと　はたらいても　いいですか。 …… ええ。でも、はたらきすぎないでください。
6. もっと　ごはんを　食べても　いいですか。 …… ええ。でも、食べすぎないでください。
7. また　テレビを　見ても　いいですか。 …… ええ。でも、見すぎないでください。
8. もう　すこし　ねていても　いいですか。 …… ええ。でも、ねすぎないでください。

3.7.9 Substitution Drill

A. 一か月に　<u>五日</u>　<u>はたらきます</u>。

1. 三週間 …… 一か月に　三週間　はたらきます。
2. 二十日 …… 一か月に　二十日　はたらきます。
3. 勉強しました …… 一か月に　二十日　勉強しました。
4. 旅行しました …… 一か月に　二十日　旅行しました。
5. 四日 …… 一か月に　四日　旅行しました。
6. 一週間だけ …… 一か月に　一週間だけ　旅行しました。

B. 一週間に　<u>何時間</u>　<u>勉強したいですか</u>。

1. 何日 …… 一週間に　何日　勉強したいですか。
2. 三日 …… 一週間に　三日　勉強したいですか。
3. アルバイトします …… 一週間に　三日　アルバイトします。
4. 十時間ぐらい …… 一週間に　十時間ぐらい　アルバイトします。

5. 日本語の　クラスが　あります　……　一週間に　十時間ぐらい　日本語の　クラスが　あります。
6. 何度（ど）　……　一週間に　何度（ど）　日本語の　クラスが　ありますか。

3.7.10 Substitution Drill

日本語を　四か月しか　習いませんでした。

1. 一年　……　日本語を　一年しか　習いませんでした。
2. 六週間　……　日本語を　六週間しか　習いませんでした。
3. 中国語　……　中国語を　六週間しか　習いませんでした。
4. 教えませんでした　……　中国語を　六週間しか　教えませんでした。
5. 九か月　……　中国語を　九か月しか　教えませんでした。
6. 漢字　……　漢字を　九か月しか　教えませんでした。
7. 百五十　……　漢字を　百五十しか　教えませんでした。
8. おぼえていません　……　漢字を　百五十しか　おぼえていません。

3.7.11 Response Drill

1. もう　ひらがなを　おぼえましたか。　……　いいえ、　まだ　おぼえていません。
2. もう　漢字は　習いましたか。　……　いいえ、　まだ　習っていません。
3. 先生に　ことわざの　いみを　聞きましたか。　……　いいえ、　まだ　聞いていません。
4. けさの　新聞を　もう　読みましたか。　……　いいえ、　まだ　読んでいません。
5. しゅくだいは　もう　しましたか。　……　いいえ、　まだ　していません。
6. もう　あの　えいがを　見ましたか。　……　いいえ、　まだ　見ていません。
7. オーストラリア人の　ジョーンズさんに　もう　あいましたか。　……　いいえ、　まだ　あっていません。
8. ホテルを　もう　よやくしましたか。　……　いいえ、　まだ　よやくしていません。

3.7.12 E-J Response Drill

1. 一日に　いくつ　新しい　漢字を　習いますか。
   ten characters　……　一日に　十（新しい　漢字を）習います。
2. 一日に　どのくらい　れんしゅうしますか。
   two hours　……　一日に　二時間　れんしゅうします。

3. 一週間に　何時間　日本語の　クラスが　ありますか。

six hours　……　一週間に　六時間（日本語の　クラスが）あります。

4. 何日で　この　本を　読みおわると　思いますか。

in about three days　……　三日ぐらいで（その　本を）読みおわると　思います。

5. あかちゃんは　何か月で　あるきはじめますか。

in twelve months　……　（あかちゃんは）十二か月で　あるきはじめます。

6. あなたは　一年で　何センチ　せいが　たかくなりましたか。

eight centimeters　……　（わたしは）一年で　八センチ（せいが）たかくなりました。

7. この　店(みせ)へ　一日に　何人ぐらい　お客(きゃく)さんが　来ますか。

fifty　……　（この　店(みせ)へ）一日に　五十人ぐらい（お客(きゃく)さんが）来ます。

8. 一年に　何週間　休みが　ありますか。

four weeks　……　一年に　四週間　休みが　あります。

9. 一か月に　何度(ど)くらい　えいがを　見に　行きますか。

twice　……　一か月に　二度(ど)くらい　見に　行きます。

3.7.13 Review Drill

1. むかしの　漢字は　書きにくかったです。思います。 → むかしの　漢字は　書きにくかったと　思います。

2. クラークさんは　きのう　テニスを　れんしゅうしすぎました。言っています。 → クラークさんは　きのう　テニスを　れんしゅうしすぎたと　言っています。

3. ひこうきの　きっぷは　よやくしやすいです。新聞で　読みました。 → ひこうきの　きっぷは　よやくしやすいと　新聞で　読みました。

4. この　こたえは　かんたんすぎました。池田(いけ)さんが　言いました。 → この　こたえは　かんたんすぎたと　池田(いけ)さんが　言いました。

5. あの　先生の　ことばは　むずかしすぎます。思います。 → あの　先生の　ことばは　むずかしすぎると　思います。

6. あねは　もう　ひるごはんを 作りはじめました。 〜そうです。 ⟶ あねは　もう　ひるごはんを　作りはじめたそうです。

7. 中国料理(りょうり)は　作りやすいです。 〜そうです。 ⟶ 中国料理(りょうり)は　作りやすい そうです。

8. あの　人は　毎日 はたらきすぎます。 〜そうです。 ⟶ あの　人は　毎日　はたらきすぎるそうです。

3.8 EXERCISES

3.8.1 Insert appropriate Relationals in the blanks and give the English equivalent:

1. ひらがなは　二週間（　　）ぜんぶ　おぼえました。
2. 英語(えい)は　まだ　五か月（　　）習っていません。
3. 一日（　　）六時間ぐらい　勉強すること（　　）たいせつだ（　　）思います。
4. ひらがな（　　）おぼえるの（　　）かんたんでした（　　）、漢字（　　）おぼえにくかったです。
5. 山田さんは　十日（　　）休みましたが、私は　二日（　　）休んでいません。

3.8.2 Say the following in Japanese:

A. 1. When did you start teaching English at a junior high school?
   2. I have been teaching English at a junior high school only for six months.
   3. How many hours a week do you teach English at a junior high school?
   4. I understand that Mr. Yamada has been teaching English at a junior high school for as many as five years.

B. 1. I think that *kan'ji* are difficult to memorize.
   2. We must memorize two hundred characters in six months. Let's do our best.
   3. I'll finish memorizing all of the *Kan'ji* for Education by next month.
   4. I memorized ten characters a day.

3.8.3 Answer the following questions in Japanese:

1. あなたは　いつ　日本語を　習いはじめましたか。
2. 日本語の　クラスは　一週間に　何時間　ありますか。
3. あなたは　一日に　何時間ぐらい　日本語を　勉強しますか。
4. うちでも　よく　れんしゅうしますか。

5. 今までに　習った　漢字の　うちで、　どの　字が　まちがえやすいですか。
6. あなたは　もう　日本語の　新聞を　読むことが　できますか。
7. 日本語の　なかで、　言いにくい　ことばは　何ですか。
8. 先生の　日本語は　はやすぎますか。

3.8.4 Write the following underlined *hiragana* in *kan'ji*:

1. <u>しょうがっこう</u>で　<u>まいにち</u>　<u>べんきょう</u>しています。
2. <u>しんぶん</u>を　<u>よ</u>むことが　できますか。
3. <u>いし</u>の　<u>うえ</u>にも　<u>さんねん</u>。
4. ぼくの　<u>し</u>っている　<u>かんじ</u>を　<u>つか</u>ってください。
5. <u>こんしゅう</u>は　まだ　森(もり)さんと　<u>はな</u>していません。

3.8.5 Distinguish the following *kan'ji*:

1. 言、語、話　　3. 近、週
2. 右、石　　4. 使、作

3.8.6 Give some examples of Japanese phenomenalism.

3.8.7 Explain the meaning of the following expressions, and using each, make a short sentence:

1. *shizen no mama*　2. *fushizen*　3. *shizen*

3.8.8 Account for what Mr. Katō says in each of the following dialogs:

Yamada: Yottsu dekimashita.
Katō: Moo yottsu mo dekimashita ka?

Ishii: Yottsu dekimashita.
Katō: Yottsu dake desu ka?

Higashi: Yottsu dekimashita.
Katō: Yottsu shika dekimasen ka?

3.8.9 After each of the following sentences, indicate which of the two expressions, *dake* or *shika . . . nai,* would be more appropriate:

1. I have just five cents.
2. I was in Japan for only ten months.
3. I invited only three people.
4. I invited twenty-five people, but only ten came.

5. I invited twenty-five people, but only one didn't come.
6. My son is twelve years old, but weighs only 65 pounds.
7. There was only one traffic accident this year.
8. Only one student got one hundred points on the test.

3.8.10 Who is at fault in the following dialog?

Tanaka: Ashita kurasu ga nai soo desu yo.

Ōkawa: Soo desu ka?

(Two days later)

Teacher: Tanaka kun to Ookawa kun, kinoo kurasu o yasumimashita ne.

Ōkawa: Ee, Tanaka kun ga nai to iimashita kara.

3.8.11 Show some examples of Japanese traditional ways of thinking, such as naturalism.

3.9 SITUATIONAL AND APPLICATION CONVERSATION

3.9.1 An American says he started learning Japanese in September. A Japanese man asks how many hours the American takes lessons a week and how many *kan'ji* he has learned.
The American answers he takes lessons ten hours a week and has memorized about 150 *kan'ji* so far. He makes a comment on studying *kan'ji, hiragana,* and so forth.

3.9.2 Tell how many hours you take Japanese lessons a week, how many *kan'ji* you have learned, etc., and ask questions on the same topic.

3.9.3 Ask a Japanese how he has studied English: institution, length of study, frequency, difficulty, etc.

3.9.4 Converse about piano lessons, sport practice, etc.

3.9.5 Fujikawa: Yokoyama kun, suiyoobi wa kurasu ga nai to iimashita ne?

Yokoyama: Iie, soo wa iimasen deshita yo. Boku wa "nai soo da" to iimashita.

Fujikawa: Suiyoobi no kurasu wa arimashita yo.

Yokoyama: Keiko san kara soo kiita to omoimashita.

3.9.6 Keiko: Okaasan, atashi, ima no shigoto ga omoshiroku nai no.

Mother: Mada ichinen han shika ima no shigoto o shite imasen yo! "Ishi no ue ni mo san'nen" desu yo, moo ni-san'nen gan'batte.

LESSON 4

洋服(ふく)[1]と　着物[2]

4.1　PRESENTATION

洋服(ふく)と　着物と、　どっちが　いいと　思いますか。　これは　日本人の　間(あいだ)で　よく　問題に　なる[3]ことです。

けっきょく　りょう方に　いい　ところが　あります。　その　いい　ところを　着る　時[4]と　場(ば)所に　合わせることが　たいせつだと　思います。

4.2　DIALOG

原(はら)の おくさん　「ミラーさん、　いらっしゃいませ。」

ミ ラ ー　「おくさん、　こんにちは。　あ、　きょうは　着物を　着ていらっしゃい[5]ますね。」

おくさん　「ええ、ミラーさんが　いらっしゃる[5]ので[6]、さっき　着かえた[7]んです[8]よ。」

ミ ラ ー　「それは　どうも。　おくさんは　着物が　よく　に合いますね。」

おくさん　「とんでもないです[9]。　おはずかしい[9]。」

ミ ラ ー　「でも、　着物は　ふべんでしょう？」

おくさん　「ええ、　そうなん[8]です。　おびを　きつく[10]　しめるので、　やっぱり　洋服(ふく)の　ほうが　ずっと　らくですわ[11]。」

原(はら)　「かないは　着物を　持っているのに[12]、　あまり　着ないん[8]です。」

おくさん　「あら、　だって[13]、　洋服(ふく)の　ほうが　働きやすいのよ[14]。」

ミ ラ ー　「日本の　若い　男の　人たちは　あまり　着物を　着ないです[8]ね。」

原(はら)　「ええ、　でも、　夏(なつ)　家で　ゆかたを　着る　人は　わりあい　多いですよ。」

ミ ラ ー　「女の　人は　パーティーに　行く　時などに　着物を　着るのに、　男の　人は　家に　いる　時に　よく　着るでしょう[15]？　ちょっと　おかしいですね。」

洋服(ようふく)　着物(きもの)　問題(もんだい)　りょう方(ほう)　着(き)る　時(とき)　場所(ばしょ)
合(あ)わせる　に合(あ)います　働(はたら)きやすい　若(わか)い　家(いえ)

4.3 PATTERN SENTENCES

4.3.1

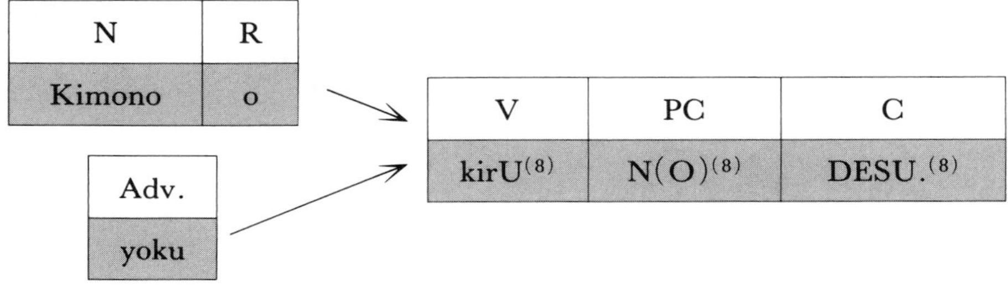

N	R
Kimono	o

Adv.
yoku

→

V	PC	C
kirU[8]	N(O)[8]	DESU.[8]

4.3.2

N	C	PC	C
Soo	NA[8]	N(O)[8]	DESU.[8]

4.3.3

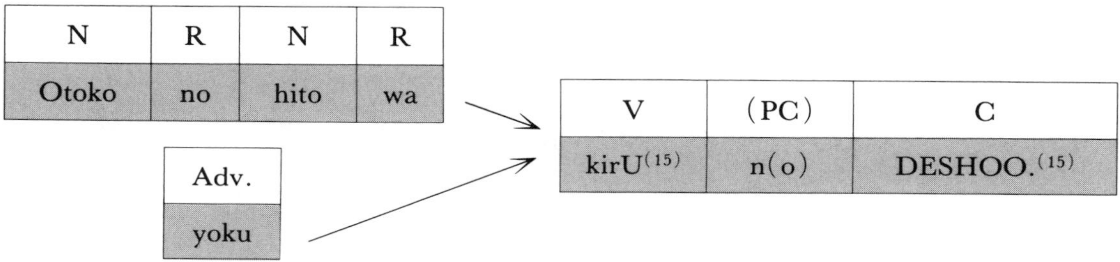

N	R	N	R
Otoko	no	hito	wa

Adv.
yoku

→

V	(PC)	C
kirU[15]	n(o)	DESHOO.[15]

4.3.4

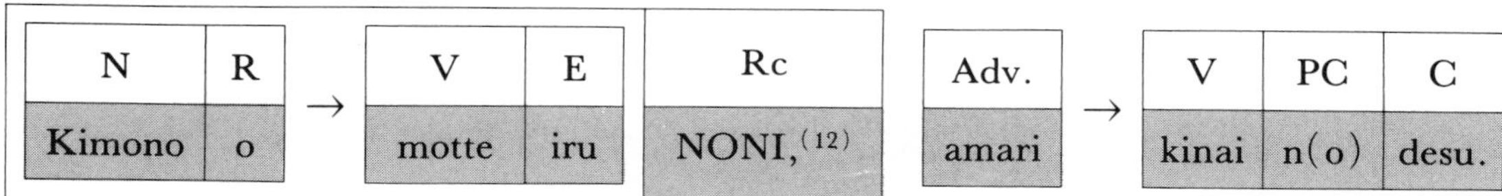

N	R	→	V	E	Rc
Kimono	o	→	motte	iru	NONI,[12]

Adv.	→	V	PC	C
amari	→	kinai	n(o)	desu.

4.3.5

N	R	→	V	Rc
Miraa san	ga	→	irassharu	NODE,[6]

V	PC	C
kikaeta	n(o)	desu.

4.4 NOTES

4.4.1 *Yoofuku*, or Western Dress in Japan

Although there was contact between Japan and the West as early as the fifteenth century, no significant Western influence in dress occurred until the last half of the nineteenth century. Such influence was at first limited to members of the upper class and high-ranking officials. It was only after 1900 that a significant shift to Western clothing among the Japanese people as a whole was evidenced. By the 1930s, such clothing could be found even in remote rural areas of Japan. From its introduction, however, Western dress was used mainly outside the home by men, and traditional dress is still commonly used in the home. Among women, Western-style dresses became common during the 1930s, and schoolchildren also began wearing Western-style uniforms during the early twentieth century. The need for simple clothing in an increasingly modern society, as well as wartime shortages, accelerated the westernization of clothing.

Western influences are also penetrating into other occupational garb. Female farmers sometimes still wear a dark blue cotton hip-length jacket and *mon'pe* trousers; raincoats with hoods, however, have completely replaced their straw cloaks on rainy days. Similarly, the vestlike apron, hip-length *happi* coat, tight trousers, and sandals of workers such as carpenters, wall painters, and *tatami* makers have given way to Western-style work clothes. Workers such as conductors, postmen, firemen, policemen, defense force personnel, and nurses as well as some pupils all wear uniforms in the Western style.

4.4.2 *Kimono*, or Traditional Japanese Clothing

The main items of traditional Japanese dress are: *kimono*, *haori*, *nagajuban*, *obi*, *hadagi*, *koshihimo*, and *tabi*.

The *kimono* has a long history of development, achieving its present form during the nineteenth century. However, its basic form dates to the seventh and eighth centuries, at which time it was worn only as an undergarment.

Throughout its development, the *kimono* has changed relative to the popular styles and fashions of the times. At court, elegance and grace were the main attributes of the *kimono*. During the Tokugawa period, the sleeves of *kimono* for young unmarried girls were sometimes as long as sixty centimeters and were called *furisode*. Similar to the *furisode*, the length of the *kimono* itself was much greater than the height of the wearer. Such features—while accenting the beauty and grace of the wearer—were quite impractical for all but the leisured classes.

During the feudal period, the use of silk was often restricted to the ruling classes; all others wore *kimono* of rough muslin or, after the seventeenth century, cotton. Variations on the basic *kimono* were made from time to time. For example, in the nineteenth century, when a whitened face, blackened teeth, and very red lips were the fashionable form of married women's make-up, a black satin collar was often added to women's *kimono* to complement this style of beauty.

Clothing bearing the family crest was first designed for the *samurai* class in the thirteenth century. *Kimono* and *haori* with the family crest are now worn on formal occasions and for mourning. Black is the usual color of both formal *kimono* and *haori*, as well as of mourning. The dead, however, are always dressed in white, symbolizing purity.

In addition to the types of clothing described above, certain types of clothing are reserved for particular professions and occupations. Shinto or Buddhist priests, for example, wear a traditional garb called *kosode*.

4.4.3 *Kore wa mon'dai ni naru koto desu* means "This is a matter which comes into question." The reason for such a discussion of clothing styles is that the simultaneous use of both traditional Japanese and Western styles in contemporary Japanese society has created some confusion. At the same time it is another instance of Japanese cultural pluralism. It is interesting, however, that Japanese men and women put these two different styles to different uses, as can be seen in the following chart:

	Kimono	Western Clothes
Male	home (relaxed)	outside (work or formal)
Female	outside (formal)	home (relaxed or work)

For the Japanese male, then, Western clothes constitute the more formal attire, whereas the Japanese female finds traditional clothing to be more formal. This generalization has its basis in role differentiation in Japanese society. In general the Japanese male works outside the home, and traditional clothing is part of his relaxation in the home and away from his work situation. The female's situation, in general, is just the opposite: *kimono* is quite inconvenient for daily work, therefore good quality *kimono* is used now as formal wear. Mrs. Hara, in this lesson, reinforces such an interpretation by stating that Western clothes are much easier for work; it would not be a common practice to wear traditional clothing at home. An amusing consequence of this situation is that Japanese people often ridicule women who own *kimono* but seldom use them by saying *tan'su no koyashi*, which implies that the women are only feeding their chest of drawers. Young children wear *kimono* for ceremonial and festival occasions such as New Year, and in celebrating their *shichi-go-san*, which are held on the fifteenth of November, of the year of their third, fifth, and seventh birthdays, although girls do not celebrate their fifth birthday while boys do not celebrate their third and seventh birthdays.

In summary, then, Western clothing has been accepted in Japanese society, and given its "proper place." However, this "place" is different for men and women. Western clothes are considered appropriate for work situations by both sexes; however, formal wear for men largely refers to Western clothing, whereas for women, traditional garb constitutes formal dress. The fact that Mrs. Hara changed into *kimono* in anticipation of Miller's visit is part of her consideration for a guest or a foreigner.

4.4.4 *Kiru toki* means "time to wear." A Noun Modifier may modify *toki*, and forms the connotation such as "time to do such and such," "when one is such and such," and so on. Noun Modifiers can be of various kinds—Pre-Noun, Noun plus *no*, plain forms of Verbs, Adjectives, and the like, and Noun plus Copula except *da*.

As already explained in Note 7.4.11, Volume II, the subject, if there is one in the Noun Modifier, should always be followed by *ga* or *no*.

Pre-Noun
Verb (plain form)
Adjective (plain form)
Noun + *no* (other than adjectival)
adjectival Noun + *na*
Noun + Copula (plain form, except *da*)
} **+ *toki***

sono toki	''that time''
au toki	''time to meet''
hataraite ita toki	''when [I] was working''
okane ga nai toki	''when one has no money''
kodomo no toki	''childhood''
raku na toki	''time of ease''
kimi ga daigakusei datta toki	''when you were a college student''

Boku ga Tookyoo Eki ni tsuita toki kara, ame ga futte imasu. — ''Since the time I arrived at Tōkyō Station, it has been raining.''

Anata ga kyonen watashi ni atta toki o oboete imasu ka? — ''Do you remember the time when you met me last year?''

Anata wa kimono o kita toki ga ichiban utsukushii desu nee. — ''You are the most beautiful when you are dressed in *kimono*.''

A so-called when clause of English may be expressed, in Japanese as a phrase, by the use of *toki* preceded by a Noun Modifier. In this case, the Relational *ni* may follow *toki* to place focus a little bit more on the time. The topic Relational *wa* may occur with or without *ni*. Also, the tense form of the Noun Modifier preceding *toki* may be either the imperfect tense form which indicates that an action has not been completed, or the perfect tense form which indicates that the action has been completed. Since the so-called sequence of tense in English does not occur in Japanese, the tense of the statement following *toki* may use either perfect tense or imperfect tense.

~ + *toki (ni) (wa)*

Nihon de wa shokuji o suru toki ni ''itadakimasu'' to iimasu. — ''In Japan, they say *Itadakimasu* when they eat a meal.''

Watakushi wa wakai toki ni iroiro na supootsu o shimashita. — ''I played various kinds of sports when I was young.''

Meriiran'do Daigaku no gakusei datta toki, nihon'go o naraimashita. — ''I learned Japanese when I was a student at the University of Maryland.''

Anata ga ohima na toki ni wa tetsudatte kudasai. — ''When you have free time, please help me.''

4.4.5 *Kimono o kite irasshaimasu ne* means ''You wear a *kimono*!'' This is a polite equivalent of *kimono o kite imasu ne*. As already explained in Note 4.4.10, Volume II, *irassharu* is a polite equivalent of *iru* ''be.'' When *iru* is used as an Extender, *irassharu* can also replace *iru*. But *irassharu* cannot be used for the speaker's and his in-group members' actions. Speech styles have been explained in Lesson 1.

Verb(*-te*) + *iru* ⟶ Verb(*-te*) + *irassharu*

sagashite imasu	⟶	sagashite irasshaimasu	''[one] is looking for''
kekkon shite iru	⟶	kekkon shite irassharu	''[he] is married''
omotte imashita	⟶	omotte irasshaimashita	''[you] were thinking''

Anata no otoosan wa doko ni tsutomete irasshaimasu ka? — ''Where does your father work?''

Okusan wa kimono o motte irasshaimasu ka?	"Does your wife have *kimono*?"
Kinoo wa nani o shite irasshaimashita ka?	"What were you doing yesterday?"

The Verb *irassharu* conjugates exactly like any other Consonant Verb such as *kaeru* except the stem form which is *irasshai(masu)*. Notice the omission of *r* before *i*. Similarly, other polite Verbs such as *kudasaru*, *ossharu*, *nasaru*, and *gozaru* also do not have *r* before *i*. *Irassharu* also means "come" or "go."

Gakkoo e irasshaimashita.	"He went to school."
Ashita watashi no uchi ni irasshaimasu ka?	"Are you coming to my home tomorrow?"

4.4.6 *Miraa san ga irassharu node, sakki kikaeta n desu* means "Since Mr. Miller was coming, I changed my clothes a short time ago." *Node* after a Predicate is a clause Relational and means "because," "since," "being that . . . ," and so forth. *Node* is frequently used interchangeably with *kara* "since," introduced in Note 5.4.8, Volume II. The main difference between these two Relationals is, however, that *node* is normally used when an "objective reason or cause" is called for while *kara* is used for a "subjective or personal" reason or cause, or is used when the speaker's judgment is rendered. Therefore, when the final Predicate suggests personal invitations, orders, requests, and the like, the reason clause is mostly followed by *kara*, although *node* is used in more formal situations.

Osoi kara, isogimashoo.	"We are late, so let's hurry."
Kutsushita ga kitanai kara, nuide kudasai.	"Your socks are dirty, so please take them off."

Since *node* is more polite than *kara*, *node* occurs more frequently in writing than in spoken language except formal or polite speech. In *Miraa san ga irassharu node, sakki kikaeta n desu*, the use of *kara* is possible, but since this speech by Mrs. Hara is polite (note the use of *irassharu*), *node* is better than *kara* in this case. The use of *kara* in the above sentence will make the statement more casual. Except in the imperfect tense of the Copula, the plain forms normally occur before the Relational *node*. The Copula *da* never occurs between a Noun and *node*, but *na*, the NA form of the Copula, does instead. Note that a Noun followed by the *na* is not necessarily an adjectival Noun but may be any other Noun in this case.

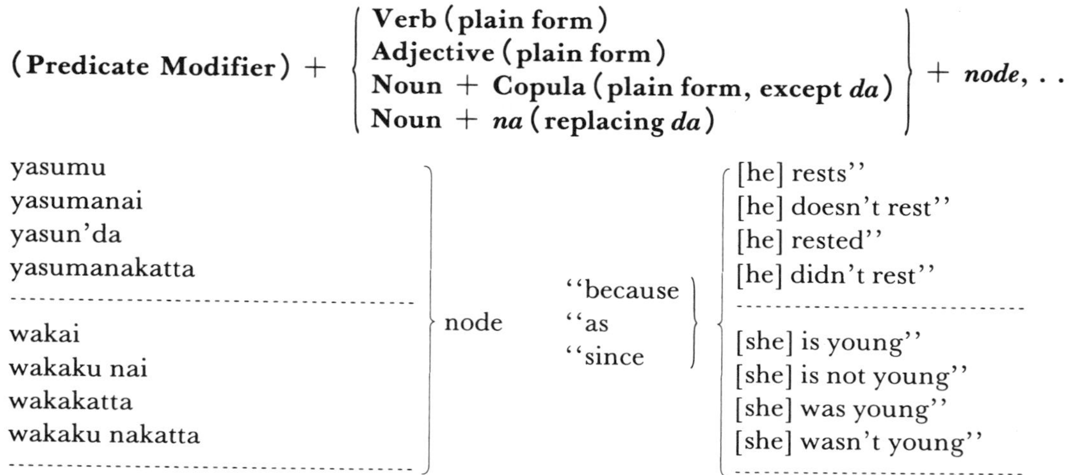

(Predicate Modifier) + { **Verb (plain form)** / **Adjective (plain form)** / **Noun + Copula (plain form, except *da*)** / **Noun + *na* (replacing *da*)** } **+ *node*, . . .**

yasumu	node	"because / "as / "since	[he] rests"
yasumanai			[he] doesn't rest"
yasun'da			[he] rested"
yasumanakatta			[he] didn't rest"
wakai			[she] is young"
wakaku nai			[she] is not young"
wakakatta			[she] was young"
wakaku nakatta			[she] wasn't young"

ben'ri na	node	"because	[it] is convenient"
ben'ri ja nai *or* ~ de wa nai		"as	[it] isn't convenient"
ben'ri datta		"since	[it] was convenient"
ben'ri ja nakatta *or* ~ de wa nakatta			[it] wasn't convenient"

Hara san wa raigetsu Furan'su e iku node, ima Furan'su no rekishi o ben'kyoo shite iru soo desu.
"Since Mr. Hara is going to France next month, I understand that he is studying French history now."

Naze kikaemashita ka?
"Why did you change your clothes?"

Machigaeta node, kakikaemashita.
"Since I made a mistake, I rewrote it."

Kutsu ga kitsui node, ashi ga itai desu.
"My shoes are so tight that my feet hurt."

Ano ryokan wa totemo yokatta node, mata tomaritai to omoimasu.
"That inn was very nice, so I'd like to stay there again."

Miraa san no okusama wa yukata ga suki na node, ichimai ageru tsumori desu.
"Since Mrs. Miller likes *yukata*, I am planning to give her one."

Mae sun'de ita ie wa fuben datta node, atarashii ie wa ben'ri ni shitai desu.
"Since the house I used to live in was inconvenient, I'd like to make my new house convenient."

4.4.7 *Kikaeta* means "one changed his clothes," and is the compound Verb consisting of the Stem form of the Verb *kiru* "wear" and *kaeta* "changed." The Verb *kaeru* "change" forms a connotation "redo," as a compound component, preceded by the Stem form of a Verb. If it is necessary to mention into what something is changed, A *o* B *ni* occurs with *kaeru*.

noru "ride" ⟶ norikaeru "change vehicles; transfer"
kaku "write" ⟶ kakikaeru "rewrite"
haku "put on (shoes, trousers, etc.)" ⟶ hakikaeru "change (shoes, trousers, etc.)"
ireru "insert; put in" ⟶ irekaeru "replace"

Dekakeru node, yoofuku o kikaemashita.
"Because I was going out, I changed my clothes."

Kyuukoo wa Kan'da ni tomarimasen kara, tsugi no eki de norikaete kudasai.
"Since the express train doesn't stop at Kanda, please transfer (cars) at the next station."

Kono zubon o atarashii hako ni irekaete kudasai.
"Please put these trousers into a new box (replacing the old box)."

Kutsushita ga kitanai kara, hakikaemashoo.
"Since my stockings are dirty, I'll change them."

Oyogi ni iku node, mizugi ni kikaemashita.
"As I am going swimming, I've changed into a swimming suit."

4.4.8 "I changed my clothes" may be expressed, in normal spoken-style Japanese, either as *kikaemashita* or *kikaeta n desu*. *Kikaemashita* is used merely to tell the fact while *kikaeta n desu* indicates some explanation to the listener's inquiry or to the statement the speaker has given or will give. Or *kikaeta n desu* may be used to show some emphasis. The difference between *kikaemashita* and *kikaeta n desu* is the same as that between *takai desu* and *takai n desu*, which has been explained in Note 8.4.3, Volume I. The ~*n desu* is a less formal equivalent of ~*no desu*. In summary, a plain form followed by *n desu* or *no desu* not only states a fact but also explains the situation. Therefore, the use of *n(o) desu* is common in conversation, and the sentence usually has a close relation with a previous or following sentence contextually. The forms that occur before *n desu* or *no desu* are the same as those which occur before the Relational *node*. Plain forms of a Verb (introduced in Lessons 4 and 9, Volume II), an Adjective (already introduced in Lessons 8 and 9, Volume I), and the Copula (except the NA form which replaces *da*) occur:

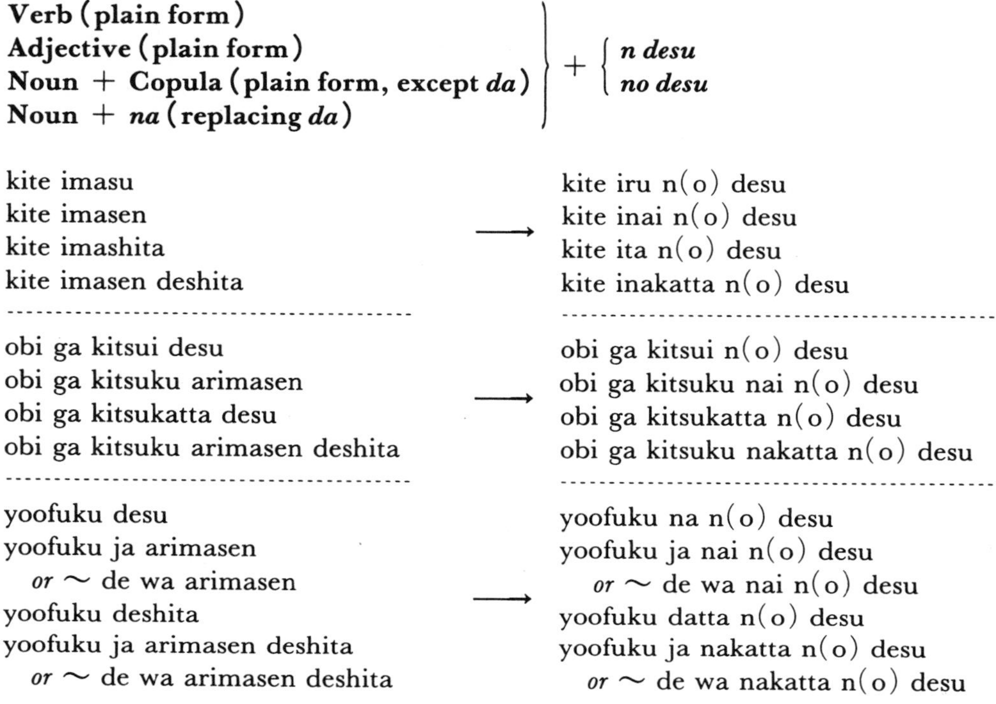

Verb (plain form)
Adjective (plain form)
Noun + Copula (plain form, except *da*)
Noun + *na* (replacing *da*)
} + { ***n desu*** / ***no desu***

kite imasu kite imasen kite imashita kite imasen deshita	⟶	kite iru n(o) desu kite inai n(o) desu kite ita n(o) desu kite inakatta n(o) desu
obi ga kitsui desu obi ga kitsuku arimasen obi ga kitsukatta desu obi ga kitsuku arimasen deshita	⟶	obi ga kitsui n(o) desu obi ga kitsuku nai n(o) desu obi ga kitsukatta n(o) desu obi ga kitsuku nakatta n(o) desu
yoofuku desu yoofuku ja arimasen *or* ~ de wa arimasen yoofuku deshita yoofuku ja arimasen deshita *or* ~ de wa arimasen deshita	⟶	yoofuku na n(o) desu yoofuku ja nai n(o) desu *or* ~ de wa nai n(o) desu yoofuku datta n(o) desu yoofuku ja nakatta n(o) desu *or* ~ de wa nakatta n(o) desu

Note that the Dictionary form and TA form of a Verb and the NA form and TA form of the Copula are never followed by *desu* directly. The Pre-Copula *n* or *no* should occur. But sometimes the plain negative forms represented by *nai* forms are directly followed by the Copula *desu* without *n* or *no*. In this case the Predicate has no meaning of explanation or emphasis. It is merely a colloquial equivalent of *-masen, -ku arimasen, de wa arimasen deshita,* and so forth.

kinai desu	......	kimasen
kinakatta desu	......	kimasen deshita
kitsuku nai desu	......	kitsuku arimasen
kitsuku nakatta desu	......	kitsuku arimasen deshita
raku ja nai desu *or* ~ de wa nai desu	......	raku ja arimasen *or* ~ de wa arimasen
raku ja nakatta desu *or* ~ de wa nakatta desu	......	raku ja arimasen deshita *or* ~ de wa arimasen deshita

But never *kiru desu, kita desu, raku na desu.*

Ashita ohima nara, uchi e asobi ni irasshaimasen ka?	"If you are free tomorrow, won't you come to visit me?"
Ashita wa shigoto ga aru n desu.	"I have work to do tomorrow."
Nara made ashi o nobashita n desu ka?	"Did you extend your trip as far as Nara?"
Iie, iku koto ga dekinakatta n desu.	"No, I couldn't do it."
Mado o akete kudasai. Totemo atsui n desu.	"Please open the window. It's very hot."
Watakushi wa mainichi yoofuku o kite imasu ga, yoofuku no hoo ga raku na n desu.	"I wear Western-style clothes every day because I feel more at ease in Western-style clothes (than in Japanese-style clothes)."

When a sentence includes an interrogative Noun such as *naze* "why" or *dooshite* "why" which asks the reason for one's action or state, the Predicate commonly has the ending *~n(o) desu*. The reason is that such a question indicates a desire to have some explanation for an assumed known fact.

Dooshite kono shitsumon no imi ga wakaranai n desu ka?	"Why don't you understand the meaning of this question?"
Anata ga omou hodo kan'tan de wa nai n desu.	"It's not as easy as you think."
Kinoo naze kurasu o yasun'da n desu ka?	"Why did you miss classes yesterday?"
Byooki datta n desu.	"Because I was sick."

4.4.9 *Ton'de mo nai desu, ohazukashii* means "Not at all! I feel embarrassed." This indicates the Japanese attitude toward compliments. Usually, the Japanese use a negative answer to respond to others' compliments.

Piano, ojoozu desu nee.	"You play piano well."
Ton'de mo nai. Mada mada heta desu.	"Not at all. I am still not good at it."
Kirei na yoofuku desu ne.	"Your dress is pretty."
Maa, hazukashii. Furui n desu yo.	"Oh, no. This is an old one."
Ii musuko san desu ne.	"You have a nice son."
Ton'de mo nai. Zen'zen ben'kyoo shinai n desu yo.	"Not at all. He doesn't study at all."

4.4.10 *Obi o kitsuku shimeru* means "An *obi* (sash) is worn tightly." *Kitsuku* is the KU form of the Adjective *kitsui*, and modifies adverbially the following Predicate *shimeru*. This is called the adverbial use of the KU form of an Adjective.

hayai	"is fast; is early"	⟶	hayaku	"fast; early"
osoi	"is slow; is late"	⟶	osoku	"slowly; late"
takai	"is expensive"	⟶	takaku	"expensively"
nagai	"is long"	⟶	nagaku	"long; for a long time"
tanoshii	"is pleasant"	⟶	tanoshiku	"happily; pleasantly"
kuwashii	"is detailed"	⟶	kuwashiku	"in detail"

asa hayai	"early morning"	⟶	asa hayaku	"early in the morning"
yoru osoi	"late night"	⟶	yoru osoku	"late at night"

Do not confuse this use of the KU form of an Adjective with the KU form followed by an Extender such as *arimasen*, *nai*, *suru*, *naru*, and the like.

Ashita wa gorufu o shi ni iku node, hayaku okinakereba narimasen.	"I must get up early tomorrow because I am going to play golf."
Nihon ni nagaku inakatta node, Nihon no koto wa yoku wakaranai n desu.	"Since I wasn't in Japan for a long time, I don't know much about Japan."
Kinoo shin'juku de beruto to saifu o yasuku kaimashita.	"I bought a belt and a wallet at a low price in Shinjuku."

4.4.11 *Yoofuku no hoo ga zutto raku desu wa* means "I feel much more comfortable with Western-style clothes on." The *wa* at the end of a sentence is a Sentence Particle frequently used by women in conversation. When this Sentence Particle *wa* is placed after *desu* or *-masu*, it gives a kind of conceited air. However, when *wa* comes after the plain form, it gives a plain, colloquial, and "as a matter of fact" tone.

Watakushi wa kimono yori yoofuku no hoo ga suki da (desu) wa.	"I prefer Western-style clothes to *kimono*."
Ben'ri na tokoro ni sumitai da (desu) wa.	"I would like to live in a convenient place."

The Particles *wa*, *yo*, and *ne* occur predominantly in the speech of women at the end of an utterance, although men also use *yo* and *ne*. Women, however, use them with much greater frequency, and also use *wa yo* and *wa ne*. Men would not use *wa*, *wa yo*, or *wa ne*. Underlying these patterns of usage is the assumption that Japanese women are supposed to refrain from asserting themselves. These Particles both modify the directness that a statement might otherwise imply, while at the same time calling attention to the fact that a statement is being made.

Furthermore, traditional Japanese women tend to use their own special style when speaking. This style may be differentiated from that of men through the use of Sentence Particles as mentioned above, or the prevalence of the *gozaimasu* style. This women's style can be seen throughout this dialog, in Mrs. Hara's speech, which is typical of most urban women's usages. *-Mase* (sentence 1), *wa* (sentence 7), and *no yo* (sentence 9), as well as *ara* are all common elements in women's speech.

4.4.12 *Kanai wa kimono o motte iru noni, amari kinai n desu* means "In spite of the fact that my wife has *kimono,* she doesn't wear them very often." *Noni,* in this instance, is a clause Relational meaning "in spite of" or "although." *Noni,* however, has a stronger reversal meaning than *keredomo.* *Noni* normally follows a plain-form Predicate, except the NA form which is used instead of the plain imperfect tense form of the Copula.

(Predicate Modifier) + { **Verb (plain form)** / **Adjective (plain form)** / **Noun + Copula (plain form, except *da*)** / **Noun + *na* (replacing *da*)** } **+ *noni*, . . .**

ame ga furu			it rains"
ame ga furanai			it doesn't rain"
ame ga futta			it rained"
ame ga furanakatta			it didn't rain"
tsumaranai			it is dull"
tsumaranaku nai			it isn't dull"
tsumaranakatta	noni, . . .	"in spite of the fact that	it was dull"
tsumaranaku nakatta		"although	it wasn't dull"
kimono na			it is a *kimono*"
kimono ja nai *or* ~ de wa nai			it isn't a *kimono*"
kimono datta			it was a *kimono*"
kimono ja nakatta *or* ~ de wa nakatta			it wasn't a *kimono*"

Ame ga futte iru noni, san'po ni iku n desu ka? — "Are you going for a walk in spite of the rain?"

Mainichi ren'shuu shita noni, joozu ni narimasen deshita. — "Although I practiced every day, I didn't progress very much."

Sono hon wa yoku nai noni, zuibun takai n desu nee. — "Though that book is not good, it's extremely expensive, isn't it?"

Kore wa totemo takakatta noni, sugu dame ni narimashita. — "In spite of being expensive, this one broke right away."

Tookyoo wa furui machi na noni, mukashi no mono ga amari nokotte imasen. — "In spite of its being an old city, there are few things left in Tōkyō from the older days."

Asa wa ii ten'ki datta noni, yoru ame ni narimashita. — "Although the weather was nice in the morning, it started to rain in the evening."

4.4.13 *Datte* means "but," "yet," "though," "because," and "why." Mr. Hara Makes a slight joke at his wife's expense in this dialog when he refers to the *kimono* which Mrs. Hara has, but rarely wears. This is quite usual, since a Japanese husband normally would kid his wife in a similar manner in front of a visitor. Such a joke, downgrading his wife, is an indication of "in-groupness." Japanese usually praise "out-group" people, and speak slightingly of their "in-group" members who are either equal or inferior. Mrs. Hara's response of *ara*, *datte* is also quite normal. Through making excuses in an attempt to get what she wants and in trying simply to stall for time, she demonstrates her "tender and dependent" (*amaeru*) attitude toward her husband (in-groupness). *Ara* and *datte* are vague expressions which can be used independently. *Datte* reveals a dependent attitude, however, and is usually used by children toward their parents, and by wives toward their husbands, and sometimes among women or a female toward a male. Those who are depended on, on the other hand, do not use this expression quite as frequently.

Dooshite ikanai no? — "Why don't you go?"

Datte (ikitaku nai no). — "Because . . ."

4.4.14 *Hatarakiyasui no yo* is the shortened, informal and colloquial equivalent of *hatarakiyasui no desu yo*. This informal expression eliminating *desu* was said by Mrs. Hara to her husband, and it is common in conversation between intimate friends, family members, and so on. The *no yo* as a sentence ending is used only by women. (See Note 4.4.11)

Dame na n(o) desu (yo). ⟶ Dame na no (yo).
Dooshite na n(o) desu ka? ⟶ Dooshite na no?

4.4.15 *Kiru deshoo* means "They wear it, don't they?" *Deshoo* appears after the plain form of a Verb. While *deshoo* may follow the plain form of a Verb directly, *desu* cannot omit *n* or *no* after the Verb.

Verb (plain form) + { *(no)* / *(n)* } + *deshoo*

iku ikanai itta ikanakatta	+ { (no) / (n) } + deshoo	"I suppose / "I imagine { [one] will go" / [one] will not go" / [one] went" / [one] did not go"

Ano hito wa kimono o kimasu ka?	"Does he wear *kimono*?"
Iie, kinai deshoo.	"No, I suppose he would not."
Minasan wa paatii ni irasshaimasu ka?	"Do they all go to the party?"
Ee, irassharu deshoo.	"Yes, I suppose they would go."

4.5 VOCABULARY

Presentation

洋服	yoofuku	......	N	Western-style clothes
着物	kimono	......	N	traditional Japanese-style clothes
間	aida	......	N	among; between
こと	koto	......	Nd	matter
りょう方	ryoohoo	......	N	both; both sides; both of them
時	toki	......	N	time; when (see 4.4.4)
合わせる	awaseru	......	V	fit; suit (transitive Verb)

Dialog

原	Hara	......	N	family name
ミラー	Miraa	......	N	Miller
いらっしゃいます	irasshaimasu	......	E	polite equivalent of *iru* (normal form of *irassharu*) (see 4.4.5)
いらっしゃる	irassharu	......	V	polite equivalent of *kuru* or *iku* (see 4.4.5)
ので	node	......	Rc	being that . . . ; since; because (see 4.4.6)

さっき	sakki	......	N	some time ago; a little while ago
かえた	kaeta	......	V	changed (TA form of *kaeru*) (compound component) (see 4.4.7)
に合います	niaimasu	......	V	match; suit; becoming (normal form of *niau*) (intransitive Verb)
とんでもないです。	Ton'de mo nai desu.	......	(exp.)	On the contrary.; Far from it. (see 4.4.9)
はずかしい	hazukashii	......	A	is ashamed; is shy; is embarrassed (see 4.4.9)
ふべん	fuben	......	Na	inconvenient
おび	obi	......	N	sash; belt (for *kimono*)
きつく	kitsuku	......	A	KU form of *kitsui* – is tight (see 4.4.10)
しめる	shimeru	......	V	tie; fasten
らく	raku	......	Na	comfortable; ease
わ	wa	......	SP	used by women (see 4.4.11)
のに	noni	......	Rc	in spite of; although (see 4.4.12)
だって	datte	......	SI	but; because (see 4.4.13)
の	no	......	PC	formal equivalent of *n* (see 4.4.8 and 4.4.14)
家	ie	......	N	house
ゆかた	yukata	......	N	summer cotton *kimono*
パーティー	paatii	......	N	party
おかしい	okashii	......	A	is funny; is strange; is laughable

Notes

くつ下	kutsushita	......	N	socks; stockings
ぬぐ	nugu	......	V	take off; put off
べんり	ben'ri	......	Na	convenient
いたい	itai	......	A	is painful; ache; is sore; hurt (The structure with *itai* is normally "(*watashi*) *wa* (*atama*) *ga itai.*")
ずぼん	zubon	......	N	trousers; pants
水着	mizugi	......	N	swimming suit
ベルト	beruto	......	N	belt (for Western-style clothes) (cf. *obi*)
(お)さいふ	(o)saifu	......	N	wallet; purse; money holder

Drills

くるしい	kurushii	......	A	is painful; is hard
ジャンパー	jan'paa	......	N	jumper; casual wear

Extra Vocabulary

ぞうり	zoori	......	N	Japanese slippers; bathroom slippers
げた	geta	......	N	wooden clogs
たび	tabi	......	N	Japanese socks
スカート	sukaato	......	N	skirt
ショートパンツ	shooto pan'tsu	......	N	short pants; shorts
ブラウス	burausu	......	N	blouse
上着(うわぎ)	uwagi	......	N	coat; jacket
オーバー	oobaa	......	N	overcoat
コート	kooto	......	N	long coat
スーツ	suutsu	......	N	suit

4.6 KAN'JI

4.6.1 洋 (1) YOO (2) ocean (3) classifier 氵 [water]
(4) (5) 洋風(ふう)、洋服(ふく)、西(せい)洋料理(りょうり)、東洋 [the Orient] (6) homonym 羊、様、養

4.6.2 着 (1) *ki(ru)* (2) wear (3) classifier 目 [eyes]
(4) (5) 着物を着ます

4.6.3 問 (1) MON (2) question; ask (3) classifier 門 (口)
(4) (5) しつ問、問題(だい)
(6) homonym 門、聞

4.6.4 題 (1) DAI (2) title; subject; topic (3) classifier 頁 [head]
(4)
(5) 宿(しゅく)題、問題、本の題は「日本文学」です
(6) homonym 醍

4.6.5 方 (1) HOO (2) direction; side; way; alternative (3) forms the classifier 方 [direction] (4) (5) 方法(ほう) [method]、右の方
(6) homonym 放、倣、訪

4.6.a 時 (2.6.10, Vol. II) (1) *toki* (2) time; when (5) その時、食事の時、時々(どき)

4.6.b 所 (5.6.6, Vol. II) (1) SHO (5) 場(ば)所、事務(む)所

4.6.6 合 (1) *a(u); a(waseru)* (2) fit; be together (3) classifier 𠆢 (口)
(4) ノ 𠆢 今 合 (5) 合わせる、に合う
(6) a mouth of a vase (ㅂ) with a top (A)

4.6.7 働 (1) *hatara(ku)* (2) work; labor (3) classifier 亻
(4) ノ 亻 亻 亻 佈 侢 偅 働 (5) デパートで働いています
(6) a man (亻) moving (動) ⟶ work

4.6.8 若 (1) *waka(i)* (2) young (3) classifier 艹 [grass]
(4) 一 十 廾 艹 芏 芐 若 若 (5) 若い人

4.6.9 家 (1) *ie* (2) house (3) classifier 宀 [roof]
(4) 丶 丷 宀 宀 宀 宁 宇 家 家 家
(5) ぼくの家を見に来てください、家々 (6) pig (豕) under the roof

4.6.c 水 (*4.6.1, Vol. II) (1) *mizu* (2) water (5) 水着(ぎ)、水をください

4.6.10 手* (1) *te* (2) hand (3) classifier ノ (手) (4) ノ 二 三 手
(5) あい手、手つだう、お手つだいさん [maid]
(6) shape of a hand (ヲ)

4.7 DRILLS

4.7.1 Transformation Drill

1. おびを　きつく　しめました。らくじゃありません。 ⟶ おびを　きつく　しめたので、　らくじゃありません。
2. 京都には　古い　お寺が　のこっています。行ってみたいです。 ⟶ 京都には　古い　お寺が　のこっているので、　行ってみたいです。
3. この　水着(ぎ)は　いろが　に合いません。ほしくありません。 ⟶ この　水着(ぎ)は　いろが　に合わないので、ほしくありません。

4. わたしは　毎日　れんしゅう
しませんでした。
じょうずに　なりませんでした。
→ わたしは　毎日　れんしゅうしなかったので、　じょうずに　なりませんでした。

5. 今ばん　お客(きゃく)さんが　来ます。
料理(りょうり)を　手つだってください。
→ 今ばん　お客(きゃく)さんが　来るので、　料理(りょうり)を　手つだってください。

6. 子どもが　ことばを
おぼえはじめました。
とても　かわいいです。
→ 子どもが　ことばを　おぼえはじめたので、　とても　かわいいです。

7. しごとが　たくさん　あります。
土曜(よう)日も　働かなければ
なりません。
→ しごとが　たくさん　あるので、　土曜(よう)日も　働かなければ なりません。

8. 新しい　くつを　はきました。
あるきやすいです。
→ 新しい　くつを　はいたので、　あるきやすいです。

4.7.2 Transformation Drill

1. 来週の　週末(まつ)は　いそがしいです。
出かけることが　できません。
→ 来週の　週末(まつ)は　いそがしいので、　出かけることが　できません。

2. ばんごはんが　おいしかったです。
食べすぎました。
→ ばんごはんが　おいしかったので、　食べすぎました。

3. 水は　今　ほしくありません。
あとで　持って来てください。
→ 水は　今　ほしくないので、　あとで　持って来てください。

4. おびが　きついです。
ちょっと　くるしいんです。
→ おびが　きついので、　ちょっと　くるしいんです。

5. せつめいが　くわしく
ありませんでした。
よく　わかりませんでした。
→ せつめいが　くわしくなかったので、　よく　わかりませんでした。

6. この　本は　あまり
ながくありません。
一日で　読みおわりますよ。
→ この　本は　あまり　ながくないので、　一日で　読みおわりますよ。

7. かたちが　よくありませんでした。
けっきょく　買いませんでした。
→ かたちが　よくなかったので、　けっきょく　買いませんでした。

8. 足が　いたいです。
くつを　はきたくありません。
→ 足が　いたいので、　くつを　はきたくありません。

4.7.3 Transformation Drill

1. ゴルフが　まだ　へたです。
はずかしいです。 → ゴルフが　まだ　へたなので、はずかしいです。
2. バスは　べんりじゃありません。
地下鉄に　のって行きましょう。 → バスは　べんりじゃないので、　地下鉄に　のって行きましょう。
3. 問題が　かんたんでは
ありませんでした。
わかりにくかったです。 → 問題が　かんたんではなかったので、わかりにくかったです。
4. ふねの　旅行は　たいへんです。
ひこうきに　したそうです。 → ふねの　旅行は　たいへんなので、ひこうきに　したそうです。
5. 奈良の　大仏は
いんしょう的でした。
また　見に　行くつもりです。 → 奈良の　大仏は　いんしょう的だったので、また　見に　行くつもりです。
6. これは　いもうとの　くつです。
ちょっと　きついです。 → これは　いもうとの　くつなので、ちょっと　きついです。
7. あの　家は　日本風
じゃありません。
すみたくありません。 → あの　家は　日本風じゃないので、すみたくありません。
8. 天気が　へんでした。
うみへ　行きませんでした。 → 天気が　へんだったので、　うみへ　行きませんでした。

4.7.4 Transformation Drill

1. 奈良まで　足を　のばしたいと
思いました。
時間が　なかったんです。 → 奈良まで　足を　のばしたいと　思ったのに、　時間が　なかったんです。
2. ドイツ語を　五か月　習いました。
まだ　じょうずに　なりません。 → ドイツ語を　五か月　習ったのに、　まだ　じょうずに　なりません。
3. ミラーさんは　中国語を
三か月しか　勉強しません。
よく　わかります。 → ミラーさんは　中国語を　三か月しか　勉強しないのに、　よく　わかります。
4. さっき　ジャンパーを　ぬぎました。
まだ　あついです。 → さっき　ジャンパーを　ぬいだのに、　まだ　あついです。
5. その　洋服は　よく　に合います。
どうして　着ないんですか。 → その　洋服は　よく　に合うのに、　どうして　着ないんですか。

6. 日本風(ふう)の　へやを　よやくしたかったんです。　もう　ありませんでした。	→ 日本風(ふう)の　へやを　よやくしたかったのに、　もう　ありませんでした。
7. 鈴木(すずき)さんに　会いたいんです。　いつも　るすなんです。	→ 鈴木(すずき)さんに　会いたいのに、　いつも　るすなんです。
8. 洋服(ふく)を　着かえたんです。　お客(きゃく)さんが　いらっしゃいませんでした。	→ 洋服(ふく)を　着かえたのに、　お客(きゃく)さんが　いらっしゃいませんでした。

4.7.5　Transformation Drill

1. この　問題は　とても　むずかしいです。　よく　わかりましたね。	→ この　問題は　とても　むずかしいのに、　よく　わかりましたね。
2. ついた　時間が　おそかったんです。　友だちは　まだ　待っていました。	→ ついた　時間が　おそかったのに、　友だちは　まだ　待っていました。
3. あの　えいがは　おもしろく　ありませんでした。　どうして　二度(ど)も　見たんですか。	→ あの　えいがは　おもしろくなかったのに、　どうして　二度(ど)も　見たんですか。
4. 手が　いたいです。　パーティーに　行かなければ　なりません。	→ 手が　いたいのに、　パーティーに　行かなければなりません。
5. くろい　ネクタイは　ほしく　ありませんでした。　あにが　くれました。	→ くろい　ネクタイは　ほしくなかったのに、　あにが　くれました。
6. この　くつは　たかく　ありませんでした。　とても　はきやすいです。	→ この　くつは　たかくなかったのに、　とても　はきやすいです。

4.7.6　Transformation Drill

1. かんたんな　ことです。　どうして　わからないんですか。	→ かんたんな　ことなのに、　どうして　わからないんですか。
2. ゆかたが　好きです。　あまり　着ないですね。	→ ゆかたが　好きなのに、　あまり　着ないですね。

3. これは　べんりじゃありません。どうして　使っているんですか。 → これは　べんりじゃないのに、どうして　使っているんですか。

4. ひらがなを　おぼえるのは　かんたんでした。かたかなは　おぼえにくかったです。 → ひらがなを　おぼえるのは　かんたんだったのに、　かたかなは　おぼえにくかったです。

5. けんぶつしたい　所は　京都でした。けっきょく　大阪(さか)へ　行きました。 → けんぶつしたい　所は　京都だったのに、けっきょく　大阪(さか)へ　行きました。

6. 週末(まつ)は　るすです。友だちが　うちへ　来るそうです。 → 週末(まつ)は　るすなのに、　友だちが　うちへ　来るそうです。

7. 原(はら)さんは　びょう気では　ありませんでした。しごとに　来なかったと　聞きました。 → 原(はら)さんは　びょう気ではなかったのに、しごとに　来なかったと　聞きました。

8. ブラウンさんは　日本語が　じょうずです。まだ　日本人と　話したことが　ないそうです。 → ブラウンさんは　日本語が　じょうずなのに、　まだ　日本人と　話したことがないそうです。

4.7.7 Transformation Drill

1. 山田さんは　びょう気なので、学校へ　来ませんでした。 ⟷ 山田さんは　びょう気なのに、　学校へ　来ました。
2. 日本語を　二年も　習ったので、話すことが　できます。 ⟷ 日本語を　二年も　習ったのに、　話すことができません。
3. この　辞(じ)書は　使いにくいので、いつも　使っていません。 ⟷ この　辞(じ)書は　使いにくいのに、　いつも使っています。
4. その　さんこう書は　せつめいがくわしかったので、　買いました。 ⟷ その　さんこう書は　せつめいがくわしかったのに、　買いませんでした。
5. あめが　ふっていたので、　花見に行かなかったそうです。 ⟷ あめが　ふっていたのに、　花見に　行ったそうです。
6. きのう　えいがの　きっぷをもらったので、　見に　行きました。 ⟷ きのう　えいがの　きっぷを　もらったのに、見に　行きませんでした。
7. 着物を　着たので、　くるしいんです。 ⟷ 着物を　着たのに、　くるしくないんです。
8. この　おさいふは　べんりなので、使っています。 ⟷ この　おさいふは　べんりなのに、　使っていません。

4.7.8 Transformation Drill

1. 新しい　自転(てん)車を　買いました。
やすかったです。 ⟶ 新しい　自転(てん)車を　やすく　買いました。
2. けさ　事務(む)所へ　行きました。
おそかったです。 ⟶ けさ　事務(む)所へ　おそく　行きました。
3. あの　店(みせ)は　物を　うります。
たかいです。 ⟶ あの　店(みせ)は　物を　たかく　うります。
4. ベルトを　しめました。
きつかったです。 ⟶ ベルトを　きつく　しめました。
5. ミラーさんは　日本に　すんでいるそうです。
ながいそうです。 ⟶ ミラーさんは　日本に　ながく　すんでいるそうです。
6. その　問題を　せつめいしてください。
くわしいです。 ⟶ その　問題を　くわしく　せつめいしてください。
7. 子どもが　にわで　あそんでいます。
たのしいです。 ⟶ 子どもが　にわで　たのしく　あそんでいます。
8. 高橋(たかはし)さんが　うちへ　来ました。
はやかったです。 ⟶ 高橋(たかはし)さんが　うちへ　はやく　来ました。

4.7.9 Transformation Drill

1. かないは　着物を　あまり　着ません。 ⟶ かないは　着物を　あまり　着ないんです。
2. なぜ　着かえますか。 ⟶ なぜ　着かえるんですか。
3. どうして　くつ下を　ぬぎましたか。 ⟶ どうして　くつ下を　ぬいだんですか。
4. あついので、　ゆかたを　着ます。 ⟶ あついので、　ゆかたを　着るんです。
5. 着物にも　洋服(ふく)にも　いい　ところが　ありますね。 ⟶ 着物にも　洋服(ふく)にも　いい　ところが　あるんですね。
6. けっきょく　旅館は　よやくしませんでした。 ⟶ けっきょく　旅館は　よやくしなかったんです。
7. つぎの　駅で　新宿(じゅく)行に　のりかえます。 ⟶ つぎの　駅で　新宿(じゅく)行に　のりかえるんです。
8. ベルトを　きつく　しめすぎました。 ⟶ ベルトを　きつく　しめすぎたんです。

9. きのう　買った　ずぼんを　はいて　みました。 ⟶ きのう　買った　ずぼんを　はいてみたんです。
10. どうして　はやく　いらっしゃい　ましたか。 ⟶ どうして　はやく　いらっしゃったんですか。

4.7.10 Transformation Drill

1. これは　ぼくの　一番　好きな　ネクタイです。 ⟶ これは　ぼくの　一番　好きな　ネクタイなんです。
2. こたえは　あなたが　言うほど　かんたんではありません。 ⟶ こたえは　あなたが　言うほど　かんたんではないんです。
3. あの　人は　学生の　間(あいだ)で　ゆうめいです。 ⟶ あの　人は　学生の　間(あいだ)で　ゆうめいなんです。
4. きのう　うちへ　いらっしゃった　お客(きゃく)さまは　ミラーさんでした。 ⟶ きのう　うちへ　いらっしゃった　お客(きゃく)さまは　ミラーさんだったんです。
5. 小学校で　教える　漢字は　教育(いく)漢字です。 ⟶ 小学校で　教える　漢字は　教育(いく)漢字なんです。
6. 先月　うみへ　行くつもりでした。 ⟶ 先月　うみへ　行くつもりだったんです。
7. 中村(むら)先生の　電話(わ)番号(ごう)は　六五八一じゃありませんでした。 ⟶ 中村(むら)先生の　電話(わ)番号(ごう)は　六五八一じゃなかったんです。
8. 洋服(ふく)を　着るのが　やっぱり　一番　らくです。 ⟶ 洋服(ふく)を　着るのが　やっぱり　一番　らくなんです。

4.7.11 Substitution Drill

子どもの　時に、　日本へ　行ったことが　あります。

1. 若い …… 若い　時に、日本へ　行ったことが　あります。
2. 学生の …… 学生の　時に、日本へ　行ったことが　あります。
3. 日本語を　習っていた …… 日本語を　習っていた　時に、日本へ　行ったことが　あります。
4. ちちが　元気(げん)だった …… ちちが　元気(げん)だった　時に、日本へ　行ったことが　あります。
5. 三年生の …… 三年生の　時に、日本へ　行ったことが　あります。
6. さくらが　さいている …… さくらが　さいている　時に、日本へ　行ったことが　あります。

7. 小さい …… 小さい　時に、　日本へ　行ったことが　あります。
8. しごとが　ひまな …… しごとが　ひまな　時に、　日本へ　行ったことが　あります。

4.7.12 E-J Response Drill

1. きのうは　なぜ　パーティーに　行かなかったんですか。
   because I was sick …… びょう気だったので、　行かなかったんです。
2. どうして　夏(なつ)　ゆかたを　着るんですか。
   because it is comfortable …… らくなので、　着るんです。
3. どうして　洋服(ふく)に　着かえたんですか。
   because a guest is coming …… お客(きゃく)さんが　いらっしゃるので、　着かえたんです。
4. あなたは　どうして　着物を　着ないんですか。
   because it doesn't suit me …… に合わないので、　着ないんです。
5. なぜ　新しい　くつを　ぬいだんですか。
   because they were too tight …… きつすぎたので、　ぬいだんです。
6. きょうは　なぜ　ネクタイを　しめないんですか。
   because it is hot …… あついので、　しめないんです。
7. なぜ　新聞を　読まないんですか。
   because *kan'ji* are difficult …… 漢字が　むずかしいので、　読まないんです。
8. どうして　パーティーの　時、　着物を　着ないんですか。
   because I don't have good *kimono* …… いい　着物を　持っていないので、　着ないんです。

4.7.13 Transformation Drill

1. 着物を　着ていますね。 ⟷ 着物を　着ていらっしゃいますね。
2. お客(きゃく)さまが　来るはずです。 ⟷ お客(きゃく)さまが　いらっしゃるはずです。
3. 原(はら)さんは　図(と)書館へ　行ったそうです。 ⟷ 原(はら)さんは　図(と)書館へ　いらっしゃったそうです。
4. 着物を　何まい　持っていますか。 ⟷ 着物を　何まい　持っていらっしゃいますか。
5. 池(いけ)田さんが　来たので、　ごちそうを　作りました。 ⟷ 池(いけ)田さんが　いらっしゃったので、　ごちそうを　作りました。
6. 何を　しているんですか。 ⟷ 何を　していらっしゃるんですか。
7. ぜひ　うちへ　来てください。 ⟷ ぜひ　うちへ　いらっしゃってください。

4.8 EXERCISES

4.8.1 Connect each of the A-group expressions with an appropriate B-group expression:

A	B
1. ゆかたは　すずしいので、	a. 着物を　持って行きたいです。
2. 洋服(ふく)の　ほうが　働きやすいので、	b. 気分が　わるくなりました。
3. アメリカへ　行く　時には、	c. あまり　に合いませんね。
4. おびを　きつく　しめたので、	d. 夏(なつ)　よく　着ます。
5. 新しい　くつと　くつ下に	e. いつも　着ているんです。
6. ネクタイを　もっと　きつく	f. はきかえたんです。
7. この　くつは　よく　に合うのに、	g. どうして　はかないんですか。
	h. しめた　ほうが　いいですよ。

4.8.2 Write the following in English:

1. この　歴史(れきし)の　本は　ゆうめいな　本なのに、　よくないんです。
2. ひこうきで　行きたかったのに、　きっぷを　よやくすることが　できませんでした。
3. あつい　時には、　ゆかたを　着ている　ほうが　らくですよ。
4. 加藤(かとう)先生の　おくさんは　着物が　好きなので、　いつも　着ていらっしゃいますわ。
5. ひらがなは　すぐ　おぼえたのに、　使わなかったので、　けっきょく　ぜんぶわすれました。
6. 京都まで　足を　のばしたのに、　一日じゅう　あめだったのよ。

4.8.3 Choose one of the two Relationals given in the parentheses to make a complete sentence:

1. しごとが　いそがしかった {のに、/ので、} 土曜(よう)日も　働きました。
2. ひらがなは　おぼえやすかった {のに、/ので、} 一週間で　おぼえました。
3. まだ　ゆきが　ふる　きせつじゃない {のに、/ので、} もう　ふりはじめました。
4. 日本風(ふう)の　家に　すみたい {のに、/ので、} さがしましたが、　ありませんでした。
5. きのう　ぼくが　いなかった {のに、/ので、} 友だちが　あいに　来たそうです。

6. 天気が　いい {ので、/から、} さんぽに　行きませんか。

7. むしあつい {のに、/から、} まどを　あけてください。

4.8.4 Choose an appropriate Verb given in the parentheses:

1. もしもし、　ご主(しゅ)人 {います/いらっしゃいます} か。
2. お客(きゃく)さまは　何時ごろ {来ました/いらっしゃいました} か。
3. ちちは　おとうとを　つれて {行く/いらっしゃる} と　言っていました。
4. おくさんは　うちへ {来た/いらっしゃった} ことが　ないんです。
5. 友だちの　林(はやし)さんは　車を　持って {いない/いらっしゃらない} はずですが。

4.8.5 Change each of the following sentences into the んです ending:

1. 洋服(ふく)の　ほうが　らくです。
2. いつ　出かけますか。
3. わたしは　着物が　に合いません。
4. よやくは　とりけしませんでした。
5. バスは　とても　こんでいました。
6. あの　アルバイトは　かんたんでした。
7. なぜ　くつを　ぬぎますか。

4.8.6 Answer each of the following questions using でしょう "I suppose":

Example: あした　あめが　ふりますか。/ええ …… ええ、 <u>ふるでしょう</u>。

1. おくさんは　もう　うちに　つきましたか。/ええ
2. 原(はら)さんは　着物を　着ますか。/いいえ
3. きのう　おとうさんは　電話(わ)を　かけましたか。/いいえ
4. ロバーツさんは　日本の　新聞を　読みますか。/いいえ
5. あの　人たちは　日光(にっこう)に　とまりますか。/ええ

4.8.7 Write the following underlined *hiragana* in *kan'ji*:

1. <u>よう</u>服(ふく)の　いい　ところを　<u>き</u>る　場(ば)<u>しょ</u>に　<u>あ</u>わせることが　たいせつです。
2. <u>いえ</u>に　いる　<u>とき</u>は　どちらが　<u>はたら</u>きやすいですか。

3. わかい　ひとは　あまり　きものを　きません。
4. はじめる　ときが　もんだいです。
5. みずを　ください。てと　あしを　あらいますから。
6. りょうほう　にあいますよ。

4.8.8 Distinguish the following *kan'ji*:

1. 間、問、聞　3. 方、旅　5. 今、合
2. 動、働　4. 洋、漢　6. 若、花

4.8.9 Change the following into more formal and/or neutral expressions:

1. Dame na no ne.
2. Ara, Miraa san. Irasshai.
3. Maa, soo?
4. Kanai wa kimono ga suki ja nai n da yo.
5. Yoshiko wa moo gakkoo e ikimashita wa.
6. Ii wa.
7. Datte, muzukashii no yo.

4.8.10 Make the following sentences more appropriate:

1. Sen'sei, sen'sei wa doko ni sun'de imasu ka?
2. Sen'sei, oniwa ni sakura ga saite irasshaimasu ne.
3. Boku, kimono ga niawanai no yo.

4.8.11 In Japanese one's speech varies according to whom one is talking to. Express the following ideas properly according to the situation given:

"I'd like to wear *yukata*, but I don't have any."

1. The speaker is talking to her husband.
2. The female speaker is talking to a guest.

4.8.12 Make appropriate changes, as if the following dialog were spoken by two men.

Sakamaki: Kyoo, Katoo san to eiga (o) mi ni iku no yo. Anata mo issho ni ikanai?

Yokozawa: Kyoo wa chotto tsugoo ga warui no.

Sakamaki: Soo. Jaa, mata ne.

Yokozawa: Gomen nasai ne.

4.8.13 Change the following sentences into men's style by replacing Sentence Particles.

1. Sugu iku wa.
2. Kyoo wa dekinai wa.
3. Ashita ni suru wa.
4. Kimono wa amari kitaku nai wa.
5. Maa, ii wa ne.
6. Kimono no hoo ga fuben da wa.

4.9 SITUATIONAL AND APPLICATION CONVERSATION

4.9.1 A foreigner is visiting his Japanese friend's home.

Looking at his friend's sister who is in a *kimono,* the foreigner asks his friend which is better, Western-style clothes or *kimono*.
The Japanese says both of them have good points and bad points.
The foreigner asks the sister what the bad points of *kimono* are.
She answers that the *kimono* is not comfortable since one has to tie the *obi* tightly.
The foreigner says he thinks it is easier to work in Western-style clothes, but *kimono* is beautiful.

4.9.2 Develop your own opinion on Western-style clothes and *kimono*.

4.9.3 Converse on clothes, shoes, etc.

4.9.4 Smith: Keiko san, kon'ban eiga o mi ni ikimasen ka?

Keiko: Kon'ban wa chotto tsugoo ga warui no. Gomen nasai ne. Demo, ashita nara ii wa.

4.9.5 Michiko: Okaasan, moo gohan o tabete mo ii?

Mother: Iie, mada dame desu yo.

Michiko: Datte.

Mother: Moo sukoshi desu kara ne.

4.9.6 Keiko: Okaasan, kore ga ii wa.

Mrs. Itō: Iie. Sore wa ikemasen.

Keiko: Datte, kore oishii no yo.

Mrs. Itō: Takai kara, dame desu yo. Wakaranai no?

LESSON 5
REVIEW AND APPLICATION

5.1 PREDICATES

5.1.1 Quotation

a. Verb

ぼくと　クラークさんは	京都で　日本の　文化(か)や でんとうを　あじわいたい		思っています
原(はら)さんは	来月から　日本語の　学生が ふえる		言っていました
みち子さんは	洋服(ふく)が　に合わない		こたえました
ミラーさんから	ニューヨークには　古い たて物が　のこっている	と	聞きました
	そこは　人や　のり物が 多すぎた		スミスさんから 聞きました
	しけんで　ぜんぜん まちがえなかった		ポールさんが 言いました

b. Adjective

ぼくは	へたなので、はずかしい		思いました
ブラウンさんは	この　問題は　むずかしくない		言いました
	高橋(たかはし)さんの　車は　あかくない		林(はやし)さんが 言ったんです
先生が	一九一五年ごろは　人口が 少なかった	と	話しました
	きのう　食べた　てんぷらは おいしかった		ブラウンさんから 聞きました
	宿(しゅく)題は　むずかしくなかった		思う

c. Copula

先生は	毎日　れんしゅうすることが たいせつだ	と	学生に 言いました
ぼくは	ここから　大使(たいし)館へ　行く みちは　かんたんだ		思います
いもうとは	おびは　らくではない		言っている
スージーさんが	東京の　タクシーは　あまり 好きじゃない		言っています
ポールさんから	ミラーさんの　家は　日本風(ふう) だった		聞きました
	スミスさんは　すきやきが きらいだった		けい子さんが 言いました
	あれは　日本の　ことわざ ではなかった		思います

5.1.2 Hearsay

a. Verb

クラークさんは　一日に　漢字を　二十　おぼえる けい子さんは　来年　アメリカへ　旅行する 日本の　男の　人は　あまり　着物を　着ない かないは　あおい　洋服(ふく)が　に合わない 主(しゅ)人は　とても　おどろいた お客(きゃく)さまが　いらっしゃったので、着かえた おとうとは　ネクタイを　しめていなかった ロバーツさんは　ホテルを　よやくしなかった	そうです そうだ

b. Adjective

いもうとの　新しい　洋服(ふく)は　きいろい 山田さんの　すんでいる　家は　せまい あしたは　天気が　よくない	そうです そうだ

この　こうちゃは　おいしくない	
あねの　くつは　ちょっと　きつかった	そうです
ミラーさんが　見た　えいがは　すばらしかった	そうだ
鎌倉の　大仏は　大きくなかった	

c. Copula

テーラーさんは　ビフテキが　大好きだ	
あの　かたは　ゆうめいな　フランス人だ	
この　さんこう書は　てき当ではない	
中国料理を　作るのは　かんたんじゃない	そうです
ひこうきの　旅行は　らくだった	そうだ
東京の　地下鉄は　べんりだった	
小山さんの　むすこは　いしゃじゃなかった	
あれは　京都を　おとずれた　時ではなかった	

5.1.3 *n desu* and *no desu* ending

a. Verb

あかちゃんは　すぐ　大きくなる	
急行の　よやくは　とりけす	
きょうは　あにの　くつを　はいている	んです
私は　着物を　ぜんぜん　着ない	のです
あなたが　いらっしゃるので、着かえた	（ん）でしょう
ぼくは　とても　おどろいた	（の）でしょう
友だちの　家には　とまらなかった	
けっきょく　毎日　れんしゅうしなかった	

b. Adjective

おとうとの　考えは　おかしい	んです
むすこの　せいは　あまり　たかくない	のです
先週の　しけんは　やさしかった	（ん）でしょう
先月の　旅行は　たのしくなかった	（の）でしょう

c. Copula

加藤先生は　アメリカ人な	んです
あの　バスは　ふべんな	のです
それは　ぼくが　学生だった　時な	（ん）でしょう
	（の）でしょう

ここが　わたしが　行った　小学校な	
〝好〟という　字は　教育(いく)漢字じゃない	んです
この　レポートは　たいせつではない	のです
ひこうきの　旅行は　らくだった	(ん)でしょう
原(はら)さんが　勉強したのは　日本の　歴史(れきし)だった	(の)でしょう
スミスさんは　メリーランド大学の　先生じゃなかった	

5.1.4 Compounds

a. "easy to do"

ひらがなの　ほうが　ずっと　書き	
わたしの　むすめは　びょう気に　なり	
この　字と　その　字は　まちがえ	やすい
加藤(かとう)先生の　せつめいは　わかり	やすいです
大使(たいし)館へ　行く　みちは　おぼえ	やすかったです
洋服(ふく)は　着	
東京は　すみ	

b. "hard to do" "difficult to do"

常用(じょうよう)漢字は　おぼえ	
よやくは　とりけし	
この　まどは　しめ	にくい
それより　この　ほうが　使い	にくいです
みち子さんの　考(かんが)えは　わかり	にくかったです
先生の　おたくへは　うかがい	
日本語では　しつ問し	

c. "excessively" "too ～"

ごちそうを　食べ さけを　のみ	すぎないでください
やさしい　漢字を　まちがえ あの　学生は　しつ問し	すぎる すぎます すぎました
あなたは　働き	すぎたのでしょう

ベルトが　きつ	
ずぼんが　みじか	すぎる
その　旅館は　とお	すぎます
来る　時間が　おそ	すぎました
くつ下が　なが	

この　へんは　ちょっと　しずか	すぎる
あの　女の　人は　ことばが　ていねい	すぎます
あなたの　こたえは　かんたん	すぎました
この　しごとは　らく	

d.　"start doing"

すぐ　ゆきが　ふり	はじめる
ロバーツさんが　ギターを　ひき	はじめます
あかちゃんが　ことばを　おぼえ	はじめた
日本は　もう　すずしく　なり	はじめました
この　町にも　自動車が　ふえ	

e.　"finish doing"

問題を　しつ問し	おわる
ぼくの　考(かんが)えを　せつめいし	おわります
さくらの　花が　もう　さき	おわった
本を　読み	おわりました
レポートは　書き	

f.　"redo" "change"

新しい　着物に　着	
きつくない　くつに　はき	かえる
新宿(じゅく)で　急(きゅう)行に　のり	かえます
名前を　書き	かえました
車が　古くなったので、買い	

5.1.5 "when" "time"

a. Verb

日本では　食事を　する	時(に)	はしを　使うそうですね
ここへ　来る		何に　のって来ますか
おととい　母(はは)が　来た		その　ことを　話しました
いそぐ		地下鉄(ちかてつ)は　べんりですよ
さくらが　さいている		日本へ　行きたいです
大学へ　行かない	時(に)は	何を　しているんですか
わたしたちが　京都を　おとずれた		あめが　ふっていました
あなたに　電話(わ)を　かけた		かないは　るすでした

b. Adjective

若い	時 時に	たくさん　スポーツを　した　ほうが　いいですよ
むすめが　小さかった		サンフランシスコに　いたことが　あります
日光(にっこう)が　一番　美しい	時は	いつですか
あつい	時には	ゆかたが　らくで　いいです
コーヒーが　ほしい		ぼくに　そう　言ってください

c. Copula

学校が　休みの	時 時に	一度(ど)　うちへ　あそびに　来てください
さくらの　花が　きれいな		上野公園(のこうえん)へ　行ってみたいです
かないが　るすだった		ミラーさんが　うちへ　いらっしゃった　そうです
ぼくが　大学の　一年生の	時は	東京に　すんでいませんでした
ひまな	時には	たいてい　テニスを　します
あねが　元気(げん)だった		よく　えいがに　いっしょに　行きました

5.2 RELATIONALS

5.2.1 "since" "because"

a. Verb

着物を　着かえる	ので、	ちょっと　おそくなります
おとうとは　まだ　小学校に　いる		英(えい)語は　知りません
あしたは　うちに　いない		勉強することが　できません
一年間　よく　れんしゅうした		日本語の　会話(かいわ)が　じょうずです
前もって　せつめいを　聞かなかった		問題が　わかりませんでした

b. Adjective

くつが　きつい	ので、	はきかえたいです
この　へんの　食事は　おいしくない		自分で　作ります
きょうは　気分が　わるかった		一日じゅう　うちで　ねていました
京都は　すばらしかった		また　おとずれたいと　思います
天気が　よくなかった		テニスを　することが　できません でした

c. Copula

ロバーツさんは　びょう気な	ので、	びょういんへ　行くそうです
この　へやの　ほうが　しずかな		ずっと　勉強しやすいです
すしは　好きじゃない		てんぷらの　ほうが　いいです
ちょうど　国へ　かえる　時だった		いそがしかったんです
常用(じょうよう)漢字じゃなかった		読むことが　できませんでした

5.2.2 "in spite of"

a. Verb

あなたは　着物が　に合う	のに、	どうして　着ないんですか
ミラーさんは　一週間も　休んだ		よく　わかりますね

あめが　ふった	のに、	花見に　行ったんですか
日本語を　六か月しか　習わなかった		じょうずですねえ

b. Adjective

ひこうきの　ほうが　もっと　はやい	のに、	のりたくないんですか
その　くつは　おかしくない		どうして　はかないんですか
ことしの　ふゆは　さむかった		ゆきが　ぜんぜん　ふりませんでした
この　カメラは　わりあい　たかかった		すぐ　だめに　なりました
コーヒーは　ほしくなかった		けい子さんが　くれました

c. Copula

日本の　ことわざな	のに、	知りませんでした
ゆかたは　らくな		着たくないんですか
むずかしい　問題ではない		わからないんですか
おひるの　おべん当(とう)だった		あさ　食べました
前は　好きじゃなかった		今は　大好きなんです

5.2.3 "per"

一時間	に	千円	もらいました
一日		三ばい	コーヒーを　のみます
一週間		四十時間	働いています
三か月		五さつぐらい	本を　読みます
一年		十日ぐらいしか	国へ　かえりません

5.2.4 "as many as" "no less than"

三か月で　漢字を	千五百	も	おぼえました
けさ　コーヒーを	四はい		のみました

あなたに　電話を	六度	も	しましたが、いませんでしたね
パーティーに　学生が	四十人		来るんですか
デパートで　買い物を	五万円		したんですよ
大学で	三年		日本語を　習っています

5.2.5 "only"

三百円	しか	持って来なかったんです
一日に　二時間		れんしゅうすることが　できません
まだ　ひらがな		習っていません
外国語は　フランス語		知らないんです
ひこうきには　一度		のったことが　ありません
スポーツは　テニス		しません
ぼくは　日曜日(に)		うちに　いません
ニューヨーク(へ)		行ったことが　ないんです

5.2.6 Apposition *no*

あれは	図書館員	の	あねです
	友だち		ポールだと　思います
あの　かたは	二年生 いしゃ 駅員 先生	の だった	ジョーンズさんです
アメリカ人		の	スミスさんが　そう　言いました
ロバーツさんの　友だち			中村さんが　来ます

5.3 REVIEW DRILLS

5.3.1 Substitution and Transformation Drills

1. A：山田さんは　旅行に　行くと　言っていましたか。

   B：いいえ、行かないと　言っていました。

A：スミスさんは　どうですか。

B：スミスさんは　行くそうです。

1. ゆかたを　着る　　2. 漢字を　おぼえた
3. 旅行が　好きだ　　4. 洋服を　着たい
5. その　問題が　わかった　　6. かたかなを　習うのが　らくだった

2. A：わたしは　着物を　着ません。

B：なぜ　着ないんですか。

A：着物は　ふべんなので、着ないんです。

1. おべん当を　持って来ませんでした、作る　時間が　なかったんです
2. 着かえました、洋服の　ほうが　らくです
3. 旅館に　とまりたいんです、日本の　でんとうを　あじわうことが　できます
4. 日本語を　勉強しています、来年　日本に行きます
5. とても　はずかしかったです、じょうずじゃないんです

3. A：ひらがなは　やさしいでしょう？

B：いいえ、やさしくないです。

A：どうして　やさしくないと　思うんですか。

B：書きにくいんです。

1. スミスさんは　来ます、しごとが　あると　言っていました
2. あしたは　あめです、ラジオで　そう　言いました
3. あの　人は　アメリカ人じゃありません、アメリカ英語を　話しています

5.4 REVIEW EXERCISES

5.4.1 Combine each pair of the following using either ので or のに：

1. ホテルに　とまりたいんです。
まだ　よやくしていません。 } →
2. 着物は　たかすぎます。
洋服に　しました。 } →
3. 今ばんの　パーティーなんです。
まだ　のみ物も　買っていないんです。 } →
4. しけんの　時、がんばりました。
あまり　よくなかったんです。 } →

5. よく　れんしゅうしました。
ぜんぜん　まちがえませんでした。 } ⟶

6. ビールが　こんなに　のこっています。
一ダースも　買うんですか。 } ⟶

7. ゆきが　ふりはじめました。
おどろきました。 } ⟶

8. これは　むずかしい　ことわざです。
よく　知っていますね。 } ⟶

9. きのうは　あめでした。
洋服(ふく)に　しました。 } ⟶

10. あそこは　日本風(ふう)じゃありません。
とまりたくありません。 } ⟶

5.4.2 Use either も or しか to express the idea given in the two sentences:

Example:

しけんは　三時間　かかりました。
ながい　しけんです。 } …… しけんは　三時間<u>も</u>　かかりました。

しけんは　三十分　かかりました。
みじかい　しけんです。 } …… しけんは　三十分<u>しか</u>　かかり<u>ませんでした</u>。

1. おさいふを　三つ　持っています。
多いです。 }

2. おさけを　二本　のみました。
のみすぎました。 }

3. きのう　ロバーツさんが　あそびに　来ました。
ロバーツさんだけです。 }

4. パーティーに　二十人　いたらしいです。
おおぜいです。 }

5. おかねは　一万円　かかるそうです。
やすいです。 }

6. 京都へ　行きました。
ほかの　所へは　行きませんでした。 }

7. 奈良(なら)で　二週間　お寺などを　けんぶつしました。
ながいですね。 }

8. 日本語を　六か月　勉強しました。
六か月は　みじかいです。 }

5.4.3 Fill in the blanks with appropriate Relationals:

1. 旅館（　　）とまりたいんですか。
2. 人口（　　）ずいぶん　ふえましたね。
3. りょうあん寺(じ)（　　）いう　お寺へ　行ったこと（　　）ありますか。
4. この　かいしゃは　一年（　　）一週間（　　）休みを　とることが　できません。
5. 鎌倉(かまくら)が　近ければ、足（　　）のばしたい（　　）思います。
6. ミラーさんは　一か月（　　）旅行しているそうです。ながい　旅行ですね。

5.4.4 Insert in each blank one of the given words:

そんなに、まだ、前もって、おどろくほど、さっき、もっと、けっきょく、わりあい、りょう方

1. よやくは（　　）とりけしたんです。
2. ゆかたを　着るのは（　　）かんたんですよ。着てみますか。
3. おどろきましたねえ。ジョージさんは（　　）知っているんですか。
4. 「どっちを　さしあげましょうか。」「（　　）ください。」
5. わたしは（　　）あつい　コーヒーが　好きなんです。
6. こちらへ　いらっしゃる　時は（　　）知らせてください。
7. 京都には　古い　お寺が（　　）たくさん　ありますよ。
8. かたかなは（　　）ぜんぶ　おぼえていません。
9. 着物を　着たかったんですが、いいのが　なかったので、（　　）洋服(ふく)に　しました。

5.4.5 What would you say when:

1. you were surprised at what someone said?
2. you think that what someone said is a good idea?
3. you want to tell your friend that a new dress is becoming to her?
4. you want to encourage someone to do his best?
5. you greet a guest at the door?
6. someone praises your suit, and your proficiency in Japanese?
7. you want to ask why?

5.4.6 Make an appropriate statement or question which will lead to each of the following responses:

1. 何が　たいへんなんですか。
2. とんでもないです。

3. そうじゃないと　思います。
4. いいえ、　おはずかしいです。
5. おどろきましたねえ。
6. そうですか。がんばってください。

5.4.7 Complete each of the following sentences:

1. 子どもの　時、__________________。
2. __________________ので、うちに　いました。
3. __________________時、食べすぎました。
4. __________________すぎると　思います。
5. きのうは　いい　天気だったのに、__________________。

5.5 MIKE HARRISON SERIES(1)

(English equivalents of new vocabulary are given in 5.5.7)

——マイク・ハリソン　日本語学校に　入る——

5.5.1 　マイク・ハリソンさんは　二十六さいの　どくしんの　アメリカ人です。カリフォルニアに　ある　アメリカの　会社(かいしゃ)に　つとめていたのですが、けんしゅうで　先月日本の　会社(かいしゃ)に　来ました。これから　二年間　東京に　いるそうです。

　ハリソンさんは　カリフォルニアに　いた　時、一年間　日本語を　勉強したそうですが、もっと　じょうずに　なりたいので、日本語学校に　入りたいと　思っています。それで、会社(かいしゃ)の　昼(ひる)休みに　どうりょうの　大石さんに　そうだんしました。

5.5.2 ——会社(かいしゃ)の　昼(ひる)休み——

ハリソン「大石さん、今　ちょっと　いいですか。」

大石「え、いいですよ。何ですか。」

ハリソン「じつは、日本語を　もっと　勉強したいので、学校を　さがしているんですが、いい　日本語学校を　知りませんか。」

大石「ええと、前　友だちだった　フランス人が　かよっていた　学校なら、知っていますけど。」

ハリソン「どこですか、その　学校は？」

大石「新宿(じゅく)の　方なんだけど、かよいにくいかな？」

ハリソン「そんな　ことは　ありません。毎日なら　むりですけど、週に　二度(ど)ぐらいなら、新宿(じゅく)でも　かまわないです。」

大石　「じゃあ、一度　電話してみますよ。きぼうの　時間や　曜日、レベルを
くわしく　教えてください、聞いてみますから。」

5.5.3　——大石　日本語学校に　電話を　かける——

女の人「日本語学校でございます。」

大石　「もしもし、日本語の　クラスの　ことを　うかがいたいんですが、つぎの
学期は　いつ　はじまるんですか。」

女の人「九月二十日からです。」

大石　「そうですか。じつは、日本語を　習いたいと　言う　アメリカ人が　いるん
ですが、どんな　クラスが　あるんですか。」

女の人「その　かたは　日本語が　はじめてですか。」

大石　「いえ、アメリカで　一年間　勉強したそうです。だから、会話は　できるん
ですが、もっと　漢字なんか　習いたいんだそうです。よるの　クラスで　週
に　二度というのは　ないでしょうか。」

女の人「ございます。ふつうの　クラスとか　新聞を　読む　クラスとか　漢字の
クラスとか　いろいろ　ございます。」

大石　「そんなに　いろいろ　あるんですか。」

女の人「その　かたに　プレイスメント・テストを　したいと　思いますので、一度
こちらへ　いらっしゃってください。初級か　中級か　上級か　きめます
から。お名前と　国籍は？」

大石　「マイク・ハリソンという　アメリカ人です。どうも　いろいろ　ありがとう
ございました。」

5.5.4　——つぎの　日、会社で——

大石　「やあ、ハリソンさん。日本語学校の　こと、すこし　わかりましたよ。」

ハリソン「そうですか。どうも　すみませんでした。」

大石　「あとで　くわしく　せつめいしますけど、一度　行ってみなければならない
と　思うんですよ。むこうは　ハリソンさんの　日本語の　力を　知りたい
そうですから。」

ハリソン「そうですか。じゃあ、今ばん　行ってみます。場所を　教えてください。」

5.5.5　——日本語学校で——

女の人　「それで、あなたが　ハリソンさん？」

ハリソン「はい、マイク・ハリソンと　いいます。」

女の人　「こちらの　へやで　プレイスメント・テストを　うけてください。三十分ぐらいで　おわりますから。」

…………………………………………………………………………………

女の人　「ハリソンさんは　上級(じょうきゅう)クラスで　だいじょうぶですね。上級(じょうきゅう)クラスは月、木の　六時半から　八時までです。」

ハリソン「そうですか。さっそく　申し込み(もうしこみ)を　したいんですが。」

女の人　「この　申し込み(もうしこみ)書に　名前、国籍(こくせき)、職業(しょくぎょう)など　書いてください。それから、月謝(げっしゃ)ですが、三か月で　六万円です。」

ハリソン「そうですか。きょう　はらいますから。」

女の人　「では、あちらで。」

5.5.6 ――つぎの　日、会社(かいしゃ)で――

ハリソン「大石さん、おかげさまで　上級(じょうきゅう)クラスに　入ることが　できました。いろいろ　お世話(せわ)に　なりました。」

大石　「よかったですね。でも、これから　たいへんだなあ。毎週　二日　かようのは。」

ハリソン「へい気ですよ。週に　二度(ど)だけですから。アメリカに　いた　時も、よる勉強に　かよったんですよ。」

大石　「とにかく、がんばってください。でも、ぼくたちと　飲みに　行く　時間はあるでしょうね。」

ハリソン「アハハハ。もちろん　だいじょうぶですよ。」

大石　「じゃあ、さっそく　入学(にゅうがく)を　いわって、いっぱい　どうですか、今ばん？」

ハリソン「いいですね。〝善(ぜん)は　急(いそ)げ〟ですね。」

大石　「え！　そんな　ことわざも　知っているんですか。おどろいたなあ！」

5.5.7 New Vocabulary (for passive learning)

1.	どくしん	dokushin	......	single; unmarried
	けんしゅう	ken'shuu	......	training
	昼(ひる)休み	hiruyasumi	......	lunchtime
	どうりょう	dooryoo	......	co-worker; colleague
	そうだんする	soodan suru	......	consult
2.	方	hoo	......	direction; toward
	かな	kana	......	I wonder ～？(normally used by men in colloquial speech)

	むり	muri	......	impossible; unreasonable
	きぼう	kiboo	......	desire; wish; hope; preference
	レベル	reberu	......	level
3.	でございます	de gozaimasu	......	polite equivalent of *desu*
	学期	gakki	......	semester; term
	はじめて	hajimete	......	(for) the first time
	なんか	nan'ka	......	and the like (colloquial equivalent of *nado*)
	ございます	gozaimasu	......	polite equivalent of *arimasu*
	ふつう	futsuu	......	regular; normal; ordinary; average
	とか	toka	......	such as ～
	プレイスメント・テスト	pureisumen'to tesuto	......	placement test
	初級	shokyuu	......	elementary level
	中級	chuukyuu	......	intermediate level
	上級	jookyuu	......	advanced level
	きめる	kimeru	......	decide
	国籍	kokuseki	......	nationality
4.	やあ	yaa	......	hi; hello (used by men)
	力	chikara	......	ability; power
5.	うける	ukeru	......	take (an exam); receive
	さっそく	sassoku	......	immediately; instantly
	申し込み	mooshikomi	......	application; entry
	申し込み書	mooshikomisho	......	application form
	職業	shokugyoo	......	occupation
	月謝	gessha	......	monthly fee; tuition
	はらう	harau	......	pay
6.	おかげさまで	okagesama de	......	thanks to god; thanks to you
	お世話になりました。	Osewa ni narimashita.	......	I am very much obliged to you.; Thank you for your kindness.
	なあ	naa	......	exclamatory sentence ending (normally used by men in colloquial speech)
	へい気	heiki	......	calm; cool; composed
	とにかく	tonikaku	......	anyway

アハハハ	a-ha-ha-ha	......	laughter (often written in *katakana*)
入学(にゅうがく)	nyuugaku	......	entering school
いわう	iwau	......	celebrate
いっぱい	ippai	......	a drink
善(ぜん)は　急(いそ)げ。	Zen wa isoge.	......	Strike while the iron is hot. (lit. When you do good, do it quickly.)

LESSON 6

自動車

6.1 PRESENTATION

1900年に、 横浜に 住んでいた 米国人が 日本で はじめての 自動車を 運転したそうです。

そのご、 日本では、 1960年ごろから 自動車の かずが どんどん[1] ふえましたが、 公害や 交通事故などの 大きな[2] 問題が おこっています。

6.2 DIALOG

—— しゅうり屋に 電話を かける ——

高木　「もしもし、 高木ですが・・・。」

しゅうり屋　「ああ、 高木さんですか。 毎度 ありがとうございます[3]。 きょうは 何でしょうか。」

高木　「じつは、 タイヤ[4]が パンク[4]してしまった[5]んですが、 あしたの 朝までに なおります[6]か。」

しゅうり屋　「なおりますよ。 車は 今 おたくですか。」

高木　「ええ、 そうなんです。 それから、 ワイパー[4]も こわれた[6]らしい[7]んですが、 それも なおして[6]おいて[8]ください。」

しゅうり屋　「かしこまりました[3]。 これから、 すぐ 取り[9]に うかがいます。」

高木　「おねがいします[3]。」

—— その 日の 夕方 ——

しゅうり屋　「ごめんください。 車を 持って来ました。」

高木　「どうも ごくろうさま[10]。 早かったですね。」

しゅうり屋　「やっぱり ワイパーが こわれていましたから、 しゅうりしておきました[8]。 それから、 だいぶ よごれて[6]いたので、 車を 洗っておきました。 これは サービス[11]です。」

高木　「どうも すみません[10]。」

住(す)んでいた　米国人(べいこくじん)　電話(でんわ)　高木(たかぎ)　毎度(まいど)　朝(あさ)
取(と)り　夕方(ゆうがた)　早(はや)かった　洗(あら)って

6.3 PATTERN SENTENCES

6.3.1

N	R
Taiya	ga

→

V	E	PC	C
pan'ku shiTE[5]	SHIMATTA[5]	n(o)	desu.

6.3.2

N	R
Kuruma	o

→

V	E
aratTE[8]	OKIMASHITA.[8]

6.3.3

N	R
Waipaa	ga

→

V	Da	(PC)	C
kowareta	RASHII[7]	n(o)	desu.

6.4 NOTES

6.4.1 *Don'don* is an Adverb meaning "rapidly" or "steadily," and is one of the many onomatopoeia used in Japan. Originating from the sound of rapidly flowing water, *don'don* means "rapid advancement." Compare this word with *dan'dan* which means "gradually."

6.4.2 *Ookina* is a derived form of *ookii* "big." *Ookina* is interchangeable with *ookii* only when it occurs immediately before a Noun and *ookina* is never used with *desu* or *da*. This replacement of the final *-i* of an Adjective is not applicable to all the Adjectives. It is limited to a few:

ooki*i* . . . ooki*na*	"big"
chiisa*i* . . . chiisa*na*	"small"
okashi*i* . . . okashi*na*	"funny; strange; laughable"
Takagi san wa ookina uchi ni sun'de iru soo desu.	"I understand that Mr. Takagi lives in a big house."
Takagi san no uchi wa ookii soo desu.	"I understand that Mr. Takagi's house is big."
Kinoo okashina koto o kikimashita.	"I heard a strange thing yesterday."
Sono shitsumon wa chotto okashii desu yo.	"That question is a little strange."

6.4.3 *Maido arigatoo gozaimasu* is an expression that is frequently used by a salesclerk or a shopkeeper to his customers. *Maido* is "every time," and the whole expression means "Thank you very much for your constant patronage," but it is used even with a customer who has purchased something there for the first time.

The difference in speech levels between Takagi and the mechanic should be noted. Although both parties use the polite style, certain words indicate their relative status. For example, *Kashikomarimashita* means "Certainly, sir" or "Certainly, I will do it as you requested." This expression is usually used when shopkeepers or store clerks are speaking to their customers, or the inferior to the superior when asked by the latter to do something. This is quite formal and polite, and is normally used by salesmen and subordinates in general toward customers and superiors. In this case, as used by the repairman, it means "I follow your instructions." *Wakarimashita* may be heard in less formal occasions.

Maido arigatoo gozaimasu is another example of typical polite speech toward customers. Originally this meant that the salesman is grateful for the continued patronage—in other words, it was used in accordance with its general meaning. Presently, however, it is used even if the customer has never patronized the store before, and will be said in parting to a customer who merely browsed and didn't purchase anything, expressing gratification for even paying attention to the store. It should also be noted that Takagi uses *Ee,* whereas the mechanic uses *Hai.*

Despite the mutually polite forms used in this dialog and indicating some distance between the two participants, Takagi appears to be a regular customer. Other examples of the relative politeness between the two are the repairman's use of *otaku* as well as Takagi's use of *Onegai shimasu*—a more polite version of *Soo shite kudasai* and *Doomo sumimasen.*

6.4.4 Because the automobile was introduced to Japan from the West, most words associated with it are *gairaigo*, or loan words, derived from English: *taiya* means "tire"; *pan'ku* means "punctured"; *waipaa* "wiper"; *oiru* "oil"; and *gasorin* "gasoline."

6.4.5 *Taiya ga pan'ku shite shimatta n desu* means "I have a flat tire" or literally "My tire has become completely flat." The combination of the TE form of a Verb and the Extender *shimaimasu* ← *shimau* means "an action is or has been completed or finished," or "is carried through to completion." *Shimau* itself means "finish," "put an end to," "conclude," "end up," "bring something to a close," and so on. In order to express a completed action, the use of *shimau* is mandatory but sometimes *shimau* occurs merely to emphasize an action which may even be a surprise to the speaker or to show that the result of an action cannot be reversed.

(Predicate Modifier) + Verb(*-te*) + *shimau*

tabete shimau	"eat up"
kaite shimaimashita	"have already written"
itte shimatta	"is gone" "has gone"
kowarete shimau	"has been broken"

Compare:

wasuremashita	"[I] forgot"
wasurete shimaimashita	"[I] have completely forgotten"
torikeshimashita	"[he] canceled"
torikeshite shimaimashita	"[he] has (already) finished canceling"

machigaemashita machigaete shimaimashita	"[I] made mistakes" "[I] have made mistakes"
"Ben'kyoo" to iu kan'ji o mata machigaete shimaimashita.	"I made a mistake on the *kan'ji* for *ben'kyoo* again!"
Katakana wa moo zen'bu oboete shimaimashita.	"I have already memorized all of the *katakana.*"
Gasorin ga kirete shimaimashita.	"Gas is used up." "Gas is out of stock."
Sono hon wa kinoo yon'de shimaimashita.	"I finished reading that book yesterday."

The difference between *hanashiowarimashita* and *hanashite shimaimashita* is that *hanashiowarimashita* merely connotes the end of a talking action with or without completing a talk or a topic while *hanashite shimaimashita* means the completion of a talk or a topic—"I have (already) talked (completely)."

The use of the TE form of a Verb plus *shimaimasu* or *shimaimashita* sometimes reveals the speaker's emotion, such as regret, pity, surprise, or dissatisfaction.

6.4.6 *Naorimasu* is an intransitive Verb meaning "something is corrected or fixed." Normally a transitive Verb is preceded by a direct object and an intransitive Verb is not preceded by any direct object. Generally speaking a direct object is followed by the Relational *o*. The distinction between the transitive Verb and the intransitive Verb will be explained in Volume IV, but there is a group of Verbs which differentiate transitive from intransitive by replacing the *-ri* or *-re* ending of a Stem form with the *-shi* ending or vice versa.

Intransitive Verb:		Transitive Verb:
kowaremasu [kowareru]	⟶	kowashimasu [kowasu]
naorimasu [naoru]	⟶	naoshimasu [naosu]
yogoremasu [yogoreru]	⟶	yogoshimasu [yogosu]
kaerimasu [kaeru]	⟶	kaeshimasu [kaesu]

6.4.7 *Waipaa mo kowareta rashii n desu* means "The windshield wipers seem to have broken." The *-rashii* is sometimes used in a meaning similar to ~*soo da* "I understand that . . ." or "I heard that. . . ." However, ~*soo da* indicates that the speaker has heard such and such, but *-rashii* carries the speaker's judgment. The forms that occur before *-rashii* are the plain forms of a Verb, an Adjective, or the Copula except *da*. *Da* is omitted before *-rashii*. Although *-rashii* is adjectival, it doesn't inflect when used in the meaning mentioned above. The other use of *-rashii*, namely a Noun plus *-rashii*, will be introduced later.

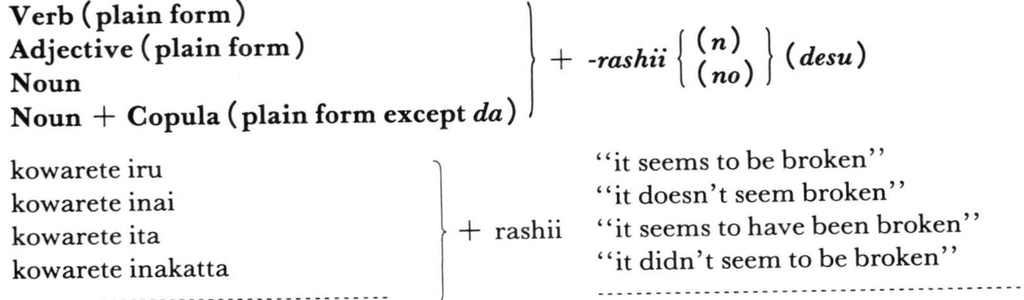

Verb (plain form)
Adjective (plain form)
Noun
Noun + Copula (plain form except *da*) } + ***-rashii*** { **(*n*)** / **(*no*)** } **(*desu*)**

kowarete iru	+ rashii	"it seems to be broken"
kowarete inai		"it doesn't seem broken"
kowarete ita		"it seems to have been broken"
kowarete inakatta		"it didn't seem to be broken"
------------------------------		------------------------------

ii	+ rashii	"it seems good"
yoku nai		"it doesn't seem good"
yokatta		"it seems to have been good"
yoku nakatta		"it seems that it was not good"
jiko (*da* never occurs)		"it seems an accident"
jiko ja nai *or* ~ de wa nai		"it seems that it is not an accident"
jiko datta		"it seems that it was an accident"
jiko ja nakatta *or* ~ de wa nakatta		"it seems that it was not an accident"

Ame ga futte iru rashii desu. — "It sounds like it is raining."

Miraa san wa Nihon e itta koto ga aru rashii desu. — "I understand that Mr. Miller has been to Japan."

Ookawa kun wa shuumatsu ni kuni e kaetta rashii desu. — "It seems to me that Mr. Ōkawa went home during the weekend."

Rajio wa kowarete inai rashii desu. — "The radio doesn't seem broken."

Sen'sei ga byooki na node, kyoo no kurasu wa nai rashii desu yo. — "Since the teacher is sick, it seems that his classes will not meet today."

Teeraa san wa Kyooto e itta noni, Nara e wa ikanakatta rashii desu. — "Although Mr. Taylor went to Kyōto, he seemingly didn't go to Nara."

Tookyoo ni wa kootsuu jiko ga ooi rashii desu. — "I heard that there are quite a few traffic accidents in Tōkyō."

Ano shuuriya wa yoku nai rashii desu. — "It is said that that repair shop is not good."

Watanabe san wa byooki rashii desu. — "Mr. Watanabe seems to be ill."

Kimura san no musuko san wa mae gakkoo no sen'sei datta rashii desu. — "I understand that Mr. Kimura's son used to be a schoolteacher."

Koyama san ga yoyaku shita heya wa nihon'fuu ja nai rashii desu. — "The room that Mr. Koyama reserved doesn't seem to be Japanese style."

Kan'ji wa oboenikukatta rashii desu. — "I understand that *kan'ji* were hard to learn."

6.4.8 *Naoshite oite kudasai* means "Please have it repaired." The combination of the TE form of a Verb and the Extender *okimasu* ← *oku* always means "do something in advance," "do such and such for a later purpose," or "do something and leave it that way," and so forth. The *oku* itself means "set aside," "put," or "leave."

(Predicate Modifier) + Verb(-*te*) + *oku*

hanashite okimasu — "talk to someone in advance"

garasu o migaite oku — "polish the glass (for a future purpose)"

mado o akete oite kudasai — "please open the window and leave it open"

kuruma o naoshite okimashita — "repaired the car (for future use)"

Osara o zen'bu aratte okimashita. — "I have washed all the dishes (for later use)."

Kyoo wa yasai ga yasukatta node, takusan katte okimashita.	"Since vegetables were cheap today, I bought a lot (for the next couple days)."
Hoteru wa hayaku yoyaku shite okimashoo.	"I think I will make a hotel reservation early."
Gasorin o irete okimashita.	"I have put gasoline in my car."
Oiru o shirabete oite kudasai.	"Please check the oil."
Ashita no asa Nikkoo e dekakemasu kara, oben'too o tsukutte oite kudasai.	"Since I am leaving for Nikkō tomorrow morning, please have a lunch prepared for me."
Kono mon'dai wa mae motte shirabete okimashita.	"I have examined this problem beforehand."
Uchi de yoku ben'kyoo shite oite kudasai.	"Please study it thoroughly at home."

6.4.9 *Tori ni ukagaimasu* in this instance means "I will go to get it" or "I will come to pick it up." *Ukagaimasu* is the polite version of *ikimasu* or *kimasu*. While *tori ni iku* is always used to mean "go to get something," *mukae ni iku* is used to mean "go to receive or meet somebody." *Tori* and *mukae* are the Stem forms of *torimasu* and *mukaemasu*, respectively. See Note 5.4.3, Volume II as to the pattern of the Stem form of a Verb plus *ni* plus a motion Verb such as *iku*, *kuru*, *kaeru*, *irassharu*, and *ukagau*.

non-human beings + *o* + *tori*	**+ *ni* +**	***iku* (*irassharu, ukagau*)**
human beings + *o* + *mukae*		***kuru* (*irassharu, ukagau*)**
		kaeru

tokei	o tori ni	iku	"go	to pick up a watch"
okane		kuru	"come	to get money"
kuruma		kaeru	"go (come) back	for a car"

isha	o mukae ni	iku	"go	for a doctor"
haha		kuru	"come	to meet my mother"
kyaku				to receive a guest"

Kuruma de eki made mukae ni ikimasu.	"I'll go to the station to pick you up in my car."
Yoofuku ga dekita n desu ga, tori ni kite kudasai.	"Your suit is ready. Please come and pick it up."
Okane o wasureta node, tori ni kaerimashita.	"As I forgot to bring my money, I went back to get it."
Kutsu o tori ni ukagatte mo ii deshoo ka?	"May I come to pick up my shoes?"

6.4.10 *Doomo gokuroo sama* is an expression used in the meaning of "Thank you very much for the work which you have done for me." This expression is said to a person of whom a service is expected. You may hear this expression said to a mailman, a repairman, a delivery man, a policeman, and the like to thank them for their work. Since the expression *Gokuroo sama* (*deshita*) includes more or less the idea that the work is expected, do not use *Gokuroo sama* as freely as *Arigatoo*.

This dialog provides a framework for analyzing the differences between *Gokuroo sama*, *Sumimasen*, and *Arigatoo*—all of which can be used to express the speaker's "gratitude." However, there are fine points of distinction in their various usages. In general, we may differentiate the three as follows.

Gokuroo sama is used when a service has been performed by the listener and that service was expected from him. It represents a type of reward given to the listener by showing the speaker's gratitude. The speaker's gratitude is, then, an appreciative gesture which focuses on the listener's effort in doing well what was expected from him. It is usually not used toward a superior. *Gokuroo sama* is used appropriately, then, by Takagi toward the mechanic for doing his job, namely, repairing Takagi's car. *Sumimasen*, on the other hand, is used when the listener has rendered some service but that service was not expected. In such a context, *Sumimasen* conveys the speaker's feeling that he has caused trouble for the listener. Consequently, this is a type of apologetic gratitude: the speaker expresses his regret that the listener has been bothered on his account by doing something which wasn't expected of him. Consequently, Takagi uses *Sumimasen* in thanking the mechanic for also washing his car, which was not expected. *Arigatoo*, however, focuses entirely on the speaker, and expresses genuine gratitude and happiness. *Arigatoo* is used when, from the point of view of expectation, the listener's action was neutral.

Comparing the three, *Gokuroo sama* is used when the speaker considers the trouble and effort of the listener, whose service had been expected; *Sumimasen* when the speaker has troubled the listener by the latter's performance of some service which had not been expected; and *Arigatoo* when no such consideration is taken of the listener's trouble and only pure, genuine thanks are being expressed by the speaker. For example, when the mailman delivers a letter, *Gokuroo sama* would be the appropriate response; if your son hands it to you, *Arigatoo*; and if your neighbor brings it, *Sumimasen*.

Furthermore, when the speaker is offered a service and the speaker wishes to accept this offer, he normally says *Onegai shimasu*—"I seek your help, I beg you." When simply accepting the offer, without demonstrating any active seeking, the appropriate response would be either *Arigatoo* or *Sumimasen*. However, one would never say *Gokuroo sama* because this would imply that the speaker expected the listener to offer this service beforehand.

Doomo also functions as a less polite form of *Doomo gokuroo sama*, as well as of *Doomo sumimasen* or *Doomo arigatoo*. To thank someone for an offer of some service in the future, either *Arigatoo gozaimasu* or *Onegai shimasu* would be appropriate. *Onegai shimasu* carries the sense of asking a favor when one is dependent upon the other person. *Arigatoo* is neutral in this respect.

6.4.11 *Kore wa saabisu desu* here means "This is free of charge." *Saabisu* is originally the English word "service," which has lots of meanings. But it is used in Japanese mostly in such expressions as "free service," "(good or bad) service," "free of charge," "bargain."

Hako o saabisu shite kudasai.	"Please give me this box free."
Ano gasorin sutan'do wa saabisu ga warui desu.	"That gasoline station offers bad service."

6.5 VOCABULARY

Presentation

横浜(よこはま)	Yokohama	......	N	a city near Tōkyō
米国	Beikoku	......	N	the United States of America
はじめて	hajimete	......	N	(for) the first time

運転(うんてん)した	un'ten shita	......	V	drove (TA form of *un'ten suru*)
運転(うんてん)	un'ten	......	N	driving
その　ご	sono go	......		after that; afterward
かず	kazu	......	N	number
どんどん	don'don	......	Adv.	rapidly; steadily (see 6.4.1)
公害(こうがい)	koogai	......	N	troubles such as air pollution, noise, etc.
事故(こ)	jiko	......	N	accident
大きな	ookina	......	A	big (see 6.4.2)
おこって	okotte	......	V	TE form of *okoru* – happen; rise; occur (intransitive Verb)

Dialog

しゅうり屋	shuuriya	......	N	repair shop; repairman; garage
高木(ぎ)	Takagi	......	N	family name
毎度　ありがとう　ございます。	Maido arigatoo gozaimasu.	......	(exp.)	Thank you for your constant patronage. (see 6.4.3)
タイヤ	taiya	......	N	tire (see 6.4.4)
パンクして	pan'ku shite	......	V	TE form of *pan'ku suru* – get a flat tire (*pan'ku* comes from an English word "puncture")
パンク	pan'ku	......	N	flat tire; puncture
しまった	shimatta	......	E	TA form of *shimau* – end up; complete (see 6.4.5)
なおります	naorimasu	......	V	is repaired; is fixed (intransitive Verb) (see 6.4.6)
ワイパー	waipaa	......	N	windshield wipers
こわれた	kowareta	......	V	was broken (TA form of *kowareru*) (intransitive Verb)
らしい	-rashii	......	Da	seem; appear; understand (see 6.4.7)
なおして	naoshite	......	V	TE form of *naosu* – fix; set right; correct (transitive Verb)
おいて	oite	......	E	TE form of *oku* – set aside; leave (see 6.4.8)
かしこまりました。	Kashikomarimashita.	......	(exp.)	Certainly, sir.; Yes, sir. (see 6.4.3)
取り	tori	......	V	Stem form of *toru* – take; pick up (see 6.4.9)
おねがいします。	Onegai shimasu.	......	(exp.)	Please do so.; I make a request of you. (see 6.4.3)

ごくろうさま。	Gokuroo sama.	......	(exp.)	Thank you for your service. (see 6.4.10)
しゅうりして	shuuri shite	......	V	TE form of *shuuri suru* – repair
しゅうり	shuuri	......	N	repairing
だいぶ	daibu	......	Adv.	quite; fairly; pretty
よごれて	yogorete	......	V	TE form of *yogoreru* – become dirty; is soiled; is stained (intransitive Verb)
サービス	saabisu	......	N	free of charge; service (see 6.4.11)

Notes

だんだん	dan'dan	......	Adv.	gradually; step by step (see 6.4.1)
小さな	chiisana	......	A	small (see 6.4.2)
おかしな	okashina	......	A	funny; strange; laughable (see 6.4.2)
オイル	oiru	......	N	oil; engine oil
ガソリン	gasorin	......	N	gasoline; gas
きれる	kireru	......	V	run out; is out of stock (intransitive Verb)
こわす	kowasu	......	V	break (transitive Verb) (see 6.4.6)
よごす	yogosu	......	V	stain; soil; spoil (transitive Verb)
ガラス	garasu	......	N	glass
みがく	migaku	......	V	polish; shine
むかえる	mukaeru	......	V	receive (a person); meet; welcome (see 6.4.9)
とけい	tokei	......	N	watch; clock
ガソリンスタンド	gasorin sutan'do	......	N	gas station

6.6 KAN'JI

6.6.1 住 (1) *su(mu)* (2) live; dwell (3) classifier 亻 (4) 亻 亻 仁 仁 住 住
(5) 東京に住んでいます

6.6.2 米 (1) BEI (2) America; rice (3) forms the classifier 米 [rice]
(4) 丶 丷 䒑 半 米 米 (5) 米国、米人、南(なん)米、北(ほく)米、日米 [Japan and U.S.A.]

6.6.a 話 (3.6.4) (1) WA (5) 電話、会話、話題 [topic]

6.6.3 高 (1) *taka(i)* (2) high; expensive (3) forms the classifier 亠 (高)
(4) 丶 亠 亠 亠 高 高 (5) 高い本、高木(ぎ)、せいが高い

6.6.4 度 (1) DO (2) degree; time(s) (3) classifier 广 [house under a roof]
(4) 丶 亠 广 产 庐 庐 庐 度 度
(5) よし子さんに一度会ったことがある、毎度ありがとうございます、今度、二、三度、熱(ねつ)が三十八度ある

6.6.5 朝 (1) *asa* (2) morning (3) classifier 卓 (月)
(4) 一 十 𠂇 古 古 吉 直 卓 朝 (5) 毎朝、朝ごはん

6.6.6 取 (1) *to(ru)* (2) take; get (3) classifier 耳 [ear]
(4) 一 丅 下 耳 取 取 (5) 取りに行きましょう
(6) hand (又⟶又) touching ear (耳⟶耳)

6.6.7 夕 (1) *yuu* (2) early evening (3) forms the classifier 夕 (4) ノ ク 夕
(5) 夕方、夕ごはん (6) the shape of (crescent) moon ⟶ evening and night

6.6.b 方[4.6.5] (1) *-kata* [*-gata*] (5) 夕方、この方は高山さんです

6.6.8 早 (1) *haya(i)* (2) early (3) classifier 日 (4) 日 早
(5) 早く来てください、朝早くおきましたか

6.6.9 洗 (1) *ara(u)* (2) wash (3) classifier 氵
(4) 氵 氵 氵 汁 洪 洗 洗 (5) お手洗い (6) homonym SEN 先

6.6.10 昼* (1) *hiru* (2) noon; daytime (3) classifier 尺 (日)
(4) コ ヨ 尸 尺 昼 昼 (5) 昼ご飯(はん)、昼ね [nap]

6.7 DRILLS

6.7.1 Transformation Drill

1. ぼくは　昼ごはんを　食べすぎました。 ⟶ ぼくは　昼ごはんを　食べすぎたらしいです。
2. 高木(ぎ)さんの　車が　パンクしました。 ⟶ 高木(ぎ)さんの　車が　パンクしたらしいです。
3. 東京から　大阪(さか)まで　けい子さんが　運転(うんてん)します。 ⟶ 東京から　大阪(さか)まで　けい子さんが　運転(うんてん)するらしいです。
4. しゅうり屋は　ラジオを　なおしませんでした。 ⟶ しゅうり屋は　ラジオを　なおさなかったらしいです。
5. 古い　おびですが、　よごれていません。 ⟶ 古い　おびですが、　よごれていないらしいです。
6. 交通(こうつう)事故(こ)などの　問題が　よく　おこります。 ⟶ 交通(こうつう)事故(こ)などの　問題が　よく　おこるらしいです。

7. おさらは　洗いませんでした。 ⟶ おさらは　洗わなかったらしいです。
8. この　とけいは　こわれていません。 ⟶ この　とけいは　こわれていないらしいです。

6.7.2 Transformation Drill

1. 漢字は　おぼえにくいです。 ⟶ 漢字は　おぼえにくいらしいです。
2. あの　えいがは　とても　おもしろかったです。 ⟶ あの　えいがは　とても　おもしろかったらしいです。
3. いもうとの　くつは　だいぶ　きつかったです。 ⟶ いもうとの　くつは　だいぶ　きつかったらしいです。
4. 小(こ)山さんは　もっと　大きな　車が　ほしいんです。 ⟶ 小(こ)山さんは　もっと　大きな　車が　ほしいらしいです。
5. この　とけいは　あまり　古く　ありません。 ⟶ この　とけいは　あまり　古くないらしいです。
6. 週末(まつ)は　いそがしくありませんでした。 ⟶ 週末(まつ)は　いそがしくなかったらしいです。
7. 高木(ぎ)さんという　人は　せいが　高いです。 ⟶ 高木(ぎ)さんという　人は　せいが　高いらしいです。
8. 一郎(ろう)くんは　あたまが　いたいんです。 ⟶ 一郎(ろう)くんは　あたまが　いたいらしいです。

6.7.3 Transformation Drill

1. アメリカの　バスは　ひじょうに　べんりです。 ⟶ アメリカの　バスは　ひじょうに　べんりらしいです。
2. ミラーさんの　言った　ことは　本当(とう)です。 ⟶ ミラーさんの　言った　ことは　本当(とう)らしいです。
3. この　とけいを　しゅうりするのは　かんたんじゃありません。 ⟶ この　とけいを　しゅうりするのは　かんたんじゃないらしいです。
4. ゆかたは　すずしいので、　らくです。 ⟶ ゆかたは　すずしいので、　らくらしいです。
5. 鎌倉(かまくら)の　うみは　あまり　きれいじゃありませんでした。 ⟶ 鎌倉(かまくら)の　うみは　あまり　きれいじゃなかったらしいです。
6. 原(はら)さんが　勉強する　へやは　しずかではありません。 ⟶ 原(はら)さんが　勉強する　へやは　しずかではないらしいです。

7. つぎの　しけんは　十月十日では　ありません。 ⟶ つぎの　しけんは　十月十日ではないらしいです。
8. ジョージさんは　米国人です。 ⟶ ジョージさんは　米国人らしいです。

6.7.4 Transformation Drill

1. タイヤが　パンクしました。 ⟶ タイヤが　パンクしてしまいました。
2. あの　かどで　大きな　事故(こ)が　おこりました。 ⟶ あの　かどで　大きな　事故(こ)が　おこってしまいました。
3. しゅうり屋さんは　パンクを　五分で　なおしました。 ⟶ しゅうり屋さんは　パンクを　五分で　なおしてしまいました。
4. あめが　ふっている　時に、　ワイパーが　こわれました。 ⟶ あめが　ふっている　時に、　ワイパーが　こわれてしまいました。
5. はじめてなので、　みちを　まちがえました。 ⟶ はじめてなので、　みちを　まちがえてしまいました。
6. 日本風(ふう)の　へやが　なかったので、　洋風(ふう)の　へやを　よやくしました。 ⟶ 日本風(ふう)の　へやが　なかったので、　洋風(ふう)の　へやを　よやくしてしまいました。
7. さっき　洗ったのに、　もう　よごれました。 ⟶ さっき　洗ったのに、　もう　よごれてしまいました。
8. 子どもは　ことばを　どんどん　おぼえました。 ⟶ 子どもは　ことばを　どんどん　おぼえてしまいました。
9. いもうとは　友だちを　むかえに　行きました。 ⟶ いもうとは　友だちを　むかえに　行ってしまいました。
10. ガソリンが　きれました。 ⟶ ガソリンが　きれてしまいました。

6.7.5 Transformation Drill

1. とても　いい　ことわざですから、　おぼえましょう。 ⟶ とても　いい　ことわざですから、　おぼえておきましょう。
2. あしたは　むずかしい　しけんが　あるので、　よく　しらべます。 ⟶ あしたは　むずかしい　しけんが　あるので、　よく　しらべておきます。
3. ガソリンが　きれたから、　入れてください。 ⟶ ガソリンが　きれたから、　入れておいてください。
4. グリーンけんを　五まい　よやくしました。 ⟶ グリーンけんを　五まい　よやくしておきました。

5. へやが　よごれていたので、きれいに　しました。 ⟶ へやが　よごれていたので、　きれいに　しておきました。
6. 屋根(ね)が　こわれたので、　なおして　ください。 ⟶ 屋根(ね)が　こわれたので、　なおしておいて　ください。
7. きたない　ガラスを　みがきましょう。 ⟶ きたない　ガラスを　みがいておきましょう。
8. 山田さんにも　話します。 ⟶ 山田さんにも　話しておきます。

6.7.6 Response Drill

1. ハンカチと　くつ下を　洗っておきましたか。
   いいえ …… いいえ、　洗っておきませんでした。
2. 大阪(さか)行の　急(きゅう)行は　もう　出てしまいましたか。
   はい …… はい、　出てしまいました。
3. しゅうり屋に　電話を　かけておきましたか。
   はい …… はい、　かけておきました。
4. ぼくの　車の　パンクを　もう　なおしてしまいましたか。
   はい …… はい、　なおしてしまいました。
5. けさの　新聞を　もう　読んでしまったんですか。
   はい …… はい、　読んでしまったんです。
6. 原(はら)さんに　あう　時間と　場(ば)所を　知らせておきましたか。
   いいえ …… いいえ、　知らせておきませんでした。
7. お客(きゃく)さんが　来ますけど、　ビールを　買っておきましたか。
   はい …… はい、　買っておきました。
8. あの　方の　名前と　所を　書いておきましたか。
   いいえ …… いいえ、　書いておきませんでした。

6.7.7 Substitution Drill

車を　洗っておきました。

1. なおしておきました …… 車を　なおしておきました。
2. しゅうりしてしまいました …… 車を　しゅうりしてしまいました。
3. こわれた　電話を …… こわれた　電話を　しゅうりしてしまいました。
4. しらべておいてください …… こわれた　電話を　しらべておいてください。
5. りょう方の　問題を …… りょう方の　問題を　しらべておいてください。
6. 読んでおいてください …… りょう方の　問題を　読んでおいてください。

7. まちがえてしまいました …… りょう方の　問題を　まちがえてしまいました。
8. 〝ぬ〟と〝ね〟を …… 〝ぬ〟と〝ね〟を　まちがえてしまいました。

6.7.8 E-J Expansion Drill

1. 洗っておきました。 …… 洗っておきました。
   a car …… 車を　洗っておきました。
   yesterday …… きのう　車を　洗っておきました。
   because it was dirty …… よごれていたので、　きのう　車を　洗って
   おきました。
2. こわれてしまいました。 …… こわれてしまいました。
   already …… もう　こわれてしまいました。
   an expensive radio …… 高い　ラジオが　もう　こわれてしまいました。
   which [I] bought last month …… 先月　買った　高い　ラジオが　もう　こわれて
   しまいました。
3. わすれてしまいました。 …… わすれてしまいました。
   kan'ji …… 漢字を　わすれてしまいました。
   that [I] learned yesterday …… きのう　習った　漢字を　わすれてしまいました。
   at school …… 学校で　きのう　習った　漢字を　わすれて
   しまいました。
4. むかえに　行ったらしいです。 …… むかえに　行ったらしいです。
   for a doctor …… いしゃを　むかえに　行ったらしいです。
   since a child is sick …… 子どもが　びょう気なので、　いしゃを　むかえに
   行ったらしいです。
5. よやくしておいてください。 …… よやくしておいてください。
   at a hotel …… ホテルを　よやくしておいてください。
   by tomorrow morning …… あしたの　朝までに　ホテルを　よやくしておいて
   ください。

6.7.9 Review Transformation Drill

A. 1. こたえを　まちがえて
   しまいました。 ⟶ こたえを　まちがえてしまったんですか。
   2. 昼ごはんを　もう　食べて
   しまいました。 ⟶ 昼ごはんを　もう　食べてしまったんですか。

3. ひらがなと　かたかなは　ぜんぶ　おぼえてしまいました。 ⟶ ひらがなと　かたかなは　ぜんぶ　おぼえてしまったんですか。
4. あめで　洋服も　くつも　よごれてしまいました。 ⟶ あめで　洋服も　くつも　よごれてしまったんですか。
5. 子どもたちに　おかしを　やってしまいました。 ⟶ 子どもたちに　おかしを　やってしまったんですか。
6. 本当の　ことを　山田さんに　話してしまいました。 ⟶ 本当の　ことを　山田さんに　話してしまったんですか。

B.

1. ワイパーも　なおしておきました。 ⟶ ワイパーも　なおしておいたんです。
2. さむくなったので、　まどを　しめておきました。 ⟶ さむくなったので、　まどを　しめておいたんです。
3. 先生の　考えを　前もって　聞いておきました。 ⟶ 先生の　考えを　前もって　聞いておいたんです。
4. 学生に　せつめいするので、　しらべておきました。 ⟶ 学生に　せつめいするので、　しらべておいたんです。
5. きっぷの　よやくを　取りけしておきました。 ⟶ きっぷの　よやくを　取りけしておいたんです。
6. ネクタイは　はこに　入れておきました。 ⟶ ネクタイは　はこに　入れておいたんです。

6.8 EXERCISES

6.8.1 Transform the following sentences into each of the ～ておきました and ～てしまいました endings and give the English equivalent for each sentence:

1. 車が　パンクしたので、　しゅうり屋に　持って行きました。
2. 昼の　食事に　使った　おさらは　洗いました。
3. あしたの　宿題は　もう　しました。
4. さむくなったので、　まどを　しめました。
5. ホテルの　よやくは　取りけします。
6. その　ことは　山本さんにも　電話で　話します。

6.8.2 Transform the following sentences into the ～らしいです ending and give the English equivalent for each sentence:

1. オイルが　よごれています。
2. むこうで　大きな　事故(こ)が　おこりました。
3. この　とけいは　こわれていません。
4. 今　いろいろな　公害(こうがい)が　おこっています。
5. この　ワイパーは　だめです。

6.8.3 Compose short sentences in Japanese by using the words given below, and then give the English equivalents for them:

1. どんどん　2. だんだん　3. はじめて　4. だいぶ

6.8.4 Insert the Relational が for intransitive Verbs and を for transitive Verbs:

1. 事故(こ)（　　）おこる
2. とけい（　　）なおす
3. ガラス（　　）こわれる
4. パンク（　　）なおる
5. オイル（　　）よごれる
6. タイヤ（　　）パンクする
7. ガソリン（　　）きれる
8. 車（　　）みがく
9. くつ（　　）よごす
10. ワイパー（　　）こわす

6.8.5 Rearrange the words given in each group to compose a good Japanese sentence:

1. なおして、　四時、　の、　ください、　までに、　あした、　ごご、　おいて
2. こわれた、　らしい、　しゅうり、　ください、　が、　に、　テレビ、　ので、　来て
3. ひらがな、　そうです、　おぼえて、　スミスさん、　一週間、　で、　を、　は、　ぜんぶ、　しまった
4. おきました、　取り、　おべん当(とう)、　来て、　作って、　から、　に、　を、　ください
5. らしい、　あめ、　ので、　花見、　は、　です、　はは、　が、　に、　ふった、　行かなかった
6. びょう気、　しまいました、　ので、　二週間、　を、　だった、　休んで、　かいしゃ、　も

6.8.6 Write the following underlined *hiragana* in *kan'ji*:

1. たか木(ぎ)さんは　べいこくに　すんでいたらしいです。
2. あの　かたに　いちど　あったことが　あります。
3. くるまを　あらっておいてください。

4. あさ　はやく　とりに　いきましたが、　ゆうがた　できるそうです。
5. ひるごろ　でんわを　ください。

6.8.7 Distinguish the following *kan'ji*:

1. 住、働　　3. 洗、洋　　5. 来、米
2. 先、洗　　4. 夕、多　　6. 早、朝

6.8.8 In what situations can *Maido arigatoo gozaimasu* be used?

6.8.9 When you order something at a restaurant, a well-trained waiter would say:

1. Kashikomarimashita.　　2. Wakarimashita.

6.8.10 When you ask your teacher to do something, he would reply:

1. Kashikomarimashita.　　2. Wakarimashita.

6.8.11 Complete the following dialogs, according to the given cues:

1. Customer: Kore onegai shimasu.
   Sales clerk:___________________.
2. Delivery boy: Maido arigatoo gozaimasu. Osake o motte kimashita.
   Customer:___________________.
3. Neighbor: Okusan, kore otaku no deshoo?
   (Okusan offers an apology to her neighbor for causing the latter inconvenience.)
   Housewife: ___________________.

6.8.12 Under the following situations which expression, *Gokuroo sama* or *Sumimasen* would be more appropriate for you to use?

1. Your typist at the office brings you her typed letter.
2. Everyone in the office is busy, and someone comes to tell you that your wife is on the phone.
3. Your teacher does something for you.
4. Your friend helps you move your furniture.
5. The mailman delivers a telegram to your house.

6.8.13 In reply to the following, would you use the expression *Arigatoo* or *Onegai shimasu*?

Repairman:　Kore kara sugu kuruma o motte ikimasu.

6.8.14 You help your mother by cooking dinner, cleaning the house, and then baby-sitting your younger sisters and brothers. Which expression(s) will she NOT use in thanking you?

1. Arigatoo gozaimasu.
2. Gokuroo sama.
3. Doomo sumimasen.
4. Arigatoo.

6.9 SITUATIONAL AND APPLICATION CONVERSATION

6.9.1 A man brings a radio to an electric repair shop and asks a repairman to check his radio. The man says it seems to have been broken. The repairman, pointing out a part of the radio, says that part has been broken.

The man asks the repairman to repair it by the following evening because he wants to listen to the radio the following night.

The repairman answers he will have the radio repaired by 5 P.M. and asks the man to come to get it.

The man agrees to come.

6.9.2 Carry on a telephone conversation acting as a car repairman and a man who has a flat tire.

6.9.3 You go to a gas station, and ask a service man to wash your car, to check the oil, to fill the gas, etc.

6.9.4

Yamaguchi:	Akita san. Ocha o nomimasen ka?
Akita:	Ee, nomitai desu ne.
Yamaguchi:	Jaa, soko e motte ikimashoo ka?
Akita:	Ee, onegai shimasu.
Yamaguchi:	Hai, doozo.
Akita:	Sumimasen.

6.9.5

Salesclerk:	Irasshaimase. Nani o sashiagemashoo ka?
Female Customer:	Are o misete kudasai.
Salesclerk:	Kashikomarimashita. . . . Hai, doozo . . . Ikaga deshoo ka?
Female Customer:	Kore o morau wa.
Salesclerk:	Hai, maido arigatoo gozaimasu. Hako ni iremashoo ka?
Female Customer:	Ee, onegai suru wa.

LESSON 7

日本研究(けんきゅう)[1]

7.1 PRESENTATION

ハワードさんは、 大学院に 入る 前[2]、 しばらくの 間[3] 高校で 歴史の 先生を して[4] いました。しかし、 東洋の 歴史に きょうみ[5]を 持ったので、 教えるのを やめた[6]そうです。そして、 七か月前に[7] 日本史を 研究(けんきゅう)しに 日本へ 来ました。

7.2 DIALOG

小林(こばやし)　「ハワードさんは、 日本へ いらっしゃってから[8]、 長いんですか。」

ハワード　「ちょうど 七か月に なります。」

小林(こばやし)　「大学を 卒業(そつぎょう)してから[8]、 すぐ いらっしゃったんですか。」

ハワード　「いいえ、 大学院に 二年ほど[9] いましたが、 その 前は[2] 教師(し)を して いました。」

小林(こばやし)　「ハワードさんの 生まれた 所は どこですか。」

ハワード　「オレゴン州の 小さな 町です。 小林(こばやし)さんは 東京生まれなんですか。」

小林(こばやし)　「いいえ、 ぼくは おととしの 三月に 長崎(さき)[10]の 高校を 卒業(そつぎょう)してから、 東京へ 来たんです。 今は 働きながら[11]、 大学に 行っています[12]。 ハワードさんは 長崎(さき)に いらっしゃったことが ありますか。」

ハワード　「いや、 ないんです。 アメリカへ 帰る 前に[2]、 一度 行ってみるつもりなんですけど[13]。」

小林(こばやし)　「じゃあ、 ぼくが 冬休みに 長崎(さき)へ 帰る 時、 いっしょに いらっしゃいませんか。 いなかの お正月(しょう)[14]を 味わうことも できますから、 ちょうど いいと思いますけど。」

ハワード　「そう できれば、 うれしいですね。 私は アメリカへ 帰ってから、 日本史を 専攻(せんこう)したいんです。 ですから、 こっち[15]に いる 間[3]に、 できるだけ[16] いろいろな ことを けいけんしておきたいと思っています。」

大学院(だいがくいん)　入(はい)る　しばらくの　間(あいだ)　高校(こうこう)　歴史(れきし)　長(なが)い
生(う)まれた　オレゴン州(しゅう)　長崎(ながさき)　帰(かえ)る　冬休(ふゆやす)み
味(あじ)わう

7.3 PATTERN SENTENCES

7.3.1

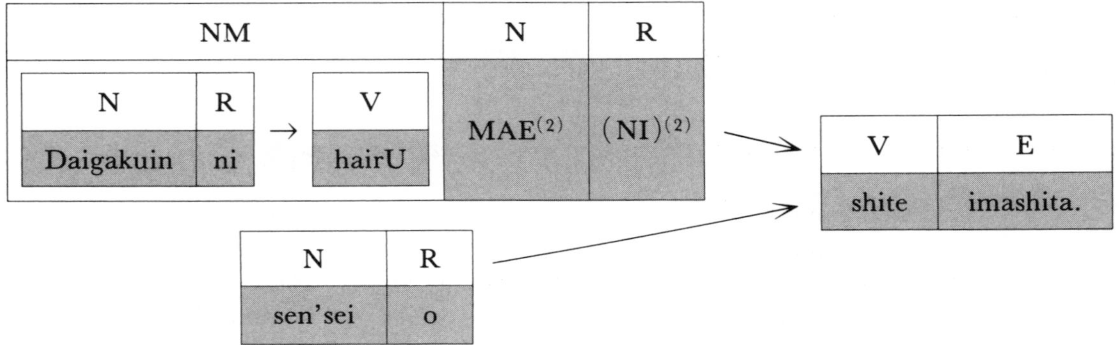

7.3.2

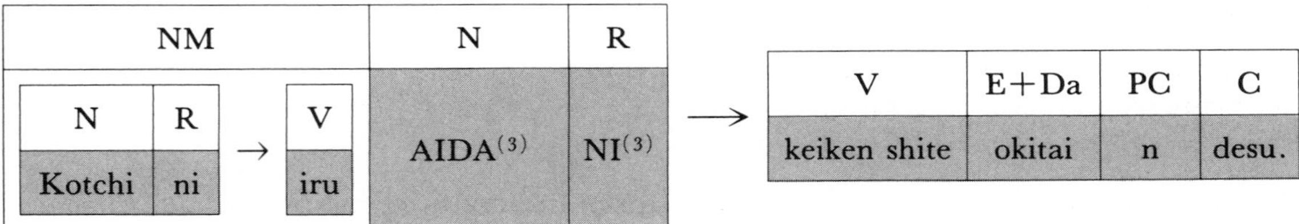

7.3.3

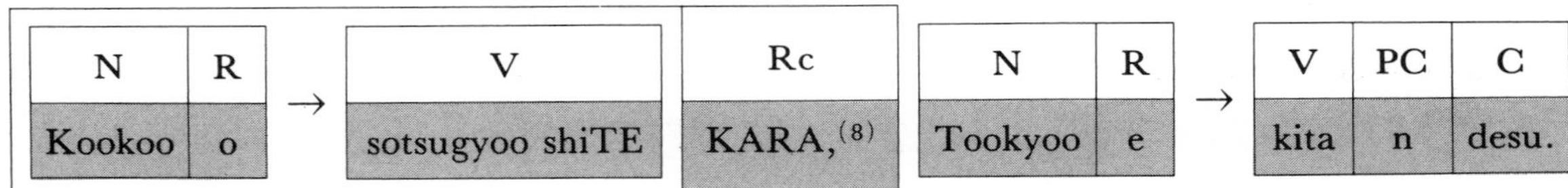

7.3.4

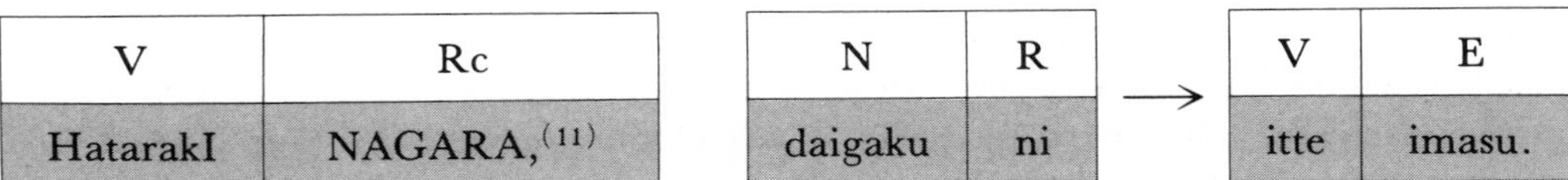

7.4 NOTES

7.4.1 Japanese language studies in the United States involved only about ten thousand college students as of 1980. When we consider the fact that millions of Japanese are studying English, we should realize the need for a national effort to increase America's interest in Japanese language study, which is not only important for communication and understanding, but also a step in the direction of liberating or emancipating the narrow mono-cultural and mono-lingual mind.

7.4.2 *Daigakuin ni hairu mae, sen'sei o shite imashita* means "Before he entered graduate school, he was a teacher." The Noun *mae* "before" may be preceded by the Dictionary form of a Verb to formulate a Predicate Modifier meaning "before one does such and such." The *mae* modified by a Noun Modifier may be followed by the Relational *ni*, which specifies or emphasizes the time more. If there is a subject exclusively for the nonfinal Predicate, the subject should be followed by *ga* or *no*. If the subject covers the final clause also, then *wa* may be used. Note that the form that occurs before *mae* is always the Dictionary form of a Verb, regardless of the tense or type of the final Predicate:

(Predicate Modifier) + Dictionary form of Verb + *mae* (*ni*) (*wa*) . . .

neru mae ni,	ha o migakimashoo	"before going to bed,	let's brush our teeth"
	ha o migakimashita		[I] brushed [my] teeth"
	ha o migaite kudasai		please brush your teeth"
	ha o migakanakatta rashii desu		it seems [he] didn't brush [his] teeth"

Ichiroo, shokuji o suru mae ni, te o arawanakereba narimasen yo.	"Ichirō, you must wash your hands before you have a meal."
Watashi ga umareru mae, chichi to haha wa Chuugoku ni ita koto ga aru soo desu.	"Before I was born, my father and mother had been in China, I understand."
Boku wa, tetsugaku o ben'kyoo shihajimeru mae, shakaigaku ni kyoomi o motte imashita.	"Before I started studying philosophy, I had an interest in sociology."
Ryokoo ni deru mae ni, hoteru o yoyaku shita hoo ga ii desu yo.	"You'd better make a hotel reservation before leaving for a trip."
Kaimono ni dekakeru mae ni, mado o shimete kudasai.	"Before you go out shopping, please close the window."

7.4.3 *Shibaraku no aida* means "for sometime" and *kotchi ni iru aida ni*, "while I am over here." *Aida*, in this instance, is a Noun meaning "while," "during," and so on, and may be modified by a Predicate or a sentence. The forms that occur before *aida* are the same as those which modify the Noun *toki*, such as a Pre-Noun, plain forms of a Verb and an Adjective, an adjectival Noun plus *na*, a Noun plus *no*, Noun plus the plain forms of the Copula (except *da*). (See Note 4.4.4.) Although the tense of the "while" phrase is normally the same as that of the final Predicate, the Predicate before *aida* often occurs in its imperfect tense form or the TE form of a Verb plus *iru*.

Aida may be used without the Relational *ni* following it, but in that case the whole sentence means "one is such and such or was doing such and such throughout the period of. . . ." When the time Relational *ni* follows *aida*, the sentence will mean "one does or did such and such within or during the period of. . . ." The Relational *wa* may occur after *aida* in both cases.

Pre-Noun	
Verb (plain form)	
Adjective (plain form)	
Noun + *no*	**+ *aida* (*ni*) (*wa*) . . .**
adjectival Noun + *na*	
Noun + Copula (except *da*)	

sono aida ni	''during that''
ken'kyuu shite iru aida	''while one is researching''
nagai aida	''for a long time''
byooki no aida	''while [I] am sick''
hima na aida ni	''while [I] am free''
gakusei datta aida	''during the time when one was a student''
Akachan ga nete iru aida ni, heya o kirei ni shimashoo.	''Let's clean the room while the baby is sleeping.''
Boku wa, Kariforunia ni iru aida ni, Buraun san ni aimashita.	''I met Mr. Brown while I was in California.''
Wakai aida ni, motto iroiro na ben'kyoo o shite okitai n desu.	''While I am still young, I'd like to study many more things.''
Hima na aida ni, ocha o ippai nomimashoo.	''Before I get busy, I'll have a cup of tea.''
Boku wa daigakusei no aida ni, Nihon e ryuugaku shitai desu.	''While I'm a college student, I'd like to go to Japan for study.''

7.4.4 *Kookoo de rekishi no sen'sei o shite imashita* means ''He was a history teacher at a high school.'' To tell one's profession or job, *~o shite imasu* may be used in the place of *~desu.*

sen'sei / kyooshi / isha / ten'in / kusuriya } o shite iru ''one is { a teacher'' / a teacher'' / a doctor'' / a salesclerk'' / a pharmacist''

Kobayashi san wa ima mo shoogakkoo no sen'sei o shite imasu ka?	''Is Mr. Kobayashi still an elementary school teacher?''
Watashi no chichi wa inaka de kusuriya o shite imasu.	''My father owns a pharmacy in my home country.''

7.4.5 *Tooyoo no rekishi ni kyoomi o motta node* means ''since he took an interest in oriental history.'' *Ni* shows the direction, objective, and some kind of relationship. *~ni kyoomi o motsu* is used quite frequently. Similarly *~ni kyoomi ga aru* and *~ni kyoomi o motte iru* mean ''[one] is interested in [something].''

Nani ni kyoomi o motte imasu ka?	''What are you interested in?''
Itsu nihon'go ni kyoomi o mochihajimeta n desu ka?	''Since when have you begun to become interested in Japanese?''

7.4.6 *Oshieru no o yameta soo desu* means ''I heard that he quit teaching.'' The Verb *yameru* means ''quit'' and is a transitive Verb. What one quits is followed by the Relational *o*. When one quits doing such and such, the nominalizer *no* will occur before *~o yameru* to nominalize the action of doing such and such. (See Note 7.4.4, Vol. II.)

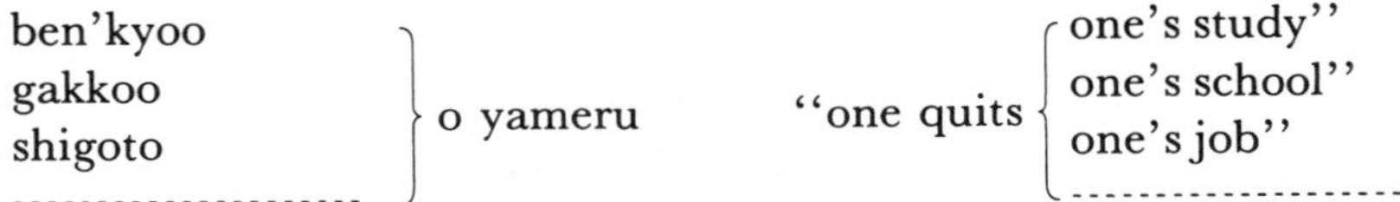

oshieru no ryuugaku suru no kuru no	o yameru	"one quits { teaching" studying abroad" coming"

This is also applicable to quite a few transitive Verbs.

motte kuru no o wasureta	"forgot to bring it with one"
hanasu no o narau	"learn speaking"
kutsu o haku no o tetsudau	"help someone put on shoes"
iku no o miru	"see someone going"

Kaeru toki, mado o shimeru no o wasurenaide kudasai.	"Please don't forget to close the window when you are going home."
Ban'gohan o tsukuru no o tetsudatte kudasai.	"Please help me in preparing supper."
Itoo san ga jogin'gu o shite iru no o mimashita.	"I saw Miss Itō jogging."

7.4.7 *Nanakagetsu mae (ni)* means "seven months ago." When *-mae (ni)* is preceded by a number which connotes time duration, it always means "ago" or "before." The time Relational *ni* may follow *-mae* to stress it.

gofun	mae (ni)	"five minutes ago"
ichijikan		"one hour ago"
futsuka		"two days ago"
isshuukan		"one week ago"
san'kagetsu		"three months ago"
gonen		"five years ago"

Otooto san wa itsu shoogakkoo o sotsugyoo shita n desu ka?	"When did your younger brother graduate from elementary school?"
Gorokunen mae ni sotsugyoo shimashita.	"He graduated five or six years ago."
Ichijikan gurai mae ni ame ga furihajimeta rashii desu.	"It seems it started raining about an hour ago."

7.4.8 *Nihon e irasshatte kara, nagai n desu ka?* means "Has it been long since your coming to Japan?" When the TE form of a Verb is followed by the clause Relational *kara,* the combination forms a clause meaning "after doing such and such," "since something happened," and so on. The final Predicate following the clause may be of any tense or of any type. If there is a subject exclusively for the nonfinal Predicate, the subject should be followed by *ga.* if the subject covers the final clause also, then *wa* may be used.

(Predicate Modifier) + Verb(*-te*) + *kara,* (*sugu*) . . .

The Adverb *sugu* may be used immediately after the *-te kara* clause, to mean "soon after. . . ." or "right after. . . ."

sotsugyoo shite kara, . . .	"after being graduated"
uchi e kaette kara, . . .	"after going home"

The *kara* after the TE form of a Verb is a clause Relational meaning "after," and should be distinguished from the *kara* after the TA form of a Verb. The latter *kara* connotes "because," "as," and so on. (See Note 5.4.8, Vol. II.)

Compare:

sotsugyoo shite kara, . . .	"after being graduated"
sotsugyoo shita kara, . . .	"as I was graduated"

Osara o aratte kara, mado garasu o migaite kudasai.	"After washing the dishes, please clean the windowpanes."
Daigaku o yamete kara, doo suru tsumori desu ka?	"What are you planning to do after quitting the university?"
Kinoo wa, uchi e kaette kara, sugu hirune o shimashita.	"Soon after going home, I took a nap yesterday."
Kyooto ni tsuite kara, nan'nichi ni narimasu ka?	"How many days has it been since arriving in Kyōto?"
Hiragana o zen'bu oboete kara, kan'ji o narau hoo ga ii desu yo.	"It is better to study *kan'ji* after memorizing all the *hiragana*."

7.4.9 *Daigakuin ni ninen hodo imashita* means "I was a graduate student for about two years." The Relational *hodo* is used in this instance in the meaning of "about," "approximately," as an equivalent for *-gurai*. *Hodo* and *-gurai* are always interchangeable when they follow a number or a numeral, although *hodo* sounds a little more formal than *-gurai*.

Nihon ni san'nen hodo imashita.	"I was in Japan for about three years."
Koko de jippun hodo matte ite kudasai.	"Please wait here for about ten minutes."

-Kurai, *-gurai*, and *hodo* are all vague expressions used quite frequently in Japanese. They mean "about" or "roughly," and such indefinites are expected to be used even in very definite situations. For example, even if you have spent exactly one hundred *yen*, one would still say *hyakuen gurai*—"roughly one hundred *yen*." Their use is practically mandatory in answering a question which has been asked with vagueness, such as *dono gurai* ("how long, how much, how many").

7.4.10 Nagasaki began as a small fishing village. Located on the west coast of Kyūshū it later developed into an important port for trade between Japan and China and, in later centuries, between Japan and the West. Its importance as Japan's window on the world became even greater during the Tokugawa isolation, when it alone remained open to Western trade, with the Dutch being allowed to maintain a small trading settlement there. It was also in the area of Nagasaki that Catholicism thrived for a short time during the early years of Western contact. However, the city is probably best known in the West because it was here, on August 9, 1945, that an atomic bomb was dropped by the United States, almost completely destroying the city. Today, Nagasaki serves Japan as a fairly large and important port city.

7.4.11 *Hatarakinagara, daigaku ni itte imasu* means "While working, I am attending a university." When the Stem form of a Verb is followed by *nagara*, the combination formulates a clause meaning "while doing such and such." *Nagara* is a clause Relational used to state "one's doing something concurrently with something else." Note that this use of *nagara* is applied only to the case in which two actions are performed by one person simultaneously. Other use of *nagara* will be introduced later. In the case of two persons' performing different actions simultaneously, *aida* should be used.

(Predicate Modifier) + Stem form of Verb + *nagara* . . .

arukinagara, . . .	"while walking"
hanashinagara, . . .	"while talking"
ren'shuu shinagara, . . .	"while practicing"
kikinagara, . . .	"while listening"
tabenagara, . . .	"while eating"

The final Predicate after the *nagara* clause may be of any tense or of any type.

Shin'bun o yominagara, gohan o tabenaide kudasai.	"Please don't eat while reading a newspaper."
Kuruma o un'ten shinagara, rajio o kikimashita.	"While driving a car, I listened to the radio."
Shokuji o shinagara, amari hanashite wa ikemasen yo.	"You shouldn't talk so much while eating."
Gin'koo ni tsutomenagara, yoru eigo no ben'kyoo o shite imasu.	"I'm working at a bank and studying English in the evenings."
Jin'ja ya otera o ken'butsu shinagara, Nihon no rekishi o ben'kyoo shimashita.	"I studied the history of Japan while visiting shrines and temples."

7.4.12 *Daigaku ni itte imasu* means "one goes to the university" or "one is attending the university." As already explained in Note 2.4.2 of Volume II, the TE form of a Verb plus *iru* may mean repeated action. When one does something repeatedly, that is, habitually, day after day, week after week, year after year, the TE form of a Verb followed by *iru* can express the idea of regular activities.

Kodomo wa shoogakkoo e itte imasu.	"My child is attending elementary school."
Ano gakusei wa mainichi toshokan ni kite imasu ne.	"That student comes to the library every day, doesn't he?"
Boku wa Asahi Shin'bun o yon'de imasu.	"I am reading the Asahi Newspaper (now or every day)."
Ichinichi ni san'do kusuri o non'de imasu.	"I've been taking medicine three times a day."

7.4.13 The softening expressions included in this dialog again indicate the Japanese characteristic indirectness and vagueness. Howard's statement *Itte miru tsumori na n desu kedo* is another example of ending a sentence with the equivalent of the English "but." However, it is not clear from the context whether he is leaving something unsaid or allowing room for contradiction.

7.4.14 *Oshoogatsu*

Originally, the Japanese people calculated age according to the first day of the New Year. At the New Year, therefore, all the nation was in fact adding one more year of age to everyone.

Although this is no longer a common practice, *oshoogatsu*, the New Year season, is still the most celebrated of all Japanese festivals.

The idea of beginning a new year with a clean slate is an important one in Japan. Consequently, by midnight of New Year's Eve, all debts are paid and everything has been thoroughly cleaned. At midnight, temple bells, called *joya no kane,* toll 108 times, symbolizing the 108 faults of mankind.

Oshoogatsu is traditionally celebrated for three days. The first day is marked by attendance at a temple or shrine, and on that day, *osechi,* festival food for the New Year, and *tosozake* or *otoso,* a thick sweet *sake,* and *ozooni,* a special rice cake in soup, are traditional elements of the festivities. Throughout the three-day holiday, there is much visiting among relatives, friends, and co-workers. This is necessary in maintaining social relations in Japan, perhaps more so than in the West. One's visit to relatives, friends, and the like is expected and it would be a breach of social etiquette to forgo such obligations.

7.4.15 *Kotchi* literally means "this side" or "in this direction." Here, *kotchi* refers to Japan, providing another illustration of the Japanese use of directions rather than concrete names in referring to places or persons.

7.4.16 *Dekiru dake* is an Adverb meaning "as much as possible," "as well as one can do," and so forth, depending upon context. This may modify Verbs, Adjectives, Adverbs as well as Nouns.

dekiru dake	hatarakimashoo	"[I] will work as hard as possible"
	ii mono	"as good things as possible"
	yukkuri	"as slowly as [you] can"
	takusan	"as many as possible"
	kan'tan na mon'dai	"as easy as questions can be"

Nihon'go no kurasu de wa dekiru dake eigo o tsukawanaide kudasai. — "Please do not use English as much as possible in Japanese class. (Please use as little English as possible in the classroom.)"

Dekiru dake hayaku naoshite okimashoo. — "We'll repair it as soon as possible."

7.5 VOCABULARY

Presentation

研究(けんきゅう)	ken'kyuu	......	N	research; study
ハワード	Hawaado	......	N	Howard
前	mae	......	N	before (see 7.4.2)
しばらく	shibaraku	......	N	some time; a while
間	aida	......	N	duration; period; while; during (see 7.4.3)
高校	kookoo	......	N	senior high school
東洋	tooyoo	......	N	the East (countries); the Orient
きょうみ	kyoomi	......	N	interest (see 7.4.5)
やめた	yameta	......	V	quit (TA form of *yameru*) (see 7.4.6)
前	-mae	......	Nd	ago; before (see 7.4.7)

研究(けんきゅう)し	ken'kyuu shi	......	V	Stem form of *ken'kyuu suru* – research; study

Dialog

小林(こばやし)	Kobayashi	......	N	family name
から	kara	......	Rc	after; since (see 7.4.8)
卒業(そつぎょう)して	sotsugyoo shite	......	V	TE form of *sotsugyoo suru* – is graduated; finish (transitive Verb)
卒業(そつぎょう)	sotsugyoo	......	N	graduation
ほど	hodo	......	R	about; approximately (see 7.4.9)
教師(し)	kyooshi	......	N	teacher
生まれた	umareta	......	V	was born (TA form of *umareru*) (intransitive Verb)
オレゴン	Oregon	......	N	Oregon
(東京) 生まれ	(Tookyoo) umare	......	N	(Tōkyō)-born; of (Tōkyō) birth
おととし	ototoshi	......	N	the year before last
長崎(さき)	Nagasaki	......	N	a historical city in Kyūshū
ながら	nagara	......	Rc	while; as (see 7.4.11)
いなか	inaka	......	N	countryside; home village
(お)正(しょう)月	(o)shoogatsu	......	N	New Year's day(s); January
うれしい	ureshii	......	A	is happy; is glad; is delighted
専攻(せんこう)し	sen'koo shi	......	V	Stem form of *sen'koo suru* – major; specialize
専攻(せんこう)	sen'koo	......	N	major
ですから	desukara	......	SI	therefore (polite equivalent of *dakara*)
できるだけ	dekiru dake	......	Adv.	as many as possible; as much as one can do (see 7.4.16)
けいけんして	keiken shite	......	V	TE form of *keiken suru* – experience
けいけん	keiken	......	N	experience

Notes

は	ha	......	N	tooth
てつ学	tetsugaku	......	N	philosophy
社会(しゃかい)学	shakaigaku	......	N	sociology
留学(りゅうがく)する	ryuugaku suru	......	V	study abroad
留学(りゅうがく)	ryuugaku	......	N	the study abroad
くすり屋	kusuriya	......	N	pharmacy; pharmacist
ジョギング	jogin'gu	......	N	jogging

昼ね	hirune	......	N	nap
昼ねする	hirune suru	......	V	take a nap
くすり	kusuri	......	N	medicine
のむ	nomu	......	V	take (medicine); smoke

7.6 KAN'JI

7.6.1 院 (1) IN (2) institution; temple (3) classifier 阝 [soil forming steps]
(4) 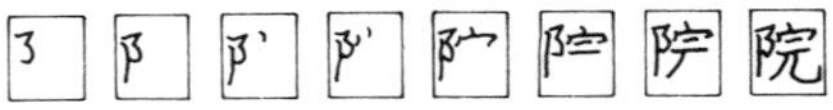 (5) 大学院、びょう院

7.6.a 入[13.6.8, Vol. II] (1) *hai(ru)* (5) 大学に入ります

7.6.b 間[7.6.3, Vol. II] (1) *aida* (2) while; during (5) みじかい間、勉強している間、仕事(しごと)の間

7.6.c 高[6.6.3] (1) KOO (5) 高校生 [high school student]

7.6.2 歴 (1) REKI (2) pass; history (3) classifier 厂 (止)
(4) 
(5) 歴史(し)、履(り)歴書 [personal history]、経(けい)歴 [career] (6) homonym 暦

7.6.3 史 (1) SHI (2) history; chronicles (3) classifier 口 (4) 
(5) 歴史、日本史、東洋史、アメリカ史
(6) a container with bamboo bars for counting numbers (中) plus a hand (又)
⟶ officer in astronomy for making calendars ⟶ recorder

7.6.4 長 (1) *naga(i)* (2) long (3) forms the classifier 長
(4)  (5) 長崎(さき)、長い間、あのえいがは長い、長さ

7.6.d 生[2.6.3, Vol. II] (1) *u(mareru)* (2) born (5) 東京で生まれる、ニューヨーク生まれ

7.6.5 州 (1) SHUU (2) province; state (U.S.A.) (3) classifier 刂 (川)
(4) 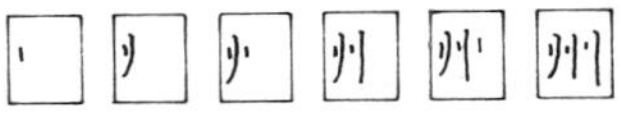 (5) オレゴン州、本州、九州
(6) islands (、、、) in a river (川); homonym 洲、酬

7.6.6 帰 (1) *kae(ru)* (2) return; go (come) back (3) classifier 刂 (巾)
(4)  (5) 国へ帰る、お帰りなさい

7.6.7 冬 (1) *fuyu* (2) winter (3) classifier 夂 (冫) (4) [ノ][ク][夂][冬][冬]
(5) 冬ゆきが多い、 冬休み、冬服(ふく) (6) ice (冫)plus gather (夂) ⟶ winter

7.6.8 味 (1) *aji* (2) taste (3) classifier 口 [mouth]
(4) [口][口一][口二][口牛][口未][味] (5) さしみを味わう (6) homonym MI 未

7.6.9 夏* (1) *natsu* (2) summer (3) classifier 一 (夂)
(4) [一][丆][百][頁][夏][夏] (5) 夏休み、夏時間、夏服(ふく)

7.7 DRILLS

7.7.1 Transformation Drill

1. 中学校を <u>卒業(そつぎょう)しました</u>。 ハワイに 来たんです。	⟶	中学校を <u>卒業(そつぎょう)してから</u>、ハワイに 来たんです。
2. 大学に 入りました。 日本語を 一年間 勉強しました。	⟶	大学に 入ってから、日本語を 一年間 勉強しました。
3. 宿(しゅく)題を してしまいます。 あそびに 行きます。	⟶	宿(しゅく)題を してしまってから、あそびに 行きます。
4. アメリカへ 帰ります。 大学院で 日本文化(か)を 研究(けんきゅう)するつもりです。	⟶	アメリカへ 帰ってから、大学院で 日本文化(か)を 研究(けんきゅう)するつもりです。
5. パンクを なおしてください。 車を 洗ってください。	⟶	パンクを なおしてから、車を 洗ってください。
6. 高校で 教えるのを やめました。 銀行に つとめはじめたそうです。	⟶	高校で 教えるのを やめてから、銀行に つとめはじめたそうです。
7. いもうとが 生まれました。 かぞくは オレゴン州へ 行きました。	⟶	いもうとが 生まれてから、かぞくは オレゴン州へ 行きました。

7.7.2 Transformation Drill

1. ぼくは <u>働きます</u>。 ぼくは 学校へ 行っています。	⟶	ぼくは <u>働きながら</u>、学校へ 行っています。
2. けさ おちゃを のみました。 日本の ざっしを 読みました。	⟶	けさ おちゃを のみながら、日本の ざっしを 読みました。

3. 京都を　けんぶつします。 日本の　古い　文化(か)を　しらべる つもりです。	→	京都を　けんぶつしながら、日本の　古い 文化(か)を　しらべるつもりです。
4. 運転(うんてん)します。 あまり　話さないでください。	→	運転(うんてん)しながら、あまり　話さないで ください。
5. ハワードさんは　東洋史を　研究(けんきゅう) します。 ハワードさんは　高校の　先生を しています。	→	ハワードさんは　東洋史を　研究(けんきゅう)しながら、 高校の　先生を　しています。
6. 日本語を　勉強します。 いなかの　お正(しょう)月を　味わうことが できます。	→	日本語を　勉強しながら、いなかの お正(しょう)月を　味わうことが　できます。
7. ミラーさんは　漢字を　書きます。 ミラーさんは　漢字を　おぼえた そうです。	→	ミラーさんは　漢字を　書きながら、 おぼえたそうです。

7.7.3 Transformation Drill

1. 食事を　します。 いつも　昼ねを　します。	→	食事を　する　前に、いつも　昼ねを します。
2. 日本を　おとずれます。 歴史の　本を　読んでおきましょう。	→	日本を　おとずれる　前に、歴史の　本を 読んでおきましょう。
3. 自動車を　取りに　行きました。 しゅうり屋に　電話を　かけて おきました。	→	自動車を　取りに　行く　前に、しゅうり 屋に　電話を　かけておきました。
4. 高校を　卒業(そつぎょう)しました。 しごとを　さがしておきました。	→	高校を　卒業(そつぎょう)する　前に、しごとを さがしておきました。
5. ホテルを　よやくします。 山田さんの　つごうを　聞いて ください。	→	ホテルを　よやくする　前に、山田さんの つごうを　聞いてください。
6. いなかへ　帰ります。 わたしに　知らせてください。	→	いなかへ　帰る　前に、わたしに 知らせてください。
7. くすりを　のみます。 せつめいを　よく　読んでください。	→	くすりを　のむ　前に、せつめいを　よく 読んでください。

7.7.4 Transformation Drill

1.	大学院に　入りました。 長崎(さき)へ　行ったことが　あります。	→	大学院に　入る　前、長崎(さき)へ　行った ことが　あります。
2.	おととし　日本へ　来ました。 カリフォルニアに　住んでいました。	→	おととし　日本へ　来る　前、 カリフォルニアに　住んでいました。
3.	ぼくが　生まれました。 ちちは　本屋を　していたそうです。	→	ぼくが　生まれる　前、ちちは　本屋を していたそうです。
4.	あなたは　先生に　なりました。 あなたは　何を　していましたか。	→	あなたは　先生に　なる　前、何を　して いましたか。
5.	おとうとが　小学校に　入りました。 いもうとは　中学校を　卒業(そつぎょう) しました。	→	おとうとが　小学校に　入る　前、 いもうとは　中学校を　卒業(そつぎょう)しました。
6.	あめが　ふりはじめました。 どこに　いたんですか。	→	あめが　ふりはじめる　前、どこに いたんですか。

7.7.5 Transformation Drill

1.	日本に　います。 いろいろな　けいけんを　したい です。	→	日本に　いる　間に、いろいろな けいけんを　したいです。
2.	中国史を　専攻(せんこう)しています。 日本史も　研究(けんきゅう)してみたいです。	→	中国史を　専攻(せんこう)している　間に、日本史も 研究(けんきゅう)してみたいです。
3.	子どもが　昼ねを　しています。 ごちそうを　作っておきましょう。	→	子どもが　昼ねを　している　間に、 ごちそうを　作っておきましょう。
4.	京都を　けんぶつしています。 日本の　でんとうを　味わって ください。	→	京都を　けんぶつしている　間に、日本の でんとうを　味わってください。
5.	おとうとが　電話を　かけています。 ぼくは　パンクを　なおしました。	→	おとうとが　電話を　かけている　間に、 ぼくは　パンクを　なおしました。
6.	あなたが　おさらを　洗います。 わたしは　ガラスを　みがきます。	→	あなたが　おさらを　洗う　間に、 わたしは　ガラスを　みがきます。
7.	かないが　着物に　着かえています。 客(きゃく)が　来てしまいました。	→	かないが　着物に　着かえている　間に、 客(きゃく)が　来てしまいました。

7.7.6 Transformation Drill

1. 高校で　教えました。
   やめました。 → 高校で　教えるのを　やめました。
2. ははが　ごちそうを　作りました。
   手つだいました。 → ははが　ごちそうを　作るのを　手つだいました。
3. ジョージさんが　あるいていました。
   見ましたよ。 → ジョージさんが　あるいているのを　見ましたよ。
4. たばこを　すいます。
   やめてください。 → たばこを　すうのを　やめてください。
5. 辞(じ)書を　持って来ます。
   わすれてしまいました。 → 辞(じ)書を　持って来るのを　わすれてしまいました。
6. パンクを　なおします。
   手つだってください。 → パンクを　なおすのを　手つだってください。
7. ハワードさんは　毎日　くすりを　のみます。
   やめたそうです。 → ハワードさんは　毎日　くすりを　のむのを　やめたそうです。

7.7.7 Substitution Drill

いなかへ　帰る　前、東京に　住んでいました。

1. 小学校を　卒業(そつぎょう)する …… 小学校を　卒業(そつぎょう)する　前、東京に　住んでいました。
2. 子どもが　生まれる …… 子どもが　生まれる　前、東京に　住んでいました。
3. オレゴン州に　行く …… オレゴン州に　行く　前、東京に　住んでいました。
4. 高校の　教師(し)に　なる …… 高校の　教師(し)に　なる　前、東京に　住んでいました。
5. けっこんする …… けっこんする　前、東京に　住んでいました。
6. この　しごとを　はじめる …… この　しごとを　はじめる　前、東京に　住んでいました。
7. 大阪(さか)へ　来る …… 大阪(さか)へ　来る　前、東京に　住んでいました。
8. アメリカへ　留(りゅう)学する …… アメリカへ　留(りゅう)学する　前、東京に　住んでいました。

7.7.8 Substitution Drill

しばらくの　間、カリフォルニアに　いました。

1. 十五年の　間 …… 十五年の　間、カリフォルニアに　いました。
2. 子どもが　中学生の　間 …… 子どもが　中学生の　間、カリフォルニアに　いました。
3. 長い　間 …… 長い　間、カリフォルニアに　いました。
4. あにが　銀(ぎん)行に　つとめていた　間 …… あにが　銀(ぎん)行に　つとめていた　間、カリフォルニアに　いました。
5. しばらくの　間 …… しばらくの　間、カリフォルニアに　いました。
6. むすこが　小さかった　間 …… むすこが　小さかった　間、カリフォルニアに　いました。
7. 夏休みの　間 …… 夏休みの　間、カリフォルニアに　いました。
8. 冬の　間 …… 冬の　間、カリフォルニアに　いました。

7.7.9 Substitution Drill

アメリカへ　帰ってから、大学院に　入りたいんです。

1. 日本へ　行く …… 日本へ　行ってから、大学院に　入りたいんです。
2. もっと　勉強する …… もっと　勉強してから、大学院に　入りたいんです。
3. 日本語が　じょうずに　なる …… 日本語が　じょうずに　なってから、大学院に　入りたいんです。
4. かいしゃを　やめる …… かいしゃを　やめてから、大学院に　入りたいんです。
5. 元(げん)気に　なる …… 元(げん)気に　なってから、大学院に　入りたいんです。
6. いろいろな　けいけんを　する …… いろいろな　けいけんを　してから、大学院に　入りたいんです。
7. すこし　働く …… すこし　働いてから、大学院に　入りたいんです。

7.7.10 Substitution Drill

七か月前に　日本へ　来たそうです。

1. 二か月 …… 二か月前に　日本へ　来たそうです。
2. 一年半 …… 一年半前に　日本へ　来たそうです。
3. 十五日 …… 十五日前に　日本へ　来たそうです。

4. 三日 …… 三日前に　日本へ　来たそうです。
5. 二週間 …… 二週間前に　日本へ　来たそうです。
6. 八週間ぐらい …… 八週間ぐらい前に　日本へ　来たそうです。
7. 十時間ほど …… 十時間ほど前に　日本へ　来たそうです。
8. 三十分ぐらい …… 三十分ぐらい前に　日本へ　来たそうです。

7.7.11 E-J Response Drill

1. いつ　日本に　きょうみを　持ちはじめましたか。
   - since I came to Japan …… 日本へ　来てから、日本に　きょうみを　持ちはじめました。
   - while I was in a graduate school …… 大学院に　いる　間に、日本に　きょうみを　持ちはじめました。
2. いつ　大学に　入ったんですか。
   - after coming to New York …… ニューヨークへ　来てから、大学に　入ったんです。
   - soon after graduating high school …… 高校を　卒業してから、すぐ　大学に　入ったんです。
3. いつ　高校を　卒業したんですか。
   - about eight months ago …… 八か月ほど前に　高校を　卒業したんです。
   - two years ago …… 二年前に　高校を　卒業したんです。
4. いつ　オレゴン州に　住んでいたんですか。
   - before my younger sister was born …… いもうとが　生まれる　前、オレゴン州に　住んでいたんです。
   - when I was five …… わたしが　五つの　時、オレゴン州に　住んでいたんです。
5. いつ　この　ざっしを　読んでしまったんですか。
   - while you were taking a nap …… あなたが　昼ねしている　間に、この　ざっしを　読んでしまったんです。
   - during the winter vacation …… 冬休みの　間に、この　ざっしを　読んでしまったんです。
6. いつ　長崎へ　行くつもりですか。
   - when Mr. Watanabe returns to his hometown …… 渡辺さんが　国へ　帰る　時、長崎へ　行くつもりです。
   - before I go home …… 国へ　帰る　前に、長崎へ　行くつもりです。

7. いつ　この　くすりを　のむんですか。

after having a meal …… ごはんを　食べてから、その　くすりを　のむんです。

before you go to bed …… ねる　前に、その　くすりを　のむんです。

7.8 EXERCISES

7.8.1 Insert an appropriate word into each blank and give the English equivalent for each sentence:

1. ハワードさんは　日本へ　来て ________、ちょうど　三年に　なるそうです。
2. 大学院に　いる ________に、一度　日本へ　行ってみたいと　思っています。
3. 高校を　卒業(そつぎょう)する ________、一年間　留学(りゅう)したいんです。
4. おんがくを　聞き ________、自動車を　運転(うんてん)する　人が　多いです。
5. テレビを　一時間ほど　見て ________、勉強しはじめます。
6. 来月　日光(にっこう)へ　行く ________は、車で　行くつもりです。
7. あるき ________、食べては　いけませんよ。

7.8.2 日本語で　書いてください。

1. Before I return to the United States next year, I intend to go to Nagasaki with Mr. Kobayashi.
2. While I was in Kyōto, I met an American who was born in Kyōto.
3. Please don't watch television while you are eating dinner.
4. After having finished elementary school in Ōsaka, I entered a junior high school in Hokkaidō.
5. I understand that my family was living in California when I was born.
6. I forgot to make a packed lunch. Therefore, I gave up going to a picnic.

7.8.3 日本語で　こたえてください。

1. あなたは　高校を　卒業(そつぎょう)してから、すぐ　働きはじめたんですか。
2. 今　働きながら、学校へ　来ていますか。
3. この　大学に　入ってから、どのぐらいに　なりますか。
4. 今　何に　一番　きょうみを　持っていますか。
5. いつごろ　日本語に　きょうみを　持ちはじめましたか。
6. 大学で　日本語を　習う　前、日本語を　習ったことが　ありますか。(どこで習ったんですか。)
7. 卒業(そつぎょう)する　前に、どんな　ことを　してみたいですか。
8. 夏休みや　冬休みの　間に、どんな　所へ　行ってみたいですか。

7.8.4 Connect each of the A-group expressions with appropriate B-group expressions:

A	B
1. 原(はら)さんは　大学を　やめてから、	a. コーヒーを　のまないでください。
2. 宿(しゅく)題を　する　前に、	b. くすり屋を　していました。
3. 池(いけ)田さんは　日本語を　教えながら、	c. もう　知っていましたよ。
4. わたしが　るすの　間に、	d. 教科(か)書を　よく　読んでください。
5. あなたから　聞く　前に、	e. 大学院へ　行っています。
6. あるきながら、	f. 何を　しているんですか。
7. ぼくは　子どもの　時、	g. 着物を　着ませんでした。
	h. 客(きゃく)が　来たそうです。

7.8.5 Choose one of the three phrases or clauses given in the parentheses to make a complete sentence:

1. 国へ　{帰る　間に、／帰りながら、／帰る　前に、}　ぜひ　ぼくの　かぞくに　あってください。

2. わたしが　夏休みに　いなかへ　{行く　時に、／行って　時に、／行く　間に、}　あなたも　いっしょに　いらっしゃいませんか。

3. 漢字は　{書くながら、／書いてながら、／書きながら、}　おぼえる　ほうが　おぼえやすいと　思います。

4. 大学を　{卒業(そつぎょう)して　時、／卒業(そつぎょう)前に、／卒業(そつぎょう)してから、}　一度　日本へ　行くつもりです。

5. わたしは　友だちと　{話しながら、／話す　時、／話す　間、}　コーヒーを　五はいも　のんで　しまいました。

6. いもうとが　{およぐ　時に、／およいでいる　間に、／およぎながら、}　わたしは　本を　一さつ　読み　おわりました。

7.8.6 Write the following underlined *hiragana* in *kan'ji:*

1. <u>だいがくいん</u>を　卒業(そつぎょう)してから、<u>なが</u>い　<u>あいだ</u>　<u>こうこう</u>で　<u>れきし</u>を　<u>おし</u>えています。

2. あなたは　ふゆやすみや　なつやすみに　いなかへ　かえりますか。
3. ぼくは　カリフォルニアしゅうで　うまれました。
4. どうぞ　はいってください。
5. でんとう的(てき)な　お正(しょう)がつを　あじわいたいです。

7.8.7 Distinguish the following *kan'ji*:

1. 史、中　　2. 口、味　　3. 川、州

7.8.8 Make the following utterances more appropriate by using softening expressions such as *sorosoro, chotto, kedo, anoo, saa, doomo, kochira, hodo,* etc.

1. Aoki: Moo kaerimasen ka?
   Satō: Matte kudasai.
   Aoki: Watashi no hoo wa owarimashita yo.
   Satō: Watashi mo jippun de owarimasu.
2. Kimura: Kono hen ni Hayashi san no otaku ga arimasu ka?
   Nakajima: Yoku wakarimasen.
   ....
   Kimura: Hayashi san no otaku wa koko desu ka?
   Hayashi: Ee, soo desu.

7.8.9 Rewrite the Dialog of Lesson 7 and make every utterance more indirect.

7.9 SITUATIONAL AND APPLICATION CONVERSATION

7.9.1 Mr. Brown asks Mr. Takagi what he has been doing since finishing high school.
Mr. Takagi says he worked at a department store for one year after he graduated from high school, then entered a college. He says he is still working at a friend's office at night while attending college.
Mr. Brown asks Mr. Takagi what he is going to major in.
Mr. Takagi answers he wants to study American literature.
Mr. Brown asks if Mr. Takagi wants to go to the United States.
Mr. Takagi says he wants to visit the United States after graduating from college.
Mr. Brown says while he is in Japan, he wants to see as many places as possible. And he wants to see Kyōto before he returns to the United States next year.

7.9.2 Ask one of your classmates where he was born, where and when he finished elementary school, junior high school, and so forth. Ask what his future plan is also.

7.9.3 Bill: Amerika e kite kara, moo ikkagetsu ni narimasu nee.
Hayashi: Ee, ikkagetsu kurai ni narimasu.

Bill: Itsumo yoku jogin'gu o shite imasu nee.

Hayashi: Ee. Nihon de wa amari shinakatta n desu ga, kotchi e kite kara wa mainichi desu. Michi ga hiroi kara, yariyasui n desu.

7.9.4 Yoshiko: Nihon e iku soo desu ne.

Betty: Ee, ichinen ryuugaku suru n desu.

Yoshiko: Sore wa yokatta desu ne. Nihon no koto o yoku ben'kyoo shite kudasai.

Betty: Dekireba, hoomu sutei (=home stay) shitai n desu kedo.

Yoshiko: Soo. Hoomu sutei sureba, nihon'jin no seikatsu o ajiwau koto ga dekimasu kara ne.

7.9.5 Jane: Keiko san, watashi wa rainen no natsu nikagetsu Amerika e kaeru n desu kedo, issho ni kimasen ka?

Keiko: Watashi mo ichido itte mitai to omotte iru n desu kedo. . . .

LESSON 8

日本の 家[1]

8.1 PRESENTATION

でんとう的(てき)な 日本の 家は おもに 木や 紙で[2] できていて[3]、 ゆかには たたみが あります。

しかし、 さいきんの 家[4]の なかには、 コンクリートや 鉄や アルミなどを 使って できているのも かなり あります。 また、日本間と 洋間の りょう方を 持つ 家が どんどん ふえています。

8.2 DIALOG

—— 青木さんの 家の げんかんで ——

おくさん 「まあ[5]、 ホールさん、 どうぞ おあがりください[6]。」

ホール 「おじゃまします[7]。 きのう ご主人[8]が、 家を 新しく たてたから、 見せると おっしゃいました[9]ので、 うかがいました。」

おくさん 「ええ、 お待ちしていました。 どうぞ こちら[10]へ。」

ホール 「ここは 広くて[11]、 あかるくて[11]、 りっぱな へやですねえ。 十じょう[12]ですか。」

おくさん 「ええ、 客間に[13] 使っています。 前に 住んでいた 家が くらくて[11]、 いやだったので、 できるだけ あかるくしたんです。」

ホール 「たたみも しょうじも 新しくて[11]、 本当に 気持ちが いいですね。 おたくは 洋間も あるんですか。」

おくさん 「ええ、 居間(いま)と 子どもべやが 洋間で[14]、 ほかは 日本間に しました。」

ホール 「おふろも 日本風ですか。」

おくさん 「ええ、 木の[2] おふろなんです。 きたなくしていますけど、 あとで 台所(だいどころ)や おふろ場(ば)へも 行って[3]、 見てください。 ちょっと しつれい。 主人を よんで 来ます[15]。」

木(き) 鉄(てつ) 日本間(にほんま) 洋間(ようま) 青木(あおき) ご主人(しゅじん) 広(ひろ)くて 客間(きゃくま) 本当(ほんとう) 日本風(にほんふう)

8.3 PATTERN SENTENCES

8.3.1

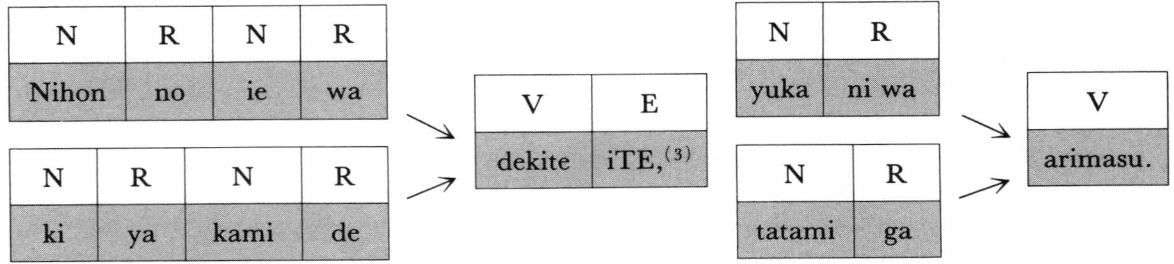

8.3.2

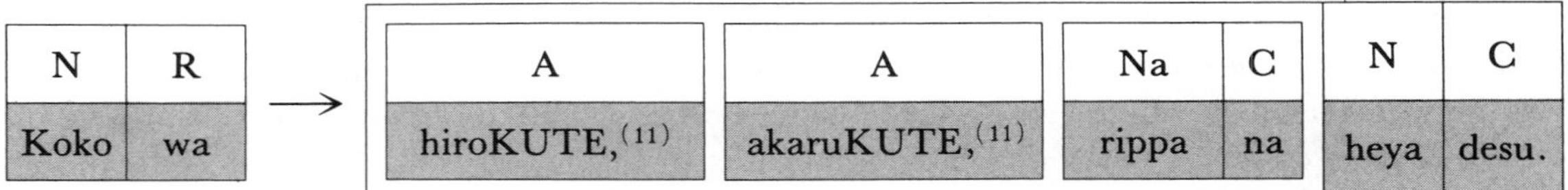

8.3.3

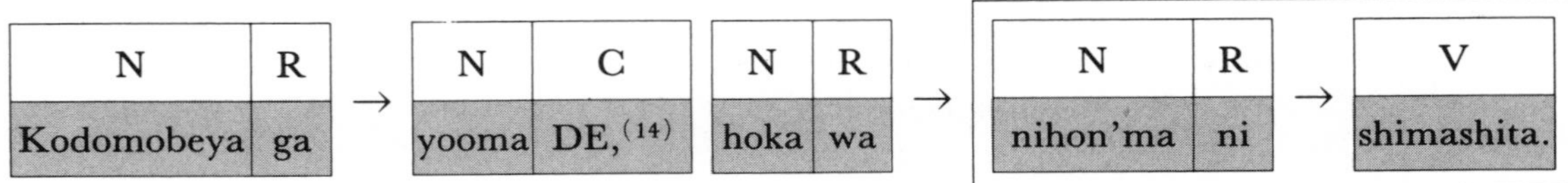

8.4 NOTES

8.4.1 Traditional Japanese-style Houses

Simplicity and elegance constitute the two main characteristics of traditional Japanese houses. The raw materials used, the wall, its open structure, the *tatami*, the interior decor, the roof, and the outer walls are some of the factors contributing to the unique Japanese architecture that structurally borders on the primitive, and yet achieves a highly refined beauty of form.

The basic framework of the house consists of the foundation, pillars and beams, and the rafters to support the roof. Not until the middle of the nineteenth century did any material other than wood begin to be used in construction. The abundant supply of timber coupled with the frequency of earthquakes necessitated a flexible structure. Thus, houses were nearly always built out of wood, showing harmony with nature, or forming a part of nature.

In European homes, sturdiness is a quality of beauty and thus often the thickness of walls is displayed. In Japan, however, the thickness of the walls is hidden, usually by being enclosed on both sides by wooden pillars, such that the two-dimensional effect is intensified. This type of beauty—that of a two-dimensional plane surface, and the beauty of the natural grain of the wood used—is one of the basic characteristics of Japanese homes constituting their style of beauty.

A characteristic uniqueness of the Japanese style of beauty in homes is the open structure—due in part to the high temperatures and humidity in Japan in summer as well as the heavy rains. The *shooji* separates the exterior from the interior of the house, and the *fusuma* separates rooms in the traditional Japanese house. The *shooji* and *fusuma* are sliding doors made of a wooden frame, with wooden strips that crisscross, upon which a special type of Japanese rice paper is pasted. The difference between them is that the latter is much thicker, using many layers of special Japanese paper which is either left plain, or painted over in a design or with a poem.

Tatami mats are made of straw that has been sewn together with linen thread to form a thickness of about 6 centimeters, a length of 180 centimeters, and a width of about 90 centimeters. These cover almost the entire floor area of the Japanese home and are used as a unit in measuring the size of a room. Thus in the dialog, Mr. Hall asks Mrs. Sasaki if it is a ten-*tatami* room.

Zabuton, or cushions, are placed upon the *tatami* for people to sit on, and at night *futon* are taken out of the *oshiire* (closet) to serve as beds. *Futon* are filled with cotton. Thus, since *zabuton* and *futon* serve the functions of furniture and can be stored away in the *oshiire* when not in use, the traditional Japanese house will have an absence of the furniture that the Westerner deems necessary. Indeed, the very few massive objects in the various rooms enhance the simple elegance of the Japanese home as well as the natural beauty of the raw materials used in construction.

The interior decoration echoes this sentiment toward simplicity. To have a house filled with furniture and decorations has been, in the past, considered bad taste. In the guest room there is a special alcove, or *tokonoma*, where a scroll or a flower arrangement is discreetly displayed.

On the exterior of the house, the beauty is a natural one. The roof is slanted at an angle of forty-five degrees or more, the best suitable for a climate of heavy rainfall. The deep eaves of the roof are characteristic of a traditional Japanese house.

8.4.2 *Ki ya kami de dekite iru* means "(traditional Japanese houses) are made from wood, paper, and so on." The *de* in this sentence is the Relational to show the preceding Noun is "material" of which or from which something is made, and is usually used with Verbs such as *tsukuru* "make," *dekite iru* "is made." To state that something is made of or made from something else, ~*de dekite iru* is often used.

ki	木				wood"
ishi	石				stone"
kon'kuriito	コンクリート				concrete"
kami	紙				paper"
take	竹				bamboo"
tetsu	鉄	de	tsukuru	"make of	iron"
kin	金		dekite iru	"is made from	gold"
gin	銀				silver"
purasuchikku	プラスチック				plastic"
biniiru	ビニール				vinyl"
kawa	かわ				leather"

Kono okashi wa nan de dekite imasu ka? — "What are these cookies made of?"

Shooji wa ki to kami de dekite imasu. — "*Shōji* is made from wood and paper."

Hako wa ki de tsukurimashoo ka, kami de tsukurimashoo ka? — "Shall I make a box with wood or with paper?"

Kono kaban wa kawa de dekite ite, takakatta desu. — "This bag is made of leather and was expensive."

In lieu of ~*de dekite iru*, the Japanese use *no* to indicate the "material" of which or from which something is made.

ki no ofuro — "wooden bathtub"
kon'kuriito no apaato — "concrete apartment building"

8.4.3 *Nihon no ie wa omo ni ki ya kami de dekite ite, yuka ni wa tatami ga arimasu* means "Japanese houses are made mainly from wood and paper and there are *tatami* on the floor." This TE form of a Verb or a Verb plus an Extender may be used as a nonfinal Predicate before a comma. This use of the TE form as a nonfinal clause carries one of the following meanings or functions in this lesson. Other meanings of the *-te* clause will be explained later.

(Predicate Modifier) + Verb(*-te*), . . .

1. Sequential action. In this case, the subject of the nonfinal clause and that of the final clause are identical. Since two or more actions are sequential, the change of the order of the Predicates stating actions affects the meaning of the whole sentence or is impossible. The whole sentence is similar to "one does something, then he does something else."

Gin'za e ikimashita. Sore kara, Gin'za de shokuji o shimashita.	⟶	Gin'za e itte, shokuji o shimashita. "I went to the Ginza and had a meal there."

2. Parallel action. The subject of the nonfinal clause and that of the final clause may be identical or different. Two or more actions are merely collected and combined, and the change of the order of those actions does not affect the meaning of the whole sentence.

Watakushi wa Gin'za e ikimashita. Kobayashi san wa uchi e kaerimashita.	⟶	Watakushi wa Gin'za e itte, Kobayashi san wa uchi e kaerimashita. "I went to the Ginza and Mr. Kobayashi went home."

3. Causal relationship. The nonfinal clause constitutes the reason for the final clause. The TE form in this use can substitute for the reason clause . . . *kara* or *node*. However, not all the *kara* or *node* clauses can be replaced by *-te* clauses. When the final clause connotes "suggestion" or "request," the reason clause should not be the *-te* clause. The final Predicate with the *-te* clause may be any kind, but the following are used frequently: *ureshii* "is glad," *taihen da* "is troublesome," *odoroku* "is surprised," and so on. The subject of the nonfinal clause and that of the final clause may be identical or different.

Ame ga futta node, gorufu ni iku no o yamemashita.	⟶	Ame ga futte, gorufu ni iku no o yamemashita. "It having rained, I quit going golfing."
Yasumi ni natta node, ureshii desu.	⟶	Yasumi ni natte, ureshii desu. "It is a vacation. I am happy."

The tense and form of the nonfinal clause *-te* are always governed by those of the final clause, and more than one *-te* clause can be used.

Tomodachi o eki made mukae ni itte, uchi e tsurete kimashita.	"I went to the station to see a friend of mine and took him home."
Kibun ga warui node, kusuri o non'de, sugu nemasu.	"Since I don't feel well, I'll take medicine and then go to bed soon."
Ichijikan gurai hirune o shite, kaimono ni ikimashita.	"I took a nap for about an hour, and went shopping."
Ofuro ni haitte, atama o araimashita.	"I took a bath and washed my hair."
Kodomobeya o hiroku shite, ima o semaku shimashoo ka?	"Shall we enlarge the children's room and make the living room smaller?"

Sono toki haha wa daidokoro ni ite, watashi wa gen'kan ni imashita.	"At that time my mother was in the kitchen and I was in the entrance."
Kuruma ga kowarete ite, tsukau koto ga dekinai n desu.	"The car is broken, and I can't use it."
Sore o kiite, odorokimashita.	"I was surprised to hear that."
Kodomo ga umarete, totemo ureshikatta desu.	"I was very glad to have a child."
Hiroi niwa ga atte, shizuka na ie ni sumitai desu.	"I want to live in a house which has a large yard and is quiet."

8.4.4 *Saikin no Ie*—Cultural Pluralism

In contemporary Japanese housing, we again find the coexistence of diverse forms in complementary fashion. There are Japanese-style wooden houses as well as Western-style concrete, stone, and steel houses. Normally many middle- and upper-middle-class families live in houses which are a combination of the two styles. For instance bedrooms are in Japanese style while living rooms and guest rooms are Western with some modifications. Similarly, there may be both Japanese- and Western-style bathrooms in such houses. *Furoba* is translated as "bathroom" and is literally that. Used only for bathing, *furoba* may contain a Western-style bath, shower, or an *ofuro*. Occasionally a sink will also be found, but usually not a toilet. This is due to the Japanese concept of cleanliness, which excludes the placing of both toilet and bath together in one room.

What Americans call "bathroom" is referred to as *otearai* (hand washing) or *ben'jo* (convenient place) or *(o)toire*. Thus, the Japanese have two rooms for the functions which are contained in one American bathroom, as the following chart illustrates:

	bathroom	furoba	otearai
toilet	+	−	+
wash basin	+	−	+
shower	+	−/+	−
tub	+	+	−

Other terms for *otearai* are *gofujoo* (unclean place), and *sen'men'jo* (face washing place). The Japanese tend to avoid direct reference to the toilet.

8.4.5 *Maa* is heard primarily in the speech of women, and is used in much the same way as the English expression "Oh!" indicating surprise. A Japanese male would be more likely to use the expression *a*, or *aa*. Aoki's use of *maa* immediately indicates that Aoki is a woman, an assumption which is confirmed later in the dialog when Hall refers to her husband.

8.4.6 *Oagari kudasai* is a polite expression meaning "Please step up." While *Ohairi kudasai* is used in the case of "entering a room from another room or entering a Western-style building," *Oagari kudasai* is used to urge someone to step up into a Japanese-style house, usually taking off his shoes. When you have a visitor outside the porch door of your Japanese-style house, you may say

Ohairi kudasai first and then *Oagari kudasai* if you want to accept the visitor in the room. *Agaru* is a Verb meaning "step up," "go up," or "rise."

The difference between *Oagari kudasai* and *Ohairi kudasai* lies in a very concrete matter, namely, the construction of a house. *Oagari kudasai* means "please come up." Houses with *tatami*-covered floors, which can be a foot or more higher than the ground, are usually entered by stepping up into the room after removing shoes in the *gen'kan*, an area just inside the front door where shoes are removed. *Ohairi kudasai*, on the other hand, may be used to invite a person to come through the main gate to a house or to enter a house constructed in such a way that floors are even with the ground. *Ohairi kudasai*, then, simply means "please enter." *Oagari kudasai* is used to invite persons who are close enough to enter the room (intimate friends, invited persons, those with whom the speaker wishes to talk for a long time, and so on). For example:

1. A: *Doozo oagari kudasai.*
   B: *Iie, koko de kekkoo desu.*
   "I shall talk to you from here."
2. C: *Doozo oagari kudasai.*
   D: *Jaa, (okotoba ni amaete) shitsurei shimasu.*
   "I'll come in," or "I'll come up."

8.4.7 *Ojama shimasu* is employed in thanking your host for inviting you into his home or room. It literally means "I'm going to disturb you," and implies modest gratitude. It exemplifies Japanese modesty and heteronomy. *Jama* means "bother" or "hindrance."

An alternative to *Ojama shimasu* is *Shitsurei shimasu*. As discussed above, *Ojama shimasu* is used when invited in and means "I'm going to disturb you." The literal translation of *Shitsurei shimasu* is "I'm going to lose etiquette." This implies that you might not be following proper etiquette. This is a very polite expression used when asked or invited into a room. When leaving the house, either expression may be used in the past tense form: *Ojama shimashita* or *Shitsurei shimashita*.

Ojama shimasu, however, seems to have a much narrower use when compared with *Shitsurei shimasu*. In a sense, *Ojama shimasu* is used when you are not a member of a group and have injected yourself into that group, whereas *Shitsurei shimasu* is not necessarily limited to such a situation.

Kon'ban ojama shite mo ii desu ka?	"May I visit you tonight?"
Ojama desu ka?	"Am I bothering you?"
Kono ookina hako wa jama da kara, atchi e motte itte kudasai.	"This big box is in the way, so please take it away."

8.4.8 The word *goshujin*, referring mainly to the second and third person's husband, is composed of the honorific prefix *go-* combined with *shujin*, which means "master." *Shujin* alone refers to one's own husband. The concept of the husband as the master of the house is not foreign to English-speaking cultures, but it is not so directly embodied in the language. Likewise, *okusan*, the wife of a person other than the speaker, means "the person deep inside the house," while *kanai*, used in referring to one's own wife, means "the one in the house." The different usages depending upon whom you are speaking to is another example of ingroupness affecting language behavior.

8.4.9 *Osshaimashita* is a polite Verb for *iimashita* and conjugates exactly like any other Consonant Verb such as *hairimasu* except the Stem form which is *osshai(masu)*. Notice the omission of *r* before *i*. *Kudasaimasu*, *irasshaimasu*, *nasaimasu*, and *gozaimasu* also omit *r* before *i*.

Dare ga soo itta n desu ka?	''Who said that?''
Sen'sei ga soo osshaimashita yo.	''The teacher said so.''

8.4.10 *Kochira*, *sochira*, *achira*, and *dochira* are polite equivalents of *kotchi*, *sotchi*, *atchi*, and *dotchi*. *Doozo kochira e* or *kochira e doozo* is an idiomatic polite expression and *kochira* is preferred to *kotchi*.

Kochira e doozo.	''Come this way, please.''
Kochira wa Kobayashi san desu.	''This is Mr. Kobayashi.''
Achira de wa ima juudoo ga sakan da soo desu ne?	''I understand that *jūdō* is popular in that place. Is that right?''

8.4.11 *Koko wa hirokute, akarukute, rippa na heya desu nee* means ''This is a large, well-lighted, and fine room.'' Like a Verb, the TE form of an Adjective may also be used, before a pause, as a nonfinal clause. The adjectival *-te* clause is usually used to indicate either the parallel relationship or the causal relationship of the two clauses. (See Note 8.4.3, nos. 2 and 3.)

The tense of the *-kute* clause is governed by that of the final Predicate.

(Predicate Modifier) + Adjective(-*kute*), . . .

Kono gen'kan wa hiroi desu. Kono gen'kan wa akarui desu.	→ Kono gen'kan wa hirokute, akarui desu. ''This entrance is large and well lighted.''
Kono gen'kan wa akarui desu. Dakara, suki desu.	→ Kono gen'kan wa akarukute, suki desu. ''This entrance is well lighted, so I like it.''
Kono heya wa kurakute, kirei ja arimasen.	''This room is dark and unclean.''
Daidokoro ga hirokute, tsukaiyasui desu.	''The kitchen is large and easy to use.''
Yasukute, oishii mise o shitte imasu ka?	''Do you know a restaurant which serves inexpensive but delicious food?''
Ohanami wa hito ga ookute, taihen deshita.	''As there were many people viewing flowers, we had a hard time.''

8.4.12 *Juujoo* means ''room matted with ten *tatami*.'' The *-joo* is a counter used to count *tatami* and to indicate the size of a room. *Ichijoo* is about 6′×3′ in width. *Tatami*-matted rooms are often called *rokujoo*, *hachijoo*, *juujoo*, and *juunijoo*, depending on the size of those rooms.

Hachijoo e itte, ocha o nomimashoo.	''Let's go to the eight-mat room and have tea.''
Boku no heya wa yojoohan na node, semasugiru n desu.	''Since my room is a four-and-a-half *tatami*-matted room, it's too small.''

8.4.13 *Kyakuma ni tsukatte imasu* means ''We are using (this room) for a guest room.'' The Relational *ni* in this instance is used in the meaning of ''for'' or ''as,'' but Verbs used with this *ni* are limited to a few. The other expressions for ''as'' or ''for'' will be explained later.

Kono heya o jimusho ni tsukaimashoo.	''Let's use this room for an office.''
Kono hon o kyookasho ni tsukatte imasu.	''We are using this book for a textbook.''

8.4.14 *Ima to kodomobeya ga yooma de, hoka wa nihon'ma ni shimashita* means "The living room and children's room are Western-style rooms, and others are made in Japanese style." The TE form of the Copula may be used before a comma and forms a nonfinal clause. Like an adjectival clause, the clause ending in *de* is used either to state parallel fact or reason. The tense of a Noun plus *de* clause is governed by that of the final Predicate.

(Predicate Modifier) + Noun + *de*, . . .

Kochira ga Katoo san de, sochira wa Kobayashi san desu.	"This is Mr. Katō, and that is Mr. Kobayashi."
Boku wa daigakuin no gakusei de, otooto wa daigakusei desu.	"I am a graduate student, and my younger brother is a college student."
Nara no daibutsu wa in'shooteki de, subarashikatta desu.	"The great image of the Buddha in Nara was impressive and wonderful."
Ano resutoran wa wariai shizuka de, kirei deshita.	"That restaurant was comparatively quiet and pretty."
Kono daidokoro wa fuben de, iya desu.	"This kitchen is not handy, so I don't like it."
Sumisu san no nihon'go ga joozu de, odorokimashita.	"Mr. Smith is good at Japanese, and I was impressed."

8.4.15 *Shujin o yon'de kimasu* means "I will go for my husband." As expressed in Note 4.4.20 of Volume II, both *kimasu* and *ikimasu* may come after the TE form of a Verb. However, when the Japanese use *kimasu*, an English speaker would emphasize the going and then the action, while a Japanese speaker would express the action and then emphasize the coming back.

Shujin o yon'de kimasu.	"I shall go for my husband."
Ato de nomu mono o katte kimashoo.	"I'll go and buy drinks later."

8.5 VOCABULARY

Presentation

でんとう的(てき)	den'tooteki	......	Na	traditional
おもに	omo ni	......	Adv.	mainly
で	de	......	R	of or from (material) (see 8.4.2)
ゆか	yuka	......	N	floor
たたみ	tatami	......	N	straw mat; straw-matted floor
さいきん	saikin	......	N	recently; lately
コンクリート	kon'kuriito	......	N	concrete
鉄	tetsu	......	N	iron

アルミ	arumi	......	N	aluminum (*arumi* or *aruminyuumu*)
かなり	kanari	......	Adv.	considerably; pretty
また	mata	......	SI	also; in addition
日本間	nihon'ma	......	N	Japanese-style room
洋間	yooma	......	N	Western-style room

Dialog

げんかん	gen'kan	......	N	entrance; front door; vestibule
まあ	maa	......	SI	oh; my (used only by women) (see 8.4.5)
ホール	Hooru	......	N	Hall
おあがりください。	Oagari kudasai.	......	(exp.)	Please come up into the house. (see 8.4.6)
あがる	agaru	......	V	step up; go up; rise (see 8.4.6)
おじゃまします。	Ojama shimasu.	......	(exp.)	I am bothering you. (see 8.4.7)
じゃま	jama	......	Na	bother; hindrance (see 8.4.7)
たてた	tateta	......	V	built (TA form of *tateru*)
おっしゃいました	osshaimashita	......	V	TA form of *ossharu* (polite equivalent of *iu* – say) (see 8.4.9)
お待ちしていました。	Omachi shite imashita.	......	(exp.)	I have been waiting for your visit.
こちら	kochira	......	N	this way; this side (see 8.4.10)
広くて	hirokute	......	A	TE form of *hiroi* – is spacious (see 8.4.11)
あかるくて	akarukute	......	A	TE form of *akarui* – is light; is well lighted; is bright (see 8.4.11)
十じょう	juujoo	......	N	(room with) ten *tatami* mats (see 8.4.12)
客間	kyakuma	......	N	parlor; guest room
に	ni	......	R	for; as (see 8.4.13)
くらくて	kurakute	......	A	TE form of *kurai* – is dark
いや	iya	......	Na	unpleasant; do not like
しょうじ	shooji	......	N	paper door
気持ち	kimochi	......	N	feeling; mood (〜 *ga ii* "feel good," 〜 *ga warui* "feel bad")
居間(い)	ima	......	N	living room (cf. *kyakuma*)
子どもべや	kodomobeya	......	N	room for children
(お)ふろ	(o)furo	......	N	bath; bathtub (*furo ni hairu* "take a bath")
台所(だいどころ)	daidokoro	......	N	kitchen
(お)ふろ場(ば)	(o)furoba	......	N	bathroom

Notes

竹	take	......	N	bamboo
金	kin	......	N	gold
銀	gin	......	N	silver
プラスチック	purasuchikku	......	N	plastic
ビニール	biniiru	......	N	vinyl
かわ	kawa	......	N	leather
かばん	kaban	......	N	bag; suitcase; briefcase
そちら	sochira	......	N	that way; that side
あちら	achira	......	N	that way; that side
じょう	-joo	......	Nd	counter for *tatami* (see 8.4.12)

8.6 KAN'JI

8.6.a 木 (4.6.9, Vol. II) (1) *ki* (5) 木のはこ、木村(むら)、青木(あお)さん

8.6.1 鉄 (1) TETSU (2) iron; steel (3) classifier 金 [metal]
(4) [金] [金] [金] [金] [金] [鉄] (5) 地下(ちか)鉄、国鉄 [Japan National Railway]

8.6.b 間 (7.6.3, Vol. II) (1) *ma* (5) 居(い)間、客(きゃく)間、日本間、洋間

8.6.2 青 (1) *ao(i)* (2) blue (3) classifier 主 (青) (4) [一] [十] [丰] [主] [青]
(5) 青い空(そら) [blue sky]、青木

8.6.3 主 (1) SHU (2) main; head (3) classifier 亠 (丶)
(4) [丶] [亠] [亍] [丰] [主] (5) 主人、女主人、店(てん)主 [store owner]

8.6.4 広 (1) *hiro(i)* (2) wide; spacious (3) classifier 广 [house under the roof]
(4) [丶] [亠] [广] [広] [広] (5) 広いみち、広島(しま) [name of a city]

8.6.5 客 (1) KYAKU (2) guest; passenger; customer; visitor (3) classifier 宀
(4) [宀] [宀] [㝉] [客] [客] (5) 客間、客車、お客様(さま)

8.6.6 当 (1) TOO (2) hit; guess; apply (3) classifier 小 (⺌)
(4) [丨] [丨丶] [⺌] [当] [当] [当] (5) 本当、てき当、べん当

8.6.7 風 (1) FUU (2) style; way; wind (3) classifier 几 (風)
(4) 丿 几 几 凧 凧 風 風
(5) 洋風、アメリカ風、むかし風、東洋風、いなか風、フランス風、台風 [typhoon] (6) homonym 諷

8.6.8 竹* (1) *take* (2) bamboo (3) forms the classifier 竹
(4) ノ 𠂉 𠂉 ⺮ ⺮ 竹 (5) 竹、竹の子 [bamboo shoot]

8.6.9 銀* (1) GIN (2) silver (3) classifier 金 (4) 金 釒 釗 釘 鉬 銀 銀
(5) 銀行、日銀 [Bank of Japan]、銀座

8.6.10 会* (1) *a(imasu); a(u)* (2) meet (3) classifier 人 [human being]
(4) ノ 人 亼 亼 会 会 (5) 先生に会います、駅で会いましょう

8.7 DRILLS

8.7.1 **Transformation Drill** (sequential)

1. きのう　ご主人に　会いました。うちを　たてたと　聞きました。	→	きのう　ご主人に　会って、うちを　たてたと　聞きました。
2. オレゴン州へ　行きました。すぐ　いもうとが　生まれました。	→	オレゴン州へ　行って、すぐ　いもうとが　生まれました。
3. きょ年　中学校の　教師を　やめました。今　大学院に　行っています。	→	きょ年　中学校の　教師を　やめて、今　大学院に　行っています。
4. くすりを　のんだ　ほうが　いいですよ。すぐ　ねた　ほうが　いいですよ。	→	くすりを　のんで、すぐ　ねた　ほうが　いいですよ。
5. 一時間ほど　昼ねするつもりです。勉強を　はじめるつもりです。	→	一時間ほど　昼ねして、勉強を　はじめるつもりです。
6. 長崎の　高校を　卒業しました。こちらへ　来たんです。	→	長崎の　高校を　卒業して、こちらへ　来たんです。
7. もっと　図書館で　しらべます。レポートを　書きます。	→	もっと　図書館で　しらべて、レポートを　書きます。
8. くつを　ぬいでください。あがってください。	→	くつを　ぬいで、あがってください。

8.7.2 Transformation Drill (parallel)

1. 青木さんは　ホテルに　とまったそうです。ハワードさんは　旅館に　とまったそうです。
   → 青木さんは　ホテルに　とまって、ハワードさんは　旅館に　とまったそう　です。
2. クラークさんは　東洋史を　専攻(せんこう)しました。ぼくは　日本文学を　研究(けんきゅう)しました。
   → クラークさんは　東洋史を　専攻(せんこう)して、ぼくは　日本文学を　研究(けんきゅう)しました。
3. きょ年は　家を　たてました。きょ年は　新しい　自動車を　買いました。
   → きょ年は　家を　たてて、新しい　自動車を　買いました。
4. 十じょうを　客間に　使いましょう。六じょうを　子どもべやに　使いましょう。
   → 十じょうを　客間に　使って、六じょうを　子どもべやに　使いましょう。
5. 台所(だいどころ)を　あかるくするつもりです。ふろ場(ば)を　広くするつもりです。
   → 台所(だいどころ)を　あかるくして、ふろ場(ば)を　広く　するつもりです。
6. ことしは　おとうとが　大学に　入ります。ことしは　ぼくが　大学を　卒業(そつぎょう)します。
   → ことしは　おとうとが　大学に　入って、ぼくが　大学を　卒業(そつぎょう)します。
7. 居(い)間と　子どもべやを　洋間に　しました。ほかは　日本間に　しました。
   → 居(い)間と　子どもべやを　洋間に　して、ほかは　日本間に　しました。

8.7.3 Transformation Drill (reason)

1. 高木(ぎ)さんは　気持ちが　わるくなりました。高木(ぎ)さんは　うちへ　帰りました。
   → 高木(ぎ)さんは　気持ちが　わるくなって、うちへ　帰りました。
2. 子どもが　生まれました。うれしいです。
   → 子どもが　生まれて、うれしいです。
3. 奈良(なら)の　大きな　大仏(ぶつ)を　見ました。とても　おどろきました。
   → 奈良(なら)の　大きな　大仏(ぶつ)を　見て、とても　おどろきました。
4. さけを　のみすぎました。あたまが　いたくなってしまいました。
   → さけを　のみすぎて、あたまが　いたく　なってしまいました。

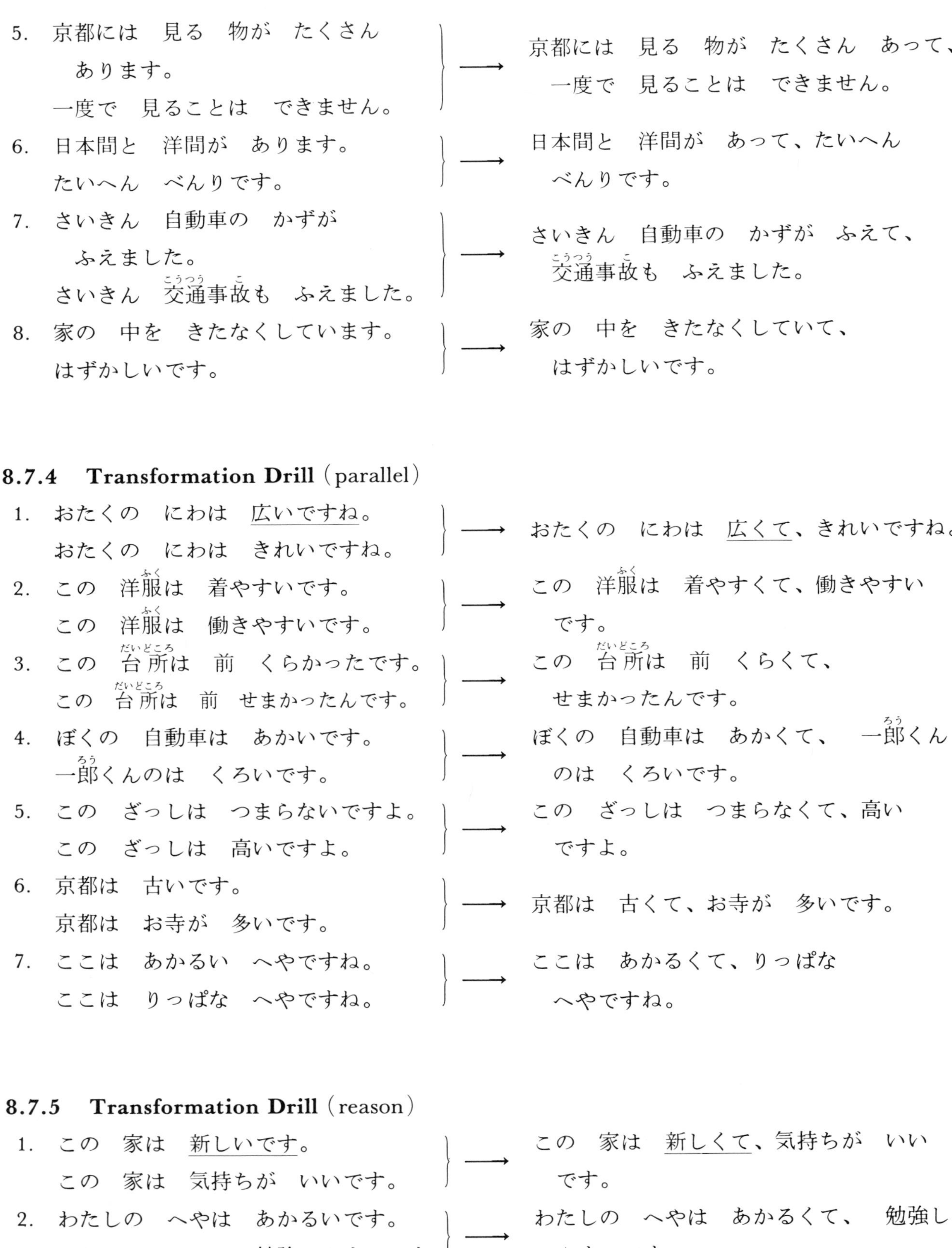

5. 京都には　見る　物が　たくさん ありります。 一度で　見ることは　できません。	⟶	京都には　見る　物が　たくさん　あって、 一度で　見ることは　できません。
6. 日本間と　洋間が　あります。 たいへん　べんりです。	⟶	日本間と　洋間が　あって、たいへん べんりです。
7. さいきん　自動車の　かずが ふえました。 さいきん　交通事故も　ふえました。	⟶	さいきん　自動車の　かずが　ふえて、 交通事故も　ふえました。
8. 家の　中を　きたなくしています。 はずかしいです。	⟶	家の　中を　きたなくしていて、 はずかしいです。

8.7.4 Transformation Drill (parallel)

1. おたくの　にわは　広いですね。 おたくの　にわは　きれいですね。	⟶	おたくの　にわは　広くて、きれいですね。
2. この　洋服は　着やすいです。 この　洋服は　働きやすいです。	⟶	この　洋服は　着やすくて、働きやすい です。
3. この　台所は　前　くらかったです。 この　台所は　前　せまかったんです。	⟶	この　台所は　前　くらくて、 せまかったんです。
4. ぼくの　自動車は　あかいです。 一郎くんのは　くろいです。	⟶	ぼくの　自動車は　あかくて、　一郎くん のは　くろいです。
5. この　ざっしは　つまらないですよ。 この　ざっしは　高いですよ。	⟶	この　ざっしは　つまらなくて、高い ですよ。
6. 京都は　古いです。 京都は　お寺が　多いです。	⟶	京都は　古くて、お寺が　多いです。
7. ここは　あかるい　へやですね。 ここは　りっぱな　へやですね。	⟶	ここは　あかるくて、りっぱな へやですね。

8.7.5 Transformation Drill (reason)

1. この　家は　新しいです。 この　家は　気持ちが　いいです。	⟶	この　家は　新しくて、気持ちが　いい です。
2. わたしの　へやは　あかるいです。 わたしの　へやは　勉強しやすいです。	⟶	わたしの　へやは　あかるくて、　勉強し やすいです。

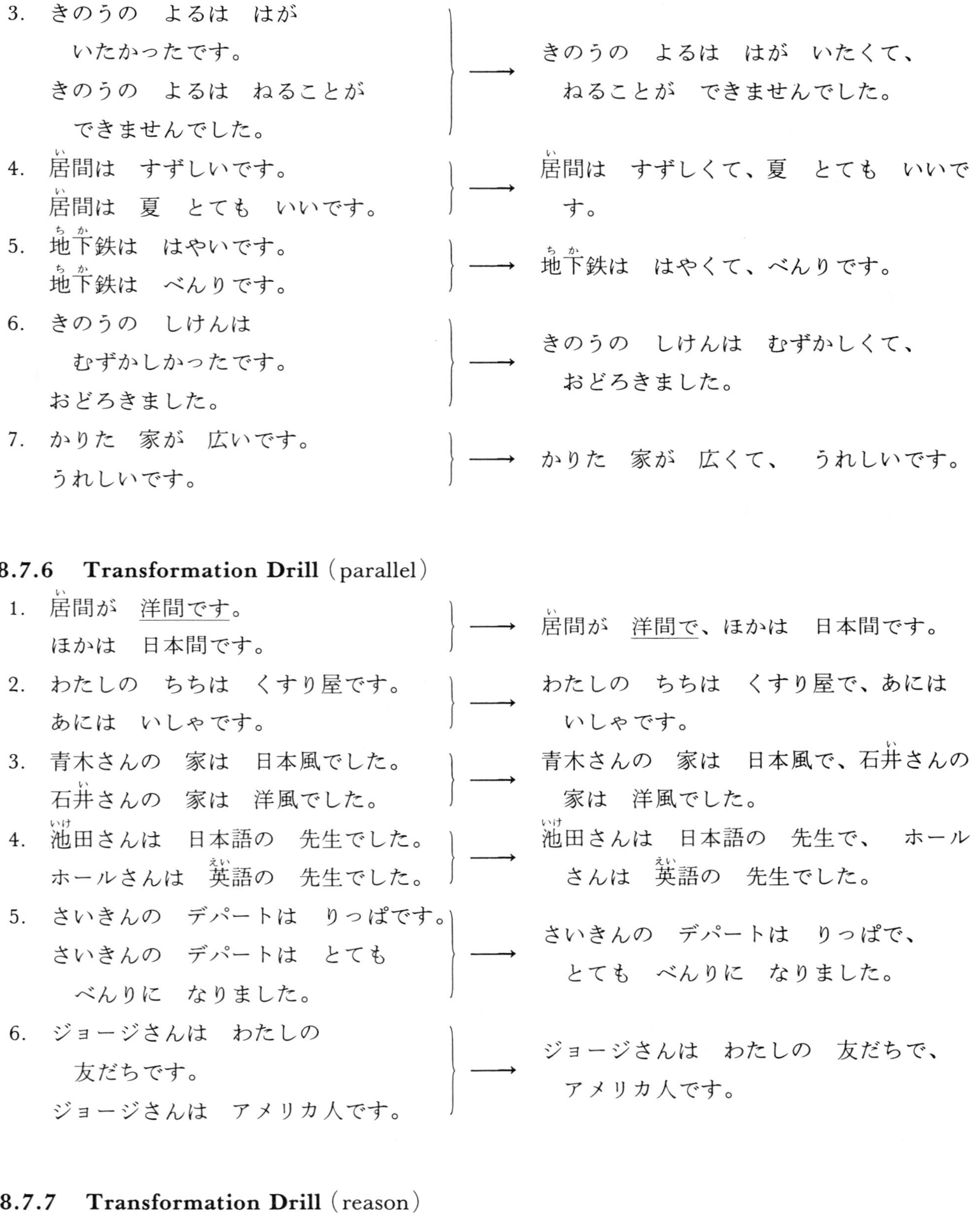

3. きのうの　よるは　はが　いたかったです。
きのうの　よるは　ねることが　できませんでした。
→ きのうの　よるは　はが　いたくて、ねることが　できませんでした。

4. 居間は　すずしいです。
居間は　夏　とても　いいです。
→ 居間は　すずしくて、夏　とても　いいです。

5. 地下鉄は　はやいです。
地下鉄は　べんりです。
→ 地下鉄は　はやくて、べんりです。

6. きのうの　しけんは　むずかしかったです。
おどろきました。
→ きのうの　しけんは　むずかしくて、おどろきました。

7. かりた　家が　広いです。
うれしいです。
→ かりた　家が　広くて、　うれしいです。

8.7.6　**Transformation Drill** (parallel)

1. 居間が　<u>洋間です</u>。
ほかは　日本間です。
→ 居間が　<u>洋間で</u>、ほかは　日本間です。

2. わたしの　ちちは　くすり屋です。
あには　いしゃです。
→ わたしの　ちちは　くすり屋で、あには　いしゃです。

3. 青木さんの　家は　日本風でした。
石井さんの　家は　洋風でした。
→ 青木さんの　家は　日本風で、石井さんの　家は　洋風でした。

4. 池田さんは　日本語の　先生でした。
ホールさんは　英語の　先生でした。
→ 池田さんは　日本語の　先生で、　ホールさんは　英語の　先生でした。

5. さいきんの　デパートは　りっぱです。
さいきんの　デパートは　とても　べんりに　なりました。
→ さいきんの　デパートは　りっぱで、とても　べんりに　なりました。

6. ジョージさんは　わたしの　友だちです。
ジョージさんは　アメリカ人です。
→ ジョージさんは　わたしの　友だちで、アメリカ人です。

8.7.7　**Transformation Drill** (reason)

1. これは　むずかしい　<u>字です</u>。
これは　おぼえにくいです。
→ これは　むずかしい　<u>字で</u>、おぼえにくいです。

2.	とても　ゆうめいな　先生です。 みんな　知っています。	→	とても　ゆうめいな　先生で、みんな 知っています。
3.	あの　セーターは　いろが いやでした。 あの　セーターは　買いませんでした。	→	あの　セーターは　いろが　いやで、 買いませんでした。
4.	これは　たいせつな　本です。 いつも　うちへ　持って帰ります。	→	これは　たいせつな　本で、いつも うちへ　持って帰ります。
5.	青木さんの　専攻（せんこう）は アメリカ文学です。 青木さんは　英（えい）語が　じょうずです。	→	青木さんの　専攻（せんこう）は　アメリカ文学で、 英（えい）語が　じょうずです。
6.	古い　車が　じゃまです。 きのう　うってしまいました。	→	古い　車が　じゃまで、きのう　うって しまいました。
7.	わたしは　お料理（りょうり）が　へたです。 はずかしいです。	→	わたしは　お料理（りょうり）が　へたで、 はずかしいです。

8.7.8 Substitution Drill

これは　木や　紙で　できているそうです。

1. コンクリートや　鉄　……　これは　コンクリートや　鉄で　できているそうです。
2. 金と　銀　……　これは　金と　銀で　できているそうです。
3. ガラス　……　これは　ガラスで　できているそうです。
4. やさいや　にくなど　……　これは　やさいや　にくなどで　できているそうです。
5. コンクリートか　石　……　これは　コンクリートか　石で　できているそうです。
6. アルミだけ　……　これは　アルミだけで　できているそうです。
7. 木と　竹の　りょう方　……　これは　木と　竹の　りょう方で　できているそうです。
8. プラスチック　……　これは　プラスチックで　できているそうです。
9. かわか　ビニール　……　これは　かわか　ビニールで　できているそうです。

8.7.9 Substitution Drill

ここを　客間に　使っています。

1. 居（い）間　……　ここを　居（い）間に　使っています。
2. 子どもべや　……　ここを　子どもべやに　使っています。
3. 客間　……　ここを　客間に　使っています。
4. 主人の　へや　……　ここを　主人の　へやに　使っています。
5. 事務（む）所　……　ここを　事務（む）所に　使っています。

6.　食堂　……　ここを　食堂に　使っています。

7.　入口　……　ここを　入口に　使っています。

8.7.10 Expansion Drill

1.　新しいですね。　……　新しいですね。
　たたみも　しょうじも　……　たたみも　しょうじも　新しいですね。
　広くて　……　広くて、たたみも　しょうじも　新しいですね。
　この　へやは　……　この　へやは　広くて、たたみも　しょうじも　新しいですね。

2.　気持ちが　いいです。　……　気持ちが　いいです。
　あかるくて　……　あかるくて、気持ちが　いいです。
　ふろ場は　……　ふろ場は　あかるくて、気持ちが　いいです。
　この　家の　……　この　家の　ふろ場は　あかるくて、気持ちが　いいです。

3.　いやでした。　……　いやでした。
　くらくて　……　くらくて、いやでした。
　ホテルは　……　ホテルは　くらくて、いやでした。
　ぼくの　とまった　……　ぼくの　とまった　ホテルは　くらくて、いやでした。

4.　わかりやすかったです。　……　わかりやすかったです。
　かんたんで　……　かんたんで、わかりやすかったです。
　一番　……　一番　かんたんで、わかりやすかったです。
　あなたの　せつめいが　……　あなたの　せつめいが　一番　かんたんで、　わかりやすかったです。

5.　また　行きたいです。　……　また　行きたいです。
　きれいなので　……　きれいなので、また　行きたいです。
　しずかで　……　しずかで　きれいなので、また　行きたいです。
　あの　きっさ店は　……　あの　きっさ店は　しずかで　きれいなので、　また　行きたいです。

6.　高かったらしいです。　……　高かったらしいです。
　古い　本で　……　古い　本で、高かったらしいです。
　ゆうめいな　……　ゆうめいな　古い　本で、高かったらしいです。
　あの　本は　……　あの　本は　ゆうめいな　古い　本で、高かったらしいです。

8.8 EXERCISES

8.8.1 Choose one of the words given in the braces to make a good sentence:

1. 先生が　そう {おっしゃいました。/言いました。}
2. この　げんかんは {せまい/せまいで/せまくて} 使いにくいです。
3. 私は　家を {新しい/新しく/新しくて} たてました。　見に {うかがいません/いらっしゃいません} か。
4. 主人が　お客さんを　よんで来ると {言っています。/おっしゃっています。}

8.8.2 つぎの　ことばを　使って、文を　作ってください。

1. かなり　2. できるだけ　3. おもに　4. さいきん

8.8.3 日本語で　書いてください。

1. The garden is spacious and pretty.
2. My room is in Western style, and the living room is in Japanese style.
3. Since it is raining, I think I'll stay at home and listen to the radio.
4. The houses in this area are made mainly from stone.
5. Yesterday I went to a department store in Tōkyō with Mr. Yamada and bought this leather bag.
6. This is very convenient, and I am using it every day.

8.8.4 日本語で　こたえてください。

1. アメリカの　家は　おもに　何で　できていますか。
2. アメリカでも　ゆかに　たたみを　使いますか。
3. あなたの　へやは　だいたい　何じょうぐらいですか。
4. あなたの　へやは　どんな　へやですか。せつめいしてください。
5. あなたは　日本風の　おふろに　入ったことが　ありますか。
6. あなたの　かばんは　どんな　物で　できていますか。

8.8.5 アメリカの　家と　日本の　家を　くらべてください。

8.8.6 この　家を　せつめいしてください。

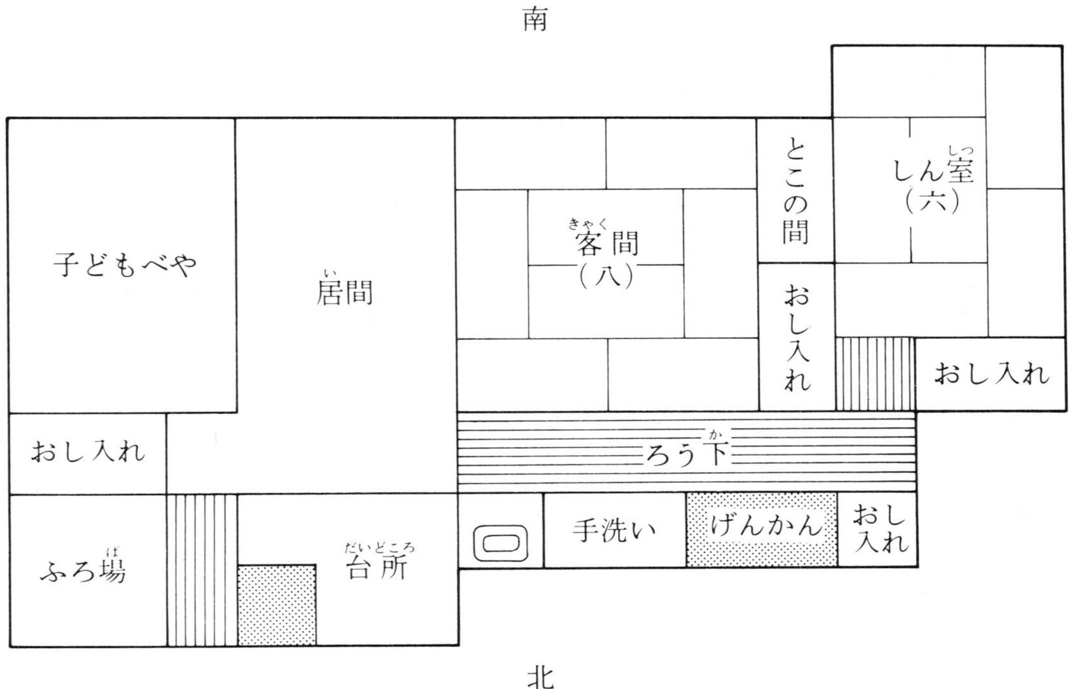

8.8.7 Write the underlined *hiragana* in *kan'ji:*

1. にほんふうの　いえは　おもに　きで　できていますが、ようふうの　たてものは　おもに　てつや　コンクリートで　できています。
2. しゅじんの　あたらしい　へやは　ひろくて、ほんとうに　きもちが　いいと　いっています。
3. 六じょうは　きゃくまに　しました。
4. まいにち　あおきさんに　あいますか。
5. むかしは　きんや　ぎんを　おかねに　つかったそうです。
6. たけの　はしが　すきです。

8.8.8 Distinguish the following *kan'ji:*

1. 金、鉄、銀
2. 主、生
3. 客、家
4. 度、広
5. 会、合、今

8.8.9 Which of the following two expressions would sound more polite?

1. Dotchi ga suki desu ka?
2. Dochira ga suki desu ka?

8.8.10 When you talk to your superior, which would be more appropriate?

1. Kotchi e itsu irasshaimashita ka?
2. Kochira e itsu irasshaimashita ka?
3. Kotchi e itsu kimashita ka?

8.8.11 When you are urged or allowed to enter one's room, you may say "Thank you" in English, but in Japanese you would say:__________.

8.8.12 Change the following dialog, using more polite forms:

A: Minoru kun imasu ka?

B: Ee, imasu. Chotto matte kudasai . . . Doozo haitte kudasai. Kotchi e doozo.

A: Ojama shimasu.

8.8.13 What would you say in the following situations?

1. When you have to use the rest room during class, and request permission from the teacher to be excused.
2. When you tell your wife that you are going to take a bath before dinner.
3. When you refer to a second person's spouse while speaking to your wife.

8.8.14 Some of the following italicized expressions can be replaced by *Ojama shimasu*, but not all of them. Replace as many as possible.

1. A: Gomen kudasai.

   B: Hai. Maa, doozo. Ohairi kudasai.

   A: Chotto *shitsurei shimasu.*

2. Yamada: Itoo san, oagari kudasai.

   Fujita: Hai, dewa, chotto *shitsurei shimasu*.

3. Paul: Katoo sen'sei! (at the office)

   Katō: A! Pooru kun, doozo.

   Paul: Hai. *Shitsurei shimasu*.

4. Satō: Moo ippai doozo.

   Sasaki: Iie, moo sorosoro *shitsurei shimasu*.

   Satō: Soo desu ka? Dewa, mata irasshai.

   Sasaki: Hai. *Shitsurei shimashita.*

8.9 SITUATIONAL AND APPLICATION CONVERSATION

8.9.1 Mr. Clark meets Mr. Aoki on the street.

Mr. Clark greets Mr. Aoki. He says that he heard from Mr. Takagi that Mr. Aoki has had a new house built.
Mr. Aoki says the new house is very spacious and well lighted.
Mr. Clark asks if it is Western style or Japanese style.
Mr. Aoki answers it is both—the children's room and living room are Western style and the others are Japanese style.
Mr. Clark says he likes a Japanese-style bathtub, as it is comfortable.

8.9.2 In Paul's room

Paul says to George that his room is noisy and dark, so he can't study hard there in spite of the fact that he has to write a report.
George asks why Paul rented this kind of room.
Paul says he rented it because it was cheap and near his school.
George says his room is new and quiet. He also says that he is planning to go home tomorrow for about one week so Paul may use his room while he is away.
Paul thanks George and says he would like to do that.

8.9.3 Talk with your friend about your house, room, apartment, etc.

8.9.4 Yamaguchi: Hino san imasu ka?

Hino: A. Yamaguchi san, doozo agatte kudasai.

Yamaguchi: Chotto ojama shimasu.

Hino no okusan: Maa. Yamaguchi san. Irasshaimase.

8.9.5 Hayashi: Kimura san, kono kata wa watashi no tomodachi no Miraa san desu.

Miller: Hajimemashite.

Kimura: Kochira koso. Doozo ohairi kudasai.

Miller: Hai, chotto ojama shimasu.

Hayashi: Jaa, Kimura san, shitsurei shimasu.

Miller: Doomo ojama shimashita.

Kimura: Iie, mata doozo.

8.9.6 Taniguchi: A, itai!

Sakamoto: A! Doomo shitsurei shimashita.

LESSON 9

おくり物[1]

9.1 PRESENTATION

日本では　十二月の　中ごろから　お正月まで　いろいろの　物を　おくり合います[2]が、これを「おせいぼ[1]」と　いいます。一年間　いろいろ[3]　世話に　なった[4]　人に　かんしゃして、物を　おくるのです。若い　人たちや　家族の　間では、クリスマスプレゼントが　とくに　さかんです。

9.2 DIALOG

吉田　「ジョーンズさん、すごい[5]　とけいを　しています[6]ね。スイス製ですか。」

ジョーンズ　「ええ、国の　母が　わたしの　たんじょう日に　おくってくれた[7]んです。」

吉田　「やさしい　お母さんですねえ。」

ジョーンズ　「わたしも　父と　母の　結婚記念日[8]に　日本的[9]な　物を　おくりたいんです けれど、何が　いいでしょうね。」

吉田　「そうですねえ。もし　ごりょうしん[10]が　絵が　お好きなら[11]、はんが[12]など[13]　いいと　思いますけど。」

ジョーンズ　「それは　いいですね。どこで　売っていますか。」

吉田　「前　友だちに　はんが専門の　いい　店を　教えてもらいました[14]。そこを　しょうかいしてあげます[7]よ。場所が　ちょっと　わかりにくいから、地図を　かいてあげましょう[7]。それとも、つれて行ってあげましょうか[7]。」

ジョーンズ　「わたしは　はんがの　ことを[15]　よく　知りませんから、つれて行って　くれませんか[7]。」

吉田　「ええ、いいですよ。」

ジョーンズ　「おねがいします[16]。」

お正月(しょうがつ)　家族(かぞく)　母(はは)　お母(かあ)さん　父(ちち)　日本的(にほんてき)　絵(え) 売(う)っています　店(みせ)　場所(ばしょ)　地図(ちず)

9.3 PATTERN SENTENCES

9.3.1

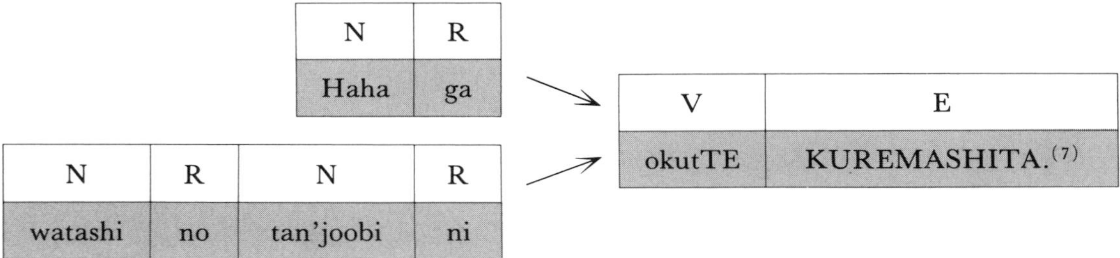

9.3.2

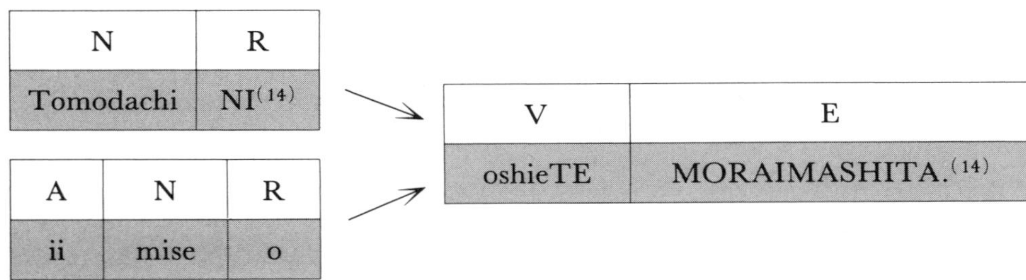

9.3.3

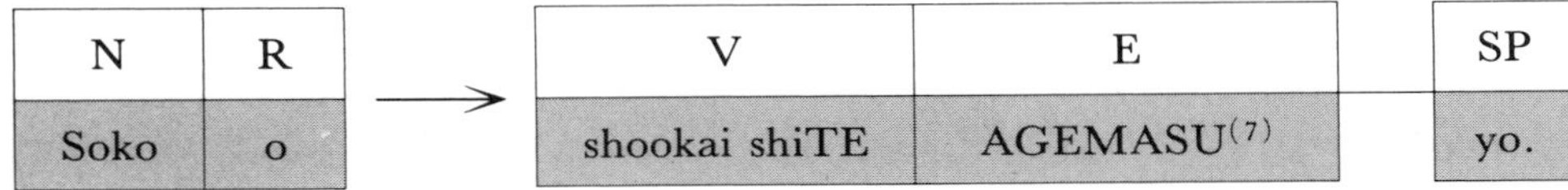

9.4 NOTES

9.4.1 In Japan, gift-giving differs from the American custom. In America, people offer Christmas and birthday presents, yet such are mainly limited to members of one's own group. In addition, such presents are offered voluntarily and without obligation except in husband-wife, parent-child, and child-parent relationships.

In Japan, the so-called *oseibo* (end-of-the-year-gift) and *ochuugen* (mid-year-present) were given in order to maintain human relationships or customer relationships both inside and outside his own group, except the intimate group. Therefore, such presents would never be given to members of one's own family, but only to those from whom favors have been received, or to business connections. A gift could be offered to your superior in the company, or to the flower arrangement teacher, or tea master under whom you studied. This type of gift-giving is commonly practiced (almost to the point of being an obligation or part of social etiquette) in Japan.

It can be seen that the very nature of gift-giving in Japan is quite different than in America. It serves as a lubrication to maintain better human relationships with formal-group and out-group people, and to seek continued cooperation and favors. For this reason, this practice can become a source of bribery.

Although the *oseibo* and *ochuugen* are given to the above-mentioned people (*sewa ni natta hito*), the Japanese also offer gifts and sometimes money to congratulate others on such happy occasions as entering a school, graduation, starting a new job, wedding, and the like. Such gifts are different, however, from those referred to above, and are also mainly given to those outside the family group. *Osen'betsu* is given to a person who is leaving or taking a long trip.

In addition to these more traditional types of gifts, the custom of exchanging Christmas presents is developing in full force in Japan at the present time.

9.4.2 *Mono o okuriaimasu* means "They give presents to each other," and *okuriaimasu* is the compound Verb consisting of the Stem form of the Verb *okuru* "present" and *aimasu* "do with each other" or "do mutually." The Verb *au* may form a connotation "do something to each other" preceded by the Stem form of a Verb.

hanashiau	"talk to each other" "discuss"
shookai shiau	"introduce each other"
oshieau	"teach mutually" "exchange instructions"
kariau	"borrow from each other"

Kurisumasu ni wa kazoku no aida de mo mono o okuriaimasu ka?	"Do you also exchange presents among the family on Christmas?"
Sono mon'dai o yoku hanashiatte kudasai.	"Please discuss that matter thoroughly."
Min'na wa kyakuma ni suwatte kara, shookai shiaimashita.	"All of them introduced each other after being seated in the guest room."

9.4.3 *Iroiro* may be used independently as a Predicate Modifier meaning "a lot," "variously," "in various ways," and so forth.

Nihon no mono o iroiro kaimashita.	"I bought various Japanese things."
Joon'zu san kara iroiro kikimashita.	"I heard many things from Mr. Jones."

9.4.4 *Sewa*—Heteronomy

The word *sewa* means "take care of; help; aid; assist" or "through the good offices of; is depended on." The various uses of *sewa* illustrate the way in which the Japanese express gratitude to their benefactors. Some of these expressions are used for greeting purposes. For example, *Tanaka san, taihen osewa ni natte imasu* means "I feel a debt of gratitude to you, Mr. Tanaka." *Taihen osewa ni narimashita* means "I'm very much obliged to you (for your kind assistance)," in connection with getting assistance in employment, marriage, lodging, or graduating from school.

Sewa (o) shimasu means "render a service to; take charge of; look after."

The Japanese repeat this expression of gratitude over and over for others' past favors; for instance, *Kinoo wa arigatoo gozaimashita* and *Kono mae wa osewa ni narimashita* are repeated expressions of gratitude for past favors, and similarly *Itsumo osewa ni natte imasu* means "for the favor you have been giving me, I am constantly grateful." Even in introductions, the Japanese tend to include their indebtedness for past favors as in *Kono kata wa watakushi ga mae ni sewa ni natta Tanaka san desu*, which translates as "This gentleman is Mr. Tanaka, from whom I have received care and service and favor in the past." When a person is transferred to another place, he/she usually says *Iroiro osewa ni narimashita* instead of saying *Sayoonara.* The word *sewa* formulates several idiomatic expressions. Here are two of them:

(Joon'zu san no) sewa ni naru	"one receives (Mr. Jones's) kindnesses"
(Joon'zu san no) sewa o suru	"look after (Mr. Jones)" "take care of (Mr. Jones)"

Iroiro osewa ni narimashita.	"I'm very much obliged to you."
Watakushi wa, Kyooto ni ita toki, Mori san no osewa ni narimashita.	"Mr. Mori took care of me when I was in Kyōto."
Kodomotachi no sewa o suru node, ichinichijuu isogashii desu.	"I'm busy all day long taking care of the children."

The use of *sewa* also reveals another characteristic Japanese posture, that of heteronomy, the tendency to promote others and demote oneself. This is done in this case by constantly praising others and remembering their good behavior. Reference to such an attitude is shown in Japanese far more frequently than in English. In this connection another Japanese concept, *on*, must be considered. *On* means kindness, favor, obligation, and a debt of gratitude toward a superior or a peer. *On* must be repaid with gratitude and should not be forgotten throughout one's life.

9.4.5 In praising Mr. Jones's watch, Mr. Yoshida uses the word *sugoi*, an Adjective which usually means "ghastly, horrible, wonderful, annoying, terrible, enormous." Such a term is considered much too strong by traditional or older Japanese to be in good taste, and they generally feel that a less extreme Adjective is much more elegant. The use of this expanded expression indicates that the above hesitation does not hold, and suggests that the speaker is a younger person.

9.4.6 *Tokei o shite imasu* means "You have a watch (on your wrist)." The *~o suru* or *~o shite iru* means "wear things such as a tie, a watch, a ring." This expression is not used for wearing clothes, footwear, hats, and the like.

tokei / nekutai / yubiwa } o { suru (action) / shite iru (state) } "wear { a watch" / a tie" / a ring"

Watashi wa tokei o shimasen.	"I don't wear a watch."
Anata wa kyoo nekutai o shite imasen ne?	"You don't have a necktie on today, do you?"
Michiko san wa taihen kirei na kin no kekkon yubiwa o shite imashita.	"Michiko had a very pretty gold wedding ring (on her finger)."

9.4.7 *Okutte kureta n desu* here means "[she] sent it to me." When a sentence indicates that someone does something for someone else or does something as a favor, it ends in the TE form of a Verb followed immediately by the Extender *ageru*, *kureru*, *yaru*, *sashiageru*, or *kudasaru*, all originally Verbs of giving. When these Verbs are used as Extenders after the TE form of another Verb, they no longer carry the original meaning of "giving things," but they nevertheless retain their function of specifying who does something and for whom it is done. Note 13.4.8 of Volume I and Notes 1.4.4 and 1.4.15 of Volume II discuss this function of these Verbs in their original sense of giving. Speech levels that determine the choice of the more polite *sashiageru* or *kudasaru* or the less polite *yaru* instead of *ageru* or *kureru* are discussed in Volume IV. The Verbs that appear in their TE form before *ageru*, *yaru*, *kureru*, and so on to convey the sense of service or favor may be either transitive or intransitive.

Person + *ni* . . . + Verb(*-te*) + { ***ageru*** / ***sashiageru*** / ***yaru*** / ***kureru*** / ***kudasaru*** }

Anata ni nihon'go o oshiete agemashoo.	"I'll teach you Japanese."
Inoue san wa Pooru san ni kuruma o kashite agemasen deshita.	"Mr. Inoue did not lend a car to Paul."
Ashita mata kite agemashoo ka?	"Shall I come again to you tomorrow?"
Imooto ni okashi o katte yarimashita.	"I bought candy for my younger sister."
Sen'sei ni ii mise o shookai shite sashiageru tsumori desu.	"I intend to introduce a good store to my teacher."
Ashita tomodachi ga Nihon no zasshi o misete kuremasu.	"My friend will show me a Japanese magazine tomorrow."
Ani ga boku ni kutsu o okutte kuremashita.	"My older brother sent shoes to me."
Yamamoto san ga sono mon'dai o setsumei shite kuremashita.	"Mr. Yamamoto explained that matter to me."

The following expressions are used quite frequently in seeking favor from others.

Verb(*-te*) + { ***kuremasen ka?*** / ***kudasaimasen ka?*** }	"Won't you do it for me?"
Gin'koo e itte kuremasen ka?	"Won't you go to the bank for me?"
Moo ichido yon'de kuremasen ka?	"Won't you please read it once more?"
Sumimasen ga, yoyaku o torikeshite kudasaimasen ka?	"I am sorry, but couldn't you cancel my reservation?"

9.4.8 *Chichi to haha no kekkon kinen'bi* means "my parents' wedding anniversary." Jones mentions that he wants to give his parents a wedding anniversary present. It is not a Japanese custom to consider such a proposal unless it is an occasion such as his parents' golden or silver anniversary. This indicates that Jones follows Western custom.

9.4.9 *Nihon'teki na mono* means "something typically Japanese." The *-teki* has a function of changing the preceding Noun into an adjectival Noun, and means "like" in nature, trend, or tradition, or "concerning." Quite a few Nouns may be changed into adjectival Nouns this way.

nihon'teki (na)	"typically Japanese"	bun'kateki (na)	"cultural"
amerikateki (na)	"typically American"	in'shooteki (na)	"impressive"
den'tooteki (na)	"traditional"	tooyooteki (na)	"oriental"
rekishiteki (na)	"historical"	keizaiteki (na)	"economical"

Kazuko san wa totemo nihon'teki na kata desu.	"Kazuko is a typical Japanese girl."
Den'tooteki na Nihon no bun'ka o ken'kyuu shitai to omotte, Nihon e kimashita.	"As I wanted to study traditional Japanese culture, I came to Japan."

9.4.10 *Goryooshin* is "your or someone else's parents." Like *kyoodai* "brothers and sisters," and *kazoku* "family," *ryooshin* may be preceded by the prefix *go-* to show politeness. Here are some more family words. These kinship terms indicate the Japanese in-groupness.

	speaking to out-group member, referring to intimate-group member	speaking to intimate-group member, referring to out-group member
grandfather	sofu	ojiisan
grandmother	sobo	obaasan
uncle	oji	ojisan
aunt	oba	obasan
older brother	ani	oniisan
older sister	ane	oneesan

In addition to the above usages, *ojiisan* and *obaasan* can be used to refer to old men and old women in general. Similarly, *ojisan* and *obasan* are often used by children, referring to, for instance, the lady next door (*tonari no obasan*) or Mrs. Tanaka (*Tanaka san no obasan*). Children may also use *oniisan* and *oneesan* referring to, for example, the young man or son next door (*tonari no oniisan*) , or Miss Tanaka (*Tanaka san no oneesan*).

In-groupness is further revealed in *haha* and *chichi*—which are intimate-group versions of *okaasan* and *otoosan*. For example, *haha* would not be used toward another's mother. Likewise, *goryooshin* refers to another's parents, and *ryooshin* refers to one's own parents.

Watashi wa moo ojiisan da kara, tenisu wa dekimasen yo.	"As I am an old man now, I won't be able to play tennis."
Are wa kusuriya no obasan deshoo?	"Isn't that the woman of the pharmacy?"
Watashi no oba wa amerikajin to kekkon shite imasu.	"My aunt is married to an American."
Ryooshin wa gen'ki desu.	"My parents are fine."

9.4.11 *Moshi goryooshin ga e ga osuki nara, . . .* means "If your parents like pictures, . . ." In an independent clause *goryooshin* may be followed by *wa*. However, the topic Relational *wa* should be replaced by *ga* in a nonfinal clause (as noted in Note 7.4.11, Vol. II), and as such the clause *moshi goryooshin ga e ga . . .* has two subject Relational *ga*'s.

Moshi Hooru san ga koohii ga iya nara, koocha o motte kite agemashoo.	"If Mr. Hall doesn't like coffee, I'll bring black tea for him."
Kodomo ga kimochi ga waruku natta toki wa, sugu isha no tokoro ni tsurete itta hoo ga ii desu yo.	"When a child gets sick, you'd better take him to the doctor immediately."

9.4.12 *Han'ga*—Woodblock Prints

The earliest specimens of the famous Japanese woodblock prints are said to be a set of sutras ordered by the Empress Kōken in 764. Pictures made from woodblocks, however, did not appear until the seventeenth century. Originally such prints were monochromatic, although color was at times added by hand. In 1764 Harunobu Suzuki developed the method of cutting separate blocks, putting exact edge marks on every block thus allowing one sheet of paper to be placed on each block in an exact position. This method is still the basic one used today.

Some of the different methods of color printing are the *sumi-e* or *sumi-zuri-e*, woodcut prints in black monochrome; the *tan-e*, or the contours black printed with vermilion color in brushwork;

the *beni-e*, or the contours black printed with a few colors in brushwork; and the *urushi-e*, or the contours woodcut printed in black with vermilion color and glossy black in brushwork. The combination of line and color creates a mosaic type of beauty of lines that flow and colors that seem to fuse gently.

9.4.13 *Nado* reveals the Japanese propensity for the non-absolute statement, as in *han'ga nado* in the dialog. *Nado* means "and so forth; etc.; such as," and makes a particular Noun less exclusive. When suggesting something, or recommending something—even a very specific thing—*nado* can still be used to demonstrate that you are not forcing your suggestion on the other person.

9.4.14 *Tomodachi ni oshiete moraimashita* means "I received that information from a friend of mine," "I had my friend inform me of it," or "I was informed of it by a friend of mine." The original idea of this pattern is that the favor of "informing" or "teaching" is received by the speaker or a member of his in-group. (See Notes 13.4.8, Vol. I and 1.4.14, Vol. II.) When the Extender immediately following the TE form is *morau* or *itadaku* the connotation is a sort of mild causative, "have someone do it for someone else" or "ask someone to do it for someone else." The person who has been asked to do something in the above pattern is followed by the Relational *ni*. The Relational *kara* that occurs with *morau* in the pattern of "(a person) *kara* (a thing) *o morau*" is not used. The Verb that occurs before *morau* may be transitive or intransitive.

person + *ni* . . . + Verb(*-te*) + { *morau* / *itadaku* } "have someone do it for the speaker or someone else"

Itoo san ni Tookyoo e itte moraimashoo.	"I think I'll ask Mr. Itō to go to Tōkyō."
Watakushi wa Joon'zu san ni hon o yon'de moraimashita.	"I had Mr. Jones read a book for me."
Ojisan ni eiga e tsurete itte moraimashita.	"I asked my uncle to take me to a movie (and he did)."
Shuuriya ni naoshite moratte kudasai.	"Please have a repairman fix it."
Sono koto wa kinoo sen'sei ni oshiete itadakimashita.	"I learned that matter from the teacher yesterday."
Boku wa tomodachi ni shashin o totte moraimashita.	"I asked my friend to take my picture, and he did it."

As an indirect way to seek another's favor, the following expressions are frequently used.

Verb(*-te*) + { *moraitai n desu (ga)* . . . / *itadakitai n desu (kedo)* . . . } "I would like to ask someone to do (a certain thing) for me"

Issho ni tsurete itte moraitai n desu kedo . . .	"I would like to ask you to take me with you . . ."
Ii desu yo. Doozo.	"It's fine with me."

9.4.15 *Han'ga no koto o yoku shirimasen* means "[I] am not too familiar with [matters] about woodblock prints." *~no koto o* is used colloquially meaning "about; concerning."

Joon'zu san no koto o kikimashita ka?	"Did you hear about Mr. Jones?"
Kodomo no koto ga shin'pai de, neru koto ga dekinai n desu.	"I am so worried about my child that I can't sleep."

9.4.16 *Onegai shimasu* and *Arigatoo*

The difference between *Onegai shimasu* and *Arigatoo* (which have been referred to in Notes 6.4.3 and 6.4.10) may be summarized in the following way:

	seeking future favor, by the speaker	speaker is depending on the listener	gratitude
onegai shimasu	yes	yes	yes
arigatoo	no	no	yes

When the speaker decided to accept the second person's favor, he could have used either expression, but *Onegai shimasu* is more proper because it shows the speaker's dependency on the second person and his deference to the latter.

9.5 VOCABULARY

Presentation

おくり物	okurimono	N	gift; present
中ごろ	nakagoro	N	middle
おくり	okuri	V	Stem form of *okuru* – present; send
合います	aimasu	V	do with each other; do mutually (compound component) (see 9.4.2)
(お)せいぼ	(o)seibo	N	year-end present
世話	sewa	N	help; kindness (see 9.4.4)
かんしゃして	kan'sha shite	V	TE form of *kan'sha suru* – thank; is grateful
かんしゃ	kan'sha	N	thanks; gratitude
クリスマス	kurisumasu	N	Christmas

Dialog

吉田	Yoshida	N	family name
すごい	sugoi	A	is terrific; is striking; is terrible; is awful (see 9.4.5)
スイス	Suisu	N	Switzerland; Swiss
製	-sei	Nd	made in ～; of (Swiss) make
くれた	kureta	E	TA form of *kureru* (see 9.4.7)
やさしい	yasashii	A	is thoughtful; is kind; is gentle
記念日	kinen'bi	N	anniversary; memorial day
日本的	nihon'teki	Na	typically Japanese (see 9.4.9)
(ご)りょうしん	(go)ryooshin	N	parents (see 9.4.10)
はんが	han'ga	N	woodblock print

に	ni	......	R	indicates the person who is asked to do something (see 9.4.14)
専門(せんもん)	sen'mon	......	N	specialty
もらいました	moraimashita	......	E	TA form of *moraimasu* ← *morau* (see 9.4.14)
あげます	agemasu	......	E	normal form of *ageru* (see 9.4.7)
地図(ず)	chizu	......	N	map
かいて	kaite	......	V	TE form of *kaku* - draw; paint
それとも	soretomo	......	SI	or (else)

Notes

ゆびわ	yubiwa	......	N	(finger) ring
さしあげる	sashiageru	......	E	Dictionary form (see 9.4.7)
やる	yaru	......	E	Dictionary form (see 9.4.7)
くださる	kudasaru	......	E	Dictionary form (see 9.4.7)
的	-teki	......	Nd	forms an adjectival Noun (see 9.4.9)
歴史的	rekishiteki	......	Na	historical
文化的	bun'kateki	......	Na	cultural
東洋的	tooyooteki	......	Na	oriental
けいざい的	keizaiteki	......	Na	economical
かず子	Kazuko	......	N	girl's name
そふ	sofu	......	N	grandfather (see 9.4.10)
そぼ	sobo	......	N	grandmother
おじいさん	ojiisan	......	N	grandfather; old man
おばあさん	obaasan	......	N	grandmother; old woman
おじ(さん)	oji(san)	......	N	uncle; man
おば(さん)	oba(san)	......	N	aunt; woman
いただく	itadaku	......	E	Dictionary form (see 9.4.14)
しゃしん	shashin	......	N	photograph (cf. *shashin o toru* "take a picture")

9.6 KAN'JI

9.6.1 正 (1) SHOO (2) right; correct (3) classifier 一 (止)
(4) [一] [丅] [下] [正] [正] (5) 正月
(6) a target (一) with feet (止) ⟶ straight ⟶ correct

9.6.a 家 [4.6.9] (1) KA (2) house (5) 家族(ぞく) (6) homonym 嫁、稼

9.6.2 族 (1) ZOKU (2) clan; relative (3) classifier 方
(4)  (5) 一族、家族、民族 [a race; a nation]
(6) arrows (矢) under military banners (方⺈)

9.6.3 母 (1) *haha* (2) mother (3) forms the classifier 母
(4)  (5) わたしの母は国にいます、母と子

9.6.b 母 [9.6.3] (1) *(o)kaa(san)* (5) お母さん、お母様(さま)

9.6.4 父 (1) *chichi* (2) father (3) forms the classifier 丷 (父)
(4)  (5) 父と母

9.6.5 的 (1) TEKI (2) similar; alike; suffix for forming adjectival Nouns
(3) classifier 白 (4) 
(5) でんとう的、歴史的、日本的

9.6.6 絵 (1) E (2) picture (3) classifier 糸 (4) 
(5) 絵をかく、絵はがき [picture postcard]、絵本

9.6.7 売 (1) *u(ru)* (2) sell (3) classifier 士 [man]
(4)  (5) 二かいで売っています、売り物 [for sale]
(6) 士 is also a simplified form of 出 [go out]. 買 means "buy," therefore 賣 ⟶ 売 means "sell."

9.6.8 店 (1) *mise* (2) store; shop (3) classifier 广 [house under a roof]
(4) 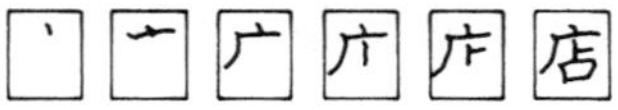 (5) ここは何の店ですか

9.6.9 場 (1) *ba* (2) place (3) classifier 土 [earth]
(4)  (5) 場所、売り場、ふろ場

9.6.10 地 (1) CHI (2) ground; earth (3) classifier 土 [earth]
(4) 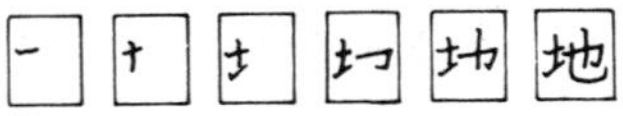 (5) 地下(か)、地下(か)鉄、地図(ず)

9.6.c 下 [*9.6.10, Vol. II] (1) KA (5) 地下鉄、地下

9.6.11 化* (1) KA (2) change (3) classifier 亻(匕) (4) 
(5) 文化、近代(きんだい)化 [modernization]、化学 [chemistry] (6) a man standing (亻) and a man fallen (匕) ⟶ change; homonym 花、訛

9.6.d 店[*9.6.8]　(1)　TEN　　(5)　きっさ店、店員

9.6.e 父[*9.6.4]　(1)　*(o)too(san)*　　(5)　お父さん、お父様(さま)

9.7 DRILLS

9.7.1 Transformation Drill

1.	吉(よし)田さんに　いい　店を　しょうかいする	⟶	吉(よし)田さんに　いい　店を　しょうかいしてあげました。
2.	青木さんの　しゃしんを　とる	⟶	青木さんの　しゃしんを　とってあげました。
3.	おじさんに　はんがを　おくる	⟶	おじさんに　はんがを　おくってあげました。
4.	ジョーンズさんに　地図(ず)を　かく	⟶	ジョーンズさんに　地図(ず)を　かいてあげました。
5.	池(いけ)田さんに　こたえを　せつめいする	⟶	池(いけ)田さんに　こたえを　せつめいしてあげました。
6.	うちの　前で　パンクを　なおす	⟶	うちの　前で　パンクを　なおしてあげました。
7.	駅へ　友だちを　むかえに　行く	⟶	駅へ　友だちを　むかえに　行ってあげました。
8.	しゅうり屋へ　電話を　かける	⟶	しゅうり屋へ　電話を　かけてあげました。

9.7.2 Transformation Drill

1.	国の　母が　わたしに　おくる	⟶	国の　母が　わたしに　おくってくれました。
2.	父が　とけいを　買う	⟶	父が　とけいを　買ってくれました。
3.	友だちが　おとうとに　さんこう書を　かす	⟶	友だちが　おとうとに　さんこう書をかしてくれました。
4.	高橋(はし)さんが　わたしに　日本語を　教える	⟶	高橋(はし)さんが　わたしに　日本語を　教えてくれました。
5.	クラークさんが　アメリカの　ことを　いろいろ　話す	⟶	クラークさんが　アメリカの　ことを　いろいろ　話してくれました。
6.	あにが　ぼくの　車を　洗う	⟶	あにが　ぼくの　車を　洗ってくれました。
7.	りょうしんが　動物園(ぶつえん)へ　つれて　行く	⟶	りょうしんが　動物園(ぶつえん)へ　つれて行ってくれました。
8.	原(はら)さんが　学校の　にわで　しゃしんを　とる	⟶	原(はら)　んが　学校の　にわで　しゃしんをとってくれました。

9.7.3 Transformation Drill

1.	友だちが　はんが専門(せんもん)の　店を　教えてくれました。	⟶	友だちに　はんが専門(せんもん)の　店を　教えてもらいました。
2.	父が　タイプライターを　おくってくれました。	⟶	父に　タイプライターを　おくってもらいました。
3.	大学の　友だちが　辞(じ)書を　かしてくれました。	⟶	大学の　友だちに　辞(じ)書を　かしてもらいました。
4.	店員が　水を　持って来てくれました。	⟶	店員に　水を　持って来てもらいました。
5.	木村(むら)さんが　いい　とけい屋を　しょうかいしてくれました。	⟶	木村(むら)さんに　いい　とけい屋を　しょうかいしてもらいました。
6.	おばさんが　家族の　しゃしんを　とってくれました。	⟶	おばさんに　家族の　しゃしんを　とってもらいました。
7.	いもうとが　子どもの　世(せ)話を　してくれました。	⟶	いもうとに　子どもの　世(せ)話を　してもらいました。
8.	主人が　結婚記念(けっこんきねん)日に　日光(にっこう)へ　つれて行ってくれました。	⟶	主人に　結婚記念(けっこんきねん)日に　日光(にっこう)へ　つれて行ってもらいました。

9.7.4 Transformation Drill

A.	1.	ロバーツさんに　地図(ず)を　かいてあげました。	⟶	ロバーツさんに　地図(ず)を　かいてさしあげました。
	2.	山本(もと)先生に　はんがを　おくってあげませんか。	⟶	山本(もと)先生に　はんがを　おくってさしあげませんか。
	3.	あなたの　ごりょうしんに　日本の　ことを　話して　あげましょう。	⟶	あなたの　ごりょうしんに　日本の　ことを　話してさしあげましょう。
B.	1.	高木(ぎ)さんに　いろいろ　世(せ)話してもらいました。	⟶	高木(ぎ)さんに　いろいろ　世(せ)話していただきました。
	2.	ミラーさんに　とけいの　しゅうりを　して　もらいませんか。	⟶	ミラーさんに　とけいの　しゅうりを　していただきませんか。
	3.	どの　先生に　外国語を　教えてもらいますか。	⟶	どの　先生に　外国語を　教えていただきますか。

C.

1. 友だちの　おじさんが　くわしく　しらべてくれました。 ⟶ 友だちの　おじさんが　くわしく　しらべてくださいました。
2. きょう　ハワードさんが　うちへ　来てくれます。 ⟶ きょう　ハワードさんが　うちへ　来てくださいます。
3. ぼくに　鈴木先生を　しょうかいしてくれませんか。 ⟶ ぼくに　鈴木先生を　しょうかいしてくださいませんか。

9.7.5 Substitution Drill

A. わたしは　母に　とけいを　買ってもらいました。

1. おくる …… わたしは　母に　とけいを　おくってもらいました。
2. 父 …… わたしは　父に　とけいを　おくってもらいました。
3. なおす …… わたしは　父に　とけいを　なおしてもらいました。
4. さがす …… わたしは　父に　とけいを　さがしてもらいました。
5. おとうと …… わたしは　おとうとに　とけいを　さがしてもらいました。
6. かす …… わたしは　おとうとに　とけいを　かしてもらいました。
7. 吉田さん …… わたしは　吉田さんに　とけいを　かしてもらいました。

B. ホールさんが　わたしに　地図を　かいてくれました。

1. さんこう書を　買う …… ホールさんが　わたしに　さんこう書を　買ってくれました。
2. 電話で　知らせる …… ホールさんが　わたしに　電話で　知らせてくれました。
3. かず子さんを　しょうかいする …… ホールさんが　わたしに　かず子さんを　しょうかいしてくれました。
4. 友だちが …… 友だちが　わたしに　かず子さんを　しょうかいしてくれました。
5. 宿題を　わたす …… 友だちが　わたしに　宿題を　わたしてくれました。
6. おちゃを　持って来る …… 友だちが　わたしに　おちゃを　持って来てくれました。
7. あの　女の人が …… あの　女の人が　わたしに　おちゃを　持って来てくれました。

C. わたしが　パンクを　しゅうりしてあげましょう。

1. 車を　みがく …… わたしが　車を　みがいてあげましょう。
2. おさらを　洗う …… わたしが　おさらを　洗ってあげましょう。
3. 動物園(ぶつえん)へ　つれて行く …… わたしが　動物園(ぶつえん)へ　つれて行ってあげましょう。
4. 駅へ　むかえに　行く …… わたしが　駅へ　むかえに　行ってあげましょう。
5. 食事を　作る …… わたしが　食事を　作ってあげましょう。
6. 大学まで　運転(うんてん)する …… わたしが　大学まで　運転(うんてん)してあげましょう。
7. あなたの　先生に　会う …… わたしが　あなたの　先生に　会ってあげましょう。

9.7.6 Expansion Drill

1. 教えてあげました。 …… 教えてあげました。
   みちを …… みちを　教えてあげました。
   知らない　人に …… 知らない　人に　みちを　教えてあげました。
   駅の　前で …… 駅の　前で　知らない　人に　みちを　教えて　あげました。
   わたしは …… わたしは　駅の　前で　知らない　人に　みちを　教えてあげました。
2. しょうかいしてもらいました。 …… しょうかいしてもらいました。
   いい　本屋を …… いい　本屋を　しょうかいしてもらいました。
   友だちに …… 友だちに　いい　本屋を　しょうかいして　もらいました。
   ぼくは …… ぼくは　友だちに　いい　本屋を　しょうかいして　もらいました。
   新宿(じゅく)へ　行った　時 …… 新宿(じゅく)へ　行った　時、　ぼくは　友だちに　いい　本屋を　しょうかいしてもらいました。
3. おくってくれるそうです。 …… おくってくれるそうです。
   すごい　ゆびわを …… すごい　ゆびわを　おくってくれるそうです。
   おじが …… おじが　すごい　ゆびわを　おくってくれるそう　です。
   たんじょう日に …… たんじょう日に　おじが　すごい　ゆびわを　おくってくれるそうです。

4. つれて行ってもらうつもりです。 …… つれて行ってもらうつもりです。

京都へ …… 京都へ　つれて行ってもらうつもりです。

主人に …… 主人に　京都へ　つれて行ってもらうつもりです。

結婚記念(けっこんきねん)日に …… 結婚記念(けっこんきねん)日に　主人に　京都へ　つれて行ってもらうつもりです。

5. 持って来てくれませんか。 …… 持って来てくれませんか。

コーヒーを …… コーヒーを　持って来てくれませんか。

わたしに …… わたしに　コーヒーを　持って来てくれませんか。

台所(だいどころ)へ　行って …… 台所(だいどころ)へ　行って、　わたしに　コーヒーを　持って来てくれませんか。

6. 手つだってあげましょう。 …… 手つだってあげましょう。

あなたの　しごとを …… あなたの　しごとを　手つだってあげましょう。

書きおわってから …… 書きおわってから、　あなたの　しごとを　手つだってあげましょう。

この　レポートを …… この　レポートを　書きおわってから、　あなたの　しごとを　手つだってあげましょう。

9.7.7 Response Drill

1. あなたは　自分で　パンクを　なおしたんですか。

いいえ、　青木さんに …… いいえ、　青木さんに　なおしてもらいました。

2. あなたは　みち子さんを　びじゅつ館へ　つれて行ってあげたんですか。

いいえ、　かず子さんを …… いいえ、　かず子さんを　つれて行ってあげたんです。

3. あなたは　いつ　ミラーさんを　しょうかいしてくれるつもりですか。

来週の　土曜(よう)日に …… 来週の　土曜(よう)日に　しょうかいしてあげるつもりです。

4. 何時に　うちへ　むかえに　来てくれますか。

三時ごろ …… 三時ごろ　むかえに　行ってあげます。

5. 地図(ず)を　かいてくれませんか。

ええ …… ええ、　かいてあげましょう。

6. だれが　とけいを　買ってくれたんですか。
   母が　…… 母が　買ってくれたんです。
7. だれに　この　問題を　せつめいしてもらいましたか。
   大学院の　学生に　…… 大学院の　学生に　せつめいしてもらいました。

9.7.8 Response Drill

1. おじいさんは　お元(げん)気ですか。 …… はい、　そふは　元(げん)気です。
2. お父さんは　銀行員を　して いらっしゃいますね。 …… はい、　父は　銀行員を　しております。
3. ごりょうしんと　いっしょに 住んでいらっしゃいますか。 …… はい、　りょうしんと　いっしょに　住んでおります。
4. おにいさんの　絵ですか。 …… はい、　あにの　絵です。
5. おばあさんは　はんがが　好き でしょう？ …… はい、　そぼは　はんがが　好きです。
6. おねえさんに　もらったんですか。 …… はい、　あねに　もらったんです。
7. お母さんの　たんじょう日だったん ですか。 …… はい、　母のたんじょう日だったんです。
8. これは　ご家族の　しゃしんですね。 …… はい、　家族の　しゃしんです。

9.7.9 E-J Response Drill

1. フランス製(せい)の　セーターを　だれに　買ってもらったんですか。
   my grandmother …… そぼに　買ってもらったんです。
2. だれに　スイスへ　つれて行ってもらったんですか。
   my father and mother …… 父と　母に　つれて行ってもらったんです。
3. どんな　物を　ハワードさんに　おくってあげたいんですか。
   something typically Japanese …… 日本的な　物を　おくってあげたいんです。
4. ポールさんに　何を　見せてあげるんですか。
   New Year's days in the countryside …… いなかの　正月を　見せてあげるんです。
5. いつ　車を　洗ってくれますか。
   after repairing the flat tire …… パンクを　なおしてから、　車を　洗ってあげます。
6. この　おみやげは　だれが　持って来てくれたんですか。
   I understand my uncle did …… おじが　持って来てくれたそうです。

7. どなたに　ピアノを　ひいていただきましょうか。
   Kazuko …… かず子さんに　ひいていただきましょう。
8. だれが　会う　時間を　知らせてくださるんですか。
   I will …… わたしが　知らせてあげます。

9.7.10 Substitution Drill

はんがの　ことを　よく　知りませんから、　教えてくれませんか。

1. 絵 …… 絵の　ことを　よく　知りませんから、　教えてくれませんか。
2. 日本の　おふろ …… 日本の　おふろの　ことを　よく　知りませんから、教えてくれませんか。
3. 東洋 …… 東洋の　ことを　よく　知りませんから、　教えてくれませんか。
4. アメリカの　公害(こうがい) …… アメリカの　公害(こうがい)の　ことを　よく　知りませんから、教えてくれませんか。
5. 着物 …… 着物の　ことを　よく　知りませんから、　教えてくれませんか。
6. 現代(げんだい)の　日本 …… 現代(げんだい)の　日本の　ことを　よく　知りませんから、教えてくれませんか。
7. 石井(い)さん …… 石井(い)さんの　ことを　よく　知りませんから、教えてくれませんか。

9.8 EXERCISES

9.8.1 日本語で　こたえてください。

1. おせいぼは　いつ　おくり合いますか。　また、　なぜ　おせいぼを　おくるのですか。
2. アメリカでは　どんな　時に　物を　おくりますか。
3. きょ年の　たんじょう日に　何を　もらいましたか。
4. クリスマスには　だれに　どんな　物を　買ってあげるつもりですか。

9.8.2 Complete each sentence, inserting in each blank one of the following words. Change forms if necessary.

あげる、　もらう、　くれる

1. わたしは　母の　たんじょう日に　着物を　おくって（　　　）つもりです。
2. きのう　おとうとは　原(はら)さんに　びじゅつ館へ　つれて行って（　　　）。

3. ミラーさんが　日本から　おもしろい　みやげを　ぼくに　持って来て（　　　）。
4. 店員に　地図（ず）を　かいて（　　　）ので、　すぐ　わかりました。
5. 吉（よし）田さんの　おくさんが　わたしたちに　おいしい　中国料理（りょうり）を　作って（　　　）そうです。
6. わたしが　運転（うんてん）して、　あなたを　駅まで　つれて行って（　　　）よ。

9.8.3 Choose one of the three phrases given to make a complete sentence:

1. あなたは　だれに　朝ごはんを　作って { くれますか。 / もらいますか。 / あげましょうか。 }
2. だれが　あなたに　日本の　ことを　話して { やりますか。 / もらいますか。 / くれますか。 }
3. きのう　私は　青木先生を　ハワードさんに　しょうかいして { あげました。 / くれました。 / やりました。 }
4. ぼくを　駅まで　つれて行って { あげませんか。 / もらいませんか。 / くれませんか。 }
5. 六時までに　わたしの　車を　しゅうりして { あげたいんですけど。 / もらいたいんですけど。 / やりたいんですけど。 }
6. 先生、　その　しゃしんを　見せて { くれませんか。 / さしあげませんか。 / くださいませんか。 }

9.8.4 日本語で　言ってください。

1. Q: Shall I go to the post office for you?

   A: Yes, please go [there].
2. Q: Will you kindly teach me Japanese?

   A: Yes, I will teach it to [for] you.
3. Q: Did you have your friend help you with your homework?

   A: No, I didn't have him help me. I did it myself.

9.8.5 Complete the family tree:

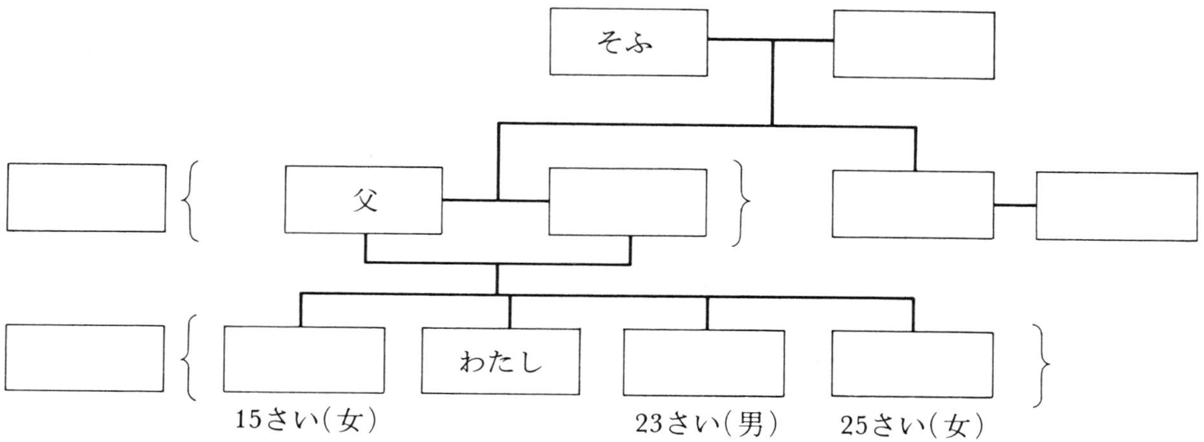

9.8.6 Write the underlined *hiragana* in *kan'ji*:

1. しょうがつに　ちちと　ははの　いる　いなかへ　かえるつもりです。
2. にほんてきな　えを　うっている　みせを　ともだちに　おしえてもらいました。
3. その　ばしょの　ち図を　かいてください。
4. かぞくと　すいぞくかん（aquarium）へ　いった。
5. おとうさんと　おかあさんは　てんいんと　ネクタイうりばで　はなしています。
6. ちかてつの　いりぐちは　どこですか。
7. ぶんかという　じを　かいてください。

9.8.7 Distinguish the following *kan'ji*:

1. 旅、族	4. 絵、紙	7. 化、花
2. 正、五	5. 店、広	8. 読、売
3. 地、場、土	6. 母、毎	9. 会、絵

9.8.8 When visiting someone's home, under what circumstances would you bring a gift? Under what circumstances would you not bring a gift (called *tebura*, or "empty-handed")?

9.8.9 If you have asked someone to fix your typewriter and he hasn't done it, which of the following would you say?

1. Taipuraitaa o naoshite kuremasen deshita.
2. Taipuraitaa o naoshimasen deshita.

9.8.10 In Japanese, how would you say the following when speaking to your younger brother; when speaking to an outsider:

1. I have prepared lunch for myself.
2. I prepared lunch for a friend.
3. My friend prepared lunch for me.

9.8.11 When your teacher has offered you an explanation in clarifying a few points which you could not understand, how would you tell your friend that your teacher has done this for you?

9.8.12 When you ask your teacher to explain more, which of the following would be most appropriate:

1. Sen'sei, motto setsumei shite kuremasen ka?
2. Sen'sei, motto setsumei shite kudasaimasen ka?
3. Sen'sei, motto setsumei shimasen ka?

9.8.13 Using the italicized phrases, rewrite the key sentence.

Key: *Boku wa tomodachi ni* shashin o totte moraimashita.

1. *Boku wa sen'sei ni* ____________________.
2. *Tomodachi wa sen'sei ni* ____________________.
3. *Watakushitachi wa shashin'ya san ni* ____________________.

9.8.14 Using the italicized phrases, rewrite the key sentence.

Key: *Boku wa chichi ni* kippu o katte moraimashita.

Chichi ga boku ni ____________________.

Key: *Watashitachi wa sen'sei ni* bijutsukan e tsurete itte itadakimashita.

Sen'sei ga watashitachi o ____________________.

Key: *Tanaka san wa watashi no haha ni* han'kachi o aratte moraimashita.

Watashi no haha wa Tanaka san ni ____________________.

9.8.15 Decide whether each of the following terms are true or false. *Iroiro osewa ni narimashita* may be said:

1. to your teacher when you graduate from school
2. to your landlady when you are moving to another place
3. to your friend, when you are leaving his house after staying there overnight
4. to your father, when you receive $100 from him
5. to your friend at his home, after you have finished eating a delicious supper there and are saying good-bye
6. to your friend, when you receive a gift from him

9.9 SITUATIONAL AND APPLICATION CONVERSATION

9.9.1 Carry on the following conversation in Japanese:

Mr. Ikeda admires Miss Kobayashi's watch and asks if it is made in Switzerland.
Miss Kobayashi says it is Japanese made and was given to her by her grandmother on her twentieth birthday.
Mr. Ikeda says his father sent him a Swiss watch when his father went to Switzerland the year before last.
Miss Kobayashi talks about the camera Mr. Ikeda has in his hand.
Mr. Ikeda says he will take her picture.
Miss Kobayashi appreciates it.

9.9.2 Carry on the following conversation in Japanese:

Kazuko shows Michiko her gold ring, saying that she bought it at a good store in Tōkyō.
Michiko wants to buy one for her mother.
Kazuko says she will introduce the store to her.
Michiko also asks Kazuko to draw a map for her.
Kazuko says that it is difficult to draw a map because the way to the store is not simple. So she suggests that she will take Michiko there.
Michiko is pleased to hear that.

9.9.3 Pretend that you are a foreigner who wants to buy a *yukata,* which you are not familiar with. Ask a favor of a Japanese friend as to how to buy it.

9.9.4

Child:	Okaasan, Keiko obasan ga kore o kureta yo.
Mrs. Mifune:	Soo. Yokatta wa ne. Obasan ni ''Arigatoo'' to itta no?
Child:	Boku, obasan ni itta yo.

9.9.5

Tanaka:	Buraun san, ashita tenisu o shi ni ikimasen ka?
Brown:	Ashita wa yama e iku kara.
Tanaka:	Hitori de desu ka?
Brown:	Soo, hitori de.
Tanaka:	Boku mo tsurete itte kuremasen ka? Boku mo yama wa daisuki na n desu.

9.9.6

Fujioka:	A. Miraa san no okusan, shibaraku desu.
Mrs. Miller:	Shujin ga itsumo osewa ni natte imasu.
Fujioka:	Iie, ton'de mo arimasen.

9.9.7 Mrs. Hall: Kodomo ga iroiro osewa ni natte imasu.

Teacher: Iie. Hooru kun wa totemo yoku yatte imasu kara . . .

9.9.8 Mrs. Akita: Minoru, sore jibun de tsukutta no?

Minoru: Tonari no oniisan ga tsukutte kureta no.

LESSON 10
REVIEW AND APPLICATION

10.1 PATTERNS

10.1.1 Guessing

a. Verb

かないは　外国人が　うちへ　来るので、着物を　着る
りょうあん寺の　にわは　石だけで　できている
山田さんの　おくさんは　車を　運転(うんてん)しない
スミスさんは　日本語が　わからない
一郎(ろう)くんは　アルバイトを　やめた
交通(こうつう)事故(こ)で　吉(よし)田さんの　自動車が　だいぶ　こわれた
くすりを　あげたのに、のまなかった
中村(むら)さんは　ハワードさんを　山本(もと)さんに　しょうかいしてあげなかった

らしいです

b. Adjective

新しい　家は　わりあい　あかるい
あしたは　つごうが　わるい
おびは　思ったほど　きつくない
よし子さんは　きのう　あたまが　いたかった
あの　えいがは　とても　おもしろかった
北海道(ほっかいどう)は　東京ほど　むしあつくなかった

らしいです

c. Copula

青木さんの　お父さんは　くすり屋
けい子さんが　もらった　すごい　とけいは　スイス製(せい)
あの　学生は　三年生じゃない
林(はやし)さんの　専攻(せんこう)は　歴史ではない
あの　たて物は　前　小学校だった
きのうの　しけんは　かんたんだった
母が　もらった　おくり物は　はんがじゃなかった
高木(ぎ)さんの　結婚記念(けっこんきねん)日は　十月三日ではなかった

らしいです

10.1.2 Doing a favor

a. TE form + *ageru*

わたしが　くつを　みがいて 駅まで　むかえに　行って	あげます
車が　よごれたから、洗って ぼくが　運転(うんてん)して	あげましょうか
とけいが　こわれたので、しゅうりして ロバーツさんに　水を　持って来て	あげてください
スミスさんの　車が　パンクしたので、なおして かんたんな　地図(ず)を　かいて	あげました
よく　わからなかったので、教えて 友だちに　宿題(しゅくだい)を　見せて	あげませんでした
お客さんに　ごちそうを　作って ジョーンズさんに　きみの　本を　かして	あげませんか
図(と)書館で　くわしく　しらべて 日本風の　へやを　さがして	あげるつもりです

b. TE form + *sashiageru*

日本語なら、わたしが　教えて	さしあげます
いい　いしゃを　しょうかいして	さしあげましょうか
クリスマスに　きくの　花を　おくって	さしあげました
先生の　あかちゃんの　世(せ)話を　して	さしあげるつもりです

c. TE form + *yaru*

小学生の　子どもには　絵本を　おくって	やります
とおいから、子どもを　つれて行って	やらないんです
おとうとの　こわれた　ラジオを　なおして	やりました
子どもたちの　しゃしんを　とって	やりませんでした
いもうとに　いぬを　買って	やるつもりです

10.1.3 Receiving a favor

a. TE form + *kureru*

母が　夏休みに　会いに　来て ジョーンズさんが　今ばん　ごちそうして	くれます
友だちが　パンクを　なおして クラークさんが　おせいぼを　おくって	くれました
原(はら)さんが　へやを　よやくしておいて たんじょう日を　教えて	くれなかったんです
名前と　所を　書いて もっと　くわしく　話して	くれませんか
りょうしんが　家を　たてて あとで　わたしの　しゃしんを　とって	くれるそうです

b. TE form + *kudasaru*

すぐ　おいしゃさんに　電話を　かけて	ください
ぼくの　カメラを　買って	くださいませんか
いつも　青木さんが　むかえに　来て	くださいます
原(はら)さんが　美しい　絵を　かいて	くださいました
先生は　わたしも　びじゅつ館へ　つれて行って	くださるはずです

c. TE form + *morau*

高木(ぎ)さん 友だち 母	に	毎月　おかねを　おくって スイス製(せい)の　ハンカチを　買って	もらいます
		車を　取りに　行って 大学まで　運転(うんてん)して	もらいましょう
		電話で　知らせて しゃしんを　とって	もらわなかったんです
		所を　書いて おさらを　洗って	もらいたいんです
		いなかの　お正月を　味わって 本当の　ことを　言って	もらいました

d. TE form + *itadaku*

あの　方 先生 お客さま	に	ゆうめいな　いしゃを　しょうかいして	いただきます
		新しい　客間に　とまって	いただきましょう
		げんかんの　ドアを　しめて	いただきました
		もっと　常用漢字を　教えて	いただきたかったんです

e. Polite request

この　ワイパーを　しゅうりして 日本語で　しつ問して すみませんが、うちまで　むかえに　来て ぼくに　山田さんを　しょうかいして ゆかと　まどガラスを　みがいて	ください くれませんか くださいませんか

10.1.4 Completion of an action

びょう気に　なって、しごとを　休んで くすりを　ぜんぶ　のんで むこうで　車が　パンクして 宿題は　もう　して おとうとは　先月　学校を　やめて	しまったんです しまいました
あめで　洋服が　よごれて たいへんな　事故が　おこって スイス製の　とけいが　こわれて	しまいますよ
早く　おさらを　洗って ごはんは　ぜんぶ　食べて この　漢字は　一日で　おぼえて あしたの　朝までに　これを　しゅうりして そんな　ことは　わすれて	しまってください しまいましょう

10.1.5 Doing in advance

よる　出かけるので、昼ねを　して 山に　行くので、おべん当を　作って	おきましょう

パンクは　四時までに　なおして しゅうり屋に　電話を　かけて	おきます
前に　旅館を　よやくして まどガラスを　みがいて、へやを　きれいに　して	おきました
ドイツへ　行く　前に、ドイツ史を　勉強して いろいろな　所を　けんぶつして	おくつもりです
池(いけ)田さんと　よく　話し合って しけんの　前に、よく　れんしゅうして	おいてください

10.1.6 Sequential action

こわれた　ワイパーを　なおして、	出かけました
くすりを　のんで、	すぐ　ねたいと　思います
着物に　着かえて、	買い物に　行きました
よやくを　取りけして、	京都まで　足を　のばしませんか
高校を　卒業(そつぎょう)して、	デパートに　つとめました
大学院を　やめて、	高校の　教師(し)を　しています
二かいに　あがって、	待っていてください
東京で　生まれて、	大阪(さか)の　小学校に　入りました

10.1.7 Parallel description

a. Verb

ぼくは　歴史を　専攻(せんこう)して、	おとうとは　てつ学を　専攻(せんこう)しています
この　たて物は　コンクリートで 　できていて、	あの　たて物は　木で　できています
一日じゅう　子どもの　世(せ)話を　して、	食事を　作らなければなりません
あには　ハワイで　生まれて、	あねは　東京で　生まれました
鈴(すず)木さんは　コーヒーを　のんで、	わたしは　こうちゃを　のみました
ぼくは　山に　行って、	おとうとは　うみに　およぎに　行くんです

b. Adjective

ぼくの　へやは　くらくて、	むしあついです
けい子さんは　あたまが　いたくて、	はも　いたいそうです
あの　レストランは　高くて、	サービスも　わるいです
りょうしんは　まだ　若くて、	とても　元(げん)気です
あの　方は　美しくて、	せいが　すごく　高いんです

c. Copula

京都は　古い　町で、	古くて　いい　物が　のこっています
居(い)間も　客間も　りっぱで、	広かったです
ミラーさんは　絵が　好きで、	はんがにも　きょうみを　持っています
高橋(はし)さんは　東京生まれで、	原(はら)さんは　長崎(さき)生まれだそうです
地下鉄は　べんりで、	はやいですよ
あの　ホテルは　しずかで、	やすいと　思います

10.1.8 Reason

a. Verb

日本文化に　きょうみを　持って、	日本語を　習いはじめました
むすめが　生まれて、	とても　うれしいです
新しい　洋服(ふく)が　に合って、	よかったですね
石井(い)さんから　りっぱな　おみやげを　もらって、	かんしゃしています
交通(こうつう)事故(こ)が　おこって、	たいへんでした
車が　パンクして、	おどろきました
人口が　ふえすぎて、	いやですね
こたえることが　できなくて、	はずかしいです
ボールペンが　こわれていて、	書くことが　できないんです

b. Adjective

へやが　くらくて、	本を　読むことが　できません
この　台所(だいどころ)は　あかるくて、	気持ちが　いいです
とても　うれしくて、	すぐ　母に　知らせました
足が　いたくて、	一日じゅう　家に　いました
旅行は　みじかくて、	おもしろくありませんでした
しごとが　いそがしくて、	えいがを　見る　時間が　ないんです
ここの　学生は　うるさくて、	教えにくいです

c. Copula

すきやきが　好きで、	食べすぎてしまいました
先生の　せつめいは　かんたんで、	よく　わかりませんでした
あの　木の　はこは　じゃまで、	むこうへ　持って行きました
あなたの　家が　りっぱで、	わたしは　おどろきました
しごとが　たいへんで、	土曜(よう)日も　働かなければなりません
地下鉄より　バスの　ほうが　べんりで、	いつも　使っています
友だちが　るすで、	会うことが　できなかったんです

10.1.9 "while" "during"

a. Verb

パンクを　なおしている	間	ぼくは　あの　きっさ店で　待っています
友だちに　電話を　かける		そこに　すわっていてください
ぼくが　加藤(かとう)さんと　話していた		きみは　どこに　いたんですか
主人が　びょう院に　入っていた		わたしも　びょう院に　とまっていたんです
日本に　いる	間に	いろいろな　所を　見ておきたいんです
子どもが　ねている		ごはんを　食べてしまいましょう
井上(いの)さんが　漢字を　十　おぼえる		森(もり)さんは　十五　おぼえるそうです
あなたを　待っている		ざっしを　一さつ　読みおわりましたよ

b. Adjective

石井(い)さんは　長い	間	英(えい)語の　先生だったそうです
子どもが　小さい		かないは　しごとを　持っていなかったんです
すずしい	間に	レポートを　書いてしまいましょう
あかるい		車を　取りに　行きます

c. Copula

お正月の	間	国に　いるつもりです
夏休みの		三十日も　アルバイトを　しました
ぼくが　るすの	間に	ブラウンさんが　来たそうです
あかちゃんが　しずかな		この　本を　読んでしまいたいです

10.1.10 "while" "as"

テレビを　見	ながら	ごはんを　食べては　いけません
自動車を　運転(うんてん)し		あまり　話さないでください
すしを　作るのを　手つだい		さかなの　名前を　おぼえました
子どもたちの　世(せ)話を　し		大学院へ　行っています
おんがくを　聞き		本を　読むのが　好きです
一郎(ろう)くんは　四年間　アルバイトを　し		大学へ　行ったそうです
高校で　英(えい)語を　教え		日本の　歴史を　研究(けんきゅう)していました
漢字は　書き		おぼえるのが　一番　はやいでしょう

10.1.11 "after"

高校を　卒業(そつぎょう)して	から、	すぐ　大学へ　行きはじめました
車を　しゅうり屋へ　取りに　行って		友だちを　むかえに　行きます
とまる　旅館を　よやくして		行った　ほうが　いいですよ
ゆかは　水で　洗って		みがくつもりです
ふろ場を　見て		新しい　台所(だいどころ)も　見てください

むすめが　生まれて	から、	東京に　来たんですよ
新しい　家を　たてて		だいぶ　べんりに　なりました
前もって　電話で　知らせて		会いに　行くつもりです

10.1.12 "before"

ぼくが　小学校を　卒業(そつぎょう)する	前	父は　銀行に　つとめはじめました
長崎(さき)へ　いらっしゃる		どこに　住んでいらっしゃいましたか
むすこが　生まれる		ドイツに　いたことが　あります
高木(ぎ)さんを　しょうかいする	前に	しゃしんを　見せてあげましょう
国へ　帰る		中村(むら)先生に　会うつもりです
ねる		はを　みがいてください
さむくなる		日光(にっこう)を　けんぶつしませんか
くすりを　のむ		せつめいを　よく　読んでください

クリスマスの　休み	の	前（に）	レポートを　書きおわりました
けい子さんの　たんじょう日			おくり物を　買っておいてください
結婚記念(けっこんきねん)日			花を　おくってもらいました
お正月			スキーに　行くつもりです
卒業(そつぎょう)			ぼくは　東京で　働きはじめました

10.2 OTHERS

10.2.1 Relational *de* "of" "from"

うちの　おふろは ゆかは	木 プラスチック	で	できています
しょうじは	木と　紙		
この　さらは	ガラス		
さいきんの　家は	コンクリートや　アルミ		

あの　人の　ゆびわは	金	で	できています
その　かたなは	竹だけ		
あの　たて物は	石と　鉄		
この　フォークは	銀		
かばん	かわ ビニール		

カレーは	やさいや　にく	で	作ります
日本風の　にわは	石と　木		
はしは	木		

10.2.2 Relational *ni* "for"

この　へやを 八じょうを 日本間を 洋間を	客間 子どもべや 居間 勉強する　へや	に	使っています 使いましょう
あの　たて物を	事務所 店 旅館 食堂	に	使っているそうです

10.2.3 Relational *hodo* "approximately"

五分	ほど	待ってください
三日		いなかに　いたことが　あります
一週間		びょう気で　ねていました
八か月		子どもの　世話を　しました
一年半		ドイツ語を　勉強しているんです
四年五か月		ハワイに　住んでいらっしゃいます

10.2.4 ～ *o shite iru*

a. "job"

りょうしん		中学校の　教師(し)		
おじ		いしゃ		
そふ	は	くすり屋	を	しています
おばあさん		花屋		していました
あの　きょうだい		自動車の　しゅうり屋		
あの　人		バスの　車しょう		

b. "wear"

よし子さん	は	すごい　とけい 高い　おび 金の　ゆびわ	を	している していた
大学生の　ポールくん あの　方		日本製(せい)の　ベルト あかい　ネクタイ		

10.2.5 "quit doing," "help someone doing," etc.

	ピアノを　習う パンクを　なおす 家を　たてる			やめます やめるつもりです やめました
わたしは	友だちが　料(りょう)理(り)する みち子さんが　着物を　着る			手つだいました
小(こ)林(ばやし)さんは	あなたが　デパートの　中を あるいている 事故(こ)が　おこる	の	を	見ました
	ポールさんが　国へ　帰る			知らなかったんです
	ホテルを　よやくする			わすれて しまいました

10.2.6 Compound

もっと　よく　話し	合ってください

学生たちが　しつ問し	合っています
しけんの　こたえを　見せ	合わないでください
日本語と　英語を　教え	合ったんです

10.3 REVIEW DRILLS

10.3.1 Substitution and Transformation Drills

1. A：上野へ　行きたいんですが、地図を　かいてくれませんか。

   B：ええ、かいてあげますよ。

   1. きっぷを　買う　2. つれて行く　3. 車を　かす

   4. みちを　教える　5. 地図を　見せる　6. バス停の　場所を　教える

2. A：だれに　フランス語を　教えてもらいましたか。

   B：石井さんに　教えてもらいました。

   A：石井さんは　じょうずなんですか。

   B：ええ、とても　じょうずです。あなたも　教えてもらいませんか。

   1. おびを　しめる　2. しゃしんを　とる　3. 絵を　かく

   4. テニスを　教える

3. A：へやは　きれいに　しましたか。

   B：はい、きれいに　しておきました。

   A：ビールも　買いましたか。

   B：あ！　いけない。買うのを　わすれてしまいました。

   1. おかしを　買う、コーヒーも　作る

   2. ガソリンを　入れる、オイルも　しらべる

   3. にくを　入れる、やさいも　洗う

   4. 車を　洗う、ガラスも　みがく

   5. ワイパーを　なおす、オイルも　入れる

4. A：あなたは　テレビを　見ながら　ごはんを　食べますか。

   B：いいえ、テレビを　見てから、ごはんを　食べます。

   A：いもうとさんたちは？

   B：いもうとたちは　テレビを　見る　前に　ごはんを　食べます。

   1. さんぽする、アイスクリームを　食べる

   2. 勉強する、おんがくを　聞く

3. コーヒーを　のむ、食事を　する
4. ねる、本を　読む
5. おんがくを　聞く、昼ねする

10.4 REVIEW EXERCISES

10.4.1 Insert appropriate Relationals into the blanks:

1. この　へやは　客間______　使っています。
2. 日本の　はんが______　きょうみ______　持っていらっしゃいますか。
3. 大学______　卒業(そつぎょう)して______、何______　なりたいですか。
4. あなたが　ねている　間______、本を　読みおわってしまいました。
5. この　はし______　プラスチック______　できている。
6. 公害(こうがい)______　おこって、いろいろ　問題______　なりました。
7. 友だち______　いい　場所を　しょうかいしてもらいました。
8. いい　ゆびわ______　していますね。
9. いろいろ　世(せ)話______　なった　人______　かんしゃして、おくり物を　するのです。
10. 電話______　こわれた______、まだ　なおさないんですか。

10.4.2 Select an appropriate word from among the words given and tell the meaning of the sentence:

1. うちでは　______　父が　車を　運転(うんてん)します。
〈だいぶ、　おもに、　だんだん〉
2. ______　洋風の　家が　ふえましたね。
〈さいきん、　できるだけ、　しばらく〉
3. あなたは　絵が　好きですか。______、おんがくが　好きですか。
〈ですから、　それとも、　その　ご〉
4. 田中さんは　______　新しい　ことばを　おぼえてしまうんです。
〈だんだん、　どんどん、　かなり〉
5. ハワードさんは　______　日本へ　いらっしゃったそうです。
〈はじめて、　しばらく、　できるだけ〉

10.4.3 Choose one of the three phrases given to make a complete sentence and give the English equivalent for each of them:

1. 父は　ぼくの　たんじょう日に　いい　かばんを　買って　{やりました。／しまいました。／くれました。}

2. 店の　ある　場所を　教えて
   - あげましょうか。
   - おきましょうか。
   - もらいましょうか。

3. すみませんが、まどを　しめて
   - しまいませんか。
   - くれませんか。
   - あげませんか。

4. ひらがなは　一週間で　おぼえて
   - やりました。
   - おきました。
   - しまいました。

5. 子どもが　帰る　時、あめが　ふっていたので、わたしは　むかえに
   行って
   - やりました。
   - くれました。
   - くださいました。

6. きみに　ぼくの　いなかへ　来て
   - しまいたいんだけど。
   - もらいたいんだけど。
   - あげたいんだけど。

7. あした　使うので、おさらを　洗って
   - やりました。
   - しまいました。
   - おきました。

10.4.4 Connect each of the A-group expressions with appropriate B-group expressions:

A	B
1. 大学院に　入る　前に、	a. 米国に　住んでいらっしゃったらしいです。
2. みち子さんと　食事を　しながら、	b. はずかしいそうです。
3. 銀行を　やめてから、	c. 住んでいる　人たちも　とても　いい人たちです。
4. わたしが　さんぽしている　間、	d. たいへんでした。
5. あの　方は　九州に　住む　前、	e. 外国旅行を　しておきたいです。
6. この　へんは　しずかで、	f. おんがくを　聞きました。
7. 山田さんは　しけんが　わるくて、	g. ほかの　人は　しゃしんを　とっていました。
8. あめの　時、ワイパーが　こわれてしまって、	h. 教師に　なったんです。

10.4.5 Make good sentences:

1. ＿＿＿＿＿＿＿＿のを　やめて、＿＿＿＿＿＿＿＿。
2. ＿＿＿＿＿＿＿＿くて、いやですね。
3. ＿＿＿＿＿＿＿＿ながら、＿＿＿＿＿＿＿＿ないでください。
4. ＿＿＿＿＿＿＿＿てから、＿＿＿＿＿＿＿＿んです。
5. ＿＿＿＿＿＿＿＿てもらって、うれしかったです。
6. ＿＿＿＿＿＿＿＿のを　手つだってくれませんか。
7. ＿＿＿＿＿＿＿＿てくださって、ありがとうございました。
8. ＿＿＿＿＿＿＿＿で、毎日　しています。

10.4.6 Choose the better Verb to fit the situation:

1. 先生の　おくさまは　着物を　着て {いました。 / いらっしゃいました。}
2. 父は　きょう　うちに {います。 / いらっしゃいます。}
3. お客さまは　何時ごろ {来ます。 / いらっしゃいます} か。
4. 青木くん、たばこを　すうのを　やめて {くれません / くださいません} か。
5. 先生、この　ことばの　いみを　教えて {もらいたい / いただきたい} んですが。
6. クリスマスは　ゆきだと　ラジオが {言いました。 / おっしゃいました。}
7. 知らない　人が　小学校を　さがしていたので、地図(ず)を　かいて {あげました。 / さしあげました。}
8. 先生が　ぼくは　歴史を　専攻(せんこう)した　ほうが　いいと {言った。 / おっしゃった。}

10.4.7 What would you say when:

1. you are going to bother someone by your visit?
2. you want to express politely and formally that you certainly will do what you have been asked to do?
3. you want to get the resident's attention at the door?
4. you ask your guest to come into the house?

5. you thank a service man for his work?
6. you want to confirm what you have asked someone to do?
7. you want to express your gratitude for a customer's constant patronage?
8. you want to express your hearty welcome to your guest, telling that you have been waiting for him?
9. you want to show the way to another room?
10. you want to ask a garage to have your car repaired by that evening?

10.4.8 Make an appropriate sentence to fit each of the following responses:

1. どうも　ごくろうさま。
2. そう　できれば、うれしいです。
3. 六か月ほどに　なります。
4. いいえ、車を　運転(うんてん)して　帰るつもりです。
5. くらくて、いやなんです。
6. 大学の　教師(し)を　していました。
7. はんがなど　いいと　思いますけど。

10.5 MIKE HARRISON SERIES (2)

——どうりょうの　大石　ハリソンを　ドライブに　さそう——

10.5.1 ——会社(かいしゃ)で——

大石　　　「ハリソンさん、今度の　土曜(よう)日　ひまですか。」

ハリソン　「ええ、べつに　よていは　ないです。」

大石　　　「ぼくの　友だちが　車を　持っていて、奥多摩(おくたま)の　方へ　ドライブに
つれて行ってくれると　言っているんですよ。」

ハリソン　「ドライブ？」

大石　　　「ええ。むこうに　おいしい　ステーキ屋も　あるので、帰りに　そこで
食事するつもりなんですけど、ハリソンさんも　行けば　たのしいだろう
と思って。」

ハリソン　「うれしいですね。ぜひ　つれて行ってください。」

大石　　　「そうですか。さそって　よかった。友だちは　林(はやし)と　いうんですが、かれが
うちまで　むかえに　来てくれるそうです。」

ハリソン　「わるいですね。」

大石　　　「じゃ、林(はやし)に　ハリソンさんが　来ると　言っておきます。かれは　ぼくの
大学の　時の　友だちなんですよ。」

ハリソン「そうですか。何か　持って行く　物は　ありますか。」

大石　　「べつに。奥多摩(おくたま)は　山が　多くて、とても　きれいな　所だから、しゃしんを　とりたければ、カメラを　持って行けば　いいでしょう。週末(まつ)は　天気が　いいらしいですよ。」

ハリソン「たのしみですね。」

大石　　「会う　時間なんか　もう　一度　かれと　そうだんして、くわしく知らせますから。」

ハリソン「ええ、おねがいします。」

10.5.2　——大石　ステーキ屋に　電話する——

大石　　「もしもし、今度の　土曜(よう)日の　よるの　よやくを　したいんですが…。」

女の人「ありがとうございます。何人さまでしょうか。」

大石　　「四人です。ステーキの　ほかにも　料理(りょうり)が　できるんですか。」

女の人「はい。さかなも　とりも　ございます。こちらに　いらっしゃってから、お好きなのを　注文(ちゅうもん)していただけば　けっこうです。前の　日に　かくにんのお電話を　したいと　思いますので、お名前と　お電話番号(ごう)を　おねがいします。」

大石　　「大石と　いいます。東京　481の　4195です。」

女の人「わかりました。では、土曜(よう)日　お待ちしています。」

10.5.3　——土曜(よう)日の　朝、林(はやし)　ガソリン・スタンドへ——

林(はやし)　「すみません。まんタンに　してください。それから、オイルも　ちょっと　見ておいてください。」

店員「はい。…オイルが　少なくて、よごれていますけど、こうかんしますか。」

林(はやし)　「いや、きょうは　時間が　ないから、オイルを　たしておいてください。いくらですか。」

店員「ガソリンは　38リッター　入りました。オイルと　ガソリンで　7,600円いただきます。…ありがとうございました。」

林(はやし)　「どうも。さあ、いそがなければ…。」

10.5.4　——大石の　うちの　前で——

大石　　「林(はやし)、おそいなあ。」

ハリソン「どう　したんでしょう？　心配(しんぱい)ですね。」

大石　　「あ、来た、来た！」

林(はやし)　「どうもどうも　おそくなって。とちゅうで　ガソリン・スタンドに　よっていたんです。さあ、のってください。はじめまして、ぼく　林(はやし)です。こちら、ぼくの　いいなずけの　かず子さんです。こちら　ハリソンさん。」

ハリソン　「はじめまして。」

かず子　「どうぞ　よろしく。」

ハリソン　「かなり　とおいんですか。奥多摩(おくたま)は？」

林(はやし)　「いや、一時間半　あれば、つくでしょう。それに、みちも　あまり　こんでいないらしいです。さあ、出かけましょうか。」

10.5.5 ——夕方、ステーキ屋で——

林(はやし)　「ああ、つかれた。たのしかったけど、つかれましたね。」

大石　「天気が　よくて、よかった。」

かず子　「本当。」

女の人　「いらっしゃいませ。お待ちしていました。おしぼりを　どうぞ。」

大石　「メニューを　見せてください。」

女の人　「はい、どうぞ。お飲(の)み物は　何を　さしあげましょうか。ビール、ワイン、おさけ、いろいろ　ございますが。」

大石　「ハリソンさんは　何に　しますか。」

ハリソン　「ぼくは　ビールに　します。」

大石　「ぼくも　ビール。きみは？」

林(はやし)　「ぼくは　運転(うんてん)するから、ジュースか　水に　しておくよ。」

かず子　「あたしも　ジュースに　するわ。」

大石　「すみません。ビールと　ジュースを　二本ずつ　おねがいします。」

10.5.6 ——食事が　おわって——

大石　「ハリソンさん、コーヒーの　おかわりは　どうですか。」

ハリソン　「いえ、ぼくは　もう　けっこうです。もう　おなかが　いっぱいです。」

林(はやし)　「ぼくは　おかわり。」

大石　「すみません。コーヒーを　二人分(ぶん)　ください。それから、おかんじょうおねがいします。」

女の人　「お待たせしました。どうぞ。」

ハリソン　「ぼくは　いくら　はらいましょうか。」

大石　「いや、ハリソンさん、きょうは　ぼくが　おごりますから、ご心配(しんぱい)なく。」

ハリソン　「いいえ、それじゃ　わるいから、わりかんに　しましょう。」

大石　　「とんでもない。きょうは　ハリソンさんは　お客さんですよ。」

ハリソン「そうですか。では、ごちそうに　なります。ありがとうございました。」

10.5.7 New Vocabulary (for passive learning)

1.	どうりょう	dooryoo	……	co-worker; colleague
	ドライブ	doraibu	……	driving
	さそう	sasou	……	invite
	よてい	yotei	……	schedule; plan
	奥多摩（おくたま）	Okutama	……	name of an area in the suburbs of Tōkyō
	ステーキ屋	suteekiya	……	steak house
	帰りに	kaeri ni	……	on one's way back
	わるい	warui	……	sorry
	だろう	daroo	……	plain equivalent of *deshoo*
	かれ	kare	……	he
	何か	nani ka	……	something
	たのしみ	tanoshimi	……	enjoyment; joy
	なんか	nan'ka	……	colloquial equivalent of *nado* – and the like
	そうだんする	soodan suru	……	consult
2.	何人さま	nan'nin sama	……	polite way of saying "how many people?"
	とり	tori	……	chicken
	ございます	gozaimasu	……	polite equivalent of *arimasu*
	注文（ちゅうもん）する	chuumon suru	……	order
	けっこう	kekkoo	……	fine
	かくにん	kakunin	……	confirmation
3.	まんタンに　する	man'tan ni suru	……	fill up the gas (tank)
	こうかんする	kookan suru	……	exchange; change
	たす	tasu	……	add
	リッター	rittaa	……	liter
4.	なあ	naa	……	exclamatory sentence ending (used usually by men)
	どう　したん　でしょう	Doo shita n deshoo?	……	I wonder what happened?
	とちゅうで	tochuu de	……	on one's way
	(〜に) よる	(ni) yoru	……	drop in (at)
	いいなずけ	iinazuke	……	fiancé

5.	つかれる	tsukareru	......	get tired
	おしぼり	oshibori	......	wet towel supplied at the table
	メニュー	menyuu	......	menu
	ワイン	wain	......	wine
	ジュース	juusu	......	juice
6.	おかわり	okawari	......	second helping; another cup
	いっぱい	ippai	......	full (ippai)
	二人分(ぶん)	futaribun	......	two persons' portion
	(お)かんじょう	(o)kan'joo	......	bill; payment
	お待たせ しました。	Omatase shimashita.	......	I'm sorry to have kept you waiting.
	はらう	harau	......	pay
	おごる	ogoru	......	treat someone (to dinner)
	ご心配(しんぱい)なく。	Goshin'pai naku.	......	Don't worry.; Never mind.
	わりかん	warikan	......	Dutch treat
	ごちそうに なる	gochisoo ni naru	......	is treated (to dinner) by someone

LESSON 11
ことば使い

11.1 PRESENTATION

日本語の 敬語の 使い方[1]は、 世界の 言語の なかで もっとも ふくざつな ものの 一つ[2]である[3]。 しかも、 男と 女は それぞれ ちがう ことば使いを する。 そのため、外国人に[4]は なかなか むずかしい。

11.2 DIALOG

ムーア 「田中先生。 きょうは 図書館で 敬語について[5] 調べてみました。 それについて ちょっと 説明してほしい[6]んですが …。 あ、まちがえました。 ていねいに[7] たのむ 時は、 説明していただきたいんですが[6]…と 言うんでしたね。」

先生 「ええ、 その とおり[8]。 でも、私には 自由に 話して いいですよ。」

ムーア 「はい。 あのう、 日本の 社会では、 話す あい手の 地位によって[5] ことば使いを 変えなければならないそうですが、 ずいぶん ふくざつなんですね。」

先生 「ええ、 以前は とくに そうでしたね。」

ムーア 「では、 さいきんは だいぶ 変わったんですか。」

先生 「ええ、 一ぱん的に 言って、 ずっと かんたんに なりましたよ。 私は 敬語が もっと かんたんに なれば いい[9]と 思っています。」

ムーア 「本当ですね。」

先生 「しかし、 むずかしくても[10]、 やはり ひつような 時が ありますから、 あなたたちにも よく 覚えてほしい[6]ですね。 けれど、 日本人でも[10]、 よく まちがえるんですよ。」

ムーア 「そうですか。 それを 聞いて、 安心しました[11]。」

使い方(つかいかた)	世界(せかい)	調べてみました(しらべてみました)	説明して(せつめいして)
社会(しゃかい)	変えなければ(かえなければ)	変わった(かわった)	覚えて(おぼえて)

11.3 PATTERN SENTENCES

11.3.1

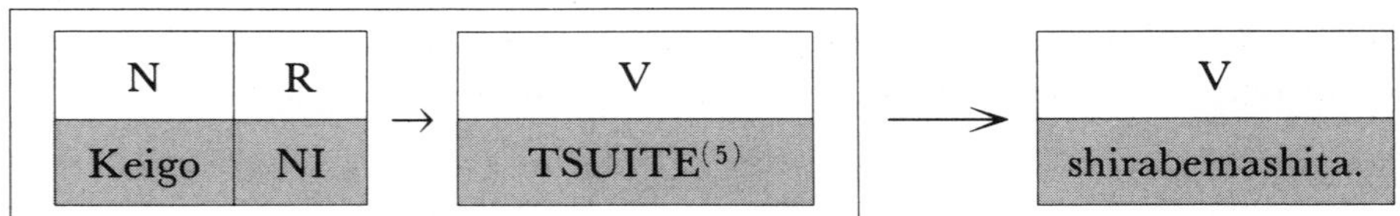

11.3.2

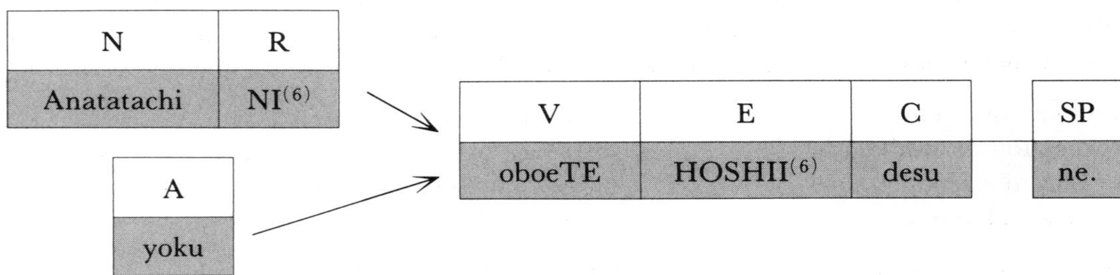

11.3.3

A	Rc	A	→	V	E	C
MuzukashikuTE	MO,[10]	yoku		oboete	hoshii	desu.

11.4 NOTES

11.4.1 *Keigo no tsukaikata* means "how to use *keigo*" or "the usage of *keigo*." The Stem form of a Verb may be followed by the dependent Noun *-kata* "method" or "way" and forms a connotation such as "how to do it," "the way one does it." Since the combination is a compound Noun, the subject or the object of the Verb, if expressed, is followed by the Relational *no* instead of *ga* or *o*. At the same time, the other Predicate Modifiers are also followed by the Relational *no*.

un'ten *o* suru	⟶	un'ten *no* shikata	"how to drive"
keigo *o* tsukau	⟶	keigo *no* tsukaikata	"how to use the honorific style"
anata *ga* hanasu	⟶	anata *no* hanashikata	"the way you talk"
Tookyoo e iku	⟶	Tookyoo e *no* ikikata	"how to go to Tōkyō"

Hashi no tsukaikata o oshiete kudasai.	"Please show me how to use the chopsticks."
Ichiroo san no hanashikata wa wakarinikui desu.	"The way Ichirō talks is difficult to understand."
Pan'ku no naoshikata o shitte imasu ka?	"Do you know how to fix a flat tire?"

11.4.2 *Mottomo fukuzatsu na mono no hitotsu* means "one of the most complicated matters." *~no hitotsu* is different from *hitotsu no~*, which means "one [thing or matter]." For example, *hitori no tomodachi* means "one friend," and *tomodachi no hitori* means "one of [my] friends."

11.4.3 *De aru* is the combination of the TE form of the Copula plus the Extender *aru*, and is the plain audience-type equivalent for the Copula *da*. The plain audience type has been explained in Lesson 1, Note 1.3.2B. When the plain audience type is used, vocabularies in the sentence are usually more formal. For example, *mottomo* is used instead of *ichiban*, *shikamo* is used in lieu of *sore ni*, and *sono tame* is used instead of *sore de*. This type is used more in written style.

11.4.4 *Gaikokujin ni wa nakanaka muzukashii* means "It is fairly difficult for foreigners." The Relational *ni* is often followed by a Predicate that connotes evaluation, such as "good," "convenient," "difficult," "important," and so forth. In this case the Relational *ni* determines that to which or to whom or for which or for whom that evaluation is true. The Relational *wa* frequently follows *ni*.

kodomo ni wa yoku nai	"it is not good for children"
gakusei ni tekitoo na san'koosho	"reference books that are suitable for students"
toshitotta hito ni wa taihen da	"it's too much (work) for aged people"
watashi ni wa wakaranai	"it's beyond my understanding"
Kono yubiwa wa watashi ni wa ookisugimasu.	"This ring is too big for me."
Keigo no tsukaikata wa nihon'jin ni wa yasashii n desu ka?	"Is the use of speech styles and levels easy for Japanese people?"
Iie, nihon'jin ni mo nakanaka muzukashii n desu yo.	"No, it is fairly difficult even for Japanese people (to use it properly)."
Kyoo wa san'po ni ii hi desu ne.	"It's a good day for a walk today, isn't it?"

11.4.5 *Keigo ni tsuite shirabete mimashita* means "I checked up on usages of the styles." The ~*ni tsuite* is used here in the meaning of "about," "concerning," "on," and so on. Some combinations of a certain Relational and the TE form of a certain Verb carry idiomatic meanings. These combinations may be called the "Relational-like function" of the TE form of a Verb. Here are some of those to be studied in this lesson:

~ni tsuite	"concerning" "about" "on"
~ni yotte	"according to" "depending upon"
~to shite	"as" "for" "in the capacity of" "by way of"

In this lesson, familiarize yourself with these combinations as they occur. These special combinations of a Relational and the TE form of a Verb formulate a Predicate Modifier.

Suzuki sen'sei ga Nihon no bun'ka ni tsuite hanashite kudasaimashita.	"Prof. Suzuki gave us a talk about Japanese culture."
Itoo san ni tsuite wa Pooru san ga kuwashii koto o shitte iru hazu desu.	"As for Mr. Itō, Paul is supposed to know the details."
Watashi no chichi wa gun'jin to shite san'nen'kan Nihon ni imashita.	"My father was in Japan for three years with the service."
Amerikajin to shite nihon'go no keigo ni tsuite doo omoimasu ka?	"As an American, what do you think of the honorific style of Japanese?"

Jikan ni yotte wa watashi mo iku koto ga dekimasu.	"I'll be able to go with you depending upon the time (if the time is right)."
Ten'ki ni yotte wa ryokoo o yamemasu.	"We'll give up traveling depending upon the weather (if the weather is bad)."

11.4.6 *Setsumei shite hoshii* means "I want you to explain it." The combination of the TE form of a Verb and the Extender *hoshii* carries the connotation "one wants someone to do such and such." This pattern should clearly be distinguished from the pattern with *-tai*. While *-tai* expresses one's wish of his own doing such and such, *-te hoshii* implies one's desire of someone else's doing such and such. The person who is wanted to do such and such is followed by the Relational *ni*. Usually ~*n desu ga* or ~*n desu kedo* is used with *-te hoshii* to soften any direct in seeking favor from others.

$$\textbf{person} + \textbf{\textit{ni}} + \textbf{Verb(\textit{-te})} + \textbf{\textit{hoshii}} + (\textbf{\textit{n}}) + (\textbf{\textit{desu}}) + \left\{ \begin{array}{l} (\textbf{\textit{ga}}) \ldots \\ (\textbf{\textit{kedo}}) \ldots \end{array} \right.$$

oniisan ni oshiete hoshii	"[he] wants his older brother to teach"
anata ni kite hoshikatta	"[I] wanted you to come"
Amerika Taishikan e iku michi o oshiete hoshii n desu.	"I want you to direct me to the American Embassy."
Boku no ryooshin ni atte hoshikatta noni, dooshite konakatta n desu ka?	"I wanted you to meet my parents; why didn't you come?"
Kuraku naru mae ni pan'ku o naoshite hoshii n desu ga.	"I want you to repair the flat tire before it gets dark."
Anatatachi ni wa moo roomaji o tsukatte hoshiku arimasen.	"I do not want you to use roman letters any more."
Ano hito ni wa kite hoshiku nakatta n desu kedo.	"I didn't want that man to come here."

The pattern ~*ni . . . -te hoshii* is almost equal to ~*ni . . . -te moraitai* in its meaning and also in its level of politeness, which is not adequate when a student asks his teacher politely to explain something for him. The pattern *-te itadakitai* is more polite than *-te moraitai*. (See Note 9.4.14.)

$$\textbf{person} + \textbf{\textit{ni}} + \textbf{Verb(\textit{-te})} + \left\{ \begin{array}{l} \textbf{\textit{moraitai}} \\ \textbf{\textit{itadakitai}} \end{array} \right\} + (\textbf{\textit{n}}) + (\textbf{\textit{desu}}) + \left\{ \begin{array}{l} (\textbf{\textit{ga}}) \ldots \\ (\textbf{\textit{kedo}}) \ldots \end{array} \right.$$

These three expressions all seek action from persons other than the speaker. However, the three may be differentiated according to degrees of politeness, and according to who is seeking the favor from whom.

Shite hoshii demonstrates the first person's wish, hoping that the second or third person would take action, while *shite itadakitai* and *shite moraitai* mean that the speaker is asking the second or third person to take action, thus favoring him. *Shite itadakitai* is more polite than both *shite hoshii* and *shite moraitai*. The action sought in all three is usually connected with favor-seeking, although *Ame ga futte hoshii* can be used, *shite moraitai* and *shite itadakitai* cannot be used for *ame* or any natural phenomenon.

11.4.7 *Teinei ni tanomu* means "one asks (someone to do) politely." When an adjectival Noun is used adverbially, the adjectival Noun should be followed by the Relational of manner *ni*. Note that the adverbial use of Adjectives, KU form, has been explained in Note 4.4.10.

shizuka ni	"quietly"	gen'ki ni	"in high spirits"
shin'setsu ni	"kindly"	teinei ni	"politely"
jiyuu ni	"freely"	kan'tan ni	"simply"
ippan'teki ni	"generally"		

Doozo jiyuu ni totte kudasai. "Please help yourself."

Suujii san wa piano o joozu ni hikimashita. "Susie played the piano very well."

Akachan ga nete imasu kara, shizuka ni aruite kudasai. "Please walk quietly since a baby is asleep."

Shiranai hito ga shin'setsu ni chizu o kaite kuremashita. "A stranger kindly drew a map for me."

11.4.8 In the sentence *Ee, sono toori*, the Copula has been omitted with a Noun ending the sentence. Such omission is quite normal in informal conversation among peers as well as from a superior toward an inferior. Although the construction is very abrupt, it is quite common or normal as a teacher's comment toward a student. A student, of course, would not address such a comment toward his teacher.

11.4.9 *Keigo ga motto kan'tan ni nareba ii to omotte imasu* means "I hope the use of *keigo* will become much simpler." The BA form, or the provisional form, of a Verb, an Adjective, or the Copula followed by *ii* formulates the connotation of "I hope that one does such and such," "I wish something to be such and such," and so on. As the Sentence Particle *ga* or *keredo* occurs after the expressions of "want" to avoid being too direct, it may also appear after the expression . . . *-ba ii (n) (desu)*. *~ to omotte imasu* at the end of the utterance, however, serves a similar purpose.

BA form of {Verb / Adjective / Copula} + *ii* (*n desu*) {(*ga*) / (*keredo*)}

yuki ga fureba ii "I wish it would snow"
yasukereba ii n desu ga "I hope it is inexpensive"
kan'tan nara ii keredo "I hope it is simple"

Kinoo no yoru wa amari ben'kyoo shinakatta n desu. Shiken ga yasashikereba ii kedo. "I didn't study well last night. I hope the examination will be easy."

Den'sha ga komanakereba ii to omoimasu. "I hope the train won't get crowded."

Yoyaku shita heya ga nihon'fuu nara ii n desu ga. "I wish the room I reserved (at the hotel) to be Japanese style."

11.4.10 *Muzukashikute mo, oboete hoshii* means "Even if it is difficult, I want you to learn it." The TE form of a Verb, an Adjective, or the Copula followed by the Relational *mo* "even" may formulate a nonfinal clause meaning "even if one does such and such," "even if something is such and such," "even though one did such and such," and so on. This clause has already been introduced in the pattern of permission: . . . *-te mo ii* or . . . *-te (mo) kamawanai*. However, note that the Relational *mo* "even" is mandatory when used other than in expressions of permission.

Verb(*-te*)
Adjective(*-kute*) } + ***mo, . . .***
Noun + *de*

teinei ni hanashite mo, . . .	"even if one speaks politely, . . ."
isoide mo, . . .	"even if one hurries, . . ."
tookute mo, . . .	"even if it is far, . . ."
osokute mo, . . .	"even if it is late, . . ."
iya de mo, . . .	"even if it is disagreeable, . . ."
fukuzatsu de mo, . . .	"even if it is complicated, . . ."
nihon'jin de mo, . . .	"even if it is a Japanese, . . ."
otona de mo, . . .	"even if it is an adult, . . ."

Kusuri o non'de mo, zen'zen gen'ki ni narimasen. — "Even though I took medicine, I haven't recovered at all."

Kono tokei wa furui node, naoshite mo, moo dame deshoo. — "Since this watch is old, it will be no use even if you have it repaired."

Ten'ki ga warukute mo, ryokoo ni iku tsumori desu ka? — "Are you planning to go traveling even if the weather is bad?"

Atama ga itakute mo, kaeru koto ga dekinai n desu ka? — "Can't you go home although you have a headache?"

Ima heta de mo, ren'shuu sureba joozu ni narimasu yo. — "Even if you are not good at it at present, you will progress in it after some practice."

Mon'dai ga fukuzatsu de mo, yoku yomeba, wakarimasu yo. — "Even if the question is complicated, you will understand it when you read it carefully."

This use of *-te mo*, *-kute mo*, or *de mo* indicates that the antecedent statement is contrary to the consequent statement.

Tanon'de mo, dame desu. — "Even if you ask (for), it wouldn't do."

Takakute mo, kau tsumori desu. — "Even if it is expensive, I intend to buy it."

In order to indicate that the antecedent statement is a condition for the following consequent statement, the BA form must be used. (See Note 13.4.11, Vol. II.)

Tanomeba, daijoobu deshoo. — "It will do if you ask (for)."

Takakereba, kawanai tsumori desu. — "If it is expensive, then I do not intend to buy it."

11.4.11 *Sore o kiite, an'shin shimashita* means "I am relieved from anxiety to hear it." There are abundant expressions revealing human sentiment in Japanese:

TE form + expression of sentiment

shin'pai suru	"is anxious (about)"
odoroku	"is surprised (by)"
ureshii	"is happy" "to be glad"
gakkari suru	"is disappointed"

Sore o kiite ureshii desu. — "I am happy to hear it."

Sore o mite gakkari shimashita. — "I was disappointed when I saw it."

11.5 VOCABULARY

Presentation

ことば使(づか)い	kotobazukai	......	N	speech; expression; wording; manner of speaking
敬(けい)語	keigo	......	N	speech levels and styles
方	-kata	......	Nd	method; way; how to ～ (see 11.4.1)
言(げん)語	gen'go	......	N	language; tongue
もっとも	mottomo	......	Adv.	the most (formal equivalent of *ichiban*)
ふくざつ	fukuzatsu	......	Na	complicated (opp. *kan'tan*)
である	de aru	......	C+E	(see 11.4.3)
しかも	shikamo	......	SI	moreover; furthermore
それぞれ	sorezore	......	Adv.	respectively
そのため	sono tame	......	SI	hence; for that reason
に	ni	......	R	with reference to (see 11.4.4)
なかなか	nakanaka	......	Adv.	fairly; quite; very

Dialog

ムーア	Muua	......	N	Moore
について	ni tsuite	......	R+V	concerning; about; on (see 11.4.5)
ほしい	hoshii	......	E	want someone to do (see 11.4.6)
に	ni	......	R	in such and such manner (see 11.4.7)
たのむ	tanomu	......	V	ask; request (～ *ni* ～ *o tanomu*)
とおり	toori	......	Nd	way; like
自由(ゆう)	jiyuu	......	Na	free; liberal
社会	shakai	......	N	society; community
あい手	aite	......	N	the other party
地位(い)	chii	......	N	status; rank; position
によって	ni yotte	......	R+V	depending upon; according to (see 11.4.5)
変え	kae	......	V	change (Stem form of *kaeru*) (transitive Verb)
以前(いぜん)	izen	......	N	former times; before
変わった	kawatta	......	V	changed (TA form of *kawaru*) (intransitive Verb)
一ぱん的	ippan'teki	......	Na	general
ひつよう	hitsuyoo	......	Na	necessary
けれど(も)	keredo(mo)	......	SI	however

安心(あんしん)しました	an'shin shimashita	......	V	feel relieved; feel easy (see 11.4.11)
安心(あんしん)	an'shin	......	N	relief; peace of mind

Notes

として	to shite	......	R+V	as; for; in the capacity of; by way of (see 11.4.5)
しんせつ	shin'setsu	......	Na	kind
心配(しんぱい)する	shin'pai suru	......	V	worry (see 11.4.11)
心配(しんぱい)	shin'pai	......	Na	worry; anxiety
がっかりする	gakkari suru	......	V	get disappointed

11.6 KAN'JI

11.6.1 世 (1) SE (2) world; generation; reign (3) classifier 一
(4) 一 十 卄 廿 世 (5) 世界(かい)、世話をする

11.6.2 界 (1) KAI (2) world; boundary; community (3) classifier 田 [rice field]
(4) 丶 冂 罒 田 田 甲 畀 界 界 (5) 世界、スポーツ界
(6) homonym 介

11.6.3 調 (1) *shira(beru)* (2) investigate; examine; check (3) classifier 言 [word]
(4) 言 訁 訂 訂 訶 調 調 (5) 調べておきます

11.6.4 説 (1) SETSU (2) opinion; theory (3) classifier 言 (4) 言 訁 訁 説
(5) 小説(しょう) [novel]、説明(めい)する、新説

11.6.5 明 (1) MEI (2) bright; clear (3) classifier 日 [sun] (4) 日 明
(5) 説明 (6) sun (日) plus moon (月); homonym 盟

11.6.6 社 (1) SHA [-JA] (2) (Shinto) shrine; (business) company (3) classifier 礻 [worship; deify] (4) 丶 ㇇ 礻 礻 社 (5) 神(じん)社、会(かい)社、社会(かい)

11.6.a 会[8.6.10] (1) KAI (2) meeting; community (5) 社会、社会学、会話、会社

11.6.7 変 (1) *ka(eru)*; *ka(waru)* (2) change; reform; move (3) classifier 夂 (亠)
(4) 丶 亠 亣 亣 亦 亦 亦 变 変 (5) 気分を変える、天気が変わる

11.6.8 覚 (1) *obo(eru)* (2) memorize; remember (3) classifier ⺍ (見 [see])
(4) ⺍ 覚 (5) あの人の名前は覚えていません、覚え方

11.6.9 雨* (1) *ame* (2) rain (3) forms the classifier 雨 [rain; weather]
(4) 一 丆 冂 帀 帀 雨 雨 雨 (5) 雨がふる、大雨

11.6.10 雪* (1) *yuki* (2) snow (3) classifier 雨 (4) 雨 雪 雪 雪
(5) 雪がふる、雪だるま [snowman]、大雪

11.6.11 英* (1) EI (2) English (3) classifier 艹
(4) 一 十 艹 艹 艿 苎 英 英 (5) 英語、英国、米英

11.7 DRILLS

11.7.1 Transformation Drill

1. 図(と)書館で 調べました。 わかりませんでした。	→ 図(と)書館で 調べても、 わかりませんでした。
2. 学校を 卒業(そつぎょう)します。 国へ 帰らないつもりです。	→ 学校を 卒業(そつぎょう)しても、 国へ 帰らないつもりです。
3. いそぎます。 もう おそいですよ。	→ いそいでも、 もう おそいですよ。
4. 説明してもらいました。 使い方が わからなかったんです。	→ 説明してもらっても、 使い方が わからなかったんです。
5. くすりを のみました。 まだ あたまが いたいんです。	→ くすりを のんでも、 まだ あたまが いたいんです。
6. 雨や 雪が ふります。 山に 出かけるつもりですか。	→ 雨や 雪が ふっても、 山に 出かけるつもりですか。
7. 三十分 待ちました。 バスは 来ませんでした。	→ 三十分 待っても、 バスは 来ませんでした。

11.7.2 Transformation Drill

1. むずかしいです。 覚えなければ なりません。	→ むずかしくても、 覚えなければ なりません。
2. 気分が わるいです。 学校を 休まないんですか。	→ 気分が わるくても、 学校を 休まないんですか。
3. スイス製(せい)の とけいが ほしいです。 今 おかねが ないんです。	→ スイス製(せい)の とけいが ほしくても、 今 おかねが ないんです。
4. おいしいです。 食べすぎないでください。	→ おいしくても、 食べすぎないでください。

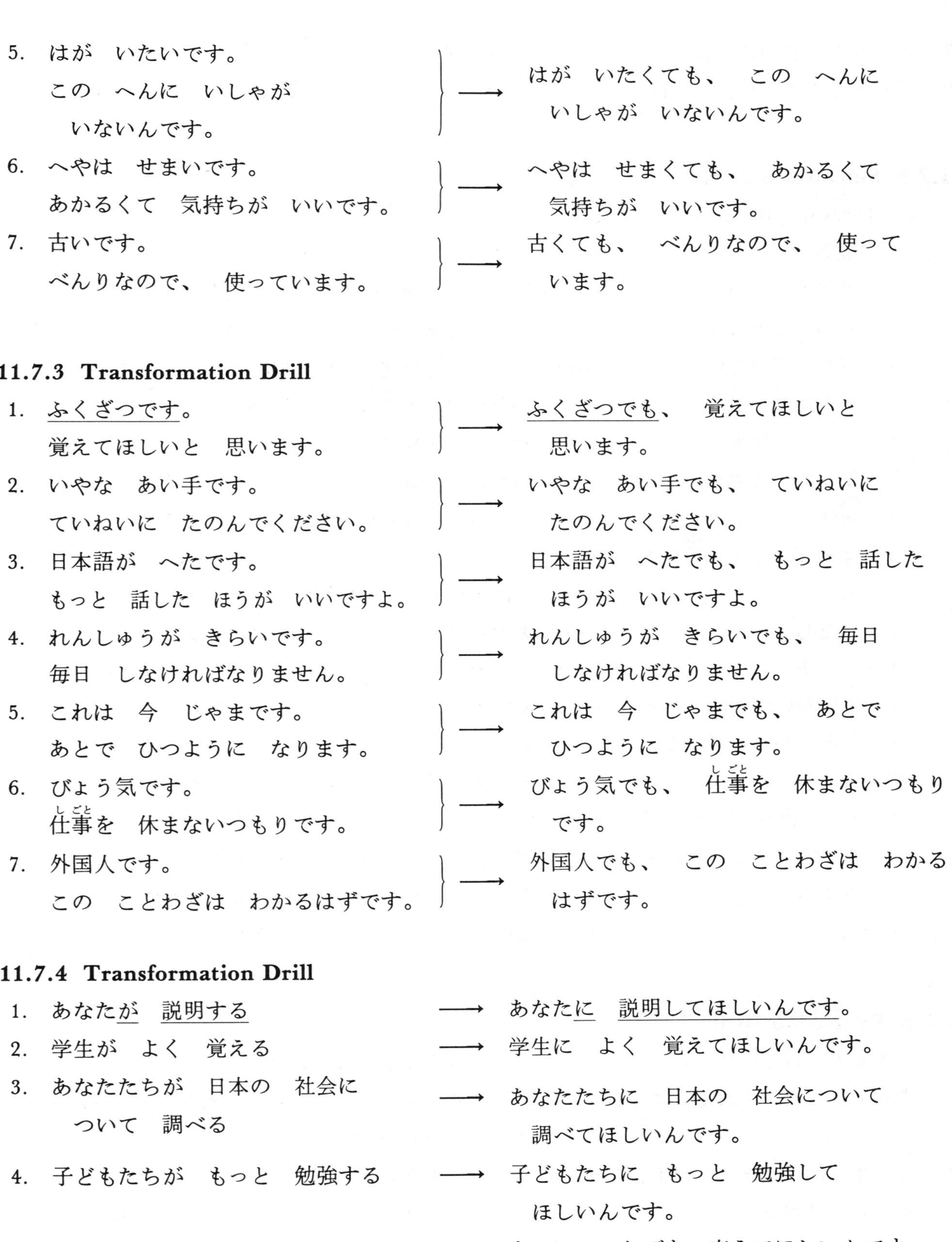

5. はが　いたいです。この　へんに　いしゃが　いないんです。 ⟶ はが　いたくても、　この　へんに　いしゃが　いないんです。

6. へやは　せまいです。あかるくて　気持ちが　いいです。 ⟶ へやは　せまくても、　あかるくて　気持ちが　いいです。

7. 古いです。べんりなので、　使っています。 ⟶ 古くても、　べんりなので、　使っています。

11.7.3 Transformation Drill

1. ふくざつです。覚えてほしいと　思います。 ⟶ ふくざつでも、　覚えてほしいと　思います。

2. いやな　あい手です。ていねいに　たのんでください。 ⟶ いやな　あい手でも、　ていねいに　たのんでください。

3. 日本語が　へたです。もっと　話した　ほうが　いいですよ。 ⟶ 日本語が　へたでも、　もっと　話した　ほうが　いいですよ。

4. れんしゅうが　きらいです。毎日　しなければなりません。 ⟶ れんしゅうが　きらいでも、　毎日　しなければなりません。

5. これは　今　じゃまです。あとで　ひつように　なります。 ⟶ これは　今　じゃまでも、　あとで　ひつように　なります。

6. びょう気です。仕事(しごと)を　休まないつもりです。 ⟶ びょう気でも、　仕事(しごと)を　休まないつもりです。

7. 外国人です。この　ことわざは　わかるはずです。 ⟶ 外国人でも、　この　ことわざは　わかるはずです。

11.7.4 Transformation Drill

1. あなたが　説明する ⟶ あなたに　説明してほしいんです。
2. 学生が　よく　覚える ⟶ 学生に　よく　覚えてほしいんです。
3. あなたたちが　日本の　社会について　調べる ⟶ あなたたちに　日本の　社会について　調べてほしいんです。
4. 子どもたちが　もっと　勉強する ⟶ 子どもたちに　もっと　勉強してほしいんです。
5. きみが　ことばを　変える ⟶ きみに　ことばを　変えてほしいんです。
6. ムーアさんが　英語を　教える ⟶ ムーアさんに　英語を　教えてほしいんです。

7. みんなが　自由に　話す　⟶　みんなに　自由に　話してほしいんです。
8. ムーアさんが　銀行へ　行く　⟶　ムーアさんに　銀行へ　行ってほしいんです。

11.7.5 Substitution Drill

A. ことば使いについて　調べたんです。

1. 敬語 …… 敬語について　調べたんです。
2. 世界の　言語 …… 世界の　言語について　調べたんです。
3. 女の　ことば使い …… 女の　ことば使いについて　調べたんです。
4. 話してください …… 女の　ことば使いについて　話してください。
5. あなたの　研究 …… あなたの　研究について　話してください。
6. 新しい　仕事 …… 新しい　仕事について　話してください。
7. 知っていますか …… 新しい　仕事について　知っていますか。
8. 現代の　日本 …… 現代の　日本について　知っていますか。

B. 地位によって　ことば使いを　変えます。

1. 人 …… 人によって　ことば使いを　変えます。
2. 友だち …… 友だちによって　ことば使いを　変えます。
3. あい手 …… あい手によって　ことば使いを　変えます。
4. ていねいに　話します …… あい手によって　ていねいに　話します。
5. ことばが　ちがいます …… あい手によって　ことばが　ちがいます。
6. 国 …… 国によって　ことばが　ちがいます。
7. 着る　物が　ちがいます …… 国によって　着る　物が　ちがいます。
8. 食べ物が　変わります …… 国によって　食べ物が　変わります。
9. きせつ …… きせつによって　食べ物が　変わります。
10. 気候 …… 気候によって　食べ物が　変わります。

11.7.6 Expansion Drill

1. はんがが　ほしいです。 …… はんがが　ほしいです。
   たんじょう日の　おくり物として …… たんじょう日の　おくり物として　はんがが　ほしいです。
2. 鈴木さんに　何を　あげましょうか。 …… 鈴木さんに　何を　あげましょうか。
   クリスマスプレゼントとして …… クリスマスプレゼントとして　鈴木さんに　何を　あげましょうか。
3. 森さんは　ハワイへ　来ました。 …… 森さんは　ハワイへ　来ました。

新しい　日本語の　先生として　……　新しい　日本語の　先生として　森(もり)さんは　ハワイへ　来ました。

4. てんぷらは　一番　ゆうめいです。　……　てんぷらは　一番　ゆうめいです。
日本の　食べ物として　……　日本の　食べ物として　てんぷらは　一番　ゆうめいです。

5. 何が　一番　さかんですか。　……　何が　一番　さかんですか。
若い　人の　スポーツとして　……　若い　人の　スポーツとして　何が　一番　さかんですか。

6. 日本の　教育(いく)について　どう　思いますか。　……　日本の　教育(いく)について　どう　思いますか。
大学生として　……　大学生として　日本の教育(いく)について　どう　思いますか。

7. どこが　一番　いんしょう的でしたか。　……　どこが　一番　いんしょう的でしたか。
アメリカ人として　……　アメリカ人として　どこが　一番　いんしょう的でしたか。

11.7.7 Substitution Drill

ていねいに　たのんでください。

1. 自由(ゆう)　……　自由(ゆう)に　たのんでください。
2. しずか　……　しずかに　たのんでください。
3. 話してくれませんか　……　しずかに　話してくれませんか。
4. 教育(いく)的　……　教育(いく)的に　話してくれませんか。
5. かんたん　……　かんたんに　話してくれませんか。
6. じょうずに　……　じょうずに　話してくれませんか。
7. なおしておきました　……　じょうずに　なおしておきました。
8. りっぱ　……　りっぱに　なおしておきました。
9. きれい　……　きれいに　なおしておきました。

11.7.8 Substitution Drill

これは　子どもには　ふくざつすぎます。

1. ぼく　……　これは　ぼくには　ふくざつすぎます。
2. 一年生　……　これは　一年生には　ふくざつすぎます。
3. むずかしい　問題です　……　これは　一年生には　むずかしい　問題です。

4. わかりにくいでしょう …… これは　一年生には　わかりにくいでしょう。
5. 小学生 …… これは　小学生には　わかりにくいでしょう。
6. ちょうど　いいと　思います …… これは　小学生には　ちょうど　いいと　思います。
7. 年取った　人 …… これは　年取った　人には　ちょうど　いいと　思います。
8. 若い　人 …… これは　若い　人には　ちょうど　いいと　思います。
9. かんたんすぎます …… これは　若い　人には　かんたんすぎます。

11.7.9 E-J Transformation Drill

A. 先生に　聞いても、　わかりませんでした。

1. even though I studied …… 勉強しても、　わかりませんでした。
2. even though I read a book …… 本を　読んでも、　わかりませんでした。
3. even though I checked on it at the library …… 図書館で　調べても、　わかりませんでした。
4. even though I asked a question …… しつ問しても、　わかりませんでした。

B. 近くても、　行きたくありません。

1. even if I am not busy …… いそがしくなくても、　行きたくありません。
2. even if the weather is nice …… 天気が　よくても、　行きたくありません。
3. even if it is warm …… あたたかくても、　行きたくありません。
4. even if tickets are inexpensive …… きっぷが　やすくても、　行きたくありません。

C. ふくざつでも、　覚えなければなりません。

1. even though you dislike it …… きらいでも、　覚えなければなりません。
2. even though it is hard …… たいへんでも、　覚えなければなりません。
3. even though it is not important …… たいせつじゃなくても、　覚えなければなりません。
4. even though it is not necessary …… ひつようじゃなくても、　覚えなければなりません。

11.7.10 Substitution Drill

あした　いい　天気に　なれば　いいんですが…。

1. 早く　しけんが　終わる …… 早く　しけんが　終われば　いいんですが…。

2. むすめが　生まれる …… むすめが　生まれれば　いいんですが…。
3. もっと　れんしゅうする …… もっと　れんしゅうすれば　いいんですが…。
4. 電話で　知らせる …… 電話で　知らせれば　いいんですが…。
5. およぐことが　できる …… およぐことが　できれば　いいんですが…。
6. かず子さんが　手つだってくれる …… かず子さんが　手つだってくれれば　いいんですが…。
7. 六時までに　なおしてしまう …… 六時までに　なおしてしまえば　いいんですが…。

11.7.11 Substitution Drill

敬語の　使い方を　教えてくれませんか。

1. カレーを　作る …… カレーの　作り方を　教えてくれませんか。
2. 運転を　する …… 運転の　し方を　教えてくれませんか。
3. レポートを　書く …… レポートの　書き方を　教えてくれませんか。
4. しゅうりを　する …… しゅうりの　し方を　教えてくれませんか。
5. おびを　しめる …… おびの　しめ方を　教えてくれませんか。
6. パンクを　なおす …… パンクの　なおし方を　教えてくれませんか。
7. 着物を　着る …… 着物の　着方を　教えてくれませんか。
8. はしを　使う …… はしの　使い方を　教えてくれませんか。

11.8 EXERCISES

11.8.1 Read the following statements and then write TRUE（T）or FALSE（F）in the space provided:

1.（　　）日本語では、　男と　女の　ことば使いは　あまり　ちがいません。
2.（　　）むかしの　ことば使いより　今の　ことば使いの　ほうが　かんたんになりました。
3.（　　）男と　女では、　一ぱん的に　女の　ほうが　ていねいに　話します。
4.（　　）日本では　あい手の　仕事や　地位によって　ことば使いを　変えます。
5.（　　）日本語の　敬語の　使い方は　英語ほど　ふくざつではありません。
6.（　　）「〜してほしい」と「〜していただきたい」とでは、「〜してほしい」の　ほうが　ていねいです。
7.（　　）日本人なら、　みんな　敬語を　じょうずに　使います。

11.8.2 つぎの　ことばを　使って、　みじかい　文(ぶん)[sentence]を　作ってください。　また、英語で　いみを　言ってください。

1. ～によって
2. しんせつに
3. ～として
4. ～について
5. ～てほしい
6. ～(て)も　''even if''
7. ～ば　いい
8. ～方　''how to''

11.8.3 Connect each of the A-group expressions with appropriate B-group expressions and tell the meaning of each sentence:

A

1. 敬語(けいご)を　使いたくても
2. ことば使(づか)いについて
3. ぼくたちには
4. アメリカ人として
5. 気候(こう)によって

B

a. せつめいしていただきたいんですが。
b. てき当ではないと　思います。
c. 着る　物が　ちがいます。
d. よく　知らないんです。
e. どう　思いますか。
f. まだ　習っていないんです。

11.8.4 Insert an appropriate Relational in each blank in the following and tell the meaning of each sentence:

1. あなたの　字は　読みにくい(　　)、もっと　きれい(　　)　書いてください。
2. あした　だれ(　　)　東京へ　行ってほしいんですか。
3. その　こと(　　)ついては　もう　友だち(　　)　知らせてもらいました。
4. アメリカ人(　　)は　敬語(けいご)の　使い方が　むずかしい(　　)　思います。
5. 来週は　いそがしい(　　)、　日曜(よう)日で(　　)、　働かなければなりません。
6. さいきんは　女の　人の　ことば使(づか)い(　　)　とても　変わりました。
7. 渡辺(わたなべ)さん(　　)　この　仕事(しごと)(　　)　たのんでみてください。
8. どんな　時に　ことば使(づか)い(　　)　変えなければなりませんか。

11.8.5 What would you say when:

1. you want to ask a lady politely to take care of your children while you are not at home? (take care of ＝ ～の　世話を　する)
2. you want a young girl to take care of your children while you are not at home?
3. you want your friends to come the following day even if it should rain?
4. you want Mr. Mori to make a reservation at a Japanese-style inn even though the rate is expensive?
5. you do not want someone to speak about that traffic accident?
6. you feel at ease to hear something?
7. you are disappointed to hear something?

11.8.6 Write the underlined *hiragana* in *kan'ji*:

1. せかいじゅうを　りょこうしてみたいですね。
2. えいごを　おぼえてほしいですね。
3. あめや　ゆきが　ふっても、　ひは　かえないつもりです。
4. にほんの　しゃかいについて　しらべて、　せつめいするつもりです。
5. この　へんの　けしきは　さいきん　かわりましたね。

11.8.7 Distinguish the following *kan'ji*:

1. 話、調、語、説
2. 明、時
3. 雨、雪、電
4. 田、界、男
5. 朝、明
6. 見、覚

11.8.8 When your teacher wants you to study more, he may say:

11.8.9 When you want your teacher to teach you Chinese, you would say:

11.8.10 When you want an outsider, who is your superior, to come to your home, you would say:

11.9 SITUATIONAL AND APPLICATION CONVERSATION

11.9.1 Kazuko asks Paul if one has to change, in English, the use of a word according to the status of the other party.

Paul says there are a few honorific expressions in English too. And he says that he understands that when the student talks to the teacher, the student must speak very politely in Japan.

Kazuko agrees. Kazuko says it is perhaps difficult for an American, but she wants Paul to memorize the use of honorific expressions.

11.9.2 Develop your own opinion on *keigo*:

11.9.3 Taniguchi: Suzuki kun, kore o sugu shite moraitai n da kedo.

Suzuki: Hai, sugu shimasu ga, sono mae ni kore o mite itadakitai n desu ga.

11.9.4 Customer: Gomen kudasai.

Salesclerk: Hai. Irasshaimase.

Customer: Kore o naoshite itadakitai n desu ga.

Salesclerk: Hai, chotto mite mimashoo.

11.9.5 Keiko: Okaasan, kore chotto mite hoshii n da kedo.

Mother: Naani?

11.9.6 Teacher: Pen ga 120 en, en'pitsu ga 30 en, soshite nooto ga 100 en . . . zen'bu de ikura desu ka?

Student: Zen'bu de 250 en desu.

Teacher: Sono toori.

LESSON 12

中村さんの　一日：うちで

12.1　PRESENTATION

中村さんは　ある[1]　会社に　つとめている　サラリーマン[2]で、　課長(かちょう)である。　年は　四十五さいで、おくさんの　まさえさんは　四十二さいである。　子どもは　むすめの　友子さんだけである。

高校生[3]の　友子さんは　考え方や　生活(かつ)たいどが　中村さん夫婦(ふうふ)と　だいぶ　ちがっている。　友子さんは　ことば使いなど　あまり　気に　しない[4,5]。

12.2　DIALOG

まさえ　「あなた[5]、　早く　起きてください。　急行に　乗るために[6]、　早く　起きるって[7]　おっしゃったでしょう？」

中村　「うん、　わかったよ。　ねむくはないんだが、　どうも[8]　さむくなれば　なるほど[9]　起きにくくなるねえ。（着かえながら）朝ご飯[10]　もう　できてる[11]かい[12]？　さむいから、　おみおつけ　あつくしてくれ[13]。　あつければ　あついほど　いいよ。」

まさえ　「ええ、　できていますよ。」

友子　「お母さん[14]。　あたし　牛乳(にゅう)が[15]　飲みたいんだけど[16]、　持って来て[13]ね。」

まさえ　「何ですねえ。　自分で　持って来なさい[17]。」

—— 朝の　食事が　終わって ——

まさえ　「友子、　急いで、　したくしなさい。　学校に[18]　おくれますよ。」

友子　「あっ、　もう　七時十分すぎ[19]だわ。　お父さん　いっしょに　出かける[12]？」

中村　「そうだね。　七時半の　急行は　こんでいて、　乗るのに[20]　たいへんだから、　そろそろ　出かけた　ほうが　いいね。」

まさえ　「じゃあ、　行ってらっしゃい。　気を　つけてね。」

中村
友子　「行ってまいります。」

中村(なかむら)さん　年(とし)　考(かんが)え方(かた)　起(お)きて　急行(きゅうこう)
乗(の)る　朝(あさ)ご飯(はん)　牛乳(ぎゅうにゅう)　飲(の)みたい　終(お)わって
急(いそ)いで

12.3 PATTERN SENTENCES

12.3.1

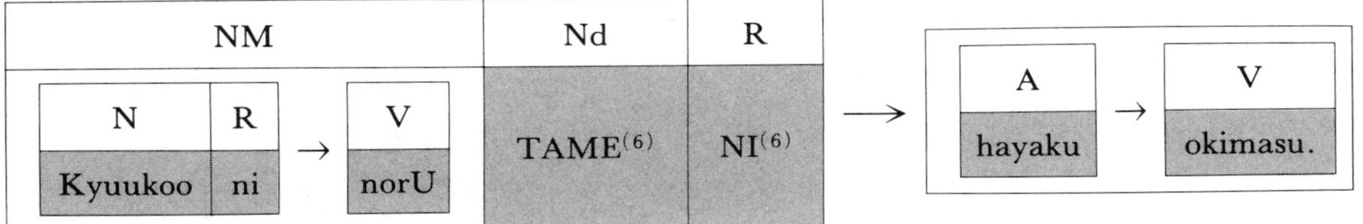

12.3.2

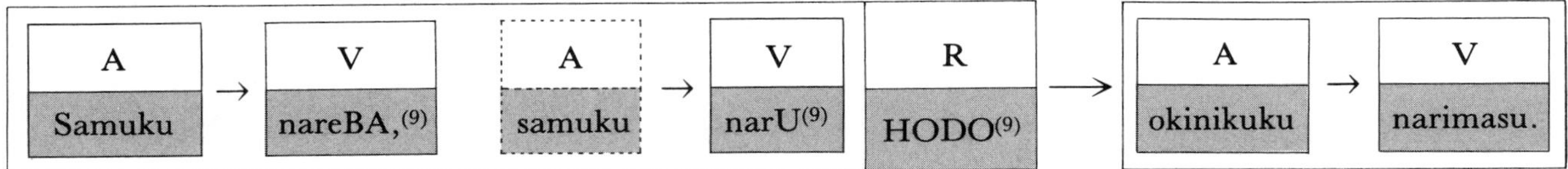

12.3.3

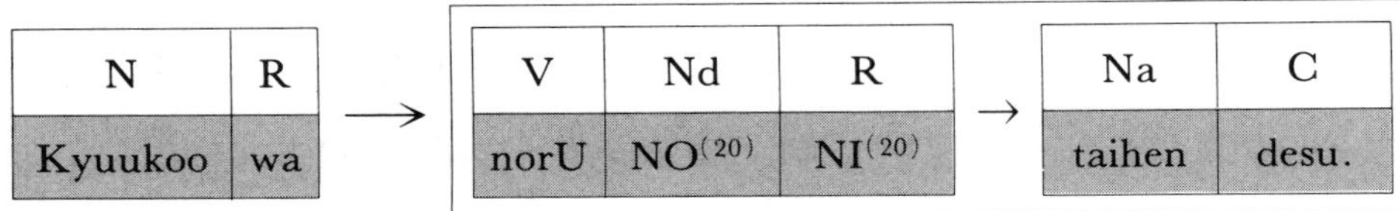

12.4 NOTES

12.4.1 *Aru kaisha* means ''a certain company'' or ''some corporation.'' *Aru* here is a Pre-Noun meaning ''a certain'' or ''some.'' This word may precede various Nouns, but here are some common combinations:

aru hi	''one day''
aru toki	''one time'' ''sometime'' ''a certain time''
aru tokoro	''some place''
aru hito	''someone''
Ani wa ima aru daigaku de kyooshi o shite imasu.	''My older brother is now teaching at a university.''
Mukashi mukashi, aru tokoro ni ojiisan to obaasan ga imashita.	''Once upon a time, there lived an old man and an old woman.''

12.4.2 The word *sarariiman* is an example of a ''made-in-Japan'' foreign loan word. It is based upon the English ''salaried man.'' In creating such a word, however, the Japanese have somewhat modified the meaning carried by the English term. In Japan, this meaning is limited to the middle-class white-collar worker. An interesting discussion of the changing situation of this middle-class white-collar worker may be found in Ezra Vogel's *Japan's New Middle Class: The Salary Man and His Family in a Tōkyō Suburb*.

12.4.3 *Kookoosei* is ''senior high school student.'' The *-sei* is attached to some Nouns to mean ''~ student.''

daigakusei	''college student''
kookoosei	''senior high school student''
chuugakusei	''junior high school student''
shoogakusei	''elementary school boy (or girl)''
ichinen'sei	''freshman'' ''the first grade boy (or girl)''
sotsugyoosei	''graduate''

12.4.4 *Kotobazukai nado amari ki ni shinai* means ''[Tomoko] does not pay much attention to the way of speaking.'' *Ki* means (1) heart, spirit; (2) an inclination; (3) mood, frame of mind; (4) temper; (5) attention; and (6) air, atmosphere, or flavor. *Ki* forms many idiomatic expressions.

(~ga) ki ni naru	''feel uneasy about~''
(~ni) ki o tsukeru	''is cautious about~''
(~o) ki ni suru	''concern [oneself] about~''

12.4.5 *Kotobazukai* means ''the way of speaking.'' Although Tomoko, the high school daughter, does not pay much attention to the way of speaking within the family group, this dialog provides an interesting setting for a study of speech styles among family members, and specifically for contrasting male and female speech styles, as well as conversation between parents and children.

The different usages employed by the husband and wife in this dialog in turn reveal the unequal status of the sexes in Japan. In general, for middle-aged people, the wife uses the polite style in addressing her husband, while the husband uses the plain style more frequently toward his wife. For example, Masae follows the custom still widely practiced by Japanese middle-aged wives. She does not address her husband by his first name. Instead, she addresses him with the pronoun *anata*. Such usage is a reflection of the Japanese tendency to not refer directly to someone of a higher status. For instance, the emperor would never be referred to by his first name. The Japanese usually prefer a title, or a respectable pronoun when addressing a superior, and since traditionally the husband is regarded as superior, a concept which still persists in present-day Japanese society, the wife still follows the traditional customs. However, it is becoming more common among younger wives to address their husbands by their first names plus *-san* or by nicknames.

The Japanese husband, on the other hand, may address his wife by her first name without any affix such as *-san*. Less polite versions of *anata* also employed by husbands toward their wives, such as *kimi* and *omae*, both mean ''you.'' These two pronouns originally were used for superiors; presently, however, they are more normally used toward inferiors.

Masae also uses the expression *osshatta deshoo*, a very polite version of *itta deshoo*. A husband, however, would never use such an expression—*osshatta deshoo*—toward his wife. The instances of female speech in this dialog provide the following contrast.

Female	Male
Soo ne.	Soo da ne.
Shichiji da wa.	Shichiji da.
Nemuku wa nai n da kedo, . . .	Nemuku wa nai n da kedo/ga, . . .
Okinikuku naru wa nee.	Okinikuku naru nee.
Asagohan dekiteru?	Asagohan dekiteru (kai)?
Omiotsuke atsuku shite.	Omiotsuke atsuku shite (kure).
Atsui hodo ii wa (yo).	Atsui hodo ii yo.
Dekaketa hoo ga ii wa ne.	Dekaketa hoo ga ii ne.

Toward her parents, however, the daughter, Tomoko, uses a more plain style than does her mother toward her father, but a less plain style than her father uses toward her mother. This style of speech as employed by Tomoko is a function of the in-groupness of an intimate group, and were an outsider present, she would normally use a more polite style toward her parents.

The mother's use of *Nan desu nee* toward her daughter is indicative of the mother's displeasure. Such an expression would not be used by a father nor would it be used by children. Under such circumstances, a father would say *Nan da nee*. The mother also used the *nasai* form in asking her daughter to do something. This form is more direct than the *kudasai* form, which she uses toward her husband.

Since the end of World War II, children in Japan have tended to use less formal forms in addressing their parents. The influence of in-groupness in language behavior, which is described above, still persists, however, and an outsider's presence would change the child's forms to more polite styles. A child's indiscriminate use of the plain form within the family may also be due to the fact that this is the first form learned by Japanese children. As such, it represents an intimate or a child's manner.

12.4.6 *Kyuukoo ni noru tame ni, hayaku okiru* means "one gets up early in order to take the express train." *Tame* is a dependent Noun meaning "account," "sake," or "purpose," and is always preceded by a Noun Modifier. The plain imperfect tense forms of a Verb or a Noun plus *no* occur before *tame ni* to formulate connotations such as "in order to do such and such," "for the purpose of something," "for someone."

plain imperfect tense form of Verb }
Noun + *no* } + ***tame ni (wa)***

shin'bun o yomu tame ni	"in order to read a newspaper"
byooki ni naranai tame ni	"so as not to be ill"
watashi no tame ni	"for me"
shigoto no tame ni	"for the sake of [my] work"
nan no tame ni	"for what?" "for what purpose?"

Nan no tame ni is often used to elicit an answer stating the purpose of an action.

Nan no tame ni hayaku okita n desu ka?	"For what purpose did you get up early?"
Kyuukoo ni noru tame ni hayaku okita n desu.	"I got up early in order to catch an express."
Jimusho de taberu tame ni oben'too o tsukutte okimashita.	"I have prepared a packed lunch in order to eat at the office."
Kore wa anata no tame ni katta hon desu.	"This is the book I bought for you."

12.4.7 *Hayaku okirutte osshatta deshoo?* means "Didn't you tell me that you would get up early?" *Okirutte* is the contracted form of *okiru to*, the Verb *okiru* plus the quotation Relational *to*. This contraction was noted in Note 1.3.2A.

Yoshida san ga ikutte osshatta n desu.	"Mr. Yoshida said that he would go."
Kurisumasu ni kimono o kurerutte itta deshoo?	"Didn't you say that you'd give me a *kimono* for Christmas?"
Dame datte.	"He said, 'No good.' "

12.4.8 Another example of Japanese vagueness is the use of *doomo*. *Doomo* carries three meanings: "very" or "much"; "by any means"; and "somehow." The use of *doomo* independently without any words following it makes *doomo* a very conveniently vague expression. For example, *Doomo arigatoo* means "many thanks" and *Doomo sumimasen* means "very sorry." Both expressions, however, can be contracted to *Doomo doomo*. Similarly, such expressions as *Doomo yokunai*—"does not seem good"—might be expressed by *doomo* alone, with the appropriate action or facial expression conveying the meaning intended, providing that such gestures would reveal the speaker's intended message.

12.4.9 *Samuku nareba naru hodo okinikuku naru nee* means "The colder it gets, the harder it is to get up." The following combination has the meaning of "the more . . . the more . . . "

(Predicate Modifier) + BA form of (1) {**Verb** / **Adjective** / **Noun + Copula**} + (2) {**Dictionary form of Verb** / **Dictionary form of Adjective** / **Noun + NA form of Copula**} + ***hodo* . . .**

The Verb, Adjective, and Noun plus the Copula under column (1) and those under column (2) must be respectively the same words with different conjugation forms. Column (1) may be omitted when understood. Extenders may follow these words.

ki ni sureba (ki ni) suru hodo	"the more you care the more . . . "
tabenakereba tabenai hodo	"the less one eats the more . . . "
nemukereba nemui hodo	"the more sleepy you are the more . . . "
atsuku nareba (atsuku) naru hodo	"the hotter it gets the more . . . "
jiyuu nara jiyuu na hodo	"the more free one is the more . . . "
Mireba miru hodo omoshiroi han'ga desu nee.	"The more I see the woodblock print, the more interesting I find it."
Gaikokugo wa ren'shuu sureba suru hodo joozu ni narimasu yo.	"The more you practice foreign languages, the more proficient you will be."
Daidokoro wa akarukereba akarui hodo hatarakiyasui desu.	"The better lighted the kitchen is, the easier you can work there."
Tsukurikata wa kan'tan nara kan'tan na hodo ii desu.	"The simpler the way to make it, the better for me."
Kotobazukai wa teinei nara teinei na hodo ii to omoimasu ka?	"Do you think the more polite one's speech is the better?"
Ie wa, eki kara chikakereba chikai hodo ben'ri desu yo.	"The nearer the house is from the station, the more convenient."

12.4.10 It is quite normal for speakers to drop the Relational after a Noun whenever the context is very clear in colloquial Japanese.

Gohan wa nai? ⟶ Gohan nai?
Omiotsuke o atsuku shite. ⟶ Omiotsuke atsuku shite.

Atashi wa iya yo.	⟶	Atashi iya yo.
Kaisha e itta?	⟶	Kaisha itta?

12.4.11 *Dekiteru* is the contracted form of *dekite iru* "is ready." The contracted form of the TE form plus *iru* was explained in Note 1.3.2A.

Doko ni sun'deru n desu ka?	"Where are you living?"
Okane motteru?	"Do you have some money?"
Wakatteta n da yo.	"I knew it."

12.4.12 *Kai* is a Sentence Particle to be used in asking a question. However, *kai* is used only by men in informal situations. The Predicate preceding *kai* is in plain form.

Kono resutoran no bifuteki wa oishii kai?	"Do they serve good beefsteak in this restaurant?"
Kimi mo kuru kai?	"Are you coming with us too?"

Male	Female
Dekakeru kai?	×
Dekakeru ka?	×
Dekakeru?	Dekakeru?

12.4.13 *Atsuku shite kure* is the imperative expression of the plain-style usage and means "Make it hot." This expression is normally used by a man to an inferior or to his close friends. Note that *kure* is omitted in women's speech. (See Note 1.3.2A.) *Kure* is the imperative form of the Extender *kureru*. The plain imperative form of Verbs will be introduced in Volume IV.

Kimi, tetsudatte kure yo.	"Help me, will you?"
Masae, chotto kite kure.	"Masae, come over here."
Chotto sono hon o misete yo.	"Let me have a look at that book."
Doobutsuen e tsurete itte ne.	"Take me to the zoo."

Motte kite ne is actually an abbreviation of *motte kite kudasai ne*, *kudasai* being omitted. This abbreviated version, however, can only be used among intimates. Women and children frequently use this form.

12.4.14 As mentioned in Notes 11.4.12 and 11.4.14 of Volume I, words to refer to family members normally have two different forms depending upon whose family members are referred to. Although *haha* is used when the speaker refers to his mother, he'll use *okaasan* with respect and familiarity, to call his mother or to talk about his mother within his family. When a child is very small, he may say *-chan* instead of *-san*.

ojiisan "grandfather"	otoosan "father"	ojisan "uncle"	oniisan "older brother"
obaasan "grandmother"	okaasan "mother"	obasan "aunt"	oneesan "older sister"

Oniisan, okane o kashite yo. — ''Lend me some money.'' (said to the speaker's older brother)

Otoosan, hayaku hayaku. — ''Papa, hurry up.''

The use of *-chan* is also common after the first name of a child, although senior members of the family often call their children or juniors by name without *-chan*.

Kazuko chan ni otan'joobi no okurimono o agemashoo. — ''I'll give you a birthday present, Kazuko.''

Ichiroo chan wa ikutsu desu ka? — ''How old is Ichirō?''

12.4.15 As explained in Note 12.4.4 of Volume I, when the Verb before *-tai* requires a direct object, the Relational *o* following the direct object may be replaced by the Relational *ga*.

Mizu ga nomitai desu. — ''I want to drink water.''

Ohiru ni nani ga tabetai desu ka? — ''What do you want to eat for lunch?''

However, such a replacement can only be made when the Verb involved represents actions to satisfy basic needs, such as *taberu*, *nomu*, or *suru*. In the case of *suru*, Verbs such as *ryokoo suru* or *ken'kyuu suru*, the Verb *suru* must be separated from the preceding component. Thus,

Ryokoo ga shitai n desu. — ''I want to take a trip.''

12.4.16 *Kedo* placed at the end of a clause and followed by a second clause does not indicate here any logical shift between the two clauses concerning the development of events. *Kedo*, *keredomo*, or *keredo* is normally translated as ''although'' or ''but.'' In many cases, it is very loosely used. For instance, the two sentences ''I want to see a movie'' and ''Don't you want to come too?'' can be connected by *kedo*. Literally translated, this sounds awkward and does not make much sense in English, ''I want to see a movie, but, don't you want to come too?''

12.4.17 *Motte kinasai* means ''Bring it in.'' The Stem form of a Verb plus *nasai* formulates a compound Verb in the connotation of command or order ''Do such and such.'' Since this is a straight and formal imperative expression, in ordinary situations *〜-te kudasai* is preferred. *Nasai* may be regularly used by parents to tell their children to do such and such. *Nasai* is a form of the Verb *nasaimasu* ← *nasaru*.

Hayaku okinasai. Okuremasu yo. — ''Get up promptly. You'll be late.''

Min'na shizuka ni shinasai. — ''Be quiet, everybody.''

Kaimono ni iku kara, yoofuku o kaenasai. — ''Change your clothes because we are going shopping.''

Motto teinei ni hanashinasai. — ''Speak more politely.''

Sugu isha o yobinasai. — ''Call a doctor right away.''

12.4.18 *Gakkoo ni okuremasu yo* means ''You will be late for school.'' The Relational *ni* preceding *okureru* is used in the meaning of ''for the purpose.''

12.4.19 *Shichiji jippun sugi* means ''ten minutes after or past seven.'' The *-sugi* used after the time is ''after'' to indicate the time after the hour, and *-mae* is used to indicate the time before the hour. The *-sugi* may be omitted, however.

goji jippun sugi *or* goji jippun	''ten minutes after five'' or ''five-ten''
kuji chotto sugi	''a little after nine''
juuji nanafun mae	''seven minutes before ten''
niji juugofun mae	''a quarter to two''
Ima kuji juuhappun (sugi) desu.	''It's nine-eighteen now.''
Moo goji ni narimashita ka?	''Is it already five o'clock?''
Iya, mada goji mae desu.	''No, it's before five yet.''

12.4.20 *Kyuukoo wa kon'de ite, noru no ni taihen da* means ''The express train is so crowded that I have a hard time getting on it.'' *Noru no ni* is a combination of the Verb *noru* plus the dependent Noun *no* plus the Relational of purpose *ni*. This combination means either ''in order to do such and such'' or ''in the process of doing such and such.'' The difference between *~tame ni* and *~no ni* is that when a sentence has the *~tame ni* phrase a stress is on the *~tame ni* while the *~no ni* phrase is less emphasized as compared with the other parts of the sentence. Therefore the sentence with *~tame ni* states for ''why one does or is such and such'' while the sentence with *~no ni* means ''how one does,'' ''how it is to do such and such,'' or ''in the process of doing such and such.''

(Predicate Modifier) + Dictionary form of Verb + *no ni*. . .

noru no ni taihen da	''have a hard time to get on''
tanomu no ni hitsuyoo da	''it is necessary for the purpose of asking someone to do that''
aruku no ni wa toosugiru	''it's too far to walk''
Mainichi gakkoo e iku no ni nan de ikimasu ka?	''What transportation do you use to go to school every day?''
Ishii san wa isogashii hito da kara, au no ni taihen desu yo.	''Mr. Ishii is a busy man, so it will be hard to meet him.''
Kono uchi o tateru no ni dono gurai okane ga kakarimashita ka?	''How much did it cost to build this house?''
Jiko de, uchi e kaeru no ni ichijikan mo kakatte shimaimashita.	''Because of an accident, it took me no less than an hour to get back home.''

12.5 VOCABULARY

Presentation

ある	aru	......	PN	a certain; some (see 12.4.1)
サラリーマン	sarariiman	......	N	salary man; company employee; white-collar worker
課長 (かちょう)	kachoo	......	N	section chief
年	toshi	......	N	age
まさえ	Masae	......	N	girl's first name
友子	Tomoko	......	N	girl's first name

高校生	kookoosei	......	N	senior high school student (see 12.4.3)
考え	kan'gae	......	V	Stem form of *kan'gaeru* – consider; think
生活(かつ)	seikatsu	......	N	life; living
たいど	taido	......	N	attitude
夫婦(ふうふ)	fuufu	......	N	married couple; husband and wife
気に　し(ない)	ki-ni-shi(nai)	......	V	Pre-Nai form of *ki-ni-suru* – care; worry; mind (transitive Verb) (see 12.4.4)

Dialog

ため	tame	......	Nd	purpose; sake; account (see 12.4.6)
うん	un	......	SI	yeah; uh-huh
ねむく	nemuku	......	A	KU form of *nemui* – is sleepy
どうも	doomo	......	Adv.	somehow; really (see 12.4.8)
かい	kai	......	SP	(see 12.4.12)
おみおつけ	omiotsuke	......	N	*miso* (bean paste) soup
くれ	kure	......	E	imperative form of *kureru* (see 12.4.13)
なさい	nasai	......	V	forms the imperative expression when used after the Stem form of a Verb (compound component) (see 12.4.17)
したくし	shitaku shi	......	V	TE form of *shitaku suru* – prepare; get ready
したく	shitaku	......	N	preparations
おくれます	okuremasu	......	V	is late; is behind time; is delayed (normal form of *okureru*) (～ *ni okureru* "is late for ～") (see 12.4.18)
すぎ	-sugi	......	Nd	after; past (the hour) (see 12.4.19)
のに	no ni	......	Nd＋R	in the process of; in order to (see 12.4.20)
気を　つけて	ki-o-tsukete	......	V	TE form of *ki-o-tsukeru* – take care; is careful

Notes

中学生	chuugakusei	......	N	junior high school student
小学生	shoogakusei	......	N	elementary school boy or girl
卒業生(そつぎょう)	sotsugyoosei	....	N	graduate
気に　なる	ki-ni-naru	....	V	feel uneasy about (see 12.4.4)
ちゃん	-chan	....	Nd	(see 12.4.14)

Drills

研究室(けんきゅうしつ)	ken'kyuushitsu	....	N	seminar room; laboratory; professor's office

12.6 KAN'JI

12.6.1 村 (1) *mura* (2) village (3) classifier 木 (4) [木][朩][村][村]
(5) 中村さん、木村さん、小さい村

12.6.2 考 (1) *kan'ga(eru); kan'ga(e)* (2) think; idea; thought (3) classifier 耂
(4) [土][耂][耂][考] (5) 問題を考える、わたしの考え

12.6.a 使[3.6.2] (1) *-zukai* (5) ことば使い

12.6.3 起 (1) *o(kiru)* (2) get up; rise (3) classifier 走 [run; walk]
(4) [土][キ][キ][走][走][起][起][起] (5) 早起き [early rising]、六時に起きた

12.6.4 急 (1) KYUU (2) hurry (3) classifier ク (心) [heart; mind]
(4) [丿][ク][ク][ク][刍][刍][急][急][急] (5) 急行電車、特急 [limited express]

12.6.5 乗 (1) *no(ru)* (2) get on; ride (3) classifier
(4) [丿][二][三][乗][乗][乗][乗][乗][乗] (5) 乗り物、車に乗る、乗りかえ

12.6.6 飯 (1) HAN (2) meal; boiled rice (3) classifier 食 [eating]
(4) [食][飠][飣][飯][飯] (5) ご飯を食べる、朝ご飯、昼ご飯、夕ご飯
(6) homonym 反、坂、阪、板、版、叛、販

12.6.7 牛 (1) GYUU (2) cow; bull (3) forms the classifier 牛 [cow]
(4) [丿][𠂉][牛] (5) 牛乳、とう牛 [a bull fight]、牛肉 [beef]
(6) shape of horns and head of a cow or a bull (ᛘ)

12.6.8 飲 (1) *no(mu)* (2) drink; take (medicine) (3) classifier 食 [eating]
(4) [食][飠][飲][飲][飲] (5) 飲み物、飲み水、酒飲み

12.6.9 終 (1) *o(waru)* (2) end; finish (3) classifier 糸 [thread] (4) [糸][終]
(5) 終わる、終わり [the end]

12.6.b 急[12.6.4] (1) *iso(gu)* (5) 急いでください、急いでしたくしなさい

12.6.10 晩* (1) BAN (2) evening; night (3) classifier 日 [sun]
(4) [日][日][晩][晩][晩] (5) 今晩、あしたの晩、晩ご飯

12.6.11 安* (1) *yasu(i)* (2) inexpensive (3) classifier 宀 [roof] (4) [宀][安]
(5) 安い車、 安田さん

12.7 DRILLS

12.7.1 Transformation Drill

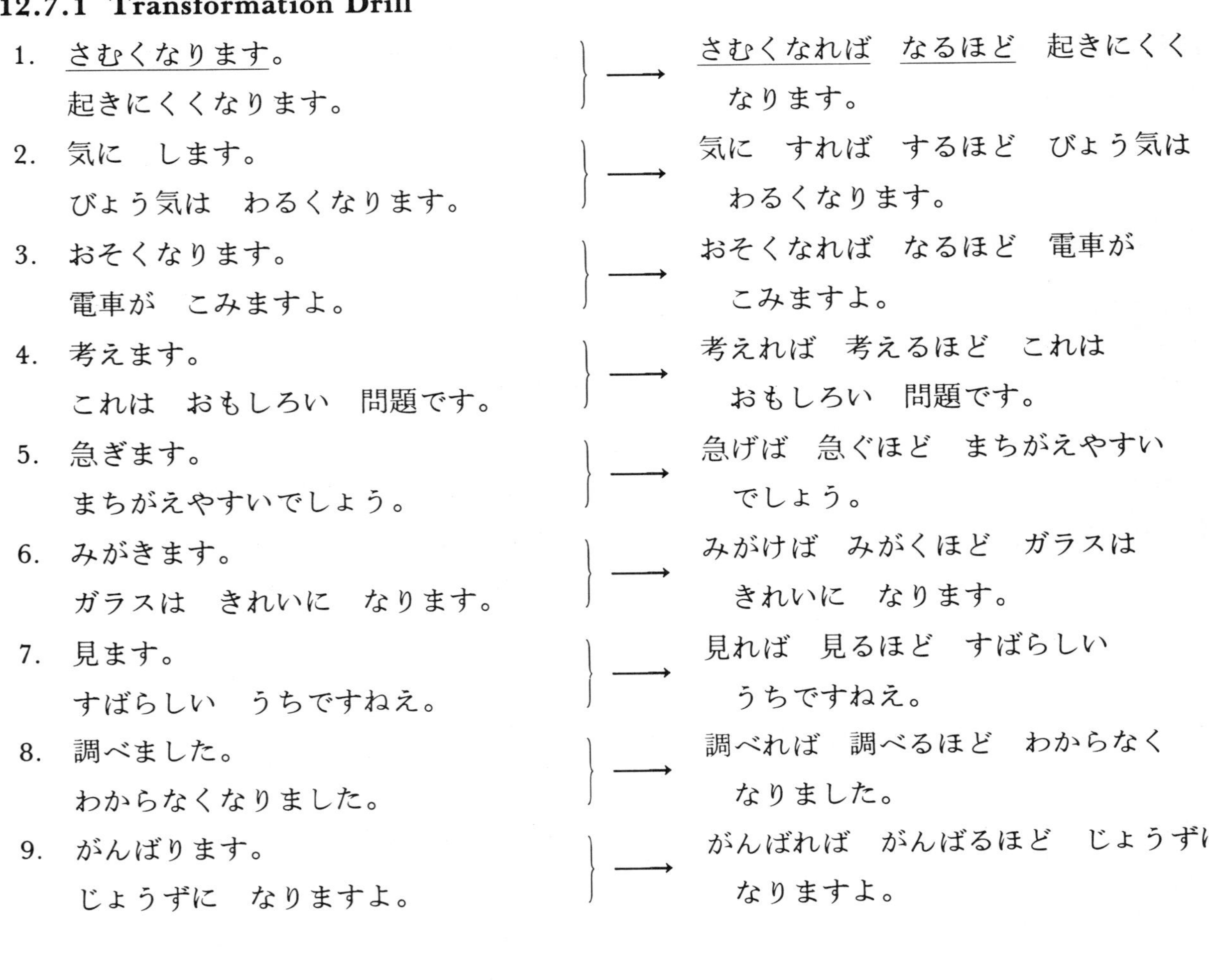

1. さむくなります。
   起きにくくなります。 → さむくなれば　なるほど　起きにくくなります。
2. 気に　します。
   びょう気は　わるくなります。 → 気に　すれば　するほど　びょう気は　わるくなります。
3. おそくなります。
   電車が　こみますよ。 → おそくなれば　なるほど　電車が　こみますよ。
4. 考えます。
   これは　おもしろい　問題です。 → 考えれば　考えるほど　これは　おもしろい　問題です。
5. 急ぎます。
   まちがえやすいでしょう。 → 急げば　急ぐほど　まちがえやすいでしょう。
6. みがきます。
   ガラスは　きれいに　なります。 → みがけば　みがくほど　ガラスは　きれいに　なります。
7. 見ます。
   すばらしい　うちですねえ。 → 見れば　見るほど　すばらしい　うちですねえ。
8. 調べました。
   わからなくなりました。 → 調べれば　調べるほど　わからなくなりました。
9. がんばります。
   じょうずに　なりますよ。 → がんばれば　がんばるほど　じょうずに　なりますよ。

12.7.2 Transformation Drill

1. さむいです。
   起きにくくなります。 → さむければ　さむいほど　起きにくくなります。
2. おみおつけは　あついです。
   おみおつけは　好きです。 → おみおつけは　あつければ　あついほど　好きです。
3. むずかしいです。
   よく　勉強しなければなりません。 → むずかしければ　むずかしいほど　よく　勉強しなければなりません。
4. 早いです。
   いいです。 → 早ければ　早いほど　いいです。
5. これは　古いです。
   これは　かちが　あります。 → これは　古ければ　古いほど　かちが　あります。

6. へやは　あかるいです。 へやは　気持ちが　いいです。	→	へやは　あかるければ　あかるいほど 気持ちが　いいです。
7. お客さんが　多いです。 たのしいです。	→	お客さんが　多ければ　多いほど たのしいです。

12.7.3 Transformation Drill

1. かんたんです。 覚えやすいです。	→	かんたんなら　かんたんなほど　覚え やすいです。
2. 勉強する　へやは　しずかです。 いいですね。	→	勉強する　へやは　しずかなら しずかなほど　いいですね。
3. ひつようです。 たいせつに　しなければなりません。	→	ひつようなら　ひつようなほど たいせつに　しなければなりません。
4. 日本的です。 うれしいのですが。	→	日本的なら　日本的なほど うれしいのですが。
5. へたです。 たくさん　れんしゅうしなければ なりません。	→	へたなら　へたなほど　たくさん れんしゅうしなければ なりません。
6. 生活(かつ)が　らくです。 いいと　思います。	→	生活(かつ)が　らくなら　らくなほど　いいと 思います。
7. 社会が　自由(ゆう)です。 いいと　思いますか。	→	社会が　自由(ゆう)なら　自由(ゆう)なほど　いいと 思いますか。

12.7.4 Transformation Drill

1. 新聞を　読みます。 毎朝　早く　起きます。	→	新聞を　読むために、　毎朝　早く 起きます。
2. 急行に　乗ります。 駅まで　はしって行きました。	→	急行に　乗るために、　駅まで　はしって 行きました。
3. おせいぼを　買います。 ごご　デパートへ　行くつもりです。	→	おせいぼを　買うために、ごご デパートへ　行くつもりです。
4. 車の　ワイパーを　なおして もらいます。 しゅうり屋に　電話を　かけたんです。	→	車の　ワイパーを　なおしてもらうために、 しゅうり屋に　電話を　かけたんです。

5.	友だちに　仕事(しごと)を　たのみます。 あした　会いに　行きます。	→	友だちに　仕事(しごと)を　たのむために、 あした　会いに　行きます。
6.	父を　むかえに　行きます。 母は　五時に　起きました。	→	父を　むかえに　行くために、　母は 五時に　起きました。
7.	うちへ　あがります。 くつを　ぬがなければなりません。	→	うちへ　あがるために、くつを ぬがなければなりません。
8.	質(しつ)問します。 山田先生の　研究室(けんきゅうしつ)へ　行きました。	→	質(しつ)問するために、山田先生の　研究室(けんきゅうしつ)へ 行きました。

12.7.5 Transformation Drill

1.	はんがを　買いました。 りょうしんの　結婚記念(けっこんきねん)日	→	りょうしんの　結婚記念(けっこんきねん)日の　ために、 はんがを　買いました。
2.	お茶(ちゃ)を　持って来てあげました。 中村さん夫婦(ふうふ)	→	中村さん夫婦(ふうふ)の　ために、　お茶(ちゃ)を 持って来てあげました。
3.	スミスさんは　日本へ 来たらしいです。 日本文化の　研究(けんきゅう)	→	日本文化の　研究(けんきゅう)の　ために、 スミスさんは　日本へ　来たらしいです。
4.	中国料理(りょうり)を　作るつもりです。 若い　人たち	→	若い　人たちの　ために、　中国料理(りょうり)を 作るつもりです。
5.	かんたんに　説明してください。 小学生	→	小学生の　ために、　かんたんに　説明 してください。
6.	いい　本だと　思います。 外国人	→	外国人の　ために、　いい　本だと 思います。
7.	いろいろ　ごちそうを　作りました。 クリスマス	→	クリスマスの　ために、　いろいろ ごちそうを　作りました。

12.7.6 Transformation Drill

1.	地下鉄に　乗ります。 毎日　たいへんです。	→	地下鉄に　乗るのに、毎日　たいへんです。
2.	うちへ　帰りました。 一時間も　かかりました。	→	うちへ　帰るのに、　一時間も かかりました。
3.	夏休みは　レポートを　書きました。 いそがしかったです。	→	夏休みは　レポートを　書くのに、 いそがしかったです。

4. 日本文学を　研究(けんきゅう)します。
どんな　さんこう書が　ひつよう
ですか。 ⟶ 日本文学を　研究(けんきゅう)するのに、　どんな　さんこう書が　ひつようですか。

5. 買い物に　行きます。
いつも　タクシーに　乗るんですか。 ⟶ 買い物に　行くのに、　いつも　タクシーに　乗るんですか。

6. パンクを　なおしてもらいます。
いくらぐらい　かかりますか。 ⟶ パンクを　なおしてもらうのに、　いくらぐらい　かかりますか。

7. 大阪(さか)へ　行きます。
ひこうきの　ほうが　べんりです。 ⟶ 大阪(さか)へ　行くのに、　ひこうきの　ほうが　べんりです。

12.7.7 Substitution Drill

あつければ　あついほど　いいです。

1. 急ぐ …… 急げば　急ぐほど　いいです。
2. ていねい …… ていねいなら　ていねいなほど　いいです。
3. みじかい …… みじかければ　みじかいほど　いいです。
4. 自由(ゆう) …… 自由(ゆう)なら　自由(ゆう)なほど　いいです。
5. 調べる …… 調べれば　調べるほど　いいです。
6. 安い …… 安ければ　安いほど　いいです。
7. 研究(けんきゅう)する …… 研究(けんきゅう)すれば　（研究(けんきゅう)）するほど　いいです。
8. ひま …… ひまなら　ひまなほど　いいです。
9. 若い …… 若ければ　若いほど　いいです。
10. 少ない …… 少なければ　少ないほど　いいです。

12.7.8 E-J Response Drill

1. 何の　ために　とけいを　買ったんですか。
for my younger brother's birthday …… おとうとの　たんじょう日の　ために　とけいを　買ったんです。

2. だれの　ために　おべん当を　作っているんですか。
for my son …… むすこの　ために　おべん当を　作っているんです。

3. どうして　きっさ店へ　行ったんですか。
in order to meet Tomoko …… 友子さんに　会うために、きっさ店へ　行ったんです。

4. 何の　ために　日本語を　習っているんですか。
for the purpose of majoring in Japanese literature …… 日本文学を　専攻(せんこう)するために、日本語を習っているんです。

5. これは　だれの　ための　本ですか。
for the children …… 子どもたちの　ための　本です。

6. どうして　おべん当が　ほしいんですか。
in order to eat it in the train …… 電車の　中で　食べるために、おべん当がほしいんです。

12.7.9 Transformation Drill

1. 朝ご飯　もう　できているかい？ ⟷ 朝ご飯は　もう　できていますか。
2. くすり　飲みたいんだけど、持って来てね。 ⟷ くすりが　飲みたいんだけど、持って来てくださいね。
3. お父さんも　買い物に　出かける？ ⟷ お父さんも　買い物に　出かけますか。
4. いい　くつ屋　しょうかいしてくれない？ ⟷ いい　くつ屋を　しょうかいしてくれませんか。
5. 気を　つけてね。 ⟷ 気を　つけてくださいね。
6. あたし　ご飯より　パンの　ほうがいいわ。 ⟷ あたしは　ご飯より　パンの　ほうがいいですわ。
7. うちの　おふろ　日本風だよ。 ⟷ うちの　おふろは　日本風ですよ。
8. 学校に　おくれるよ。 ⟷ 学校に　おくれますよ。
9. ゆっくり　言ってくれ。 ⟷ ゆっくり　言ってください。
10. 名前　ちがっているよ。 ⟷ 名前が　ちがっていますよ。
11. そうだね。 ⟷ そうですね。

12.7.10 Transformation Drill

A. 1. 早く　<u>起きるって</u>　おっしゃったでしょう？ ⟷ 早く　<u>起きると</u>　おっしゃったでしょう？
2. ジャックは　学校に　おくれたって　言いました。 ⟷ ジャックは　学校に　おくれたと　言いました。
3. スージーさんは　とても　せいが　高いって　聞きました。 ⟷ スージーさんは　とても　せいが　高いと　聞きました。

4. 旅行は　わりあい　たのしかったって　ホールさんが　言いました。 ←→ 旅行は　わりあい　たのしかったと　ホールさんが　言いました。

5. 漢字の　読み方は　ふくざつだって　聞いたんです。 ←→ 漢字の　読み方は　ふくざつだと　聞いたんです。

6. 鎌倉(かまくら)は　いんしょう的だったって　言っていましたよ。 ←→ 鎌倉(かまくら)は　いんしょう的だったと　言っていましたよ。

B. 1. 朝ご飯は　もう　できてるかい？ ←→ 朝ご飯は　もう　できているかい？

2. 毎日　日本語を　れんしゅうしてるんです。 ←→ 毎日　日本語を　れんしゅうしているんです。

3. 何を　考えてるの？ ←→ 何を　考えているの？

4. 原(はら)さんは　今　大学院に　行ってるそうです。 ←→ 原(はら)さんは　今　大学院に　行っているそうです。

5. きょ年まで　長崎(さき)に　住んでたんです。 ←→ きょ年まで　長崎(さき)に　住んでいたんです。

6. ミラーさん夫婦(ふうふ)と　げんかんで　話してたんです。 ←→ ミラーさん夫婦(ふうふ)と　げんかんで　話していたんです。

12.7.11 Transformation Drill

1. あなた、起きてください。
   友子 ⟶ 友子、起きなさい。

2. あなた、急いで、したくしてください。
   友子 ⟶ 友子、急いで　したくしなさい。

3. あなた、気を　つけてください。
   友子 ⟶ 友子、気を　つけなさい。

4. お母さん、牛乳(にゅう)　持って来て。
   友子 ⟶ 友子、牛乳(にゅう)　持って来なさい。

5. みなさん、早く　してください。
   友子 ⟶ 友子、早く　しなさい。

6. 山田さん、がんばってください。
   友子 ⟶ 友子、がんばりなさい。

7. みなさん、もっと　ていねいに　話してください。
   友子 ⟶ 友子、もっと　ていねいに　話しなさい。

12.7.12 E-J Response Drill

1. 今　何時ですか。
   ten to nine …… 九時十分前です。
2. 何時に　学校へ　来たんですか。
   fifteen after eight …… 八時十五分すぎに　来たんです。
3. 何時に　会いましょうか。
   twenty to four …… 四時二十分前に　会いましょう。
4. 仕事(しごと)は　何時ごろ　終わりますか。
   about forty after five …… 五時四十分すぎごろ　終わります。
5. 東京行の　ひこうきは　何時に　出ますか。
   sixteen after eleven P.M. …… ごご　十一時十六分すぎに　出ます。
6. えいがは　何時から　何時までですか。
   from ten after ten to twelve …… 十時十分すぎから　十二時までです。

12.8 EXERCISES

12.8.1 Combine a set of the following sentences into one sentence using the ～ば～ほど pattern and give the English equivalent for each sentence:

Example: あついです。 いいです。 } ⟶ あつければ　あついほど　いいです。

1. パーティーは　にぎやかです。 たのしいです。 } ⟶
2. 考えます。 むずかしい　問題ですね。 } ⟶
3. おふろは　新しいです。 気持ちが　いいです。 } ⟶

12.8.2 Combine each pair of the following into one sentence according to the instruction given and give the English equivalent:

1. 東京から　横浜(よこはま)まで　行きました。 二時間も　かかりました。 } ⟶ (～のに)
2. 京都を　けんぶつします。 毎年　たくさんの　米国人が　おとずれます。 } ⟶ (～の　ために)
3. タクシーを　よびます。 何番に　電話すれば　いいですか。 } ⟶ (～のに)

4. 高校の 歴史の 先生に なります。
どんな 勉強が ひつようですか。 } ⟶ （～のに）

5. 先生に 質(しつ)問します。
研究室(けんきゅうしつ)に 行きました。 } ⟶ （～ために）

12.8.3 Transform the following sentence as indicated in the given English:

早く 起きます。

1. The earlier you get up, the better.
2. Go to bed earlier in order to get up early.
3. Get up early! You'll be late for school!
4. The colder it gets, the harder it is to get up early.
5. I have a hard time getting up early every morning.

12.8.4 Tell which of the two, man or woman, said each of the following sentences and give the English equivalent for each; then transform each sentence into the normal polite form:

1. 晩ご飯は もう できてるかい？
2. 早く 起きた ほうが いいわよ。
3. 学校に おくれるよ。
4. お茶(ちゃ)を 持って来てくれ。
5. あたしと いっしょに 出かけない？
6. 今 新聞を 読んでるんだよ。
7. 七時の 急行に 乗るつもりなのよ。
8. さむくなれば なるほど 起きにくくなるねえ。

12.8.5 つぎの ことばを 使って、 文[sentence]を 作りなさい。 それから、 いみを 言いなさい。

1. 気に する
2. ～なさい
3. ～ば ～ほど
4. ～すぎ
5. ～に おくれる
6. （～分）前

12.8.6 Write the underlined *hiragana* in *kan'ji*:

1. なかむらくんの としは いま じゅうはちです。
2. まいばん はやく おきますか。
3. いそいで よじはんの きゅうこうに のってください。
4. ごはんを たべて、 おちゃを のみました。
5. もう いちど かんがえてみましょう。

6. やすければ　やすいほど　いいよ。
7. ぎゅう乳(にゅう)　のみおわった？

12.8.7 Distinguish the following *kan'ji*:

1. 冬、終
2. 食、飲、飯、館
3. 牛、手
4. 来、乗
5. 晩、日、明
6. 女、安
7. 村、校
8. 考、教
9. 安、家
10. 思、急

12.8.8 On what occasions or to whom may the expression *Hayaku shinasai* be used?

12.8.9 Change the following dialog into a casual one between two boys, then change it into that of two girls.

A: A, moo shichiji juugofun desu ne. Issho ni dekakemasen ka?

B: Ee, sorosoro dekaketa hoo ga ii desu ne.

A: Basu ni notte ikimasu ka?

B: Amari jikan ga arimasen kara, takushii o yobimasu yo.

12.8.10 Can you say *Watashi ga soo sen'sei ni osshaimashita?* If not, how would you correct the given expression?

12.8.11 Describe to whom you may say each of the following.

1. Koohii motte kite yo.
2. Niwa o kirei ni shinasai.
3. Ashita kuni e kaerutte kiita kedo, hon'too kai?
4. Kimi wa ninen'sei da ne.

12.9 SITUATIONAL AND APPLICATION CONVERSATION

12.9.1 At a breakfast table

Mother urges her son, Paul, to go to school right away. He will be late for school, she says.
Looking at a watch, Paul is surprised because it's already 8:10.
Mother says to Paul that in order to catch the 8:20 bus he has to get up at 7:30.
Paul says the colder it gets, the harder it is to get up. He says he will get up earlier after tomorrow.
Mother gives him a packed lunch and they greet each other at the door.

12.9.2 At a supper table

Father asks his daughter how her Japanese lessons are.
Daughter says the lessons are getting harder rapidly.
Father says the more difficult they get, the more she has to study.
Daughter says there will be an examination on *kan'ji* on Thursday next week. She suddenly realizes it's 7:15, so she says she will go to her room and study for the exam.
Father encourages her.

12.9.3 Mr. Yamada: Kimiko, ima nan'ji da?

Mrs. Yamada: Moo shichiji desu yo. Hayaku shitaku shite kudasai.

Mr. Yamada: Chotto shin'bun o totte kurenai kai?

12.9.4 Keiko: Okaasan, atashi no han'kachi doko?

Mrs. Yamada: Nan desu ka! Son'na mono jibun de sagashinasai.

12.9.5 Minoru: Otoosan, eki made issho ni ikanai?

Father: Ii yo. Hayaku shinasai.

12.9.6 Suzuki: Shibaraku.

Mifune: Yaa, doomo. Nagaku matta?

Suzuki: Iiya.

12.9.7 Sasaki: Shigoto wa doo?

Yamamoto: Sore ga doomo nee.

12.9.8 A: Chotto ukagaimasu ga, kono hen ni Yamada san to iu otaku wa arimasen ka?

B: Yamada san nara asoko desu yo.

A: Doomo.

12.9.9 Ishida: Oyama kun, boku no nooto (o) motte kite kureta?

Oyama: Aa, gomen. Wasureta!

Ishida: Jaa, ashita motte kite yo. Wasurenaide ne.

12.9.10 Paul: Kon'ban eiga o mi ni ikanai?

Toshiko: Soo ne, ikitai kedo.

Paul: ''Ikitai kedo'' doo shita no?

Toshiko: Anoo. Shukudai ga nee.

LESSON 13

中村さんの　一日：会社で

13.1　PRESENTATION

会社では、　社長[1]、　重役(じゅうやく)、　部長、　課長、　ふつうの　社員[2]などの　地位の　じゅんじょが　はっきりしていて、　ことば使いについても　なかなか　きびしい。　戦争後(せんそうご)[3]　日本の　社会は　大きく　変わったが、　多く[4]の　日本人は　まだまだ　ことば使いの　くべつを　大切だと　思っている。

13.2　DIALOG

石川(女)　「課長さん[5]、　おはようございます。」

中村　「やあ、　おはよう。　けさは　こまったよ。　地下鉄が　なかなか[6]　来ないので、　タクシーに　乗ろう[7]と　した[7]んだが、　タクシーも　ないんだ。」

石川　「毎朝　大変ですねえ。」

中村　「ところで、　石川さん、　後で　この　手紙を　出してください。」

石川　「ちょうど　今　切(きっ)手と　はがきを　買いに　ゆうびん局(きょく)[8]へ　行こう[9]と　思っています。　そくたつか　かきとめに　しますか。」

中村　「いや、　ふつうで　かまわない。」

石川　「わかりました。　それから、　あのう、　社長が　お呼びです[10]が…。」

中村　「あ、　そう。　ありがとう。」

—— 社長室(しつ)[11]で ——

中村　「社長、　お呼びに　なりましたか[12]。」

社長　「ああ、　中村君か。　すわりたまえ[13]。　じつは、　松本(まつもと)君に　やって[14]もらっている仕事なんだが、　急ぐ　仕事なので、　君にも　協力(きょうりょく)してほしいんだ。　忙しくて大変だろう[15]と　思うが、　よろしく[16]　たのむよ。」

中村　「はい、　かしこまりました。　いっしょうけんめい　やります。」

社長(しゃちょう)	部長(ぶちょう)	課長(かちょう)	地位(ちい)	大切(たいせつ)だ	大変(たいへん)です
後(あと)で	出(だ)して	お呼(よ)びです		中村君(なかむらくん)	仕事(しごと)
君(きみ)	忙(いそが)しくて				

13.3 PATTERN SENTENCES

13.3.1

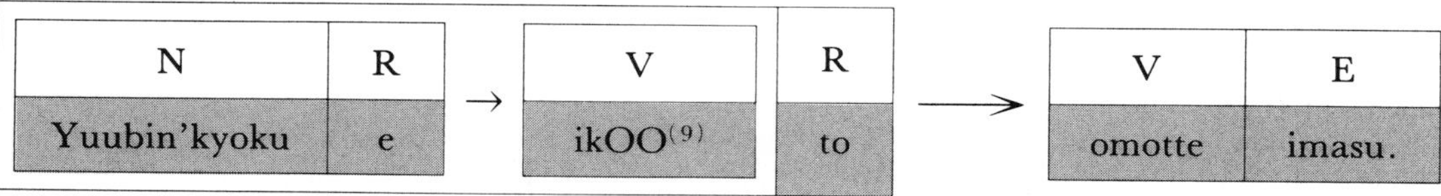

13.3.2

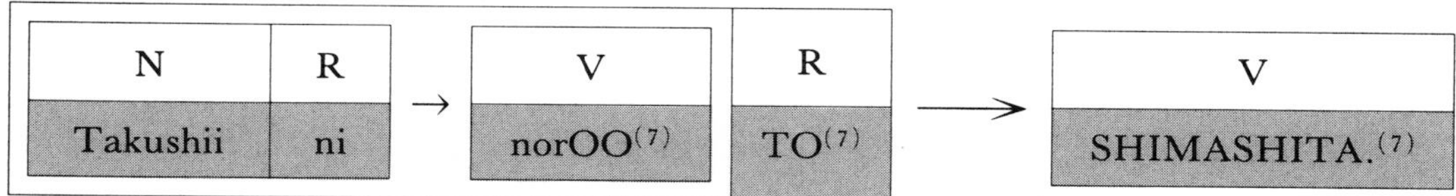

13.3.3

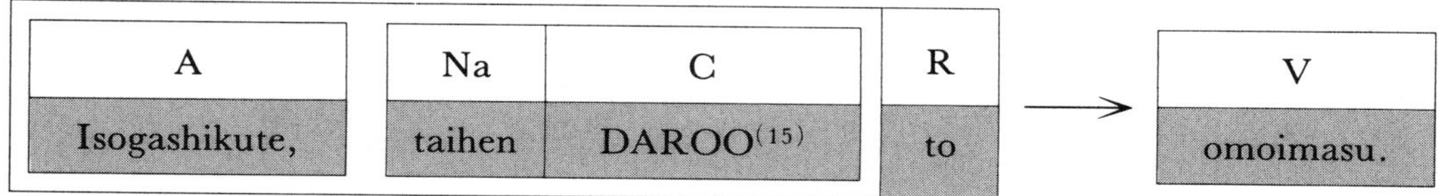

13.4 NOTES

13.4.1 *Shachoo* means ''president of a corporation.'' Likewise, *buchoo* ''director of a department,'' *kachoo* ''section chief.'' The *-choo* forms quite a few words of the meaning of ''head or chief ~.''

gakuchoo	''president of a university''	shachoo	''president of a corporation''
gakubuchoo	''dean''	buchoo	''department head''
koochoo	''principal''	kachoo	''section chief''

People in the position of *shachoo*, *buchoo*, *kachoo*, and the like may be called with or without *-san* after the position name instead of their own names. Female employees may prefer using *-san*.

Kachoo, shigoto ga owarimashita.
Kachoo san, shigoto ga owarimashita. — ''Chief, the work is finished.''

Suzuki buchoo ga yon'de imashita yo. — ''Mr. Suzuki, a department head, wanted to see you.''

13.4.2 *Shain* means ''company employee.'' The *-in* is attached to form quite a few words meaning ''employee of ~'' or ''member of ~.''

ten'in	''salesclerk''	jimuin	''office clerk''
ekiin	''station employee''	kooin	''factory worker''
kaishain	''company employee''	toshokan'in	''library employee''
gin'kooin	''bank employee''		

13.4.3 *Sen'soogo* means ''postwar'' or ''after the war.'' Sometimes *sen'go* is used. As far as Japan is concerned, ''the war'' means ''the last war,'' which was ended in 1945. Since Japanese society and culture have been affected tremendously by the various postwar reforms, this word, *sen'go*, has been used widely in contrast with *sen'zen*, "prewar," although Japanese youths may not use this word as often.

13.4.4 *Ooku no nihon'jin* means "quite a few Japanese" or "many Japanese." In formal or written Japanese *takusan* is often replaced by *ooku*, which sounds more formal than *takusan*. *Ooku* is the Noun use of the KU form of an Adjective *ooi*. This will be explained later.

13.4.5 *Kachoo*, meaning "section chief," is a form of address mainly used by male company employees. *Kachoo san* is used by female employees. Groupism also strongly affects the addressing system in general. For instance, if referring to one's section chief while speaking to an outsider of the company, one would say *uchi no kachoo* or *uchi no kachoo no Yamada* (without *-san*). Such usage is a function of in-groupness. To refer to the second person's company section chief, one would use *otaku no kachoo* or *otaku no kachoo no Yamada san*.

13.4.6 *Nakanaka* is an Adverb and means here "not easily," "not readily," "not nearly," or "far from" before a negative expression.

Shiken wa doo deshita ka?	"How was the exam?"
Nakanaka muzukashikatta desu.	"It was quite difficult."
Shigoto o sagashite iru n desu kedo, nakanaka ii no ga nai n desu.	"I have been looking for a job, but it is rather difficult to find a good one."

13.4.7 *Takushii ni noroo to shita n da ga* means "I tried to catch a taxi, but I couldn't." *Noroo* is the OO form of the Verb *noru* and is the plain equivalent of *norimashoo*. The plain OO form of a Verb is formulated as follows:

1. Vowel Verb. . . . Stem form plus *-yoo* or replace *-ru* by *-yoo*

ake-*ru*	⟶	ake-*yoo*	oki-*ru*	⟶	oki-*yoo*
dekake-*ru*	⟶	dekake-*yoo*	shime-*ru*	⟶	shime-*yoo*
i-*ru*	⟶	i-*yoo*	tabe-*ru*	⟶	tabe-*yoo*
kan'gae-*ru*	⟶	kan'gae-*yoo*	wasure-*ru*	⟶	wasure-*yoo*
mi-*ru*	⟶	mi-*yoo*	yame-*ru*	⟶	yame-*yoo*

2. Consonant Verb. . . . Base form plus *-oo* or replace *-u* by *-oo*

kaer-*u*	⟶	kaer-*oo*	das-*u*	⟶	das-*oo*
tor-*u*	⟶	tor-*oo*	hanas-*u*	⟶	hanas-*oo*
			naos-*u*	⟶	naos-*oo*
ara-*u*	⟶	ara-*oo*			
a-*u*	⟶	a-*oo*	nom-*u*	⟶	nom-*oo*
ka-*u*	⟶	ka-*oo*	tanom-*u*	⟶	tanom-*oo*
nara-*u*	⟶	nara-*oo*	yom-*u*	⟶	yom-*oo*
mats-*u*	⟶	mat-*oo*	asob-*u*	⟶	asob-*oo*
tats-*u*	⟶	tat-*oo*	yob-*u*	⟶	yob-*oo*
aruk-*u*	⟶	aruk-*oo*	isog-*u*	⟶	isog-*oo*
kak-*u*	⟶	kak-*oo*	nug-*u*	⟶	nug-*oo*
migak-*u*	⟶	migak-*oo*	oyog-*u*	⟶	oyog-*oo*

3. Irregular Verb

suru	⟶	shiyoo	kuru	⟶	koyoo

The plain OO form of a Verb can be used at the end of a sentence in plain style mainly by men. Women usually use ~*mashoo* at the end of a sentence.

Eiga o mi ni ikoo yo.	"Let's go see a movie."
Koko ni iyoo ka?	"Shall we stay here?"

The OO form can be used to show the intention of the subject person "to do or be such and such" or "is about to do/become such and such." In many cases steps leading to such an action might have been taken but the action itself has not been taken. In this meaning the plain OO form of a Verb is followed by the quotation Relational *to* and *suru.*

Predicate Modifier + Verb(*-oo*) + *to suru*

Note that the TE form of a Verb plus *miru* (see Note 1.4.13, Vol. II) is usually translated as "try to do such and such." In the case of ~*-te mimashita*, however, the action has already been tried, and yet the action has not been taken in the case of ~*-oo to shita.*

Compare:

Osushi o tabete mimashita.	"I ate *sushi* once."
Osushi o tabeyoo to shimashita.	"I tried to eat *sushi* (but I couldn't)." "I was about to eat *sushi*."

The following are some examples of the OO form.

Ima dekakeyoo to shite imasu.	"I am now about to leave."
Watanabe sen'sei ni kikoo to shimashita ga, sen'sei wa orusu deshita.	"I wanted to ask Prof. Watanabe, but he was out."
Tegami o dasanakatta n desu ka?	"Didn't you mail the letter?"
Dasoo to shita n desu ga, yuubin'kyoku ga yasumi datta n desu.	"I tried to, but the post office was closed."
Ishikawa san ni den'wa o kakeyoo to shita toki, Ishikawa san ga kimashita.	"When I was about to make a phone call to Mr. Ishikawa, he showed up."

13.4.8 *Yuubin'kyoku*

A postal system in Japan was first established during the Kamakura period; it linked the Bakufu in Kamakura with the Imperial Court of Kyōto. Mail would reach Kyōto seven days after leaving Kamakura, and the service was called *hikyaku* (flying legs) or *hayauma* (fast horses). Kublai Khan's attempted invasion of Japan in 1274 led to the extension of the system to Dazaifu, Kyūshū. Much like the American Pony Express, relays of horses and riders were used in this system.

Hikyaku remained operative until the establishment of a modern postal system in 1871, and today Japan's postal system is one of the best in the world. Mail is delivered seven days a week, including holidays. In many areas delivery is twice daily, and many main branches of the post office remain open twenty-four hours a day, although most ordinary branches are open nine to five.

The method of addressing mail differs in Japan from the United States. If mail is being sent to one of the prefectures, you place the name of the prefecture first, then the name of the city, the name of the town, the name of the residence, and finally the name of the person to receive the letter.

The issuance of stamps and the supervision of postal matters comes under the direction of the Ministry of Postal Services and the Postal Services Advisory Council. Denominations of all kinds are issued. Registered mail, or *kakitome,* can be sent either for regular purposes or for the purposes of sending money, called *gen'kin kakitome*. Since in Japan the checking account system is not as popularized as it is in America, many people send cash through the mail using *gen'kin kakitome*.

As compared with other industrialized countries, Japan has produced more designs of stamps showing animals, birds, fish, and national treasures. Special issue stamps often feature the places of scenic beauty such as the Fuji-Hakone National Park. These reveal the feeling of closeness with nature of the Japanese.

13.4.9 *Ikoo to omotte imasu* means "I am thinking of going there." The plain OO form of a Verb (Note 13.4.7), as well as other plain forms, may occur in quotation phrases, such as follow:

(Predicate Modifier) + Verb(*-oo*) + *to* + { ***omou*** / ***iu*** / ***hanasu*** / ***kan'gaete iru*** }

As in the quotation expressions already introduced in Note 2.4.6, when the sentence to be quoted or reported is ~*-mashoo*, the plain OO form of a Verb must be used.

Kono tegami o sokutatsu de dasoo to omou n desu ga, yuubin'kyoku wa doko deshoo ka?	"I am thinking of sending this letter by special delivery; where can I find a post office?"
Tsugi no doyoobi ni issho ni gorufu o shiyoo to tomodachi to hanashiaimashita.	"My friend and I agreed to play golf together next Saturday."
Sotsugyoo shite kara, don'na shigoto o yaroo to kan'gaete imasu ka?	"What sort of work are you thinking of doing after being graduated?"
Ashita wa ichinichijuu uchi ni iyoo to omoimasu.	"I think I'll stay home all day tomorrow."
Gakubuchoo ga ken'kyuushitsu de aoo to osshaimashita.	"The dean said he would meet me in his office."

13.4.10 *Shachoo ga oyobi desu* means "The president is calling for you" or "You are wanted by the president." In polite speech or in order to show respect to the person who performs, the polite prefix *o-* plus the Stem form of a Verb plus *desu* is often used in the meaning of "someone is doing such and such" or "someone is going to do such and such." The person who is doing such and such cannot be the speaker, since this pattern is used to show the speaker's respect to the actor.

o-* + Stem form of Verb + *desu

However, the Verbs used in this combination are rather limited. Here are some common expressions:

Oyobi desu.	"He wants you to come to see him."
Odekake desu ka?	"Are you going out?"

Otetsudai desu ka?	"Are you helping someone?"
Okaeri desu yo.	"She is leaving."
Donata o omachi desu ka?	"Who are you waiting for?"
Okomari deshoo!	"You must be in trouble!"
Owakari desu ne?	"I am sure you understand this (?)"

Oyobi desu, *yon'de imasu*, and *yon'de irasshaimasu* all refer to someone "calling" someone of a different status. However, the three terms carry different connotations. *Yon'de irasshaimasu* and *oyobi desu* are much more polite than *yon'de imasu*. Japanese has, in fact, more than just these three terms which function in this capacity, and all carry varying degrees of politeness. For example, *yobu* is less polite than *oyobi ni naru*. (See Note 13.4.12.)

13.4.11 *Shachooshitsu* means "the room of the president." The *-shitsu* is a word to formulate words meaning "room for ~" or "~ room."

kyooshitsu	"classroom"	shachooshitsu	"president's office"
toshoshitsu	"library"	shin'shitsu	"bedroom"
ken'kyuushitsu	"seminar room"		
	"laboratory"		

13.4.12 *Oyobi ni narimashita ka?* means "Did you call for me?" The polite prefix *o-* plus the Stem form of a Verb followed by *ni naru* is a polite equivalent of "someone does such and such." It is more polite than *o~desu*. The person who does such and such cannot be the speaker.

o-* + Stem form of Verb + *ni* + *naru

Oyobi ni narimashita ka?	"Did you call for me?"
Owakari ni narimasu ka?	"Is that clear to you?"
Koochoo sen'sei ga okaeri ni narimashita.	"The principal came back."
Omachi ni narimasu ka?	"Do you (want to) wait?"

13.4.13 *Suwaritamae* means "Sit down." The Verb *tamae* (←*tamau*) preceded by the Stem form of a Verb formulates an imperative expression of a compound Verb. However, it is used by men of far higher position and greater age than those to whom the command is directed and is much more high-handed than the form *nasai*. On the other hand, *~te kudasai* is a polite request form which does not convey much sense of command. In general, the use of *tamae* should be avoided because it shows arrogance and your own self-image as a superior. *Tamae* is usually limited to superior-inferior command situations, and it is not normally used today.

	father → son	superior → inferior (office)	male teacher → pupil
tamae	not used	used	debatable
nasai	used	not used	used

13.4.14 *Yatte* is the TE form of *yaru* that is the colloquial equivalent of *suru* "do." Men use *yaru* more often than women. It should be noted that *yaru* is not always interchangeable with *suru*. *Suru* in the Noun plus *suru* formulations such as *kaimono suru*, *sen'koo suru*, cannot be replaced by *yaru*.

Kyonen kara tenisu o yatte imasu.	"I've been playing tennis since last year."
Shukudai o issho ni yarimasen ka?	"Don't you want to do homework with me?"
Nani o yatteru no?	"What are you doing?"

13.4.15 *Isogashikute taihen daroo to omou* means literally "I think that you are busy and it will be hard for you." *Daroo* is the OO form of the Copula *da* or the plain equivalent of *deshoo*. Like the plain OO form of a Verb, *daroo* may occur at the end of a sentence in plain style or in quotation phrases. In conversation women do not use *daroo* at the end of a sentence, even in informal situations; instead they use *deshoo*. Women can use *daroo* if it appears in the nonfinal position. *Daroo* does not necessarily occur after a Noun, but it may occur after a Verb and an Adjective.

Noun **Noun + Copula (plain form, except *da*)** **Verb (plain form)** **Adjective (plain form)**	+ ***daroo*** + ***to*** +	***omou*** ***iu*** ***hanasu*** ***kiku*** ***kan'gaeru*** ***kotaeru***

Chikatetsu no hoo ga ben'ri daroo to iimashita.	"He said that the subway might be more convenient."
Okane ga motto hitsuyoo datta daroo to omoimasu.	"I think he must have needed more money."
Ano gakusei wa ninen'sei ja nai daroo to omoimasu yo.	"I don't think that student is a sophomore."
Watashitachi wa Keiko san no otoosan wa sarariiman daroo to hanashite imashita.	"We have been saying that Keiko's father must be a salary man."
Buraun san wa osake o nomu daroo to min'na ga itte imasu.	"They say that Mr. Brown will drink *sake*."
Ishikawa san wa kitte o kai ni yuubin'kyoku e itta n daroo to kachoo ga iimashita.	"The section chief said that Miss Ishikawa must have gone to the post office to buy stamps."
Moo juuji da kara, kodomo wa neta daroo to omoimasu.	"Since it's already ten o'clock, I think the children might have gone to bed."
Atarashii tetsugaku no sen'sei wa hijoo ni kibishii daroo to omoimasu.	"I think that the new professor of philosophy will be extremely strict."
Ashita wa atsuku nai daroo to rajio ga iimashita.	"The radio said that it would not be hot tomorrow."

13.4.16 *Yoroshiku* is a very convenient word exemplifying Japanese heteronomy, vagueness, and the tendency to seek other's favor. It has no exact English equivalent. For example, *Yoroshiku tanomu* or *Yoroshiku onegai suru* can only literally translate as "I leave it entirely to you, at your own discretion.'' *Yoroshiku*, in fact, could mean almost anything. Its frequent use indicates Japanese heteronomy, but especially heteronomy's by-product, namely, leaving decision-making to others.

Yoroshiku or *Doozo yoroshiku* can be used as a greeting when one is introduced, meaning ''How do you do?'' or ''I'm glad to make your acquaintance.'' *Doozo minasama ni yoroshiku* means ''Please remember me to everyone''; *Yamada san ga yoroshiku to itte imashita* means ''Mr. Yamada sent his best regards.''

Yamada Kazuo o yoroshiku onegai shimasu.	''Please take good care of Kazuo Yamada.''
Sen'sei, kono ko o yoroshiku onegai shimasu.	''Teacher, please take good care of this child.''

13.5 VOCABULARY

Presentation

社長	shachoo	......	N	company president (see 13.4.1)
重役(じゅうやく)	juuyaku	......	N	director; high executive
部長	buchoo	......	N	head of a department
ふつう	futsuu	......	N	average; normal; ordinary
社員	shain	......	N	company employee (see 13.4.2)
じゅんじょ	jun'jo	......	N	order; sequence
はっきり	hakkiri	......	Adv.	clearly; distinctly
きびしい	kibishii	......	A	is strict; is severe
戦争(せんそう)	sen'soo	......	N	war (see 13.4.3)
後(ご)	-go	......	Nd	post ～; after ～
くべつ	kubetsu	......	N	distinction

Dialog

石川	Ishikawa	......	N	family name
やあ	yaa	......	SI	hi; hello (used by men)
こまった	komatta	......	V	was troubled; had a hard time (TA form of *komaru*)
なかなか	nakanaka	......	Adv.	easily (used with negation) (see 13.4.6)
乗ろう	noroo	......	V	OO form of *noru* – get on (see 13.4.7)
出して	dashite	......	V	TE form of *dasu* – mail; put out; submit
切手(きっ)	kitte	......	N	postage stamp
はがき	hagaki	......	N	postcard
行こう	ikoo	......	V	OO form of *iku* – go
そくたつ	sokutatsu	......	N	special delivery

かきとめ	kakitome	......	N	registered mail
社長室	shachooshitsu	......	N	president's office (see 13.4.11)
たまえ	tamae	......	V	(compound component) (← *tamau*) (see 13.4.13)
松本	Matsumoto	......	N	family name
やって	yatte	......	V	TE form of *yaru* – do; perform (equivalent for *suru*) (see 13.4.14)
協力して	kyooryoku shite	......	V	TE form of *kyooryoku suru* – cooperate
協力	kyooryoku	......	N	cooperation
だろう	daroo	......	C	OO form of *da* (see 13.4.15)
よろしく	yoroshiku	......	A	KU form of *yoroshii* – is all right; is good; is agreeable (see 13.4.16)
いっしょうけんめい	isshooken'mei	......	Adv.	with utmost effort; as hard as one can do; eagerly

Notes

長	-choo	......	Nd	chief ～; ～ head (see 13.4.1)
学長	gakuchoo	......	N	university president
学部長	gakubuchoo	......	N	dean
校長(先生)	koochoo (sen'sei)	......	N	principal; headmaster
員	-in	......	Nd	member; employee (see 13.4.2)
会社員	kaishain	......	N	company employee
銀行員	gin'kooin	......	N	bank employee
事務員	jimuin	......	N	office clerk
工員	kooin	......	N	factory worker; mechanic
図書室	toshoshitsu	......	N	library room
しん室	shin'shitsu	......	N	bedroom

13.6 KAN'JI

13.6.a 長 [7.6.4] (1) CHOO (2) chief (5) 社長、課長、部長、駅長、学長、学部長、校長 (6) homonym 帳、張、脹

13.6.1 部 (1) BU (2) department; part (3) classifier 阝 [places where people reside] (4) 丶 亠 亠 亣 立 咅 咅 部 (5) 部長、学部長、東部、語学部 [language department]、文学部 [department of literature]、全部

13.6.2 課 (1) KA (2) section; division (3) classifier 言 [word]
(4) 言 訂 訂 詚 誤 課 課 (5) 課長、課目(もく) [course]
(6) word (言) and result (果)(KA) ⟶ order; 果 also indicates pronunciation; homonym 果、菓

13.6.3 位 (1) I (2) position; rank (3) classifier 亻 [people]
(4) 亻 亻' 亻亠 位 位 (5) 地位、一位 [the first rank]、方位 [direction]
(6) man (亻) standing (亼) ⟶ 立 ⟶ place where man stands ⟶ position

13.6.b 大 [2.6.1, Vol. II] (1) TAI (5) 大変(へん)だ、大切(せつ)な物

13.6.4 切 (1) SETSU (2) cut (3) classifier ⺈ (刀 [sword; knife])
(4) 一 ⺈ 切 切 (5) 大切、親切(しん) (6) cut a horizontal line by a vertical line (⺈) plus a knife (刀)

13.6.c 変 [11.6.7] (1) HEN (5) 変化 [change]、大変だ、変な事(こと)

13.6.5 後 (1) *ato* (2) after; behind (3) classifier 彳 [passage]
(4) ノ 彡 彳 彳' 彳幺 彳幺 後 後 後 (5) 仕事(しごと)の後、 後で

13.6.d 出 [7.6.8, Vol. II] (1) *da(su)* (2) send out (5) そくたつで出す、宿(しゅく)題を出す

13.6.6 呼 (1) *yo(bu)* (2) call; name (3) classifier 口
(4) 口 口' 口ン 口㐅 口乎 呼 (5) 医者(いしゃ)を呼ぶ

13.6.7 君 (1) KUN (2) Mr.; Ms. (3) classifier 尹 (口) (4) フ ヨ 尹 君
(5) 松本(まつもと)君 (6) hold a bar (丨) with a hand (ヨ) ⟶ 尹 ⟶ command with a bar in a hand

13.6.8 仕 (1) SHI (2) serve (3) classifier 亻 (4) 亻 仁 什 仕
(5) 仕事(ごと)、仕方 [way of doing] (6) officer (士) ⟶ to serve

13.6.e 事 [12.6.4, Vol. II] (1) *koto* [*-goto*] (5) 仕事

13.6.f 君 [13.6.7] (1) *kimi* (2) you (to peer or inferior) (5) 君にあげるよ

13.6.9 忙 (1) *isoga(shii)* (2) busy (3) classifier 忄 [heart]
(4) 丿 丷 忄 忄丶 忄亠 忙 (5) 忙しい (6) heart (忄) with
亡 (BOO) pronunciation; homonym BOO 亡、芒、忘、茫

13.6.10 茶* (1) CHA (2) tea; brown (3) classifier 艹 [grass] (4) 艹 艹人 茶
(5) お茶を飲む、こう茶、茶色、茶の湯(ゆ) [tea ceremony]

13.7 DRILLS

13.7.1 Transformation Drill

A. 1. カレーライスを　食べましょう。 ⟶ カレーライスを　食べようと　思います。

2. もう　一度　考えましょう。 ⟶ もう　一度　考えようと　思います。

3. ここで　待っていましょう。 ⟶ ここで　待っていようと　思います。

4. 課長さんに　たのんで　みましょう。 ⟶ 課長さんに　たのんでみようと　思います。

5. 東京へ　つれて行って　あげましょう。 ⟶ 東京へ　つれて行ってあげようと　思います。

6. 新しい　洋服(ふく)に　着かえましょう。 ⟶ 新しい　洋服(ふく)に　着かえようと　思います。

7. 九月から　日本語を　習いはじめましょう。 ⟶ 九月から　日本語を　習いはじめようと　思います。

B. 1. 今晩　友だちに　会いましょう。 ⟶ 今晩　友だちに　会おうと　思います。

2. 本当の　ことを　話しましょう。 ⟶ 本当の　ことを　話そうと　思います。

3. 沖縄(おきなわ)の　うみで　およぎましょう。 ⟶ 沖縄(おきなわ)の　うみで　およごうと　思います。

4. 今度は　先生に　たのみましょう。 ⟶ 今度は　先生に　たのもうと　思います。

5. いしゃを　呼びましょう。 ⟶ いしゃを　呼ぼうと　思います。

6. 母に　そくたつを　出しましょう。 ⟶ 母に　そくたつを　出そうと　思います。

7. 急ぐから、　タクシーに　乗りましょう。 ⟶ 急ぐから、　タクシーに　乗ろうと　思います。

8. これから　テープを　聞きましょう。 ⟶ これから　テープを　聞こうと　思います。

9. もうすこし　待ちましょう。 ⟶ もうすこし　待とうと　思います。

10. 十二時十分前に　来ましょう。 ⟶ 十二時十分前に　来ようと　思います。

11. これは　かきとめに しましょう。 ⟶ これは　かきとめに　しようと　思います。

13.7.2 Transformation Drill

1. 事務(む)員が　切(きっ)手を　買います。 ⟶ 事務(む)員が　切(きっ)手を　買おうと　しています。
2. 友だちは　来年　ヨーロッパへ 行きます。 ⟶ 友だちは　来年　ヨーロッパへ　行こうと しています。
3. おとうとは　サラリーマンに なります。 ⟶ おとうとは　サラリーマンに　なろうと しています。
4. 石川さんが　今　電話を　かけます。 ⟶ 石川さんが　今　電話を　かけようと しています。
5. 六時に　なったので、　みんなは 仕事を　やめます。 ⟶ 六時に　なったので、　みんなは　仕事を やめようと　しています。
6. ポールさんは　パンクを なおします。 ⟶ ポールさんは　パンクを　なおそうと しています。
7. みち子さんは　ていねいな ことば使いに　変えます。 ⟶ みち子さんは　ていねいな　ことば使いに 変えようと　しています。
8. ハワードさんは　はんがを 買います。 ⟶ ハワードさんは　はんがを　買おうと しています。

13.7.3 Transformation Drill

1. 急行に　乗ることが できませんでした。 ⟶ 急行に　乗ろうと　しましたが、 乗ることが　できませんでした。
2. すぐ　いしゃを　呼ぶことが できませんでした。 ⟶ すぐ　いしゃを　呼ぼうと　しましたが、 呼ぶことが　できませんでした。
3. いっしょうけんめい　働くことが できませんでした。 ⟶ いっしょうけんめい　働こうと　しましたが、 働くことが　できませんでした。
4. 青木さんに　協力(きょうりょく)することが できませんでした。 ⟶ 青木さんに　協力(きょうりょく)しようと　しましたが、 協力(きょうりょく)することが　できませんでした。

5. 友子さんに　ゆびわを　おくって　あげることが　できませんでした。 ⟶ 友子さんに　ゆびわを　おくってあげようと　しましたが、　おくってあげることが　できませんでした。

6. 一郎(ろう)君に　辞(じ)書を　かしてもらう　ことが　できませんでした。 ⟶ 一郎(ろう)君に　辞(じ)書を　かしてもらおうと　しましたが、　かしてもらうことが　できませんでした。

7. かきとめで　出すことが　できませんでした。 ⟶ かきとめで　出そうと　しましたが、　出すことが　できませんでした。

8. 母に　買い物を　たのむことが　できませんでした。 ⟶ 母に　買い物を　たのもうと　しましたが、　たのむことが　できませんでした。

13.7.4 Transformation Drill

1. みんなが　協力(きょうりょく)するでしょう。 ⟶ みんなが　協力(きょうりょく)するだろうと　思います。

2. 松本(まつもと)さんは　ぜんぜん　気に　しないでしょう。 ⟶ 松本(まつもと)さんは　ぜんぜん　気に　しないだろうと　思います。

3. 部長は　旅行に　行かないでしょう。 ⟶ 部長は　旅行に　行かないだろうと　思います。

4. 忙しくて　こまるでしょう。 ⟶ 忙しくて　こまるだろうと　思います。

5. 東京では　およぐことが　できないでしょう。 ⟶ 東京では　およぐことが　できないだろうと　思います。

6. 吉(よし)田さんは　だいぶ　こまったでしょう。 ⟶ 吉(よし)田さんは　だいぶ　こまっただろうと　思います。

7. むすめは　けさ　学校に　おくれたでしょう。 ⟶ むすめは　けさ　学校に　おくれただろうと　思います。

8. 重役(じゅうやく)には　たのまなかったでしょう。 ⟶ 重役(じゅうやく)には　たのまなかっただろうと　思います。

9. 原(はら)さんは　大学を　卒業(そつぎょう)しなかったでしょう。 ⟶ 原(はら)さんは　大学を　卒業(そつぎょう)しなかっただろうと　思います。

10. 課長は　いっしょうけんめい　仕事を　やるでしょう。 ⟶ 課長は　いっしょうけんめい　仕事を　やるだろうと　思います。

13.7.5 Transformation Drill

1. 会社では　ことば使いが
   きびしいでしょう。
   思います。
   → 会社では　ことば使いが　きびしいだろうと　思います。

2. この　紙は　後で
   ひつようでしょう。
   部長が　おっしゃいました。
   → この　紙は　後で　ひつようだろうと　部長が　おっしゃいました。

3. 子どもたちは　まだ
   ねむくないでしょう。
   思いました。
   → 子どもたちは　まだ　ねむくないだろうと　思いました。

4. 高木さんは　せいが
   高かったでしょう。
   けい子さんが　言いました。
   → 高木さんは　せいが　高かっただろうと　けい子さんが　言いました。

5. 小林さんは　しんせつな
   人でしょう。
   思います。
   → 小林さんは　しんせつな　人だろうと　思います。

6. ジョーンズさんは
   三十さいじゃないでしょう。
   言っていました。
   → ジョーンズさんは　三十さいじゃないだろうと　言っていました。

7. あの　たて物は　ゆうびん局
   じゃないでしょう。
   思います。
   → あの　たて物は　ゆうびん局じゃないだろうと　思います。

8. これは　ちょっと　おかしい
   でしょう。
   思います。
   → これは　ちょっと　おかしいだろうと　思います。

9. あかい　自転車が　ほしかった
   のでしょう。
   ジョージさんが　言ってましたよ。
   → あかい　自転車が　ほしかったのだろうと　ジョージさんが　言ってましたよ。

10. 今度の　仕事は　かんたんでしょう。
    社長が　おっしゃいました。
    → 今度の　仕事は　かんたんだろうと　社長が　おっしゃいました。

13.7.6 Expansion Drill

1. おかねが　ありませんでした。 …… おかねが　ありませんでした。
   足を　のばそうと　しましたが …… 足を　のばそうと　しましたが、　おかねが　ありませんでした。

ニューヨークまで …… ニューヨークまで　足を　のばそうと　しましたが、　おかねが　ありませんでした。

2. 言ったんですか。 …… 言ったんですか。
学校を　休もうと …… 学校を　休もうと　言ったんですか。
だれが …… だれが　学校を　休もうと　言ったんですか。
きのう …… きのう　だれが　学校を　休もうと　言ったんですか。

3. しています。 …… しています。
地図を　かいてもらおうと …… 地図を　かいてもらおうと　しています。
みちが　わからないので …… みちが　わからないので、　地図を　かいてもらおうと　しています。
伊藤さんは …… 伊藤さんは　みちが　わからないので、　地図を　かいてもらおうと　しています。

4. 聞きました。 …… 聞きました。
むしあついだろうと …… むしあついだろうと　聞きました。
京都の　ほうが …… 京都の　ほうが　むしあついだろうと　聞きました。
山本さんから …… 山本さんから　京都の　ほうが　むしあついだろうと　聞きました。

5. ジョーンズさんが　言いました。 …… ジョーンズさんが　言いました。
じょうずだろうと …… じょうずだろうと　ジョーンズさんが　言いました。
日本語が …… 日本語が　じょうずだろうと　ジョーンズさんが　言いました。
あなたは …… あなたは　日本語が　じょうずだろうと　ジョーンズさんが　言いました。

6. 思います。 …… 思います。
大変だっただろうと …… 大変だっただろうと　思います。
仕事が　多くて …… 仕事が　多くて　大変だっただろうと　思います。

事務員が　少ないので　…… 事務員が　少ないので、　仕事が　多くて　大変だっただろうと　思います。

7. だめでした。　…… だめでした。
入ろうと　しましたが　…… 入ろうと　しましたが、　だめでした。
大学院に　…… 大学院に　入ろうと　しましたが、　だめでした。
もっと　勉強したくて　…… もっと　勉強したくて、　大学院に　入ろうと　しましたが、　だめでした。

13.7.7 Substitution Drill

ご飯を　食べようと　した　時、　友だちが　来ました。

1. 買い物に　出かける　…… 買い物に　出かけようと　した　時、　友だちが　来ました。
2. 林さんに　電話を　かける　…… 林さんに　電話を　かけようと　した　時、　友だちが　来ました。
3. 日本語の　宿題を　やる　…… 日本語の　宿題を　やろうと　した　時、　友だちが　来ました。
4. 着物を　着かえる　…… 着物を　着かえようと　した　時、　友だちが　来ました。
5. パンクを　なおす　…… パンクを　なおそうと　した　時、　友だちが　来ました。
6. ビールを　飲む　…… ビールを　飲もうと　した　時、　友だちが　来ました。
7. ゆうびん局へ　行く　…… ゆうびん局へ　行こうと　した　時、　友だちが　来ました。

13.7.8 Substitution Drill

部長が　お呼びですよ。

1. 休む　…… 部長が　お休みですよ。
2. 出かける　…… 部長が　お出かけですよ。
3. 帰る　…… 部長が　お帰りですよ。
4. 待つ　…… 部長が　お待ちですよ。

5. むかえる …… 部長が　おむかえですよ。
6. 読む …… 部長が　お読みですよ。
7. 飲む …… 部長が　お飲みですよ。

13.7.9 Substitution Drill

社長が　お呼びに　なりました。

1. 駅に　つく …… 社長が　駅に　おつきに　なりました。
2. 学長 …… 学長が　駅に　おつきに　なりました。
3. 課長 …… 課長が　駅に　おつきに　なりました。
4. 急行に　乗る …… 課長が　急行に　お乗りに　なりました。
5. 仕事を　やめる …… 課長が　仕事を　おやめに　なりました。
6. 校長先生 …… 校長先生が　仕事を　おやめに　なりました。
7. 図書室(としつ)に　入る …… 校長先生が　図書室(としつ)に　お入りに　なりました。

13.7.10 Response Drill

1. ジャックさんは　アメリカ人ですか。 …… ええ、　アメリカ人だろうと　思います。
2. 森(もり)さんの　おたんじょう日は　四月八日でしょうか。 …… ええ、　四月八日だろうと　思います。
3. 鈴(すず)木さんの　むすこさんは　小学生ですか。 …… ええ、　小学生だろうと　思います。
4. ムーアさんは　日本語が　じょうずでしょうか。 …… ええ、　じょうずだろうと　思います。
5. えんぴつで　書いても　いいですか。 …… ええ、　いいだろうと　思います。
6. この　着物は　おかしくないでしょうか。 …… ええ、　おかしくないだろうと　思います。
7. 小林(こはやし)さんは　二時ごろ　いらっしゃるでしょうか。 …… ええ、　いらっしゃるだろうと　思います。
8. あした　およぎに　行きたいんですが、　雨が　ふるでしょうか。 …… ええ、　ふるだろうと　思います。
9. 井上(いの)さんは　日本語を　教えてくれるでしょうか。 …… ええ、　教えてくれるだろうと　思います。
10. 先生は　そう　おっしゃったんですか。 …… ええ、　そう　おっしゃったんだろうと　思います。

13.8 EXERCISES

13.8.1 日本語で　言いなさい。

1. I'm about to send a letter by registered mail.
2. I think you will have lots of work (to do) and have a hard time.
3. My younger brother tried to master ten *kan'ji* every day (but he couldn't).
4. Mr. Watanabe said that, because of an accident, Mr. Ishii will be late for school.
5. George tried to repair a radio himself, but, after all, he took it to *den'kiya* [electric shop].

13.8.2 Transform the following sentences according to the examples given:

Example:　お茶を　お飲みです。　⟶　お茶を　飲んでいます。

　　　　　お食べに　なります。　⟶　食べます。

1. 学部長が　あなたを　お呼びですよ。
2. ご主人は　何時に　お出かけに　なりましたか。
3. きょう　課長さんは　びょう気で　お休みなんです。
4. お客さまは　社長室(しつ)で　お待ちだそうです。
5. この　新聞は　もう　お読みに　なりましたか。

13.8.3 Fill in the blanks with appropriate conjugation forms:

1. 母が　一郎(ろう)君は　大学の　三年生______と　言っていました。
2. 地下鉄に　乗______と　したが、　こんでいて、　乗______が　できなかった。
3. 松本(まつもと)さんは　やっぱり　行かない______と　思いますよ。
4. 日本文学を　研究(けんきゅう)______と　しましたが、　やめました。
5. この　絵本は　中村さんの　お子さんに　あげ______と　思っています。
6. 小(こ)山さんが　いしゃを　呼______と　しましたが、　いしゃは　るすでした。

13.8.4 つぎの　ことばを　使って、文[sentence]を　作りなさい。それから、　いみを言いなさい。

1. なかなか...(ない)
2. ふつう
3. きびしい
4. いっしょうけんめい
5. はっきり

13.8.5 Write the underlined *hiragana* in *kan'ji*:

1. <u>ぶちょう</u>、　<u>しゃちょう</u>、　<u>かちょう</u>の　<u>ちい</u>の　じゅんじょが　わかりますか。
2. <u>たいせつ</u>な　<u>しごと</u>なので、　<u>きみ</u>にも　<u>て</u>つだってほしいんだ。
3. <u>やまだくん</u>に　<u>あと</u>で　やってもらおう。
4. お<u>ちゃ</u>の　<u>じかん</u>だと　<u>はは</u>が　<u>よ</u>んでいます。
5. <u>いそが</u>しくて　<u>たいへん</u>でしょうが、　これを　そくたつで　<u>だ</u>してください。

13.8.6 Distinguish the following *kan'ji*:

1. 位、住、仕
2. 課、調
3. 後、行
4. 呼、味
5. 都、部
6. 茶、英、若、花

13.8.7 After each of the following situations mark P if the plain style would be appropriate, N if the *desu-masu* style should be used, or PN if either will do:

1. male teacher to male student in a class
2. male teacher to female student in a class
3. student to teacher in a class
4. housewife to deliveryman at home
5. husband to wife at home
6. husband to mailman at home
7. father to children at home
8. man to close friend in a restaurant
9. man to store clerk in a department store
10. woman to close friend in a coffee house
11. company president to young visitor in the former's office

13.8.8 A female employee may call the president of the company ______ or ______, while a male employee may call him ______.

13.8.9 Which expression would you use to tell your section chief most politely that the company president is waiting for him?

1. Shachoo ga achira de matte imasu.
2. Shachoo ga atchi de omachi desu.
3. Shachoo ga achira de omachi desu.

13.8.10 When you are the speaker, who can be the subject of ～ *ga oyobi ni narimashita*?

1. you
2. your friend
3. your teacher
4. your father
5. your employer

13.8.11 What is the relationship (superior, inferior, equal) of the following three people: Tanaka san, the speaker, and the listener?

1. Tanaka san ga mukoo no heya de omachi da yo.
2. Tanaka san ga mukoo no heya de omachi desu ga.
3. Tanaka san ga mukoo no heya de matteru yo.

13.8.12 When the company president is not around, is it mandatory for the speaker to use the honorific expression referring to him?

13.9 SITUATIONAL AND APPLICATION CONVERSATION

13.9.1 At the office

One of the company employees tells his friend that he was late for work in the morning because of a train accident. He adds that the train he took was very crowded.
The friend says it is hard to get on a train every day.
He agrees and says he tried to come in a taxi but he couldn't.
His friend says he thinks a bus might have been better than a taxi.
The man says it is inconvenient to come to the office by bus; he has to change buses twice.

13.9.2 A section chief asks a clerk when she is going to the post office.

The clerk says she is thinking of going to the post office at the moment.
The section chief asks the clerk to send a letter by special delivery then.
The clerk receives it and tells the section chief that the president of the company is asking for him.
The section chief thanks the clerk.

13.9.3 Yamazaki: Anoo, kochira wa Yamada san no otaku deshoo ka?

Mrs. Yamada: Hai, soo desu ga.

Yamazaki: Watakushi, Yamazaki to iimasu ga, goshujin wa irasshaimasu ka?

Mrs. Yamada: Ima chotto dekakete imasu ga.

13.9.4 Kojima: Otaku no kachoo wa nan to iu namae desu ka?

Takeshita: Uchi no kachoo wa Katoo to iimasu ga.

13.9.5 Takeda: Kachoo san, Katoo san ga yoroshiku to ittemashita.

Katō: A, soo.

Takeda: A! Kachoo san, ohayoo gozaimasu.

Department Head: Ohayoo. Katoo kun, chotto kore o shirabete kuretamae.

Katō: Hai, wakarimashita.

13.9.6 Nakano: Kachoo, oyobi desu ka?

Section Chief: A, Nakano kun. Kimi wa Keioo Daigaku o sotsugyoo shita soo da ne.

Nakano:	Hai, kotoshi sotsugyoo shimashita.
Section Chief:	Jitsu wa, watashi mo Keioo o deta n da yo.
Nakano:	Soo deshita ka. Jaa, sen'pai desu ne. Kon'go tomo yoroshiku onegai shimasu.
Section Chief:	Kochira mo yoroshiku.

LESSON 14
RECEPTIVE COMPREHENSION

14.1 GENERAL INTRODUCTION

Generally speaking, production and comprehension are different skills. In producing oral utterances or written sentences, the speaker (or the writer) is given enough opportunity to choose expressions to transmit certain messages, while the listener (or the reader), in listening to a speaker's oral utterances or reading a writer's written sentences, must try to comprehend the speaker's (or the writer's) intended messages from the product. Sometimes, the speaker's (or the writer's) products may be muffled or blurred; a portion of them may not be audible or decipherable; some parts of an utterance or sentence may be omitted; a sentence may not be complete; and sometimes the sentence may be so complicated that even the subject cannot be located. There might be redundancies, duplications, and even misuses by speaker or writer.

In this lesson, linguistic problems such as the ones just described will be examined, and techniques in developing aural and reading comprehension will be explored. In addition, cultural factors affecting comprehension will be discussed. Please keep in mind that Lesson 14 is a lesson for passive learning and therefore the student should not be asked to prepare for any examination. The learner should try, however, to practice some of the techniques listed below and apply them to the various live situations which the learner might encounter.

14.2 LINGUISTIC FACTORS

Linguistic factors which enable the listener or the reader to comprehend the Japanese language better are listed below, then described individually.

1. Phrase Relationals
2. Clause Relationals
3. Phrase and Clause Omissions
4. Nonfinal Clause Endings
5. Sentence Interjectives and Conjunctive Functions
6. Noun Modifiers
7. Speech Levels and Styles
8. Some Clues

14.2.1 Phrase Relationals

Relationals, especially phrase Relationals, are important because they indicate the relationship between a Predicate Modifier and the Predicate. Listed below are some major functions of some important phrase Relationals studied so far:

PHRASE RELATIONALS

Relational	Lesson	Functions	Example Sentences
dake	II 9	limitation [only; just; no more than]	*Kotae dake kaite kudasai.* *Kono kudamono wa Kariforunia ni dake arimasu.*
de	I 3, 4	place of action [in; at; on, etc.]	*Gakkoo de naraimashita.*
	I 11, 12	means [by means of; with]	*Den'sha de kaerimashita.*
	II 1	totalizing	*Mittsu de hyakuen desu.* *Zen'bu de ikura desu ka?*
	II 7	limiting the length of time [within; in]	*Ichijikan de kaku koto ga dekimasu ka?* *Nan'pun de tsukurimashita ka?*
	II 11	designation of scope [among; of]	*Sono naka de ichiban ookii desu.* *Amerika de ichiban yuumei na hito wa dare desu ka?*
	III 8	material [from; of]	*Kore wa kin de dekite imasu.*
e	I 3	direction [to]	*Umi e ikimasen ka?*
ga	I 4	subject	*Den'wa ga arimasu.*
hodo	II 11, 12	[as much as]	*Watakushi wa anata hodo joozu ja arimasen.*
	III 7	[about; approximately]	*Nanakagetsu hodo mae ni Nihon e kita n desu.*
ka	I 11	[or]	*Koohii ka ocha o nomimashoo.*
kara	I 12	place of departure [from]	*Doko kara kimashita ka?*
	I 13	source [from]	*Tomodachi kara moraimashita.*
made	II 7	time or place of goal [until; as far as]	*Eki made arukimashoo.* *Asa goji made ben'kyoo shimashita.*
made ni	II 8	[by (the time given); not later than]	*Tooka made ni den'wa o kudasai.*
mo	I 4, 7, 12	inclusion [also; too]	*On'gaku mo suki desu.* *Kyooto e mo ryokoo shimashita.* *Koohii mo nomimasu.*
	I 8	[(not) either]	*Rekoodo mo yoku arimasen.* *Uchi ni mo imasen.* *Shin'bun mo yomimasen.*
	II 9	[even]	*Itte mo ii desu ka?*
	III 2	[as many as; no less than]	*Kan'ji o gohyaku mo shitte iru n desu.*
ni	I 5	location [in; at; on, etc.]	*Soko ni arimasu.*
	I 13	indirect object [to (a person)]	*Anata ni agemashoo.*
	II 2	target time [at; in; on]	*Yoji ni dekakemashoo.*
	II 4	direction [to]	*Uchi ni kaeritai desu.*
	II 5	purpose (of going) [for; to]	*San'po ni ikimasen ka?* *Gohan o tabe ni kaerimashita.*

Relational	Lesson	Functions	Example Sentences
ni	II 12	goal (to become) (to make) (to choose)	*Sen'sei ni naritai n desu.* *Kirei ni shimashoo.* *Ban'gohan wa bifuteki ni shimasu.*
	III 3	time and unit reference [per]	*Ichinichi ni san'do kusuri o non'de kudasai.* *Hitori ni yottsu ageyoo to omoimasu.*
	III 8	purpose [for; as]	*Rokujoo wa kodomobeya ni tsukatte imasu.*
	III 9, 11	indicates the person who is asked or wanted to do something	*Haha ni kippu o katte moraimashita.* *Anata ni itte hoshii n desu.*
	III 11	manner	*Doozo jiyuu ni hanashite kudasai.*
	III 11	reference	*Kono hon wa kodomo ni wa muzukashii desu.*
no	I 7, 9	qualification or modification of Noun, including possessive [of; in, etc.]	*Kore wa watakushi no heya desu.* *Nihon'go no hon o kaimasu.* *Gin'za no mise de kaimashita.*
	II 7	follows the subject in a Noun Modifier	*Kyuukoo no tsuku jikan o shitte imasu ka?* *Sei no takai hito wa dare desu ka?*
	III 2	appositional	*Tomodachi no Ichiroo kun ga uchi e kimasu.*
o	I 3	direct object	*Terebi o mimasu ka?*
	II 13	place through which action has taken place [through; along; in, etc.]	*Kono toori o tsugi no kado made arukimasu.* *Kooen o san'po shimashita.*
shika	III 3	limitation [only; just]	*Kyooshitsu ni wa gakusei shika imasen deshita.*
to	I 5	exhaustive listing [and]	*Kami to en'pitsu o kaimashita.*
	I 13	involvement [with]	*Okusan to issho ni kimasen ka?*
	III 2	quotation	*Kono shigoto wa taihen da to omoimasu yo.*
wa	I 7, 12	topic	*Kore wa hon desu.* *Kinoo wa Nikkoo ni imashita.*
	I 9, 12	in negation	*On'gaku wa kikimasen.* *Osake wa suki ja arimasen.* *Nikkoo e wa ikimasen deshita.*
	I 9, 12	contrast	*Ima wa suki desu ga, mae wa kirai deshita.* *Hon wa yomimasu ga, zasshi wa yomimasen.*
ya	I 9	sample listing [and (the like)]	*Kyooto ya Nara e ikimashoo.*
yori	II 11	comparison [than]	*Kyooto yori Tookyoo no hoo ga ookii desu.* *Soto de taberu yori uchi de tsukuru hoo ga ii desu.*

Try to identify the relationship between the Predicate Modifiers and the Predicate by interpreting the function of phrase Relationals. Notice that *ga* is mainly used as a subject marker. *O* is mainly used as a direct object marker; *ni* is mainly used as a target marker involving person, location, time, purpose, goal, direction, manner; *de* is mainly used to designate place of action and instrument; *kara* means "from" and indicates source of place, time, or person; *to* after a Noun functions as "and" or "with," and *to* after a Predicate is used to indicate a quotation; *wa* serves as a topic marker which can also serve as a subject; and *mo* means "(not) either (or)" and "also," which may replace *ga, wa,* or *o*.

14.2.2 Clause Relationals

Most of the clause Relationals studied so far function as connectors which relate the clause that precedes the connector with the one that follows the connector. The following are the clause Relationals which appeared in our Volume I through Volume III texts.

CLAUSE RELATIONALS

Relational	Lesson	Functions	Example Sentences
ga	I 9	reversal reasoning [but; although]	*Ten'ki ga warukatta desu ga, dekakemashita.*
	I 9	neutral connector [and]	*Sono eiga o mimashita ga, omoshirokatta desu.*
kara	II 5	reason [because; since]	*Sugu kimasu kara, matte ite kudasai.* *Yasui (desu) kara, kau tsumori desu.*
	III 7	sequential action [after; since]	*Amerika e kaette kara, nani o suru tsumori desu ka?*
kedo	I 4, 12	neutral connector [and]	*Sono eiga o mimashita kedo, omoshirokatta desu.*
kedo *keredo* *keredomo*	I 4, 12 II 11	reversal [but; although; however]	*Takai keredo, sore ni shimasu.* *Ikitai n desu kedo, tsugoo ga warui n desu.*
nagara	III 7	simultaneous action [while; as]	*Gakkoo e ikinagara, hataraite imasu.*
node	III 4	expected result [since; because]	*Yasumi na node, ashita wa hima desu.*
noni	III 4	reverse result [in spite of; although]	*Yasui noni, kawanakatta n desu ka?*

Some clause connectors (such as *ga, kedo, keredo, keredomo,* and *noni*) show either that the clause with these Relationals are reasons for the reversed result indicated in the second clause, or the result shown in the second clause is a reversed one despite the situation described in the clause with these Relationals. They can be translated as "although." Sometimes, *ga* or *kedo* serves as a mere neutral connector, while *noni* indicates a strong reversal.

Another group of clause Relationals, such as *kara* (except *kara* after the TE form of a Verb) and *node* mean "because," while *kara* after the TE form of a Verb indicates that actions are sequentially listed. *Ga* and *kedo* as clause Relationals also serve as casual clause connectors without much meaning or as a softener.

14.2.3 Phrase and Clause Omissions

The Japanese have a tendency to omit one or more phrases if the reference is understood by both parties. Since Japan has been a homogeneous nation, normally misunderstandings are fewer.

Kinoo gakkoo e ikimashita ka?

Hai, ikimashita.

In Japanese, the final clause can also be omitted if the listener understands what the rest might be. Sometimes, however, the listener must guess what should be filled in. This kind of communication by implication may create ambiguity, which reveals traditional Japanese cultural traits stated elsewhere.

Anata ga ikanakereba . . .

Ikitai n desu ga . . .

Yamada desu ga . . .

14.2.4 Nonfinal Clause Endings

When there are two or more clauses in a sentence, the nonfinal clause may have a clause Relational ending or may have the TE form, BA form, or Stem form ending of a Verb; the TE form, KU form, and BA form ending of an Adjective; and the TE form and BA form ending of the Copula. (TARI form and TARA form will be studied in Vol. IV.)

The nonfinal clause ending with the clause Relational has been discussed in Note 14.2.2. In this section, other endings will be studied.

The TE form of a Verb at the end of a nonfinal clause may carry one of the following functions, as indicated in Note 8.4.3 of this volume.

1. sequential action, if the subjects for both clauses are identical;

   Watashi wa Gin'za e itte, shokuji o shimashita.

2. parallel action, if the subject for each clause is different;

   Watashi wa Gin'za e itte, Kobayashi san wa uchi e kaerimashita.

3. causal relationship, when the subject for each clause is different and the events for both clauses are sequential;

   Ame ga futte, gorufu ni iku no o yamemashita.

The TE form of an Adjective at the end of a nonfinal clause may carry, as indicated in Note 8.4.11 of this volume, one of the following functions:

1. parallel relationship;

   Kono gen'kan wa hirokute, akarui desu.

2. causal relationship;

   Kono gen'kan wa hirokute, suki desu.

The TE form of the Copula at the end of a nonfinal clause may indicate, as stated in Note 8.4.14 of this volume, that the two or more clauses

1. show parallel facts;

   Kochira wa Katoo san de, sochira wa Kobayashi san desu.

2. or are in causal relationship;

   Kono daidokoro wa fuben de, iya desu.

The BA form of a Verb, an Adjective, or the Copula is described in Notes 13.4.6, 13.4.9, and 13.4.11 of Volume II. As the ending of a nonfinal clause, it functions as a statement of provision or condition for the final clause.

Chikakereba, aruite ikimasu.

Basu de ikeba, taishikan no soba ni tomarimasu.

Furan'su Taishikan nara, yoku shitte imasu.

The Stem form of a Verb at the end of a nonfinal clause functions exactly like the TE form of a Verb. The KU form of an Adjective at the end of a nonfinal clause functions exactly like the TE form of an Adjective. Both will be introduced in Volume IV. The use of the Stem form of a Verb and the KU form of an Adjective at the end of a nonfinal clause is more common in formal written Japanese.

14.2.5 Sentence Interjectives and Conjunctive Functions

Many Sentence Interjectives have been introduced in the three volumes of this text series. Some of them can serve to establish a relationship between two sentences.

1. continuation and addition (then; furthermore);

   sore kara, sore ni, soshite, mochiron, tokoro de, jaa, dewa, mata, shikamo

2. disagreement;

   demo, datte, shikashi

3. hesitation and halting;

   anoo, eeto, saa, maa, yaa, soretomo

4. reason;

   dakara, datte, doori de, desukara, sore de, sono tame

5. recollection;

   soosoo, hora, jitsu wa

6. response;

   a, aa, ee, hai, iie, iya

7. sequence;

   sore kara, suruto

8. surprise;

   oya! ara! maa! a!

There are many other words which can perform conjunctive functions.

14.2.6 Noun Modifiers

Pre-Noun, Noun + *no*, and adjectival Noun + *na* as Noun Modifiers are not by themselves sentences. However, other Noun Modifiers which end with Adjective or Verb endings can be independent sentences. It is the Verb ending which creates some difficulties for English speakers because the Noun after the Noun Modifier may be followed by (1) a subject *ga*; (2) a direct object *o*; (3) a place *de*; (4) an indirect object *ni*; (5) a direction *e*; or (6) an instrument *de*. Therefore, ambiguity may be created as a result. For instance, *korosu tora* may mean (1) the tiger that kills someone, (*tora ga*) *hito o korosu;* or (2) the tiger to be killed by someone, (*tora o*) *hito ga korosu.*

It is important to find out the Noun Modifier before the Noun; pinpoint the Predicate; distinguish the various kinds of Predicate Modifiers by checking Relationals; and if it is still ambiguous, then try to find out the context and situation.

14.2.7 Speech Levels and Styles

The Japanese have many special expressions and grammatical structures indicating the various kinds of speech levels and styles which have been discussed in Lesson 1 of this volume, and will be discussed further in Volume IV. Styles are determined by the speaker's evaluation of the relative status of the speaker and the listener, and levels are determined by the speaker's evaluation of the relative status relationship of the subject-person with the object-person involved in his talk or with other people. Ordinarily, levels are formulated by using special lexical items, affixing prefixes or suffixes, or using special structural forms. It will be, however, necessary to understand Japanese cultural traits in order to be able to understand appropriate human relationships involved in different styles and levels.

14.2.8 Some Clues

There are some other clues to enable the listener or reader to comprehend fully. For instance, Japanese Counters such as *-hon* or *-satsu* may be of help in deciding what object is being counted. The following are some of the Counters, although some of them have not been studied so far:

-dai (mechanical objects such as automobiles)

-do (times)

-hiki (small animals, insects, and fish)

-hon (long objects such as pencils)

-joo (*tatami* mats)

-kai (floors)

-ken (houses)

-kyaku (chairs and tables)

-mai (flat objects such as paper)

-me (order)

-nin (persons)

-sai (age)

-satsu (bound papers such as books)

-soku (footwear such as socks)

-too (big animals such as horses)

-tsuu (documents)

-wa (birds)

14.3 CULTURAL FACTORS

As described in the forward, nine traditional cultural traits have been set up for the purpose of students' understanding of social and cultural background in comprehending and producing Japanese expressions. The following cultural factors have been observed through Japanese language behavior.

1. Phenomenalism
2. Eclecticism
3. Naturalism
4. Secularism
5. Transitoriness
6. Groupism
7. Hierarchy
8. Familialism
9. Heteronomy

Notes on these traditional cultural traits which still affect the Japanese language usage have appeared in many places in this text series. The following are some of those notes where such traits were treated:

Volume I: 1.5.5; 2.5.4; 3.4.4; 5.4.11; 7.4.9; 7.4.10; 7.4.15; 7.4.17; 7.4.18; 8.4.12; 11.4.1; 11.4.12; 11.4.15; 12.4.13; 13.4.1; 13.4.8; 13.4.9.

Volume II: 1.4.3; 1.4.4; 1.4.5; 1.4.8; 1.4.14; 1.4.15; 2.4.6; 4.4.10; 4.4.11; 4.4.18; 5.4.1; 5.4.6; 7.4.8; 7.4.13; 8.4.7; 11.4.14; 12.4.1; 12.4.5; 12.4.7; 12.4.8; 12.4.13; 14.4.3; 14.4.4; 14.4.5.

Volume III: Lesson 1; 2.4.7; 2.4.8; 2.4.16; 3.4.10; 4.4.11; 4.4.13; 6.4.10; 7.4.13; 8.4.4; 9.4.4; 9.4.13; 12.4.5; 12.4.8; 13.4.16.

1. *Phenomenalism—Japanese approach toward abstraction.* The Japanese are willing to accept the phenomenal world as absolute rather than to make any abstraction. There is a tendency among the Japanese to comprehend a universal law only in reference to some particular or specific phase of things. They emphasize historical and topographical particularity or specificity. They place emphasis upon concrete objects and events rather than universals or generalizations. This leads to their emphasis on intuitiveness and lack of pursuit of the Western type of logic to its thorough end or consequence. They leave much room for sentiment and emotion. We may call this trait "alogical."

Isso, doose, yahari, sasuga are used quite frequently. They show the speaker's abandonment of thinking, logic, or personal judgment, as Gen Itasaka described in his book *Nihon'jin no Ron'ri Koozoo.*

2. *Eclecticism—Japanese approach to selection.* The Japanese have a tendency to introduce foreign cultures with vigor, digesting them, adapting them, and letting them coexist with their traditional and already adopted cultures. The cultural pluralism results in a variety of cultures coexisting in Japan:

Clothing—Japanese (*wafuku, kimono*), Western (*yoofuku*)

Food—Chinese (*chuuka ryoori*), Japanese (*washoku* or *Nihon ryoori*), Western (*seiyoo ryoori*)

Housing—Japanese (*wafuu, nihon'fuu*), Western (*seiyoofuu, yoofuu*)

Writings-*kan'ji, hiragana, katakana, roomaji, on, kun, tooon, kan'on, goon, kan'yooon*

Sports-baseball, basketball, golf, *juudoo, ken'doo, karate*

Music-classical, *gagaku*, jazz, *kayookyoku, kouta, min'yoo, nagauta, naniwabushi, yookyoku, hoogaku, yoogaku*

Religion-Buddhism, Christianity, Confucianism, Shinto

Vocabularies-*kan'go, wago, gairaigo*

We find thousands of vocabularies representing these cultural items and various types of expressions describing or representing the various cultural features. Superficially they seem to be chaotic and confused, but the Japanese give each one its proper place and allow them to coexist. The eclectic selection or cultural pluralism itself is an important feature of Japanese culture. They have their own characteristics but they have been open and embracive in adapting other cultures.

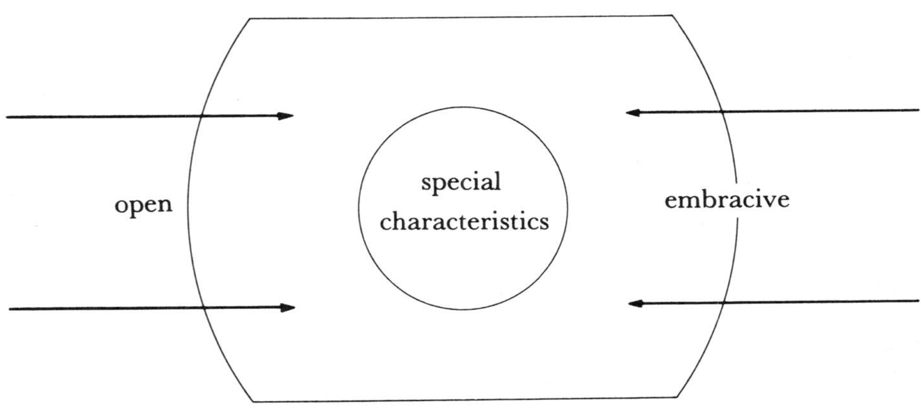

3. *Naturalism—Japanese approach to nature.* This trait has already been described in detail elsewhere. Therefore, only a few examples will be listed here.

"rain" *harusame, murasame, samidare, tsuyu, yuudachi, shigure, nihyakutooka*

"snow" *watayuki, botan'yuki, konayuki, sasameyuki*

"is wet" *shippori, shittori, jimejime, shimeyaka, bishobisho, gushogusho, pichapicha, jitojito*

"season" *harumeku, sakura zen'sen*

Haruhiko Kin'daichi in his *Nihon'go* listed rich vocabularies in the areas of weather, season, topography, water, fish, plants, and flowers. This phenomenon coincides with the Japanese love of flowers, birds, mountains and rivers, grass and trees. The patterns of Japanese *kimono*, their efforts in preserving the natural forms of their food in cooking; their *ikebana* and *bon'sai*; their painting of birds and natural scenery on their screens and *fusuma*, and their emphasis on nature in composing the syllable *haiku*, and so on reflect their love of nature.

4. *Secularism—Japanese approach to religion.* The Japanese tend to pay more attention to secular matters than things supernatural, and to transform "things in nature" to "human relationships." Since all spirits or gods reside in peaks, ridges, pines, trees, mountains, rivers, villages, plains, fields, and seas; since those objects are things in nature; and since they rely heavily on human relationships, the Japanese tend to pay more attention to human matters, namely, secular matters, than to supernatural things.

5. *Transitoriness—Japanese approach to life.* Influenced by Buddhism and its view of nature as impermanent and transient, traditionally the Japanese have viewed life as ephemeral and fatalistic, although Japan's younger generation has been moving away from this trait. The transitoriness leads to the sense of the uncertainty and frailty of life. Therefore, *akirame ga yoi* (resigned to), *tan'paku* (ardor, simple), *kodawari o mizu ni nagasu* (to reconcile), *kirei sappari* (neat), *bun o mamoru* (keep within one's bounds), *isagiyoku* (with a good grace), and *yukashii* (tasteful) are regarded to be good because they indicate the above-stated trait. Similarly, *shitsukoi* (persistent), *shuunen bukai* (tenancious), *kodawaru* (scrupulous), *namaiki* (conceited), *bun o mamoranai* (does not keep within one's bounds) carry bad connotations. *Shikata ga nai* (cannot be helped), *yamu o enai* (unavoidable), *munashii* (empty, void), *hakanai* (transient), and the like appear often in Japanese expressions. Since this world is impermanent, everything is imperfect. People must recognize that there is a limit and should be satisfied with what they already have. As a result, some Japanese find beauty in the impermanence and imperfection of beauty. *Yuugen* (subtle profundity), *wabi* (taste for the simple and quiet), and *sabi* (tranquility and antiquity) are prized. Unaccomplished love, *kanawanu* or *shinobu koi*, is valued. The more emotion and feeling are suppressed, the more they are purified. *Noo* drama shows this kind of sentiment and emotion. Tea ceremony, especially *wabi cha*, advocates this trait. *Taru o shiru* or *fusoku ni aman'jiru* (satisfied with insufficiency), *yojoo* (lingering sentiment), and *akirame* (give up) lead to human happiness. *Doose* or *mamayo* show that unhappiness is quite natural; therefore, nothing can be done, and thus, everything is fated, destined, and predesignated.

The famous *naru* philosophy emphasizes that things "become" such, rather than *suru*, which "makes" things such. The traditional Japanese seem to prefer *naru* to *suru* in making a statement. This leads to arationalism and abandonment of decision-making responsibility. *In'nen* means the source of fate or destiny. This trait has become less obvious today in Japan, and more positive and aggressive attitudes toward life are widely accepted, especially by the young generation.

6. *Groupism.* In Japan, unlike in America, "ego" or individualism is still weak. The individual exists because of the group that he is in or he belongs to. Therefore, autonomy, independence of individuals, is still weak and dependency on the group is expected in Japan. *Ga o korosu* has a good connotation, and *jibun katte, shishin* (egoism, selfishness) are bad. *Amae* (depend and expect others' favor or benevolence), *giri* (obligation), *nin'joo* (humanity), *haji* (shame) can only be understood under this consideration. Actually *haji* means that you put your group to shame or disgrace; therefore, *hajishirazu, hajisarashi, haji ni naru, haji o*

sarasu, uchi no haji o soto ni sarasu are regarded to be bad. *Tabi no haji wa kaki sute* (a man away from home need feel no shame) shows the nature of "group consciousness." *Seken* (the community) is one type of "group," *seken'tei* (decency, reputation), *seken'tei ga warui* (be discreditable, injurious to one's reputation), *seken'tei o tsukurou* (put up a good front), *seken'tei o gomakasu* (sail under false colors), *taimen* (respectability) show the importance of "group consideration."

Ruth Benedict described Japanese culture as shame oriented rather than guilt oriented. *Yahari* and *sasuga* reveal Japanese dependency on groups and group values in rendering judgment. Guilt is felt only within a group and shame is felt when *seken*, which is dealing with a group, is hurt by the behavior of a member of that group. Those who have nothing to do with that group are called *yoso mono*, those who are placed outside of both guilt and shame.

7. *Hierarchy*. As Chie Nakane stated in her *Tateshakai no Nin'gen Kan'kei*, Japanese society is a vertical society. During the Tokugawa period, there were four major classes: samurai, farmers, artisans, and merchants. Since merchants, who were ranked lowest in society, must deal with money, expressions related to money used to convey bad connotations, for example, *keisan'dakai, kin'sen ni hakkiri shite iru, chakkari shite iru, okane no koto o ukagatte shitsurei desu ga. . . .*

Inferiors must be obedient to superiors, resulting in a "peace-at-any-price" attitude, for instance, *Nagai mono ni wa makarero, Futoi mono ni nomare yo, Sawaranu kami ni tatari nashi, Gomuri gomottomo.*

It is therefore necessary for the inferior to protect himself or herself against the superior. The only alternative to social revolution or human emancipation would be to become a practical, self-centered person. Traditionally, ego in Japan did not have its origin in self-dignity but self-interest.

A hierarchic society may develop a concept called *bun*, which means one's lot, one's place, and one's social standing. Traditionally the Japanese emphasize the importance of *bun*, as in *bun soooo ni kurasu* (live within one's means), *bun ni sugita* (undue, undeserved), *bun ni yasun'jiru* (be contented with one's lot), *bun o mamoru* (keep one's sphere in life), *bun o wakimaeru* (know one's place), and *bun ni oojite, hon'bun* (one's duty).

8. *Familialism.* Traditionally, the family has been the basic social unit in Japan. But the important role played in Japanese society by family relationships is not confined to individual families. A similar pattern has spread to every human relationship. Thus, consanguine groups, such as families, and pseudo-consanguine groups, such as professionals and political parties, are formed and treated alike. The Japanese tend to treat a company as a family and treat superiors as fathers or elder brothers. The traditional composition of a family was not a nuclear family type but rather an extended family type with father and sons, especially the oldest son as the core. The features of groupism and hierarchy stated above play an important role here. For instance, *oya*, *oyabun*, *oyagokoro*, and *oyaji* are viewed as the source of authority and *kobun* must be obedient.

This male-centered family system leads to a tradition of treating men as superior in status, as exemplified in such phrases as *otoko to shite, otoko rashiku, otoko to otoko no hanashiai, otoko o ageru, otoko no yakusoku*. This familialism also leads to paternalism (*on'jooshugi*), and to a parental affection approach in managing nonfamily groups.

9. *Heteronomy*. Heteronomy can be described as the "other-directed" or listener-centered approach. The Japanese tend to pay attention to the feelings and emotions of the listener and are concerned with how the talk would be received by the listener. The following tendencies are often observable in their verbal behavior.

a) The attempt to avoid definitive statements and make them rather ambiguous and indirect: They prefer suggestiveness and implied intentions, for example, *nan to naku, betsu ni doo to iu koto mo nai kedo, hodo yoku, ~to kan'jirareru, ~to omowareru, ~to kan'gaerareru, Tadaima kirashite orimasu ga . . . , Ome ni kakaritai n desu ga . . . , Kore kara maishuu suiyoobi ni atsumaru koto ni narimashita, Anata no ossharu koto wa machigai de wa nai to omoimasu keredomo, watakushi no mijuku na ken'kai de wa . . . , sorosoro, shooshoo, Ocha demo nomimasen ka?*

b) The emphasis on *sasshi* (conjecturing sensitivity and reading others' minds) and *omoiyari* (being considerate and empathetic toward others): Generally speaking, they attach more value to harmony, understanding, modesty, and considerateness. Therefore, *omoiyari*, *ki ga kiku*, *kokorozukai*, *sashihikaeru*, *en'ryo suru* are viewed as good qualities, and *deshabari*, *minohodo shirazu*, *osekkai o yaku* carry bad connotations.

c) The attempt to forestall possible accusation: *Warukatta ne*, *Sumimasen*, *Ojama shimasu*, *Shitsurei desu ga*.

d) The use of softener as buffers: *Jiman ja nai ga . . .*, *Itcha warui kedo . . .*, *Soo itcha nan da kedo . . .*, *Kon'na koto ga ieta gara ja nai n desu ga . . .*

e) The use of the double negative to soften the tone: *Ao ni naranai uchi ni wataranakereba abunaku arimasen*, *Yamada san wa yoji ni naranakereba kaerimasen*, *~de wa nai deshoo ka?*, *~ja nai ka to omoimasu keredo. . . .*

14.4 EXERCISES

14.4.1 Indicate the subject for the second and the third sentences.

マイク・ハリソンさんは　二十六さいの　どくしんの　アメリカ人です。　カリフォルニアに　ある　アメリカの　会社に　つとめていたのですが、　けんしゅうで　先月　日本の　会社に　来ました。　これから　二年間　東京に　いるそうです。

14.4.2 Supply an omitted clause or Predicate after the underlined incomplete sentences.

女の人　「ハリソンさんは　上級(じょうきゅう)クラスで　だいじょうぶですね。　上級(じょうきゅう)クラスは　月木の　六時半から　八時までです。」

ハリソン　「そうですか。　さっそく　申(もう)し込(こ)みを　したいんですが。」

女の人　「この　申(もう)し込(こ)み書に　名前、　国籍(せき)、　職業(しょくぎょう)など　書いてください。　それから、　月謝(げっしゃ)ですが、　三か月で　六万円です。」

ハリソン　「そうですか。　きょう　はらいますから。」

女の人　「では、　あちらで。」

14.4.3 Explain the function of the following underlined Relationals.

ハリソン　「はい、　マイク・ハリソンと　いいます。」

女の人　「こちらの　へやで　プレイスメント・テストを　うけてください。　十五分ぐらいで　終わります。」

14.4.4 Explain the function of the following underlined clause Relationals.

ハリソンさんは　カリフォルニアに　いた　時、　一年間　日本語を　勉強したそうですが、　もっと　じょうずに　なりたいので、　日本語学校に　入りたいと思っています。　それで、　会社の　昼休みに　どうりょうの　大石さんに　そうだんしました。

14.4.5 Describe the use of the underlined *jitsu wa* and *nara*. Also indicate Noun Modifiers modifying the underlined Nouns.

ハリソン 「大石さん、 今 ちょっと いいですか。」

大石 「え、 いいですよ。 何ですか。」

ハリソン 「じつは、日本語を もっと 勉強したいので、学校を さがしているんですが、いい 日本語学校を 知りませんか。」

大石 「ええと、 前 友だちだった フランス人が かよっていた 学校なら、知っていますけど。」

ハリソン 「どこですか、 その 学校は？」

14.4.6 State the relative status of *on'na no hito* and Ōishi, and indicate reasons (style and level) in support of your statement.

女の人 「日本語学校でございます。」

大石 「もしもし、 日本語の クラスの ことを うかがいたいんですが、つぎの 学期(がっき)は いつ はじまるんですか。」

女の人 「九月二十日からです。」

大石 「そうですか。 じつは、 日本語を 習いたいという アメリカ人が いるんですが、どんな クラスが あるんですか。」

女の人 「その 方は 日本語が はじめてですか。」

大石 「いいえ、 アメリカで 一年間 勉強したそうです。 だから、 会話はできるんですが、 もっと 漢字なんか 習いたいんだそうです。 よるのクラスで 週に 二度というのは ないでしょうか。」

女の人 「ございます。」

14.4.7 Describe the relationships among the four: Hayashi, Ōishi, Kazuko, and *on'na no hito.*

林(はやし) 「ああ、 つかれた。たのしかったけど、 つかれましたね。」

大石 「天気が よくて、 よかった。」

かず子 「本当。」

女の人 「いらっしゃいませ。 お待ちしていました。 おしぼりを どうぞ。」

大石 「メニューを 見せてください。」

女の人 「はい、 どうぞ。 お飲み物は 何を さしあげましょうか。 ビール、ワイン、 おさけ、 いろいろ ございますが。」

大石 「ハリソンさんは 何に しますか。」

ハリソン 「ぼくは ビールに します。」

大石 「ぼくも ビール。 君は？」

林　　「ぼくは　運転するから、　ジュースか　水に　しておくよ。」
かず子　「あたしも　ジュースに　するわ。」
大石　　「すみません。ビールと　ジュースを　二本ずつ　おねがいします。」

14.4.8 Describe the functions of the following underlined words.

ハリソン「かなり　とおいんですか、奥多摩は？」
林　　「いや、　一時間半　あれば　つくでしょう。　それに、　みちも　あまり
こんでいないらしいです。　さあ、　出かけましょうか。」

14.4.9 Describe different attitudes taken by Harrison and Ōishi toward paying the bill. Can those differences be attributed to the cultural differences between America and Japan?

——食事が　終わって——

大石　　「ハリソンさん、　コーヒーの　おかわりは　どうですか。」
ハリソン「いいえ、ぼくは　もう　けっこうです。　もう　おなかが　いっぱいです。」
林　　「ぼくは　おかわり。」
大石　　「すみません。　コーヒーを　二人分　ください。　それから、　おかんじょう
おねがいします。」
女の人　「お待たせしました。　どうぞ。」
ハリソン「ぼくは　いくら　はらいましょうか。」
大石　　「いや、　ハリソンさん、　きょうは　ぼくが　おごりますから、
ご心配なく。」
ハリソン「いいえ、　それじゃ　わるいから、　わりかんに　しましょう。」
大石　　「とんでもない。　きょうは　ハリソンさんは　お客さんですよ。」
ハリソン「そうですか。　では、　ごちそうに　なります。　ありがとう
ございました。」

14.4.10 Describe the use of *node, kedo, ikeba,* and omission of the final clause, all underlined below.

大石「ええ。　むこうに　おいしい　ステーキ屋も　あるので、　帰りに　そこで
食事するつもりなんですけど、　ハリソンさんも　行けば　たのしいだろうと
思って。」

14.4.11 Describe the use of *betsu ni, ookute, dakara, toritakereba,* and *motte ikeba,* underlined below.

大石「べつに。奥多摩(おくたま)は　山が　多くて　とても　きれいな　所だから、しゃしんを　とりたければ、カメラを　持って行けば　いいでしょう。週末(まつ)は　天気が　いいらしいですよ。」

14.4.12 Study Mike Harrison Series (3) appeared in Lesson 15, Section 5. Describe the various relationships among Okusan, Buchō, Harrison, Ōishi, and Un'ten'shu in relation to familialism, groupism, hierarchy, and heteronomy.

LESSON 15
REVIEW AND APPLICATION

15.1 PATTERNS

15.1.1 "want someone to do"

a.

いい　店を　しょうかいして	
クリスマスプレゼントを　おくって	ほしいんです
よく　考えて	
もっと　協力(きょうりょく)して	
この　はがきは　まだ　出して	
あまり　くすりを　飲んで	ほしくないんです
よやくを　取りけして	
クラスに　おくれて	
早く　取りに　来て	
漢字を　もっと　おぼえて	ほしかったんです
げんかんで　くつを　ぬいで	
車を　きれいに　みがいて	
洋風の　家を　たてて	
仕事を　やめて	ほしくなかったんです
わたしの　うちに　とまって	

b.

母		むかえに　来て	
おとうと		地図(ず)を　かいて	
		もっと　れんしゅうして	ほしいんです
友だち		すぐ　知らせて	
君	に	この　くつを　はいて	ほしくないんです
あなた		ラジオを　なおして	ほしかったんです
		ニューヨークを　おとずれて	
課長		事務(む)所に　のこっていて	ほしくなかったんです
お客さん		二かいへ　あがって	

15.1.2 ''hope'' ''wish''

生活たいどを　変えれば	
ことば使いが　変われば	
はっきり　たのめば	
敬(けい)語は　もっと　かんたんに　なれば	
雨が　ふらなければ	
問題が　やさしければ	いい
天気が　よければ	いいけど
へやが　あかるければ	いいんですが
しけんが　なければ	いいと　思いますが
先生が　きびしくなければ	
校長先生が　女なら	
父が　部長なら	
教室(しつ)が　広くて、しずかなら	
交通(こうつう)が　べんりなら	

15.1.3 ''even if''

車が　よごれてしまって		洗う　時間が　ありません
電車が　こんでいて	も、	乗らなければなりません
すぐ　わからなくて		よく　考えてみてください
よやくしておかなくて		ホテルに　とまることが　できますよ
あたまが　いたくて		くすりが　ないんです
うちが　とおくて	も、	あるくんですか
ねむくて むずかしくて 忙しくて		宿(しゅく)題を　しなければなりません やってみてください
小学生で		この　問題の　いみが　わかりますよ
日曜(よう)日で		働くんですか
いやで	も、	しなければなりません
今　ひつようじゃなくて		買っておいてください
好きじゃなくて		やってみませんか

15.1.4 "the more . . . the more"

みちが　こめば	こむ		おそくなります
早く　行けば	（早く）　行く		すわるのが　らくです
気に　すれば	（気に）　する	ほど	あたまが　いたくなります
この　問題は　考えれば	考える		
会話は　れんしゅうすれば	（れんしゅう）する		じょうずに　なるでしょう

仕事が　忙しければ	忙しい		いっしょうけんめい　やります
むずかしければ	むずかしい		
人が　多ければ	多い	ほど	うれしいです
食事は　あたたかければ	あたたかい		
天気が　よければ	よい		たのしいでしょう

説明は　かんたんなら	かんたんな		わかりやすいです
へやは　しずかなら	しずかな		いいと　思います
仕事は　らくなら	らくな	ほど	
交通(こうつう)は　べんりなら	べんりな		よろしいですね
みやげは　日本的なら	日本的な		

15.1.5 OO form of Copula "probably"

a. Verb

クラスに　おくれるだろう		
三月に　子どもが　生まれるだろう		
きっと　おどろくだろう		
安いから、すぐ　こわれるだろう		思います
学校に　おくれないだろう	と	（友だちが）　言いました
かないが　世話を　しただろう		（先生が）　おっしゃいました
一九七五年に　卒業(そつぎょう)しただろう		
中村さんが　運転(うんてん)しただろう		
この　洋服が　一番　に合っただろう		

b. Adjective

つぎの　しけんは　たぶん　やさしいだろう
原(はら)さんの　おくさんは　美しいだろう
北海道(ほっかいどう)は　東京より　すずしいだろう
石川さんの　レポートは　あまり　長くないだろう
この　こたえは　おかしいだろう
いもうとも　うれしかっただろう
あなたが　思うほど　きびしくなかっただろう
外国人には　とても　わかりにくかっただろう

と

思います
（松本(まつもと)さんが）言っています
（山田先生が）おっしゃいました

c. Copula

子どもが　あそんでいるので、じゃまだろう
こんな　仕事は　いやだろう
いなかは　交通(こうつう)が　ふべんだろう
この　さんこう書は　あなたに　ひつようだろう
ジョージさんは　大学の　三年生ではないだろう
これは　銀の　ゆびわだろう
あの　旅館は　日本風だっただろう
山田さんは　大きな　会社の　部長だっただろう
しけんは　十月六日ではなかっただろう

と

思います
（友だちが）言っています
（先生が）おっしゃいました

15.1.6 OO form of Verb ＋ *to omou,* etc.

あした　学校を　休もう
車の　パンクを　自分で　なおそう
よし子さんに　会おう
八時ごろ　出かけよう
もっと　考えてみよう
日本文学を　研究(けんきゅう)しよう
来年　家を　たてよう
銀行に　つとめるのを　やめよう
松本(まつもと)さんに　協力(きょうりょく)してもらおう
地図(ず)を　かいてやろう

と

思います
（友だちが）言いました
（先生が）おっしゃいました

15.1.7 OO form of Verb + *to suru*

a. "try to do"

かきとめで　出そう	と	しました(が...)
ゆかを　洗おう		
吉(よし)田さんに　たのもう		
その　仕事を　やろう		
くすりを　飲もう		
学校へ　いもうとを　むかえに　行こう		
七時の　急行に　乗ろう		
ぼくも　協力(きょうりょく)しよう		
お客さんが　来るので、　着かえよう		
もっと　いっしょうけんめい　勉強しよう		
友だちに　みやげを　買ってあげよう		

b. "about to do"

ミラーさんは ジョージが	本当の　ことを　話そう	と	しています した　時
	いすに　すわろう		
	車を　なおそう		
	ガラスを　みがこう		
	いしゃを　呼ぼう		
	しずかな　へやで　昼ねしよう		
	げんかんの　ドアを　しめよう		
	常用(じょうよう)漢字を　ぜんぶ　おぼえよう		
	松本(まつもと)さんに　電話を　かけよう		

15.1.8 *Tame ni* and *no ni*

a. "in order to"

漢字を　覚える	ために	日本語学校に　入りました
急行に　乗る		早く　家を　出た
銀座(ざ)へ　行く		地下鉄に　乗りました
駅の　中に　入る		きっぷを　買ったんですか

b. ''in the process of''

漢字を　覚える	のに	時間が　かかります
急行に　乗る		大変でしょう
銀座(ざ)へ　行く		三十分も　電車に　乗らなければなりません
駅の　中に　入る		二百円　かかります

15.1.9 Relational-like function of TE form

a. ''concerning''

はんがの　作り方
戦争(せんそう)前の　生活(かつ)
男と　女の　ことば使い
敬語(けい)
その　ことばの　いみ
日本の　でんとう的な　社会
アメリカの　文化
戦争(せんそう)後(ご)の　社会
「石の　上にも　三年」という　ことわざ

について

教えてください
話してください
説明してくださいませんか
知っていますか
調べようと　思います
書こうと　しています

b. ''depending upon'' ''according to''

それぞれの　専攻(せんこう) 研究(けんきゅう)する　人	によって	きょうみが　ちがいます
戦争(せんそう) 教育(いく)		わたしの　考えは　変わりました
あい手の　地位 あい手の　たいど		ことば使いを　変えます
山本(もと)さんの　協力(きょうりょく) あなたの　しんせつ		レポートを　書くことが　できました

c. "as" "for"

あなたは	この　大学の　卒業(そつぎょう)生 外国人 軍(ぐん)人	として	この　問題について　どう　思いますか
私は	社長 重役(じゅうやく) 部長 課長		ある　会社に　つとめています
あの　人は	いしゃ サラリーマン 会社員 銀行員		りっぱです
父は	学長 学部長 校長		八年間　仕事を　しました

15.1.10 Relational of reference *ni*

敬(けい)語の　使い方は	外国人 わたし	には	むずかしすぎます わかりにくいです
この　本は その　問題は	小学生 けい子ちゃん	にも	やさしいでしょう かんたんだと　思います
この　食べ物は	あかちゃん おばあさん	には	よくありません
くだ物は	子ども	に	いいそうです
これは	びょう気の　人		てき当でしょう
この　本は	サラリーマン 学生		とくに　ひつようです

15.1.11 Relational of manner *ni*

らく かんたん 自由(ゆう) ていねい	に	話してください
りっぱ 元(げん)気		やります
しんせつ ていねい		みちを　教えてくれました
しずか		たのみました
ふくざつ きれい		作りました
文化的		かちが　あります
歴史的 一ぱん的		言えば、そうでしょう

15.1.12 Time words "before" "after"

今　一時五分 四時十八分	前 すぎ	です	
七時二、三分 午前(ごぜん)　十一時二十分 午後(ごご)　九時十五分	前 すぎ	に	来てください

百年ぐらい	前(に)	米国人が　自動車を　運転(うんてん)したそうです
三年半 四か月		日本語を　習いはじめました
二週間 五日ほど		大学で　よし子さんに　会いました

三時間 二、三十分 五分か　六分ぐらい	前(に)	そくたつで　出しました 友だちが　来ました 汽車は　出てしまいましたよ

15.2 SPEECH STYLE

15.2.1 Imperative expressions

a.

牛乳を　持って来て ていねいに　話して くわしく　説明して もう　一度　やって かきとめで　出して 早く　ご飯を　食べてしまって 車を　なおしておいて ゆっくり　読んであげて まさえさんに　たのんで はっきり　言って	(ね) (よ) くれ くれない？

b.

牛乳を　持って来 ていねいに　話し くわしく　説明し もう　一度　やり かきとめで　出し 早く　ご飯を　食べてしまい 車を　なおしておき ゆっくり　読んであげ まさえさんに　たのみ はっきり　言い	なさい (たまえ)

15.2.2 Polite expressions

a. ''someone is doing''

あの　方 校長先生	が	お呼び お帰り	です

社長	が	お出かけ	です
部長		お休み	
林さん		お待ち	
お客さま		おとまり	

b. ''someone did something''

あの　方	が	お呼び	に	なりました
校長先生		お帰り		
社長		お出かけ		
部長		お休み		
林さん		お待ち		
お客さま		おとまり		

15.3 REVIEW DRILLS

15.3.1 Transformation and Substitution Drills

1. A：何の　ために　日本へ　来たんですか。
   B：日本文化を　研究する　ために　来たんです。
   A：どのくらい　いるつもりですか。
   B：一年ぐらい　いようと　思っています。
   1. いろいろな　けいけんを　する　　2. 仕事を　する
   3. 英語の　教師に　なる　　4. 日本的な　生活を　味わう
   5. 日本の　おんがくを　勉強する　　6. じゅうどうを　習う

2. A：お正月の　休みに　何を　するつもりですか。
   B：国へ　帰ろうと　思っています。
   A：おとうとさんも　帰るんですか。
   B：おとうとは　帰らないだろうと　思います。
   1. スキーを　する　　2. 京都へ　あそびに　行く
   3. 旅行に　出かける　　4. 毎日　ジョギングを　する
   5. 父の　仕事を　手つだう

3. A：どうして　手紙を　書かなかったんですか。
   B：手紙を　書こうと　した　時、友だちが　来てしまったんです。
   1. 電話を　かける　　2. おふろに　入る　　3. 出かける
   4. したくを　する　　5. 手紙を　出す　　6. 地図を　かいてあげる

4. A：れんしゅうすれば、 じょうずに なるでしょうか。
   B：れんしゅうすれば するほど じょうずに なりますよ。
   1. がんばる、いい 仕事が できる
   2. 少ない、覚えやすい
   3. あつい、おいしい
   4. カレーライスは からい、いい
   5. 手つだう、早く 終わる

5. A：れんしゅうすれば、 じょうずに なりますか。
   B：さあ、れんしゅうしても、じょうずに ならないだろうと 思いますけど。
   1. いっしょうけんめい やる、できる
   2. がんばる、一番に なる
   3. くすりを 飲む、よく なる
   4. 手つだう、早く 終わる
   5. 安い、たくさん 買う
   6. 天気が よい、およぐ

15.4 REVIEW EXERCISES

15.4.1 Insert an appropriate Relational in each blank, and then give the English equivalent for each sentence:

1. もっと ていねい____ 話してくれませんか。
2. 着物____ 着方は 外国人____は むずかしいでしょう。
3. 急行____ 乗ろう____ したんだ____、 だめだった。
4. 気____ つけてくださいね。
5. あまり 気____ しないでください。
6. 今晩は 君____ あそび____ 来てほしいんです。
7. 一ぱん的____ 言って、 地位____ じゅんじょ____ はっきりしている。
8. 先生____ しゃしんを とっていただきたいのですが。
9. あの えいがは 子ども____は おもしろいが、おとな____ は つまらないだろう。

15.4.2 Select an appropriate word from among the words given and tell the meaning of the sentence:

1. 国によって 文化は（ ）ちがいます。
   <そろそろ、 それぞれ、 どんどん>
2. 一度 奈良(なら)へ 行ってみたいんですが、 時間が ないので、（ ）行くことができません。
   <なかなか、 だいぶ、 もっとも>
3. 池(いけ)田さんが（ ）りっぱな 家を たてたそうです。
   <どうも、 そろそろ、 なかなか>

4. 日本語は（　　）むずかしいですね。でも、（　　）勉強すれば、（　　）
じょうずに　なりますよ。
<いっしょうけんめい、　わりあい、　はっきり、　だんだん、　それぞれ>
5. よく　わかりませんから、（　　）（　　）言ってください。
<はっきり、　もっとも、　いっしょうけんめい、　もっと>
6. 「お元(げん)気ですか。」「いや、（　　）あまり　元(げん)気じゃないんです。」
<どうぞ、　どうも、　はっきり>
7. 「わかれば、（　　）知らせます。」「（　　）おねがいします。」
<よろしく、　いっしょうけんめい、　前もって>

15.4.3 What would you say when:

1. you feel relieved to hear something?
2. you see your children leaving for school?
3. you want to ask your boss politely to give an instruction about the work to do?
4. you want to tell your chief that the president wants to meet him?
5. you want to wake your children up?
6. you want to warn someone that he will be late for work unless he hurries?
7. you want to ask your friend to go to mail out a postcard?
8. you want your employee to go to mail out a postcard?

15.4.4 Transform the following sentences, if necessary, according to the situation given in English:

1. 「この　仕事を　ちょっと　手つだってください。」
   a. A father speaks to his son.
   b. A daughter speaks to her mother.
   c. A company employee speaks to his colleague.
   d. A company president speaks to his employee.
   e. A man speaks to a stranger.
2. 「わたしは　林(はやし)さんに　手紙を　書きました。」
   a. A husband speaks to his wife.
   b. A son speaks to his father.
   c. An older brother speaks to his younger brother.
   d. An employee speaks to his section chief.

3. 「しゃしんを　とりましたか。」
   a. You ask to your boss.
   b. A man asks to a child.
   c. A mother asks to her daughter.

15.4.5 Complete each of the following sentences:

1. 人によって ________________________________。
2. ________________について　くわしく　話してください。
3. スミスさんは　アメリカ人としては ________________________。
4. ________________のに、大変ですね。
5. ________________________うと　思っている。
6. 雨が　ふっても、________________________。
7. いしゃを　呼ぶために、________________。
8. ____________________くても、自分で　やりなさい。
9. ____________________うと　しましたが、だめでした。
10. __________ば __________ほど __________　なりますね。

15.4.6 Give the reading of each *kan'ji* in parentheses and then connect each of the A-group words with its antonym or related word listed in the B group by putting the appropriate B-group letter in the A-group blank.

A			B	
1. 戦争前(せんそう)	(　　　)	______	a. 休む	(　　　)
2. 日本風	(　　　)	______	b. 冬	(　　　)
3. 朝	(　　　)	______	c. 着物	(　　　)
4. 買う	(　　　)	______	d. 電車	(　　　)
5. 先週	(　　　)	______	e. 安い	(　　　)
6. 夏	(　　　)	______	f. 戦争後(せんそうご)	(　　　)
7. 社長	(　　　)	______	g. 洋風	(　　　)
8. 洋服(ふく)	(　　　)	______	h. 売る	(　　　)
9. 働く	(　　　)	______	i. 金	(　　　)
10. 父	(　　　)	______	j. 社員	(　　　)
11. 急行	(　　　)	______	k. 夕方	(　　　)
12. 高い	(　　　)	______	l. 母	(　　　)
13. 若い	(　　　)	______	m. 手	(　　　)
14. 足	(　　　)	______	n. 年取った	(　　　)
15. 銀	(　　　)	______	o. 来週	(　　　)

15.4.7 Write two readings of each of the following *kan'ji*:

1. 新 ______、______		14. 下 ______、______	
2. 変 ______、______		15. 出 ______、______	
3. 事 ______、______		16. 長 ______、______	
4. 大 ______、______		17. 会 ______、______	
5. 間 ______、______		18. 家 ______、______	
6. 方 ______、______		19. 入 ______、______	
7. 話 ______、______		20. 高 ______、______	
8. 今 ______、______		21. 生 ______、______	
9. 来 ______、______		22. 時 ______、______	
10. 木 ______、______		23. 所 ______、______	
11. 行 ______、______		24. 小 ______、______	
12. 年 ______、______		25. 聞 ______、______	
13. 水 ______、______			

15.4.8 In which case(s) can you use *Sore wa mon'dai de aru?*

1. in casual speech
2. in an article
3. in formal speech

15.4.9 In what situations can *Kirei de aru* be used?

1. in casual speech
2. in writing articles

15.4.10 By whom might the following expressions be used?

1. Chotto matte kure yo.
2. Ii wa nee.
3. Yoku wakatta.
4. Toshokan made aruita n da yo.
5. Kinoo gakkoo ni kita?

15.4.11 Change the sentences listed in 15.4.10 into a student's utterances made to his teacher.

15.4.12 Transform the following contracted forms and simplified sentences into their original forms and sentences.

1. Nihon e itte doo datta?
2. Kimi, Jooji kun?
3. Soo na no ka?
4. Maa, kowareteta no ne.
5. Itsumo dare to ason'deru?
6. Kekkon shitatte kiita kedo, hon'too?

15.4.13 In writing a diary, which version would you adopt?

1. Kyoo mita eiga wa omoshirokatta.
2. Kyoo mita eiga wa omoshirokatta desu.
3. Kyoo mita eiga wa omoshirokatta ne.

15.4.14 When a politician is making a speech in front of the Diet, which of the following expressions would he use?

1. Kore wa hijoo ni ookina mon'dai de aru.
2. Kore wa hijoo ni ookina mon'dai desu.
3. Kore wa hijoo ni ookina mon'dai de arimasu.
4. Watashi wa Yamada de aru.
5. Watakushi wa Yamada de arimasu.
6. Boku wa Yamada desu.

15.4.15 In an editorial article for a newspaper, which version would you expect to be used?

1. Nihon'jin wa yoku mono o okuriau ga . . .
2. Nihon'jin wa yoku mono o okuriau n desu ga . . .
3. Nihon'jin wa yoku mono o okuriaimasu ga . . .
4. Nihon'jin wa yoku mono o okuriau n da ga . . .

15.5 MIKE HARRISON SERIES (3)

——マイク・ハリソン　日本の　正月を　味わう——

15.5.1 ——部長の　家で——

おくさん 「それで、 マイクさんも　お正月に　よぼうと　思っているのね。」
部長 「そう、 日本の　正月を　味わってもらうのも　いいと　思って。」

おくさん 「それは いいけど、 マイクさん 日本の お正月の 食べ物 食べるかしら。 もし 好きじゃなければ、 洋風の 物 作りましょうか。」

部長 「そんな ひつよう ないだろうと 思うよ。 かれ よく 大石君なんかと すし屋や やきとり屋へ 行ってるらしいよ。」

おくさん 「それなら いいわ。 それから、 その マイクさん 日本語が わかるの？」

部長 「もちろん、 なかなか うまいよ。 会社では ほとんど 日本語で 話してるよ。 ふくざつな 仕事の 話は やっぱり まだ むりだけどね。」

おくさん 「そう、 よかったわ。 あたし 英語に よわいから。 それで、 よぶ 日は 二日ね。」

部長 「そう。 あした みんなに 話してみるよ。」

15.5.2 ——会社で (1)——

部長 「ハリソンさん、 お正月は 東京に いますか。」

ハリソン 「はい、 その つもりです。」

部長 「一月の 二日に 会社の 若い 人を 何人か うちに よぼうと 思ってるんだけど、いっしょに 来ませんか。 あまり ごちそうは ないけど…。」

ハリソン 「日本の お正月は はじめてです。 よろこんで うかがいます。」

部長 「そう。 大石君たちも 来るから、 いっしょに 来れば いいでしょう。」

ハリソン 「はい。 どうも ありがとうございます。」

15.5.3 ——会社で (2)——

ハリソン 「大石さん。 お正月に 部長が 家に よんでくれるんですけど、 大石さんも 来るそうですね。」

大石 「ええ。 部長は 毎年 正月に われわれを よんで、 ごちそうしてくれるんですよ。」

ハリソン 「そうですか。 行く 時、 何か 持って行った ほうが いいですか。」

大石 「ぼくは よく おかしとか のりとか ウイスキーとか 持って行くけど、 日本の しゅうかんだから、 ハリソンさんは 持って行かなくても いいと 思いますけど。」

ハリソン 「アメリカでも よく 花とか チョコレートとか プレゼントします。」

大石 「そうですか。 それで、 二日の 日、 新宿駅の 西口で 会いましょうか。 新宿から タクシーで すぐなんです。」

ハリソン 「西口ですね。 何時ですか。」

大石 「二時すぎに 部長の おたくに つけば いいから、 一時半に しますか。」

ハリソン 「西口、 一時半ですね。 わかりました。」

15.5.4 ——二日、タクシーの　中で——

大石　「大久保四丁目まで　行ってください。」

タクシー運転手　「四丁目の　どの　へんですか。」

大石　「三十八番地なんだけど、わかりにくいから、四丁目の　かどに　スーパーが　あるでしょう？　まず　あそこまで　行ってください。」

大石　「つぎの　かどを　右へ　入って、すこし　行ってください。…あの　はしを　わたって、すぐ　左に　まがってください。…ああ、あそこに　ポストが　あるでしょう？　あの　前で　とめて。…どうも。おいくら？」

運転手　「七百八十円です。」

大石　「じゃあ、これで　おつり　取っておいて。」

運転手　「どうも　すみません。」

15.5.5 ——一月二日、部長の　家で——

大石　「ごめんください。」

おくさん　「あ、いらっしゃいませ。どうぞ　おあがりください。スリッパを　どうぞ。」

大石　「おじゃまします。…部長、あけまして　おめでとうございます。」

部長　「やあ、おめでとう。」

ハリソン　「あけまして　おめでとうございます。」

部長　「おめでとう。ハリソンさん、これ　かないです。」

おくさん　「まあ、よく　いらっしゃいました。」

大石、ハリソン　「おめでとうございます。今年も　よろしく　おねがいいたします。」

おくさん　「こちらこそ。さあ、どうぞ　らくに　してください。」

大石　「はい。これ　つまらない　物ですが、どうぞ。」

おくさん　「まあ、いつも　すみません。」

部長　「さあ、らくに　して、まず　一ぱい　どうぞ。ハリソンさん、お酒は？」

ハリソン　「ええ、大石さんたちと　よく　会社の　帰りに　飲みに　行きます。」

おくさん　「ハリソンさん、ここから　お好きなのを　取ってください。」

ハリソン　「はい、いただきます。おいしそうですね。これは　何ですか。」

おくさん　「かまぼこ、きんとんなんかです。大石さんも、どうぞ。」

大石　「えんりょなく、いただきます。」

15.5.6 New Vocabulary (for passive learning)

1.

よぶ	yobu	…… invite; call for
かしら	kashira	…… I wonder (used by women)
かれ	kare	…… he
なんか	nan'ka	…… and the like (colloquial equivalent of *nado*)
やきとり	yakitori	…… small pieces of chicken, onions, liver, heart, etc., skewered on bamboo
うまい	umai	…… delicious
ほとんど	hoton'do	…… mostly
むり	muri	…… impossible; difficult
よわい	yowai	…… weak

2.

何人か	nan'nin ka	…… some (people)
よろこぶ	yorokobu	…… is pleased; is delighted

3.

われわれ	wareware	…… we (formal equivalent of *watashitachi*)
ごちそうする	gochisoo suru	…… treat someone (to dinner)
何か	nani ka	…… something
とか	toka	…… such as ～
のり	nori	…… dried seaweed
ウイスキー	uisukii	…… whisky
しゅうかん	shuukan	…… habit; custom
チョコレート	chokoreeto	…… chocolate
西口	nishiguchi	…… west gate; west entrance

4.

大久保（おおくぼ）	Ookubo	…… name of a town in Shinjuku
四丁（ちょう）目	yon'choome	…… fourth district of a town
運転手（うんてんしゅ）	un'ten'shu	…… driver (professional)
三十八番地	san'juu hachiban'chi	…… No. 38
スーパー	suupaa	…… supermarket
はし	hashi	…… bridge
わたる	wataru	…… cross
とめる	tomeru	…… stop

	おつり	otsuri	......	change
	とる	toru	......	take; keep
5.	スリッパ	surippa	......	slipper
	あけまして おめでとう ございます。	Akemashite omedetoo gozaimasu.	......	A Happy New Year.
	いたします	itashimasu	......	humble equivalent of *shimasu*
	こちらこそ。	Kochira koso.	......	It is I who should say so.
	つまらない	tsumaranai	......	trifle; little
	一ぱい	ippai	......	a drink
	帰りに	kaeri ni	......	on one's way back
	おいしそう	oishisoo	......	look delicious
	かまぼこ	kamaboko	......	boiled fish paste
	きんとん	kin'ton	......	mashed sweet potato
	えんりょなく	en'ryo naku	......	without reservation

APPENDIX I
ABBREVIATIONS

A	……	Adjective	*kitsui, okashii*
Adv.	……	Adverb	*mottomo, nakanaka*
B	……	Base	*yame(ru), akaru(i)*
C	……	Copula	*da, datta, daroo*
D	……	Derivative	
{ Da	……	adjectival Derivative	*-rashii*
{ Dv	……	verbal Derivative	*-masu, -mashoo*
E	……	Predicate Extender	*(-te) shimau, (-te) ageru*
I	……	Inflection	*(yasum)u, (akaru)i*
N	……	Noun	
{ Na	……	adjectival Noun	*jiyuu, shin'setsu*
{ Nd	……	dependent Noun	*-kagetsu, -kata, soo*
{ Ni	……	interrogative Noun	*naze*
{ N	……	ordinary Noun	*kimono, keigo, ototoshi*
NM	……	Noun Modifier	*kaeru (mae), isha datta (hito)*
P	……	Predicate	
PC	……	Pre-Copula	*n (desu), no (da)*
PM	……	Predicate Modifier	(Adverb, time Noun, N + R, number)
PN	……	Pre-Noun	*aru*
R	……	Relational	
{ Rc	……	clause Relational	*kara, node, noni*
{ Rp	……	phrase Relational	*to, shika*
S	……	Sentence	
SI	……	Sentence Interjective	*iya, yaa*
SP	……	Sentence Particle	*kai, wa, ne*
V	……	Verb	*iku, arukoo*

APPENDIX II
SENTENCE STRUCTURE
PHRASE STRUCTURE

$$\mathrm{S}=\mathrm{SI}+\mathrm{PM}\left\{\begin{array}{l}(\mathrm{NM})^{*1}\left\{\begin{array}{l}\mathrm{PN}\\ \mathrm{N}+(\mathrm{R})^{*2}\\ \mathrm{Adv.}^{*3}\\ \mathrm{P}^{*4}\end{array}\right\}^{*5}+\mathrm{N}+(\mathrm{R})\\ (\mathrm{Adv.})+\mathrm{Adv.}+(\mathrm{R})\\ \mathrm{P}^{*6}+(\mathrm{R})\end{array}\right\}//\mathrm{P}\left\{\begin{array}{l}\left\{\begin{array}{l}\mathrm{V}\{\mathrm{B}+\mathrm{I}+\mathrm{D}\}\\ \mathrm{A}\{\mathrm{B}+\mathrm{I}+\mathrm{D}\}\\ (\mathrm{NM})+\mathrm{N}+(\mathrm{R})+\mathrm{C}\end{array}\right\}+(\mathrm{R})+(\mathrm{E})^{*7}+(\mathrm{PC})^{*8}+(\mathrm{C})^{*9}\end{array}\right\}+\mathrm{SP}$$

*1 (NM)=NM optional

*2 (R)=R optional

*3 Adv. is only followed by Na such as *kirei*, adverbially used N such as *san'nin*, *kyoo*, or place N such as *ushiro*, *ue*.

*4 limited to final-clause Predicate such as *iku*, *itta*.

*5 { }=specification or limitation

*6 limited to TE, KU, TARI, Stem forms. R is obligatory for TARI, Stem forms, but optional for TE, KU forms.

*7 (E)=E optional

*8 (PC)=PC optional

*9 (C)=C optional

APPENDIX III
RELATIONALS

Relational		Lesson	Functions	Example Sentences
de	Rp	8	material [from; of]	*Kore wa kin de dekite imasu.*
hodo	Rp	7	[about; approximately]	*Nanakagetsu hodo mae ni Nihon e kita n desu.*
kara	Rc	7	sequential action [after; since]	*Amerika e kaette kara, nani o suru tsumori desu ka?*
mo	Rp	2	[as many as; no less than]	*Kan'ji o gohyaku mo shitte iru n desu.*
nagara	Rc	7	simultaneous action [while; as]	*Gakkoo e ikinagara, hataraite imasu.*
ni	Rp	3	time and unit reference [per; at the rate of]	*Ichinichi ni san'do kusuri o non'de kudasai.* *Hitori ni mittsu ageyoo to omoimasu.*
ni	Rp	8	purpose [for; as]	*Rokujoo wa kodomobeya ni tsukatte imasu.*
ni	Rp	9 11	indicates the person who is asked or wanted to do something	*Haha ni kippu o katte moraimashita.* *Anata ni itte hoshii n desu.*
ni	Rp	11	manner	*Doozo jiyuu ni hanashite kudasai.*
ni	Rp	11	reference	*Kono hon wa kodomo ni wa muzukashii desu.*
no	Rp	2	appositional	*Tomodachi no Ichiroo kun ga uchi e kimasu.*
node	Rc	4	expected result [since; because]	*Yasumi na node, ashita wa hima desu.*
noni	Rc	4	reverse result [in spite of; although]	*Yasui noni, kawanakatta n desu ka?*
shika	Rp	3	limitation [only; just]	*Kyooshitsu ni wa gakusei shika imasen deshita.*
to	Rp	2	quotation	*Kono shigoto wa taihen da to omoimasu yo.*

APPENDIX IV
CONJUGATION TABLE

FORM

1. Verb

a. Vowel Verb

ageru	I, 13	iru	I, 5	kowareru	III, 6	okiru	II, 4	sugiru	III, 3
akeru	II, 9	kaeru	III, 4, 11	kuraberu	II, 11	okureru	III, 12	taberu	I, 3
awaseru	III, 4	kakeru	II, 4	kureru	I, 13	oriru	II, 7	tateru	III, 8
dekakeru	I, 4	kan'gaeru	III, 12	machigaeru	III, 3	oshieru	II, 13	tsureru	II, 4
dekiru	II, 5, 7, 12	kariru	I, 9	miru	I, 4	otozureru	III, 2	tsutomeru	II, 2
deru	II, 7	ki-o-tsukeru	III, 12	miseru	II, 1	sashiageru	II, 1	umareru	III, 7
fueru	III, 2	kireru	III, 6	mukaeru	III, 6	shimeru	II, 9; III, 4	wasureru	II, 9
hajimeru	II, 9; III, 3	kiru	II, 1	neru	II, 4	shiraberu	II, 8	yameru	III, 7
ireru	II, 1	kotaeru	II, 9	oboeru	III, 3	shiraseru	III, 2	yogoreru	III, 6

Conjugation

Neutral Form					Plain Form		
Stem Form	Base Form	TE Form	BA Form	Pre-Nai Form	Dictionary Form	TA Form	OO Form
age(masu)	age	agete	agereba	age(nai)	ageru	ageta	ageyoo

b. Consonant Verb

Group 1 /r/ group

agaru	III, 8	*irassharu	II, 4; III, 4	magaru	II, 13	okoru	III, 6	toru	II, 4; III, 6
aru	I, 4	kaeru	I, 3	mitsukaru	II, 8	okuru	III, 9	tsukuru	II, 12
furu	I, 11	kakaru	II, 7	naoru	III, 6	*ossharu	III, 8	uru	II, 1
gan'baru	III, 3	kawaru	III, 11	naru	II, 11, 12	owaru	II, 4; III, 3	wakaru	II, 4, 13
hairu	I, 8	ki-ni-naru	III, 12	*nasaru	III, 12	shiru	II, 2	yaru	I, 13; III, 13
hajimaru	II, 4	komaru	III, 13	nokoru	III, 2	suwaru	II, 9		
hashiru	II, 7	*kudasaru	II, 1	noru	II, 7	tomaru	II, 13; III, 2		

*The Stem forms of *irassharu, nasaru, ossharu, kudasaru,* and *gozaru* are *irasshai, nasai, osshai, kudasai,* and *gozai* respectively. Notice the omission of *r* before *i*.

Group 2 /w/ group

ajiwau	III, 2	iu	I, 11; III, 2	kayou	II, 2	niau	III, 4	tetsudau	II, 12
arau	II, 12	kamau	II, 8	morau	I, 13	omou	II, 12	tsukau	II, 8
au	II, 4; III, 9	kau	I, 3	narau	I, 7	suu	II, 9	ukagau	II, 2, 7
chigau	II, 4								

Group 3 /t/ group

matsu	I, 13	motsu	II, 2	tatsu	II, 9

Group 4 /k/ group

aruku	II, 7	hiku	II, 7	kaku	I, 4; III, 9	ochitsuku	II, 11	suku	II, 13
haku	II, 1	iku	I, 3	kiku	I, 4; II, 7	odoroku	III, 2	tsuku	II, 7
hataraku	II, 2	itadaku	II, 1	migaku	III, 6	saku	II, 5		

Group 5 /s/ group

dasu	III, 13	kasu	II, 8	naosu	III, 6	sagasu	I, 9	watasu	II, 9
hanasu	I, 7	kowasu	III, 6	nobasu	III, 2	torikesu	III, 2	yogosu	III, 6
kaesu	II, 8								

Group 6 /m/ group

komu	II, 13	sumu	II, 2	yasumu	II, 4
nomu	I, 3; III, 7	tanomu	III, 11	yomu	I, 9

Group 7 /b/ group

asobu	II, 5	yobu	I, 5

Group 8 /g/ group

isogu	II, 12	nugu	III, 4	oyogu	I, 11

Group 9 /n/ group

shinu —

Conjugation

Neutral Form						Plain Form		
Group	Stem Form	Base Form	TE Form	BA Form	Pre-Nai Form	Dictionary Form	TA Form	OO Form
1	uri(masu)	ur	utte	ureba	ura(nai)	uru	utta	uroo
2	arai(masu)	ara(w)	aratte	araeba	arawa(nai)	arau	aratta	araoo
3	mochi(masu)	mot	motte	moteba	mota(nai)	motsu	motta	motoo
4	haki(masu)	hak	haite	hakeba	haka(nai)	haku	haita	hakoo
5	dashi(masu)	das	dashite	daseba	dasa(nai)	dasu	dashita	dasoo
6	nomi(masu)	nom	non'de	nomeba	noma(nai)	nomu	non'da	nomoo
7	yobi(masu)	yob	yon'de	yobeba	yoba(nai)	yobu	yon'da	yoboo
8	nugi(masu)	nug	nuide	nugeba	nuga(nai)	nugu	nuida	nugoo
9	shini(masu)	shin	shin'de	shineba	shina(nai)	shinu	shin'da	shinoo

c. Irregular Verb

kuru	I, 3	gochisoo suru	II, 12	ken'kyuu suru	III, 7	san'po suru	II, 5	shokuji suru	I, 4
suru	I, 3; II, 12	hirune suru	III, 7	ki-ni-suru	III, 12	sen'koo suru	III, 7	shookai suru	I, 7
an'shin suru	III, 11	kaimono suru	I, 4	kyooryoku suru	III, 13	setsumei suru	II, 8	shuuri suru	III, 6
arubaito suru	II, 2	kan'sha suru	III, 9	pan'ku suru	III, 6	shigoto suru	II, 2	sotsugyoo suru	III, 7
ben'kyoo suru	I, 4	keiken suru	III, 7	ren'shuu suru	III, 3	shin'pai suru	III, 11	un'ten suru	III, 6
den'wa suru	I, 12	kekkon suru	II, 2	ryokoo suru	I, 12	shitaku suru	III, 12	yoyaku suru	III, 2
gakkari suru	III, 11	ken'butsu suru	I, 12	ryoori suru	II, 12	shitsumon suru	II, 9		

Conjugation

Neutral Form					Plain Form		
Stem Form	Base Form	TE Form	BA Form	Pre-Nai Form	Dictionary Form	TA Form	OO Form
ki(masu)	k	kite	kureba	ko(nai)	kuru	kita	koyoo
shi(masu)	s	shite	sureba	shi(nai)	suru	shita	shiyoo

2. Adjective

akai	II, 13	atsui	I, 11	hazukashii	III, 4	isogashii	I, 8	kitanai	I, 8
akarui	III, 8	chairoi	II, 13	hikui	II, 7	itai	III, 4	kitsui	II, 1
amai	II, 12	chiisai	I, 8	hiroi	II, 11	karai	II, 12	kurai	III, 8
aoi	II, 13	chikai	I, 8	hoshii	II, 1	kawaii	II, 5	kuroi	II, 13
atarashii	II, 5	furui	II, 5	hosonagai	II, 11	kibishii	III, 13	kurushii	III, 4
atatakai	I, 11	hayai	I, 13; II, 7	ii	I, 8; II, 8	kiiroi	II, 13	kuwashii	II, 8

mazui I, 8
mijikai II, 9
mushiatsui I, 11
muzukashii I, 9
nagai II, 9
nai I, 9
nemui III, 12
nikui III, 3
oishii I, 8
okashii III, 4
omoshiroi I, 9
ooi II, 5
ookii I, 8
osoi I, 13; II, 9
samui I, 11
semai II, 11
shiroi II, 13
subarashii I, 12
sugoi III, 9
sukunai II, 5
suppai II, 12
suzushii I, 11
takai I, 9; II, 7
tanoshii I, 12
tooi I, 8
tsumaranai I, 9
tsumetai I, 11
ureshii III, 7
urusai I, 8
utsukushii II, 5
wakai II, 12
warui I, 8
yasashii I, 9; III, 9
yasui I, 9; III, 3
yoi I, 8
yoroshii III, 13

Conjugation

Plain Form		Neutral Form			
Dictionary Form	TA Form	TE Form	KU Form	BA Form	Base Form
itai	itakatta	itakute	itaku	itakereba	ita

3. Adjectival Derivative

Plain Form		Neutral Form			
Dictionary Form	TA Form	TE Form	KU Form	BA Form	Base Form
-rashii*	-rashikatta	-rashikute	-rashiku	-rashikereba	-rashi

*-*Rashii* in this volume was introduced with no conjugation as shown above. These conjugation forms will be introduced later.

4. Copula

Normal Form			Neutral Form			Plain Form		
Dictionary Form	TA Form	OO Form	TE Form	NA* Form	BA Form	Dictionary Form	TA Form	OO Form
desu	deshita	deshoo	de	na	nara(ba)	da	datta	daroo

*NA Form is used mainly with adjectival Nouns such as follow:

ben'ri III, 4
bun'kateki III, 9
daijoobu II, 4
daikirai I, 8
daisuki I, 8
dame I, 8
den'tooteki III, 8
fuben III, 4
fukuzatsu III, 11
gen'ki I, 8
hen II, 5
heta I, 7
hima I, 5
hitsuyoo III, 11
in'shooteki III, 2
ippan'teki III, 11
iroiro II, 5
iya III, 8
jama III, 8
jiyuu III, 11
joozu I, 7
kan'tan III, 3
keizaiteki III, 9
kirai I, 8
kirei I, 7
nigiyaka I, 7
nihon'teki III, 9
raku III, 4
rekishiteki III, 9
rippa I, 9
sakan II, 11
shin'pai III, 11
shin'setsu III, 11
shitsurei II, 5
shizuka I, 7
suki I, 8
taihen II, 7
taisetsu III, 3
teinei II, 1
tekitoo II, 8
tokui II, 12
tooyooteki III, 9
yutaka II, 11
yuumei II, 5

APPENDIX V
PRESENTATION AND DIALOG

ROMANIZATION AND ENGLISH EQUIVALENT

2.1 ——Kan'sai Ryokoo——

Kyooto ya Nara ni wa Nihon no furui bun'ka ga nokotte iru. Kyooto, Nara o otozureru hitobito wa rekishi o jibun no me de miru koto ga dekiru. Shikashi, mae motte rekishi o shitte ireba, Kyooto nado o otozureru kachi ga motto fueru to omou.

——A Trip to the Kansai District——

The ancient culture of Japan is preserved in Kyōto and Nara. People visiting Kyōto and Nara can see the history there with their own eyes. However, if one knows the history in advance, the value of visiting such spots as Kyōto will increase further, I think.

2.2

Robaatsu: Raishuu no shuumatsu ni Kyooto e ikitai to omotte imasu.

Ikeda: Sore wa ii desu ne. Kyooto to iu [=yuu] tokoro ni wa miru mono ga odoroku hodo takusan arimasu yo. Tera ya jin'ja ga sen gohyaku mo aru soo desu.

Robaatsu: Son'na ni ooi n desu ka↗ Odorokimashita nee.

Ikeda: Soo deshoo. Hoteru wa moo yoyaku shimashita ka↗

Robaatsu: Iya, mukoo de chiisai ryokan o sagasu tsumori desu.

Ikeda: Naze desu ka↗

Robaatsu: Hon'too no Nihon o shiritai kara, nihon'fuu no chiisai ryokan ni tomaritai n desu.

Ikeda: Sore wa ii kan'gae da to omoimasu ne. Yoofuu no hoteru de wa Nihon no den'too o ajiwau koto ga dekimasen kara ne.

Robaatsu: Ee. Tokoro de, Nara wa Kyooto kara chikai soo desu ne↗

Ikeda: Ee, tokkyuu nara, san'jippun gurai da soo desu yo↗

Robaatsu: Son'na ni chikakereba, ashi o nobashitai desu ne. Boku no tomodachi no Joon'zu san wa, Nara no daibutsu ga totemo in'shooteki datta to itte imashita.

Mr. Roberts: I think I would like to go to Kyōto the weekend after next.
Mr. Ikeda: That would be nice. In the city of Kyōto, there are many things to see, to your surprise. There are as many as 1,500 temples and shrines, I understand.
Mr. Roberts: Are there that many? I am surprised!
Mr. Ikeda: I suppose you are. Have you already made hotel reservations?
Mr. Roberts: No, I am planning to find a small inn there.
Mr. Ikeda: Why?
Mr. Roberts: I want to stay at a small Japanese-style inn because I want to know the real Japan.

Mr. Ikeda:	I think that's a good idea. You can't taste the traditions of Japan at a Western-style hotel.
Mr. Roberts:	That's right. By the way, I understand that Nara is near Kyōto.
Mr. Ikeda:	Yes, I understand it is about thirty minutes if you take a limited express.
Mr. Roberts:	If it's that close, I want to extend the trip to Nara. My friend, Mr. Jones, said that the great image of the Buddha in Nara was very impressive.

3.1 ——Kan'ji——

Gen'dai no nihon'go de yoku tsukau kan'ji wa sen kyuuhyaku yon'juu goji arimasu. Kore o "Jooyoo Kan'ji" to iimasu. Shoogakkoo to chuugakkoo de wa, kono uchi kyuuhyaku kyuujuu roku no kan'ji o oshiemasu ga, kore wa "Kyooiku Kan'ji" to iimasu.

——Chinese Characters——

The *kan'ji* used frequently in modern Japanese are 1,945 characters. These are called "*Jooyoo Kan'ji*" [*Kan'ji* for Common Use]. In the elementary school and the junior high school, 996 *kan'ji* out of 1,945 are taught, and these are called "*Kyooiku Kan'ji*" [*Kan'ji* for Education].

3.2

Takahashi:	Kuraaku san, Mori san ga hanashite imashita kedo, nihon'go o ben'kyoo shihajimeta soo desu ne ↗
Kuraaku:	Ee. Demo, mada yon'kagetsu shika naratte imasen.
Takahashi:	Isshuukan ni nan'jikan desu ka ↗
Kuraaku:	Rokujikan desu.
Takahashi:	Ima made ni kan'ji wa ikutsu gurai naraimashita ka ↗
Kuraaku:	Soo desu nee. Hyaku gurai deshoo. Dakara, mada shin'bun ya hon o yomu koto ga dekimasen.
Takahashi:	Soo, mada sukunasugimasu ne. Kan'ji wa oboenikui desu ka ↗
Kuraaku:	Oboeyasui no mo oboenikui no mo arimasu.
Takahashi:	Hiragana wa moo zen'bu oboemashita ka ↗
Kuraaku:	Ee. Nishuukan de oboemashita. Hiragana o oboeru no wa wariai kan'tan deshita. Demo, hajime wa, "a" to "o" ya, "nu" to "me" nado ga machigaeyasukatta desu.
Takahashi:	Kekkyoku, kan'ji mo hiragana mo mainichi ren'shuu suru koto ga taisetsu desu ne. Nihon ni wa "Ishi no ue ni mo san'nen" to iu kotowaza ga arimasu yo. Gan'batte kudasai.

Mr. Takahashi:	Mr. Clark, according to Mr. Mori, [I understand that] you started studying Japanese at the university. Is that right?
Mr. Clark:	Yes. But I have been studying it only four months.
Mr. Takahashi:	How many hours do you take lessons a week?
Mr. Clark:	Six hours.

Mr. Takahashi:	How many *kan'ji* have you learned so far?
Mr. Clark:	Let me see . . . About one hundred, I suppose. So I am not able to read a newspaper and a book yet.
Mr. Takahashi:	Yes, a hundred characters are still too few (to read it). Are *kan'ji* difficult to memorize?
Mr. Clark:	There are both easy ones and difficult ones to memorize.
Mr. Takahashi:	Have you already mastered all of the *hiragana*?
Mr. Clark:	Yes. I mastered them in two weeks. To learn *hiragana* was comparatively easy. But, at the beginning, it was easy to confuse *a* and *o* and *nu* and *me*.
Mr. Takahashi:	At any rate, it is important to practice *hiragana* as well as *kan'ji* every day. In Japan, we have a proverb saying "Three years on top of a stone" (=Be patient and you'll be successful). Please do your best.

4.1 ——Yoofuku to Kimono——

Yoofuku to kimono to, dotchi ga ii to omoimasu ka↗ Kore wa nihon'jin no aida de yoku mon'dai ni naru koto desu.

Kekkyoku, ryoohoo ni ii tokoro ga arimasu. Sono ii tokoro o kiru toki to basho ni awaseru koto ga taisetsu da to omoimasu.

——Western Clothes and *Kimono*——

Which are better, Western-style clothes or *kimono*? This frequently comes into question among the Japanese people.

After all, both of them have good points. I think that it is important to adjust the good points of each of them to the occasions and places of wearing them.

4.2

Hara san no Okusan:	Miraa san, irasshaimase.
Miraa:	Okusan, kon'nichi wa A, kyoo wa kimono o kite irasshaimasu ne↗
Okusan:	Ee, Miraa san ga irassharu node, sakki kikaeta n desu yo.
Miraa:	Sore wa doomo. Okusan wa kimono ga yoku niaimasu ne.
Okusan:	Ton'de mo nai desu. Ohazukashii.
Miraa:	Demo, kimono wa fuben deshoo↗
Okusan:	Ee, soo na n desu. Obi o kitsuku shimeru node, yappari yoofuku no hoo ga zutto raku desu wa.
Hara:	Kanai wa kimono o motte iru noni, amari kinai n desu.
Okusan:	Ara, datte, yoofuku no hoo ga hatarakiyasui no yo.
Miraa:	Nihon no wakai otoko no hitotachi wa amari kimono o kinai desu ne↗
Hara:	Ee, demo, natsu ie de yukata o kiru hito wa wariai ooi desu yo.
Miraa:	On'na no hito wa paatii ni iku toki nado ni kimono o kiru noni, otoko no hito wa ie ni iru toki ni yoku kiru deshoo↗ Chotto okashii desu ne↗

Mrs. Hara: It's nice of you to have come, Mr. Miller.
Miller: Good afternoon, Mrs. Hara. Ah, you are wearing a *kimono* today, aren't you?
Mrs. Hara: Yes, I changed clothes a while ago because you were coming.
Miller: That's nice of you. You look very fine in a *kimono,* Mrs. Hara.
Mrs. Hara: Not at all. I'm embarrassed.
Miller: But isn't a *kimono* inconvenient?
Mrs. Hara: Yes, that's right. After all, Western clothes are much more comfortable than *kimono,* since we have to tie the *obi* tightly (when we wear *kimono*).
Mr. Hara: My wife doesn't wear *kimono* often despite the fact that she has some *kimono.*
Mrs. Hara: Oh, that is because it is easier to work in Western-style clothes, you know.
Miller: Young Japanese men do not wear *kimono* often, do they?
Mrs. Hara: No, but men wear *yukata* at home during the summer quite often.
Miller: Although women are dressed in *kimono* on such occasions as going to parties, men often wear *kimono* when they are at home, don't they? It's a little funny, isn't it?

6.1 ——Jidoosha——

Sen kyuuhyakunen ni, Yokohama ni sun'de ita beikokujin ga Nihon de hajimete no jidoosha o un'ten shita soo desu.

Sono go, Nihon de wa, sen kyuuhyaku rokujuunen goro kara jidoosha no kazu ga don'don fuemashita ga, koogai ya kootsuu jiko nado no ookina mon'dai ga okotte imasu.

——Automobiles——

In 1900 it is said that an American who was living in Yokohama drove an automobile which was the first in Japan.

After that, since about 1960 the number of automobiles has increased rapidly in Japan, and there are big problems such as pollution and traffic accidents occurring.

6.2 ——Shuuriya ni den'wa o kakeru——

Takagi: Moshi moshi, Takagi desu ga . . .
Shuuriya: Aa, Takagi san desu ka. Maido arigatoo gozaimasu. Kyoo wa nan deshoo ka ↗
Takagi: Jitsu wa, taiya ga pan'ku shite shimatta n desu ga, ashita no asa made ni naorimasu ka ↗
Shuuriya: Naorimasu yo ↗ Kuruma wa ima otaku desu ka ↗
Takagi: Ee, soo na n desu. Sore kara, waipaa kowareta rashii n desu ga, sore mo naoshite oite kudasai.
Shuuriya: Kashikomarimashita. Kore kara, sugu tori ni ukagaimasu.
Takagi: Onegai shimasu.

——Sono hi no yuugata——

Shuuriya: Gomen kudasai. Kuruma o motte kimashita.
Takagi: Doomo gokuroo sama. Hayakatta desu ne.

Shuuriya: Yappari waipaa ga kowarete imashita kara, shuuri shite okimashita. Sore kara, daibu yogorete ita node, kuruma o aratte okimashita. Kore wa saabisu desu.

Takagi: Doomo sumimasen.

——Making a phone call to a repair shop——

Takagi: Hello, this is Takagi . . .
Mechanic: Ah, Mr. Takagi? Thank you for your continued patronage. What can I do for you today?
Takagi: The reason why I called you is that I have a flat tire. Will it be fixed by tomorrow morning?
Mechanic: Yes, it will be fixed (by tomorrow morning). Is your car at your house now?
Takagi: That's right. Besides, it seems like the windshield wipers are broken. Please have them fixed also.
Mechanic: Yes, we'll certainly do that. I'll come to pick the car up right away.
Takagi: Please.

——In the early evening of the same day——

Mechanic: Excuse me. I have brought your car.
Takagi: Thank you for your trouble. You did your job very early.
Mechanic: As you thought, the wipers were broken, so we have repaired them. And we have washed your car because it was quite dirty. This is free of charge.
Takagi: Thank you.

7.1 ——Nihon Ken'kyuu——

Hawaado san wa, daigakuin ni hairu mae, shibaraku no aida koo koo de rekishi no sen'sei o shite imashita. Shikashi, tooyoo no rekishi ni kyoomi o motta node, oshieru no o yameta soo desu. Soshite, nanakagetsu mae ni nihon'shi o ken'kyuu shi ni Nihon e kimashita.

——Japanese Study——

Mr. Howard was a history teacher at a high school for some time before entering a graduate school. I heard, however, that he quit teaching, as he took an interest in oriental history. Then he came to Japan seven months ago in order to study Japanese history.

7.2

Kobayashi: Hawaado san wa, Nihon e irasshatte kara, nagai n desu ka↗

Hawaado: Choodo nanakagetsu ni narimasu.

Kobayashi: Daigaku o sotsugyoo shite kara, sugu irasshatta n desu ka↗

Hawaado: Iie, daigakuin ni ninen hodo imashita ga, sono mae wa kyooshi o shite imashita.

Kobayashi: Hawaado san no umareta tokoro wa doko desu ka↗

Hawaado: Oregon Shuu no chiisana machi desu. Kobayashi san wa Tookyoo-umare na n desu ka↗

Kobayashi:	Iie, boku wa ototoshi no san'gatsu ni Nagasaki no kookoo o sotsugyoo shite kara, Tookyoo e kita n desu. Ima wa hatarakinagara, daigaku ni itte imasu. Hawaado san wa Nagasaki ni irasshatta koto ga arimasu ka ／
Hawaado:	Iya, nai n desu. Amerika e kaeru mae ni, ichido itte miru tsumori na n desu kedo.
Kobayashi:	Jaa, boku ga fuyuyasumi ni Nagasaki e kaeru toki, issho ni irasshaimasen ka ／ Inaka no oshoogatsu o ajiwau koto mo dekimasu kara, choodo ii to omoimasu kedo.
Hawaado:	Soo dekireba, ureshii desu ne. Watakushi wa Amerika e kaette kara, nihon'shi o sen'koo shitai n desu. Desukara, kotchi ni iru aida ni, dekiru dake iroiro na koto o keiken shite okitai to omotte imasu.

Mr. Kobayashi:	Have you been long in Japan, Mr. Howard?
Mr. Howard:	I have been here exactly seven months.
Mr. Kobayashi:	Did you come to Japan immediately after being graduated from a university?
Mr. Howard:	No, I was in a graduate school for about two years, but I was a teacher before that.
Mr. Kobayashi:	Where were you born, Mr. Howard?
Mr. Howard:	In a small town in the state of Oregon. Were you born in Tōkyō, Mr. Kobayashi?
Mr. Kobayashi:	No, after graduating from a senior high school in Nagasaki in March of the year before last, I came to Tōkyō. Now I'm attending college while working. Have you ever been to Nagasaki?
Mr. Howard:	No, I haven't. I plan to go there once before I return to America though.
Mr. Kobayashi:	Then won't you join me when I return to Nagasaki during the winter vacation? I think it will be a good chance for you to experience the New Year in the countryside.
Mr. Howard:	I'll be happy if I can do so. I want to major in Japanese history after I return to America. Therefore, I want to experience as many things as possible while I am over here.

8.1 ——Nihon no Ie——

Den'tooteki na Nihon no ie wa omo ni ki ya kami de dekite ite, yuka ni wa tatami ga arimasu.

Shikashi, saikin no ie no naka ni wa, kon'kuriito ya tetsu ya arumi nado o tsukatte dekite iru no mo kanari arimasu. Mata, nihon'ma to yooma no ryoohoo o motsu ie ga don'don fuete imasu.

——Japanese House——

Traditional Japanese houses are made mainly from wood and paper, and there are straw mats on the floor.

However, among the modern houses there are quite a few that are built using concrete, iron, aluminum, etc. Also, houses having both Japanese-style rooms and Western-style rooms have been increasing rapidly.

8.2 ——Aoki san no ie no gen'kan de——

Okusan:	Maa, Hooru san, doozo oagari kudasai.
Hooru:	Ojama shimasu. Kinoo goshujin ga, ie o atarashiku tateta kara, miseru to osshaimashita node, ukagaimashita.

Okusan: Ee, omachi shite imashita. Doozo kochira e

Hooru: Koko wa hirokute, akarukute, rippa na heya desu nee. Juujoo desu ka↗

Okusan: Ee, kyakuma ni tsukatte imasu. Mae ni sun'de ita ie ga kurakute, iya datta node, dekiru dake akaruku shita n desu.

Hooru: Tatami mo shooji mo atarashikute, hon'too ni kimochi ga ii desu ne. Otaku wa yooma mo aru n desu ka↗

Okusan: Ee, ima to kodomobeya ga yooma de, hoka wa nihon'ma ni shimashita.

Hooru: Ofuro mo nihon'fuu desu ka↗

Okusan: Ee, ki no ofuro na n desu. Kitanaku shite imasu kedo, ato de daidokoro ya ofuroba e mo itte, mite kudasai. Chotto shitsurei. Shujin o yon'de kimasu.

——At the entrance of Aoki's house——

Mrs. Aoki: Oh, Mr. Hall, please come in.
Mr. Hall: Excuse me. Yesterday your husband told me that he would show me his house as it was newly built, so I came to see it.
Mrs. Aoki: Yes, we have been expecting you. Please come this way.
Mr. Hall: This is a spacious, well-lighted, and gorgeous room! Is this a ten-*tatami* room?
Mrs. Aoki: Yes; we are using this for a guest room. We didn't like the house we used to live in because the house was dark. So we made this house as well lighted as possible.
Mr. Hall: I feel really good because the *tatami* as well as the *shooji* are new. Do you have any Western-style rooms too?
Mrs. Aoki: Yes, the living room and the children's room are in Western style, and the others are made in Japanese style.
Mr. Hall: Is the bath (tub) Japanese style too?
Mrs. Aoki: Yes, it is a wooden bathtub. Please go and see the kitchen and the bathroom later, although they are messy. Excuse me for a while. I'll go and call my husband.

9.1 ——Okurimono——

Nihon de wa juunigatsu no naka goro kara oshoogatsu made iroiro no mono o okuriaimasu ga, kore o "oseibo" to iimasu. Ichinen'kan iroiro sewa ni natta hito ni kan'sha shite, mono o okuru no desu. Wakai hitotachi ya kazoku no aida de wa, kurisumasu purezen'to ga toku ni sakan desu.

——Presents——

In Japan, people give presents to each other from the middle of December through New Year's Day. This is called *oseibo*. They give presents with gratitude to those people who were especially helpful during the year. Among the young people and family members, (exchange of) Christmas presents are especially popular.

9.2

Yoshida: Joon'zu san, sugoi tokei o shite imasu ne. Suisu-sei desu ka↗

Joon'zu: Ee, kuni no haha ga watashi no tan'joobi ni okutte kureta n desu.

Yoshida: Yasashii okaasan desu nee.

Joon'zu: Watashi mo chichi to haha no kekkon kinen'bi ni nihon'teki na mono o okuritai n desu keredo, nani ga ii deshoo ne↗

Yoshida: Soo desu nee. Moshi goryooshin ga e ga osuki nara, han'ga nado ii to omoimasu kedo.

Joon'zu: Sore wa ii desu ne. Doko de utte imasu ka↗

Yoshida: Mae tomodachi ni han'ga sen'mon no ii mise o oshiete moraimashita. Soko o shookai shite agemasu yo. Basho ga chotto wakarinikui kara, chizu o kaite agemashoo. Soretomo, tsurete itte agemashoo ka↗

Joon'zu: Watashi wa han'ga no koto o yoku shirimasen kara, tsurete itte kuremasen ka↗

Yoshida: Ee, ii desu yo↗

Joon'zu: Onegai shimasu.

Mr. Yoshida: Mr. Jones, you have an awfully good watch. Is it Swiss made?
Mr. Jones: Yes, my mother in my hometown sent it to me for my birthday.
Mr. Yoshida: You have a thoughtful mother.
Mr. Jones: I also would like to send something Japanese to my parents for their wedding anniversary. What do you think would be good?
Mr. Yoshida: Well . . . If your parents like pictures, I will recommend woodblock prints and the like.
Mr. Jones: That's good. Where can I buy them?
Mr. Yoshida: Sometime ago I was introduced to a good specialized store on woodblock prints by a friend of mine. I will introduce you to the store. Since it's a little hard to find the place, I'll draw a map for you. Or, shall I take you to the place with me?
Mr. Jones: I don't know much about woodblock prints. Won't you please take me there with you?
Mr. Yoshida: Yes, certainly.
Mr. Jones: Thank you. [Please do so.]

11.1 ——Kotobazukai——

Nihon'go no keigo no tsukaikata wa, sekai no gen'go no naka de mottomo fukuzatsu na mono no hitotsu de aru. Shikamo, otoko to on'na wa sorezore chigau kotobazukai o suru. Sono tame, gaikokujin ni wa nakanaka muzukashii.

——Usage of Words——

The Japanese honorific-style usage is one of the most complicated ones among the languages of the world. Furthermore, men and women use different ways of speaking respectively. Therefore, it is fairly difficult for foreigners (to use the honorific style).

11.2

Muua: Tanaka sen'sei. Kyoo wa toshokan de keigo ni tsuite shirabete mimashita. Sore ni tsuite chotto setsumei shite hoshii n desu ga . . . A, machigaemashita. Teinei ni tanomu toki wa, setsumei shite itadakitai n desu ga . . . to iu n deshita ne↗

Sen'sei: Ee, sono toori. Demo, watakushi ni wa jiyuu ni hanashite ii desu yo.

Muua: Hai. Anoo, Nihon no shakai de wa, hanasu aite no chii ni yotte kotobazukai o kaenakereba naranai soo desu ga, zuibun fukuzatsu na n desu ne/

Sen'sei: Ee, izen wa toku ni soo deshita ne.

Muua: Dewa, saikin wa daibu kawatta n desu ka/

Sen'sei: Ee, ippan'teki ni itte, zutto kan'tan ni narimashita yo. Watakushi wa keigo ga motto kan'tan ni nareba ii to omotte imasu.

Muua: Hon'too desu ne.

Sen'sei: Shikashi, muzukashikute mo, yahari hitsuyoo na toki ga arimasu kara, anatatachi ni mo yoku oboete hoshii desu ne. Keredo, nihon'jin demo, yoku machigaeru n desu yo/

Muua: Soo desu ka/ Sore o kiite, an'shin shimashita.

Mr. Moore: Prof. Tanaka, today I studied on the Japanese styles at the library. I would like you to explain [about] it to me . . . Oh, it's wrong. When I ask you politely, I should say, "I would like you to render me your explanation on such and such . . . ," shouldn't I?

Professor: Yes, that's right. But please feel free to talk to me.

Mr. Moore: Yes. Well, I understand that in Japanese society one has to change from one style of speaking to another depending on the status of the other party. It's very complicated, isn't it?

Professor: Yes, and it was especially so before.

Mr. Moore: Then, has it recently changed a great deal?

Professor: Yes, generally speaking, it became far more simple. I hope that the honorific style becomes even more simple.

Mr. Moore: Yes, indeed.

Professor: However, even though it is difficult, still there are some occasions when it is necessary (for you to use it), so I want you to memorize it well. But even Japanese people make mistakes [in its use], you know.

Mr. Moore: Really? I'm relieved to hear that.

12.1 ——Nakamura san no Ichinichi: Uchi de——

Nakamura san wa aru kaisha ni tsutomete iru sarariiman de, kachoo de aru. Toshi wa yon'juu gosai de, okusan no Masae san wa yon'juu nisai de aru. Kodomo wa musume no Tomoko san dake de aru.

Kookoosei no Tomoko san wa kan'gaekata ya seikatsu taido ga Nakamura san fuufu to daibu chigatte iru Tomoko san wa kotobazukai nado amari ki-ni-shinai

——A Day with Mr. Nakamura: At Home——

Mr. Nakamura is a salary man who works at a certain company and a section chief. He is forty-five years old and his wife, Masae, is forty-two. Their only child is a daughter, Tomoko.

Tomoko, a senior high school student, has a quite different way of thinking and way of living from those of Mr. and Mrs. Nakamura's. Tomoko does not pay much attention to the way of speaking.

12.2

Masae: Anata, hayaku okite kudasai. Kyuukoo ni noru tame ni, hayaku okirutte osshatta deshoo ↗

Nakamura: Un, wakatta yo. Nemuku wa nai n da ga, doomo samuku nareba naru hodo okinikuku naru nee. (Kikaenagara) Asagohan moo dekiteru kai ↗ Samui kara, omiotsuke atsuku shite kure. Atsukereba atsui hodo ii yo.

Masae: Ee, dekitemasu yo.

Tomoko: Okaasan. Atashi gyuunyuu ga nomitai n da kedo, motte kite ne ↗

Masae: Nan desu nee. Jibun de motte kinasai.

——Asa no shokuji ga owatte——

Masae: Tomoko, isoide, shitaku shinasai. Gakkoo ni okuremasu yo.

Tomoko: A, moo shichiji jippun sugi da wa. Otoosan issho ni dekakeru ↗

Nakamura: Soo da ne. Shichijihan no kyuukoo wa kon'de ite, noru no ni taihen da kara, sorosoro dekaketa hoo ga ii ne.

Masae: Jaa, itterasshai. Ki-o-tsukete ne ↗

Nakamura:
Tomoko: Itte mairimasu.

Masae: Honey, please get up at once. You said you'd get up early to take an express train, didn't you?

Mr. Nakamura: Yeah, I know. I'm not sleepy, but the colder it gets the harder it is to get up, isn't it? (While changing clothes) Is breakfast ready now? Make the *omiotsuke* hot, since I'm cold. The hotter the better.

Masae: Yes, it's ready.

Tomoko: Mother. I want to drink milk; please bring it to me.

Masae: What's that? Bring it yourself.

——After breakfast——

Masae: Hurry up and get ready, Tomoko. You'll be late for school.

Tomoko: Oh, it's already seven-ten! Are you going out with me, father?

Mr. Nakamura: Well. The seven-thirty express is crowded, and it's hard getting on, so I'd better be going with you.

Masae: Then, so long. Take care.

Mr. Nakamura:
Tomoko: See you.

13.1 ——Nakamura san no Ichinichi: Kaisha de——

Kaisha de wa, shachoo, juuyaku, buchoo, kachoo, futsuu no shain nado no chii no jun'jo ga hakkiri shite ite, kotobazukai ni tsuite mo nakanaka kibishii. Sen'soogo, Nihon no shakai wa ookiku kawatta ga, ooku no nihon'jin wa mada mada kotobazukai no kubetsu o taisetsu da to omotte iru.

——A Day with Mr. Nakamura: At the Company——

In a business company, the positions of the president, the top executives, department chiefs, section chiefs, and ordinary employees are clearly in order and the company members' way of talking to each other is quite strictly defined. Since the (Second World) War Japanese society has undergone a large-scale change. Many Japanese people still think that it is important to differentiate their way of talking (according to the persons involved).

13.2

Ishikawa: (On'na) Kachoo san, ohayoo gozaimasu.

Nakamura: Yaa, ohayoo. Kesa wa komatta yo. Chikatetsu ga nakanaka konai node, takushii ni noroo to shita n da ga, takushii mo nai n da.

Ishikawa: Maiasa taihen desu nee.

Nakamura: Tokoro de, Ishikawa san, ato de kono tegami o dashite kudasai.

Ishikawa: Choodo ima kitte to hagaki o kai ni yuubin'kyoku e ikoo to omotte imasu. Sokutatsu ka kakitome ni shimasu ka ↗

Nakamura: Iya, futsuu de kamawanai.

Ishikawa: Wakarimashita. Sore kara, anoo, shachoo ga oyobi desu ga. . . .

Nakamura: A, soo. Arigatoo.

——Shachooshitsu de——

Nakamura: Shachoo, oyobi ni narimashita ka ↗

Shachoo: Aa, Nakamura kun ka Suwari tamae. Jitsu wa, Matsumoto kun ni yatte moratte iru shigoto na n da ga, isogu shigoto na node, kimi ni mo kyooryoku shite hoshii n da. Isogashikute taihen daroo to omou ga, yoroshiku tanomu yo.

Nakamura: Hai, kashikomarimashita. Isshooken'mei yarimasu.

Miss Ishikawa: Good morning, section chief, sir.
Mr. Nakamura: Oh, good morning. I was in trouble this morning. The subway didn't come soon, so I was going to catch a taxi, but there was no taxi either.
Miss Ishikawa: We have a hard time every morning, don't we?
Mr. Nakamura: By the way, Miss Ishikawa, please mail this letter later.
Miss Ishikawa: I'm thinking of going to the post office now to buy stamps and postcards. Shall I send it out by special delivery or registered mail?
Mr. Nakamura: No, the ordinary mail will be fine.
Miss Ishikawa: All right, sir. Well, the president is calling for you.
Mr. Nakamura: Oh, yeah? Thank you.

——In the president's office——

Mr. Nakamura: Mr. President, did you ask for me?

President: Ah, Mr. Nakamura. Sit down. The reason why I've called you is that I wanted to talk about some work I've asked Mr. Matsumoto to deal with. I want you to cooperate with him since it's urgent work. I imagine you will get busier and will have a hard time because I am assigning you more work to do, but please do it for me.

Mr. Nakamura: Yes, certainly. I'll do my best, sir.

APPENDIX VI
GLOSSARY

(A)

achira	あちら	N	8	that way; that side
agaru	あがる	V	8	step up; go up; rise (see 8.4.6)
ageru	あげる	E	9	(see 9.4.7)
aida	間	N	4	among; between
aida	間	N	7	duration; period; while; during (see 7.4.3)
aite	あい手	N	11	the other party
ajiwau	味わう	V	2	taste; appreciate
akachan	あかちゃん	N	3	baby
akarui	あかるい	A	8	is light; is well lighted; is bright
an'na ni	あんなに	Adv.	2	that (many; much)
an'shin	安心(あんしん)	N	11	relief; peace of mind
an'shin suru	安心(あんしん)する	V	11	feel relieved; feel easy
aru	ある	PN	12	a certain; some (see 12.4.1)
arumi(nyuumu)	アルミ(ニューム)	N	8	aluminum (*arumi* or *aruminyuumu*)
au	合う	V	9	do with each other; do mutually (compound component) (see 9.4.2)
awaseru	合わせる	V	4	fit; suit (transitive Verb)

(B)

Beikoku	米国	N	6	the United States of America
ben'ri	べんり	Na	4	convenient
(o)ben'too	(お)べん当	N	3	packed lunch; a lunch
beruto	ベルト	N	4	belt (for Western-style clothes) (cf. *obi*)
biniiru	ビニール	N	8	vinyl
boorupen	ボールペン	N	3	ball-point pen
buchoo	部長	N	13	head of a department
bun'ka	文化	N	2	culture
bun'kateki	文化的	Na	9	cultural (see 9.4.9)

(C)

-chan	ちゃん	Nd	12	(see 12.4.14)
chii	地位(い)	N	11	status; rank; position
chiisana	小さな	A	6	small (see 6.4.2)
chizu	地図(ず)	N	9	map
-choo	長	Nd	13	chief ～; ～ head (see 13.4.1)
chuugakkoo	中学校	N	3	junior high school
chuugakusei	中学生	N	12	junior high school student

(D)

da	だ	C	2	plain equivalent of the Copula *desu* (see 2.4.17)
daibu	だいぶ	Adv.	6	quite; fairly; pretty
daibutsu	大仏(ぶつ)	N	2	a great image of the Buddha
daidokoro	台所(だいどころ)	N	8	kitchen
dan'dan	だんだん	Adv.	6	gradually; step by step (see 6.4.1)
daroo	だろう	C	13	OO form of *da* (see 13.4.15)
dasu	出す	V	13	mail; put out; submit
datta	だった	C	2	TA form of *da* (plain equivalent of the Copula *deshita*) (see 2.4.17)
datte	だって	SI	4	but; because (see 4.4.13)
de	で	R	8	of or from (material) (see 8.4.2)
de aru	である	C+E	11	(see 11.4.3)
dekiru dake	できるだけ	Adv.	7	as many as possible; as much as one can do (see 7.4.16)
den'too	でんとう	N	2	tradition
den'tooteki	でんとう的	Na	8	traditional
desukara	ですから	SI	7	therefore (polite equivalent of *dakara*)
de wa nai	ではない	C+R+E	2	negative of *da* (see 2.4.17)
don'don	どんどん	Adv.	6	rapidly; steadily (see 6.4.1)
don'na ni	どんなに	Adv.	2	how (many; much)?
doomo	どうも	Adv.	12	somehow; really (see 12.4.8)

(F)

fuben	ふべん	Na	4	inconvenient
fueru	ふえる	V	2	increase (intransitive Verb)
fukuzatsu	ふくざつ	Na	11	complicated (opp. *kan'tan*)
(o)furo	(お)ふろ	N	8	bath; bathtub (*furo ni hairu* "take a bath")
(o)furoba	(お)ふろ場	N	8	bathroom
futsuu	ふつう	N	13	average; normal; ordinary
fuufu	夫婦(ふうふ)	N	12	married couple; husband and wife

(G)

gakkari suru	がっかりする	V	11	get disappointed
gakubuchoo	学部長	N	13	dean
gakuchoo	学長	N	13	university president
gan'baru	がんばる	V	3	do one's best; buck up; persist (see 3.4.11)
garasu	ガラス	N	6	glass
gasorin	ガソリン	N	6	gasoline; gas
gasorin sutan'do	ガソリンスタンド	N	6	gas station
gen'dai	現代(げんだい)	N	3	the present age; today
gen'go	言語(げん)	N	11	language; tongue
gen'kan	げんかん	N	8	entrance; front door; vestibule
gin	銀	N	8	silver
gin'kooin	銀行員	N	13	bank employee

-go	後(ご)	Nd	13	post- 〜; after 〜
Gokuroo sama.	ごくろうさま。	(exp.)	6	Thank you for your service. (see 6.4.10)

(H)

ha	は	N	7	tooth
hagaki	はがき	N	13	postcard
hajimeru	はじめる	V	3	start (doing); begin (doing) (compound component) (see 3.4.2)
hajimete	はじめて	N	6	(for) the first time
hakkiri	はっきり	Adv.	13	clearly; distinctly
han'ga	はんが	N	9	woodblock print
Hara	原(はら)	N	4	family name
Hawaado	ハワード	N	7	Howard
hazukashii	はずかしい	A	4	is embarrassed; is shy; is bashful (see 4.4.9)
hirune	昼ね	N	7	nap
hirune suru	昼ねする	V	7	take a nap
hitobito	人々	N	2	people (more commonly used in formal speech or in writing than *hitotachi*) (see 2.4.3)
hitsuyoo	ひつよう	Na	11	necessary
hodo	ほど	R	7	about; approximately (see 7.4.9)
Hooru	ホール	N	8	Hall
hoshii	ほしい	E	11	want someone to do (see 11.4.6)
hoteru	ホテル	N	2	(Western-style) hotel

(I)

ie	家	N	4	house
Ikeda	池田(いけ)	N	2	family name
ima	居間(い)	N	8	living room (cf. *kyakuma*)
imi	いみ	N	2	meaning
-in	員	Nd	13	member; employee (see 13.4.2)
inaka	いなか	N	7	countryside; home village
in'shooteki	いんしょう的	Na	2	impressive
ippan'teki	一ぱん的	Na	11	general
irassharu	いらっしゃる	E	4	polite equivalent of *iru* (see 4.4.5)
irassharu	いらっしゃる	V	4	polite equivalent of *kuru* or *iku* (see 4.4.5)
Ishikawa	石川	N	13	family name
isshooken'mei	いっしょうけんめい	Adv.	13	with utmost effort; as hard as one can do; eagerly
itadaku	いただく	E	9	(see 9.4.14)
itai	いたい	A	4	is painful; ache; is sore; hurt (The structure with *itai* is normally "*(watashi) wa (atama) ga itai.*")
iu (yuu)	いう	V	2	is called; is named (see 2.4.9)
iya	いや	SI	2	no (used normally by men)
iya	いや	Na	8	unpleasant; do not like
izen	以前(いぜん)	N	11	former times; before

(J)

ja nai	じゃない	C+R+E	2	negative of *da* (see 2.4.17)
jama	じゃま	Na	8	bother; hindrance (see 8.4.7)
jiko	事故(こ)	N	6	accident
jimuin	事務(む)員	N	13	office clerk
jin'ja	神社(じんじゃ)	N	2	Shinto shrine
jiyuu	自由(ゆう)	Na	11	free; liberal
jogin'gu	ジョギング	N	7	jogging
-joo	じょう	Nd	8	counter for *tatami* (see 8.4.12)
Joon'zu	ジョーンズ	N	2	Jones
jooyoo kan'ji	常用(じょうよう)漢字	N	3	*Kan'ji* for Common Use
jun'jo	じゅんじょ	N	13	order; sequence
juuyaku	重役(じゅうやく)	N	13	director; high executive

(K)

kaban	かばん	N	8	bag; suitcase; briefcase
kachi	かち	N	2	value
kachoo	課長	N	12	section chief
kaeru	変える	V	4	change (compound component) (see 4.4.7)
kaeru	変える	V	11	change (transitive Verb)
-kagetsu	か月	Nd	3	Counter for months (see 3.4.4)
kai	かい	SP	12	(see 12.4.12)
kaishain	会社員	N	13	company employee
kakitome	かきとめ	N	13	registered mail
kaku	かく	V	9	draw; paint
-kan	間	Nd	3	period (see 3.4.6)
kanari	かなり	Adv.	8	considerably; pretty
kan'gae	考え	N	2	idea; thought
kan'gaeru	考える	V	12	consider; think
kan'sha	かんしゃ	N	9	thanks; gratitude
kan'sha suru	かんしゃする	V	9	thank; is grateful
kan'tan	かんたん	Na	3	easy; simple; short
kara	から	Rc	7	after; since (see 7.4.8)
Kashikomari-mashita.	かしこまりました。	(exp.)	6	Certainly, sir.; Yes, sir. (see 6.4.3)
-kata	方	Nd	11	method; way; how to (see 11.4.1)
katana	かたな	N	2	sword
kawa	川	N	2	river; stream
kawa	かわ	N	8	leather
kawaru	変わる	V	11	change (intransitive Verb)
kazu	かず	N	6	number
Kazuko	かず子	N	9	girl's name
keigo	敬(けい)語	N	11	speech levels and styles
keiken	けいけん	N	7	experience
keiken suru	けいけんする	V	7	experience

keizaiteki	けいざい的	Na	9	economical
kekkyoku	けっきょく	Adv.	3	after all; in conclusion
ken'kyuu	研究	N	7	research; study
ken'kyuu suru	研究する	V	7	research; study
ken'kyuushitsu	研究室	N	12	seminar room; laboratory; professor's office
keredo(mo)	けれど(も)	SI	11	however; but
kibishii	きびしい	A	13	is strict; is severe
kiku	きく	N	2	chrysanthemum
kimochi	気持ち	N	8	feeling; mood (〜 *ga ii* "feel good," 〜 *ga warui* "feel bad")
kimono	着物	N	4	traditional Japanese-style clothes
kin	金	N	8	gold
kinen'bi	記念日	N	9	anniversary; memorial day
ki-ni-naru	気に　なる	V	12	feel uneasy about (see 12.4.4)
ki-ni-suru	気に　する	V	12	care; worry; mind (transitive Verb) (see 12.4.4)
ki-o-tsukeru	気を　つける	V	12	take care; is careful
kireru	きれる	V	6	run out; is out of stock (intransitive Verb)
kisha	汽車	N	2	steam train; railroad train
kitte	切手	N	13	postage stamp
Kobayashi	小林	N	7	family name
kochira	こちら	N	8	this way; this side (see 8.4.10)
kodomobeya	子どもべや	N	8	room for children
komaru	こまる	V	13	is troubled; have a hard time
kon'kuriito	コンクリート	N	8	concrete
kon'na ni	こんなに	Adv.	2	this (many; much)
koochoo (sen'sei)	校長（先生）	N	13	principal; headmaster
koogai	公害	N	6	troubles such as air pollution, noise, etc.
kooin	工員	N	13	factory worker; mechanic
kookoo	高校	N	7	senior high school
kookoosei	高校生	N	12	senior high school student (see 12.4.3)
koto	こと	Nd	4	matter
kotobazukai	ことば使い	N	11	speech; expression; wording; manner of speaking
kotowaza	ことわざ	N	3	proverb
kowareru	こわれる	V	6	is broken (intransitive Verb)
kowasu	こわす	V	6	break (transitive Verb) (see 6.4.6)
kubetsu	くべつ	N	13	distinction
kudasaru	くださる	E	9	(see 9.4.7)
Kuraaku	クラーク	N	3	Clark
kurai	くらい	A	8	is dark
kureru	くれる	E	9	(see 9.4.7 and 12.4.13)
kurisumasu	クリスマス	N	9	Christmas

kurushii	くるしい	A	4	is painful; is hard
kusuri	くすり	N	7	medicine
kusuriya	くすり屋	N	7	pharmacy; pharmacist
kutsushita	くつ下	N	4	socks; stockings
kyakuma	客間	N	8	parlor; guest room
kyooiku kan'ji	教育漢字	N	3	*Kan'ji* for Education
kyoomi	きょうみ	N	7	interest (see 7.4.5)
kyooryoku	協力	N	13	cooperation
kyooryoku suru	協力する	V	13	cooperate
kyooshi	教師	N	7	teacher
(M)				
maa	まあ	SI	9	oh; my (used only by women) (see 8.4.5)
machigaeru	まちがえる	V	3	make a mistake; error; mistake (transitive Verb)
-mae	前	Nd	7	ago (see 7.4.7)
mae motte	前もって	Adv.	2	in advance
Maido arigatoo gozaimasu.	毎度　ありがとう ございます。	(exp.)	6	Thank you for your constant patronage. (see 6.4.3)
Masae	まさえ	N	12	girl's first name
mata	また	SI	8	also; in addition
Matsumoto	松本	N	13	family name
migaku	みがく	V	6	polish; shine
Miraa	ミラー	N	4	Miller
mizugi	水着	N	4	swimming suit
mo	も	R	2	as many as; no less than; no fewer than (see 2.4.13)
morau	もらう	E	9	(see 9.4.14)
motto	もっと	Adv.	2	some more; more; longer; farther (see 2.4.5)
mottomo	もっとも	Adv.	11	the most (formal equivalent of *ichiban*)
mukaeru	むかえる	V	6	receive (a person); meet; welcome (see 6.4.9)
mukoo	むこう	N	2	over there; the other side
Muua	ムーア	N	11	Moore
(N)				
nagara	ながら	Rc	7	while; as (see 7.4.11)
Nagasaki	長崎	N	7	a historical city in Kyūshū
nakagoro	中ごろ	N	9	middle
nakanaka	なかなか	Adv.	11	fairly; quite; very
nakanaka	なかなか	Adv.	13	easily (used with negation) (see 13.4.6)
naoru	なおる	V	6	is repaired; is fixed (intransitive Verb) (see 6.4.6)
naosu	なおす	V	6	fix; set right; correct (transitive Verb) (see 6.4.6)

Nara	奈良	N	2	a historical spot in Kansai
nasai	なさい	V	12	forms the imperative expression when used after the Stem form of a Verb (compound component) (see 12.4.17)
naze	なぜ	Ni	2	why?
nemui	ねむい	A	12	is sleepy
ni	に	R	3	per (see 3.4.7)
ni	に	R	8	for; as (see 8.4.13)
ni	に	R	9	indicates the person who is asked or wanted to do something (see 9.4.14 and 11.4.6)
ni	に	R	11	with reference to (see 11.4.4)
ni	に	R	11	in such and such a manner (see 11.4.7)
niau	に合う	V	4	match; suit; becoming
nihon'fuu	日本風	N	2	Japanese style
nihon'ma	日本間	N	8	Japanese-style room
nihon'teki	日本的	Na	9	typically Japanese (see 9.4.9)
nikui	にくい	A	3	hard (to do); difficult (to do) (compound component) (see 3.4.9)
ni tsuite	について	R+V	11	concerning; about; on (see 11.4.5)
ni yotte	によって	R+V	11	depending upon; according to (see 11.4.5)
no	の	PC	4	formal equivalent of *n* (see 4.4.8 and 4.4.14)
no	の	R	2	(see 2.4.19)
nobasu	のばす	V	2	extend; stretch
node	ので	Rc	4	being that . . . ; since; because (see 4.4.6)
nokoru	のこる	V	2	remain; is left (intransitive Verb)
nomu	飲む	V	7	drink; take (medicine); smoke
noni	のに	Rc	4	in spite of; although (see 4.4.12)
no ni	のに	Nd+R	12	in the process of; in order to (see 12.4.20)
nugu	ぬぐ	V	4	take off; put off

(O)

Oagari kudasai.	おあがりください。	(exp.)	8	Please come up into the house. (see 8.4.6)
oba(san)	おば(さん)	N	9	aunt; woman
obaasan	おばあさん	N	9	grandmother; old woman
obi	おび	N	4	sash; belt (for *kimono*)
oboeru	覚える	V	3	memorize; master
odoroku	おどろく	V	2	is surprised (intransitive Verb)
oiru	オイル	N	6	oil; engine oil
Ojama shimasu.	おじゃまします。	(exp.)	8	I am bothering you. (see 8.4.7)
oji(san)	おじ(さん)	N	9	uncle; man
ojiisan	おじいさん	N	9	grandfather; old man
okashii	おかしい	A	4	is funny; is strange; is laughable
okashina	おかしな	A	6	funny; strange; laughable (see 6.4.2)
okoru	おこる	V	6	happen; rise; occur
oku	おく	E	6	set aside; leave (see 6.4.8)

okureru	おくれる	V	12	is late; is behind time; is delayed (see 12.4.18)
okurimono	おくり物	N	9	gift; present
okuru	おくる	V	9	present; send
Omachi shite imashita.	お待ちしていました。	(exp.)	8	I have been waiting for your visit.
omiotsuke	おみおつけ	N	12	*miso* (bean paste) soup
omo ni	おもに	Adv.	8	mainly
Onegai shimasu.	おねがいします。	(exp.)	6	Please do so.; I make a request of you. (see 6.4.3)
ookina	大きな	A	6	big (see 6.4.2)
Oregon	オレゴン	N	7	Oregon
ossharu	おっしゃる	V	8	say (more polite equivalent of *iu*) (see 8.4.9)
ototoshi	おととし	N	7	the year before last
otozureru	おとずれる	V	2	visit (transitive Verb) (normally used in formal speech or in writing)
owaru	終わる	V	3	finish (doing) (compound component) (see 3.4.2)
(P)				
paatii	パーティー	N	4	party
pan'ku	パンク	N	6	a flat tire; puncture
pan'ku suru	パンクする	V	6	get a flat tire (*pan'ku* comes from the English word ''puncture'')
purasuchikku	プラスチック	N	8	plastic
(R)				
raku	らく	Na	4	comfortable; ease
-rashii	らしい	Da	6	seem; appear; understand (see 6.4.7)
rekishiteki	歴史的	Na	9	historical
ren'shuu	れんしゅう	N	3	practice; drill
ren'shuu suru	れんしゅうする	V	3	practice; drill
Robaatsu	ロバーツ	N	2	Roberts
ryokan	旅館	N	2	Japanese-style hotel or inn
ryoohoo	りょう方	N	4	both; both sides; both of them
(go)ryooshin	(ご)りょうしん	N	9	parents (see 9.4.10)
ryuugaku	留(りゅう)学	N	7	study abroad
ryuugaku suru	留(りゅう)学する	V	7	go to study abroad
(S)				
saabisu	サービス	N	6	free of charge; service (see 6.4.11)
(o)saifu	(お)さいふ	N	4	wallet; purse; money holder
saikin	さいきん	N	8	recently; lately
sakki	さっき	N	4	some time ago; a little while ago
sarariiman	サラリーマン	N	12	salary man; company employee; white-collar worker
sashiageru	さしあげる	E	9	(see 9.4.7)

-sei	製	Nd	9	made in ～; of (Swiss) make
(o)seibo	(お)せいぼ	N	9	year-end present
seikatsu	生活	N	12	life; living
sen'koo	専攻	N	7	major
sen'koo suru	専攻する	V	7	major; specialize
sen'mon	専門	N	9	specialty
sen'soo	戦争	N	13	war (see 13.4.3)
sewa	世話	N	9	help; kindness (see 9.4.4)
shachoo	社長	N	13	company president (see 13.4.1)
shachooshitsu	社長室	N	13	president's office (see 13.4.11)
shain	社員	N	13	company employee (see 13.4.2)
shakai	社会	N	11	society; community
shakaigaku	社会学	N	7	sociology
shashin	しゃしん	N	9	photograph (cf. *shashin o toru* "take a picture")
shibaraku	しばらく	N	7	some time; a while
shika	しか	R	3	only; nothing but (see 3.4.5)
shikamo	しかも	SI	11	moreover; furthermore
shikashi	しかし	SI	2	however; but (formal equivalent of *demo*) (see 2.4.4)
shimau	しまう	E	6	end up; complete (see 6.4.5)
shimeru	しめる	V	4	tie; fasten
shin'pai	心配	Na	11	worry; anxiety
shin'pai suru	心配する	V	11	worry
shin'setsu	しんせつ	Na	11	kind
shin'shitsu	しん室	N	13	bedroom
shiraseru	知らせる	V	2	inform; let someone know
shitaku	したく	N	12	preparations
shitaku suru	したくする	V	12	prepare; get ready
shoogakkoo	小学校	N	3	elementary school
shoogakusei	小学生	N	12	elementary school boy (or girl)
(o)shoogatsu	(お)正月	N	7	NewYear's Day; January
shooji	しょうじ	N	8	paper door
-shuukan	週間	Nd	3	counter for weeks (see 3.4.6)
shuuri	しゅうり	N	6	repairing
shuuri suru	しゅうりする	V	6	repair; fix
shuuriya	しゅうり屋	N	6	repair shop; repairman; garage
sobo	そぼ	N	9	grandmother
sochira	そちら	N	8	that way; that side (see 8.4.10)
sofu	そふ	N	9	grandfather (see 9.4.10)
sokutatsu	そくたつ	N	13	special delivery
son'na ni	そんなに	Adv.	2	so (many); that (much) (see 2.4.15)
sono go	その後	Adv.	6	after that; afterward
sono tame	そのため	SI	11	hence; for that reason
soo	そう	Nd	2	I heard; I understand (see 2.4.14)
soretomo	それとも	SI	9	or (else)

sorezore	それぞれ	Adv.	11	respectively
sotsugyoo	卒業(そつぎょう)	N	7	graduation
sotsugyoo suru	卒業(そつぎょう)する	V	7	is graduated; finish (transitive Verb)
sotsugyoosei	卒業(そつぎょう)生	N	12	graduate
-sugi	すぎ	Nd	12	after; past (the hour) (see 12.4.19)
sugiru	すぎる	V	3	excess; over (do)ing; too (few); excessively (compound component) (see 3.4.8)
sugoi	すごい	A	9	is terrific; is striking; is terrible; is awful (see 9.4.5)
Suisu	スイス	N	9	Switzerland; Swiss
(T)				
taido	たいど	N	12	attitude
taisetsu	大切	Na	3	important
taiya	タイヤ	N	6	tire (see 6.4.4)
Takagi	高木(ぎ)	N	6	family name
Takahashi	高橋(はし)	N	3	family name
take	竹	N	8	bamboo
tamae	たまえ	V	13	(compound component) (see 13.4.13)
tame	ため	Nd	12	purpose; sake; account (see 12.4.6)
tanomu	たのむ	V	11	ask; request (〜 *ni* 〜 *o tanomu*)
tatami	たたみ	N	8	straw mat; straw-matted floor
tateru	たてる	V	8	build
-teki	的	Nd	9	forms an adjectival Noun (see 9.4.9)
tetsu	鉄	N	8	iron
tetsugaku	てつ学	N	7	philosophy
to	と	R	2	quotation Relational (see 2.4.6)
tokei	とけい	N	6	watch; clock
toki	時	N	4	time; when (see 4.4.4)
tokkyuu	特急(とっきゅう)	N	2	limited express
tomaru	とまる	V	2	stop (at); stay (at) (〜 *ni tomaru*)
Tomoko	友子	N	12	girl's first name
Ton'de mo nai desu.	とんでもないです。	(exp.)	4	On the contrary.; Far from it. (see 4.4.9)
toori	とおり	Nd	11	way; like
tooyoo	東洋	N	7	the East (countries); the Orient
tooyooteki	東洋的	Na	9	oriental
torikesu	取りけす	V	2	cancel
toru	取る	V	6	take; pick up (see 6.4.9)
toshi	年	N	12	age
to shite	として	R+V	11	as; for; in the capacity of; by way of (see 11.4.5)
toshoshitsu	図(と)書室(しつ)	N	13	library room
(U)				
-uchi	うち	Nd	3	among; out of
umare	生まれ	N	7	〜 -born; of 〜 birth

umareru	生まれる	V	7	is born (intransitive Verb)
un	うん	SI	12	yeah; uh-huh
un'ten	運転(うんてん)	N	6	driving
un'ten suru	運転(うんてん)する	V	6	drive
ureshii	うれしい	A	7	is happy; is glad; is delighted
(W)				
wa	わ	SP	4	used by women (see 4.4.11)
waipaa	ワイパー	N	6	windshield wipers
wariai	わりあい	Adv.	3	comparatively
(Y)				
yaa	やあ	SI	13	hi; hello (used by men)
yameru	やめる	V	7	quit (see 7.4.6)
yaru	やる	E	9	(see 9.4.7)
yaru	やる	V	13	do; perform (equivalent for *suru*) (see 13.4.14)
yasashii	やさしい	A	9	is thoughtful; is kind; is gentle
yasui	やすい	A	3	easy (to do) (compound component) (see 3.4.9)
yogoreru	よごれる	V	6	become dirty; is soiled; is stained (intransitive Verb) (see 6.4.6)
yogosu	よごす	V	6	stain; soil; spoil (transitive Verb)
Yokohama	横浜(よこはま)	N	6	a city near Tōkyō
yoofuku	洋服(ふく)	N	4	Western-style clothes
yoofuu	洋風	N	2	Western style
yooma	洋間	N	8	Western-style room
yoroshii	よろしい	A	13	is all right; is good; is agreeable (see 13.4.16)
Yoshida	吉(よし)田	N	9	family name
yoyaku	よやく	N	2	reservation
yoyaku suru	よやくする	V	2	reserve
yubiwa	ゆびわ	N	9	(finger) ring
yuka	ゆか	N	8	floor
yukata	ゆかた	N	4	summer cotton *kimono*
(Z)				
zubon	ずぼん	N	4	trousers; pants

APPENDIX VII
INDEX TO NOTES